Crack in America

Crack in America

Demon Drugs and Social Justice

EDITED BY

Craig Reinarman
and
Harry G. Levine

UNIVERSITY OF CALIFORNIA PRESS

Berkeley   Los Angeles   London

University of California Press
Berkeley and Los Angeles, California

University of California Press, Ltd.
London, England

© 1997 by
The Regents of the University of California

Library of Congress Cataloging-in-Publication Data

Crack in America: demon drugs and social justice / edited by Craig
Reinarman and Harry G. Levine.
    p.   cm.
  Includes bibliographic references and index.
      ISBN 978-0-520-20242-9 (pbk. : alk. paper)

   1. Crack (Drug)—United States.   2. Cocaine habit—United States.
3. Narcotics, Control of—United States.   4. Drugs and mass media—
United States.   I. Reinarman, Craig.   II. Levine, Harry Gene.
HV5810.C73   1997
362.29'8'0973—dc21   96-47765
                                                              CIP

CONTENTS

FIGURES AND TABLES

FIGURES

TABLES

ACKNOWLEDGMENTS

There is an old saying about orthodox politics being "the art of the possible." There is also a newer saying about radical politics being "the art of making possible what is necessary." So, first, we thank all needle exchange workers and other harm reduction pioneers who forced open the political space in which it became possible to do what is necessary. We thank all the scholars and scientists from Alfred R. Lindesmith on who have challenged the biases underlying orthodox drug policy and searched for more just, humane, and effective alternatives. We thank the Drug Policy Foundation, Arnold Trebach, and Kevin Zeese for creating the annual conferences where many of us met and planned this book. We thank the International Conferences on the Reduction of Drug-Related Harm and Pat O'Hare for making harm reduction a growing international movement. We thank the American Civil Liberties Union, especially Ira Glasser and Loren Siegel, for courageously cutting against the grain of national prejudice in the interest of justice and rights and for being out front when few others dared. We thank Ethan Nadelmann for extraordinary leadership, for establishing first the Princeton Working Group on the Future of Drug Policy and then The Lindesmith Center, and for showing that science and scholarship fused with courage and compassion can create social change. And we thank Ray Smart and the Smart Family Fund whose generous financial support to the Princeton Working Group made this book possible.

We thank the chapter contributors for their extraordinary work without pay and their patience. We thank Naomi Schneider of the University of California Press for her courage, her confidence, and her patience and Rose Anne White and Sylvia Stein Wright for their excellent editorial work. We thank Howard S. Becker, Lester Grinspoon, and James Inciardi for insightful reviews of an early draft of this book. We thank the many interview respondents whose voices are heard in several of these chapters for their time and their honesty. We thank our colleagues in our home departments of sociology—at the University of California, Santa Cruz, and Queens College and the Graduate Center at the City University of New York—who have encouraged us to teach and write what we found to be true, wherever that led. Last here, but first in our hearts, we thank our families and our friends for their steadfast support and love. As they know too well, we could not have done it without them. We especially thank Laurie Phillips, who did not live to see this book finished but who would have been very proud. All of these people deserve partial credit for whatever is worthwhile in these pages. As for whatever flaws remain, the editors and authors deserve full credit.

· · · · · · ·

The editors also gratefully acknowledge grant support for parts of their research from the Social Sciences Division and the Faculty Senate of the University of California, Santa Cruz; the PSC-CUNY Faculty Research Fund of the City University of New York; the Michael Harrington Center at Queens College; and, for the research reported in Chapter 4, the National Institute on Drug Abuse (grant #1R01-DA03791–01). The views expressed in this book do not necessarily reflect those of any of these granting agencies.

Earlier versions of several of the chapters in this book first appeared as articles or chapters in various scholarly journals or books. The editors and authors are grateful to the following publishers for granting permission to print updated versions of them here; in each case, all rights are reserved to them. The core materials in Chapters 2, 3, and 6 first appeared in a special issue of *Contemporary Drug Problems,* volume 16, 1989 (copyright Federal Legal Publications), edited by Professor Jeffrey Fagan. Some of Chapter 4 first appeared in *Cocaine Changes,* by Dan Waldorf, Craig Reinarman, and Sheigla Murphy (copyright Temple University Press, 1991). An early version of Chapter 5 first appeared in the *Journal of Psychoactive Drugs,* volume 24, 1992 (copyright Haight Ashbury Publications, San Francisco). Chapter 12 first appeared in *Drug Law Report,* volume 2, number 15, 1990 (copyright Clark Boardman Callaghan). A portion of the introduction to Chapter 13 first appeared in *American Sociologist,* volume 26, 1995 (copyright Transaction Publishers). An earlier version of Chapter 14 first appeared in *Science,* volume 245, 1989 (copyright American Association for the Advancement of Science).

CONTRIBUTORS

Patricia A. Bellucci is a clinical psychologist and substance abuse therapist at the Metropolitan Center for Mental Health in New York City. She was a predoctoral fellow of the National Institute on Drug Abuse and a researcher on a twenty-five-year follow-up study of addicts at UCLA and at Narcotic and Drug Research, Inc., in New York City. She has published articles on the relationship between drugs and violence in the *Journal of Community Psychology, Advances in Alcohol and Substance Abuse,* and the *Journal of Psychoactive Drugs.*

Phillipe Bourgois is a professor of anthropology at San Francisco State University and a research fellow at the San Francisco Urban Institute. He is the author of *In Search of Respect: Selling Crack in El Barrio* (Cambridge University Press, 1995), which won the 1996 C. Wright Mills Award from the Society for the Study of Social Problems, and *Ethnicity at Work* (Johns Hopkins University Press, 1989). Dr. Bourgois has also written numerous articles and essays in such publications as the *New York Times Magazine, Contemporary Drug Problems, Anthropology Today,* and *American Ethnologist.*

Henry H. Brownstein is chief of the Bureau of Statistical Services for the New York State Division of Criminal Justice Services and an adjunct professor of sociology at Russell Sage College. He has been principal investigator on research grants from the National Institute of Justice and the National Institute on Drug Abuse. Dr. Brownstein is the principal author of *Crime and Justice Annual Report* (1992 and 1993) to the State of New York and co-author of *Drug-Related Crime Analysis—Homicide,* a report to the National Institute of Justice. He also has written about drug-related crime and violence in the *International Journal of the Addictions,* the *Journal of Crime and Justice, Criminal Justice Review,* and *Humanity and Society.*

Yuet W. Cheung was a research scientist at the Addiction Research Foundation in Toronto and a fellow in the Faculty of Medicine at the University of Toronto until 1992. He is now professor of sociology at the Chinese University of Hong Kong. He has been the recipient of research grants on drug issues from the Canadian and Hong Kong governments. Dr. Cheung is the author of *Missionary Medicine in China* (University Press of America, 1988) and has written on substance use and crime in the *International Journal of the Addictions, Social Science and Medicine, Contemporary Drug Problems,* and *Medical Anthropology.*

Peter D. A. Cohen is a professor of social psychology in the Faculty of Environmental Sciences at the University of Amsterdam. He is the author of *Cocaine Use in Amsterdam in Non-Deviant Subcultures* (1989) and *Drugs as a Social Construct* (1989), and co-author of *Licit and Illicit Drug Use in Amsterdam* (1991, 1994) and *Ten Years of Cocaine* (1994), all published by the University of Amsterdam. Dr. Cohen is the Dutch representative on the Drug Expert Committee of the Council of Europe. In 1993, he won the Lindesmith Award for scholarship on drug issues from the Drug Policy Foundation. He is also the author of numerous articles and essays on drug use and policy in such journals as the *International Journal of Drug Policy, Tijdschrift voor Criminologie, Addiction Research,* and *Contemporary Drug Problems.*

Troy Duster is professor of sociology and director of the Institute for the Study of Social Change at the University of California, Berkeley. He has been the recipient of research fellowships from the Guggenheim Foundation, the Ford Foundation, and the Swedish government and has served as a member of the President's Commission on Mental Health and the National Academy of Sciences Committee on Habitual Behavior and Substance Abuse. He is the author of *The Legislation of Morality: Law, Drugs, and Moral Judgment* (Free Press, 1970) and *Backdoor to Eugenics* (Routledge, 1990) and co-editor of *Cultural Perspectives on Biological Knowledge* (Alex Publishing, 1984). Dr. Duster has written widely in the areas of race relations, the sociology of science, and poverty and the underclass in such journals as *Society, Black Scholar, Philosophy and Social Action, Actes de Recherche en Sciences Sociales, Politics and the Life Sciences, Crime and Delinquency,* and *American Sociologist.*

Patricia G. Erickson is senior scientist at the Addiction Research Foundation in Toronto, adjunct professor of sociology at the University of Toronto, and a consultant to the Canadian government and the World Health Organization Programme on Substance Abuse. She is the author of *Cannabis Criminals* (ARF Books, 1980), co-author of *The Steel Drug: Cocaine and Crack in Perspective* (Lexington Books, 1994), and co-editor of *Illicit Drugs in Canada* (Nelson, 1988). Dr. Erickson has also published widely on drug issues in such journals as the *International Journal of the Addictions, Criminology,* the *British Journal of Addictions, Social Pharmacology,* the *Journal of Criminal Law and Criminology,* and *Addiction Research.*

Ira Glasser is the executive director of the American Civil Liberties Union. He has taught at Queens College and Sarah Lawrence College. He is the author of *Visions of Liberty: A Bill of Rights for All Americans* (Arcade, 1991) and co-author of *Doing Good: The Limits of Benevolence* (Pantheon, 1978). Mr. Glasser has written numerous essays on civil liberties, including the impact of drug policy on civil liberties, in the *New York Times, The Nation,* the *Wall Street Journal, Harper's,* the *Washington Post, Christianity and Crisis, Police, Social Policy,* and *New Republic.* Mr. Glasser has been the recipient of the Martin Luther King, Jr., Award and the American Bar Association Gavel Award.

Paul J. Goldstein is professor of public health at the University of Illinois, Chicago. He has been the principal investigator on a number of research grants from the National Institute on Drug Abuse and has served as an expert on substance use and crime for the National Research Council of the National Academy of Sciences and the Centers for Disease Control. Dr. Goldstein is the author of *Prostitution and Drugs* (1979) and co-author of *Taking Care of Business: The Economics of Crime by Heroin Abusers* (1985), both published by Lexington Books. He has written numerous scientific articles on the epidemiology of drugs, crime, and violence in such journals as *Public Health Reports,* the *American Journal of Preventive Medicine, Criminology,* and the *International Journal of the Addictions.*

Harry G. Levine is professor of sociology at Queens College and the Graduate Center of the City University of New York. He has been researching and writing about the history, sociology, and anthropology of drug issues for over twenty years. Professor Levine has been director of research at the Alcohol Research Group of the University of California, Berkeley, and is currently a director of drug projects at the Michael Harrington Center of Queens College. He has received a number of awards for scholarship, including the Keller Award from the *Journal of Studies on Alcohol* for his article "The Discovery of Addiction." His many articles and book chapters have appeared in journals such as the *British Journal of Addiction, Contemporary Drug Problems,* the *Journal of Drug Issues,* the *Milbank Quarterly, Alkoholpolitik, The Journal of Contemporary Ethnography,* and *Public Opinion* as well as on a number of websites.

John P. Morgan is a physician and professor of pharmacology at City University of New York Medical School and adjunct professor at Mount Sinai School of Medicine. He has been a captain in the U.S. Air Force and a fellow in clinical pharmacology at Johns Hopkins and the University of Rochester medical schools. Dr. Morgan is the author of the chapter on drug addiction in the *Merck Manual* (Merck & Co., 1977) and co-editor of *Society and Medication* (Lexington Books, 1983). He has published widely in the medical science literature on central nervous system stimulants, opiates, hypnotics, and chemical dependency in such journals as the *New England Journal of Medicine*, the *Journal of the American Medical Association*, the *British Medical Journal*, *Archives of Neurology*, and the *Annals of Internal Medicine*. In 1996, Dr. Morgan won the LeDain Award for contributions to drug policy reform in the field of law from the Drug Policy Foundation.

Stephen K. Mugford is a professor of sociology at the Australian National University. He is an associate editor of the *International Journal of Drug Policy* and co-editor of *An Unwinnable War: The Politics of Drug Decriminalization* (Pluto Press, 1991) and of a special issue of *Addiction Research* devoted to community studies of cocaine use. Dr. Mugford was the principal author of a special report on cocaine use to the Australian government's National Campaign Against Drug Abuse. He has also published on drug use and policy in the *Australian and New Zealand Journal of Criminology*, *Social Justice*, and the *Journal of Drug Issues*.

Sheigla B. Murphy is a medical sociologist and senior research associate at the Institute for Scientific Analysis in San Francisco. She is the principal investigator of a research grant on needle exchange as an AIDS prevention strategy from the National Institute on Drug Abuse, for which she also serves as a consultant. Dr. Murphy is author of a forthcoming book about women and crack and co-author of *Cocaine Changes: The Experience of Using and Quitting* (1991), both published by Temple University Press. She has published widely on drug use, abuse, and treatment in such journals as the *British Journal of Addiction*, *Contemporary Drug Problems*, the *International Journal of Drug Policy*, and the *Journal of Psychoactive Drugs*.

Ethan A. Nadelmann is a political scientist and attorney who was a professor at the Woodrow Wilson School at Princeton University until 1994, when he left to establish the Lindesmith Center, an independent drug policy research institute in New York City of which he is now director. He is the author of *Cops Across Borders: The Internationalization of U.S. Criminal Law Enforcement* (Penn State University Press, 1993) and co-editor of *Psychoactive Drugs and Harm Reduction* (Whurr Publishers, 1993). Dr. Nadelmann has published widely on the domestic and comparative international aspects of drugs, crime, and law enforcement in such journals as *Science, Foreign Policy, International Organization, American Heritage, Rolling Stone, The Public Interest,* and *Daedalus.*

Craig Reinarman is professor of sociology and adjunct faculty in legal studies at the University of California, Santa Cruz. He has served on the board of directors of the College on Problems of Drug Dependence and as a consultant to the World Health Organization Programme on Substance Abuse. Dr. Reinarman is the author of *American States of Mind* (Yale University Press, 1987) and co-author of *Cocaine Changes* (Temple University Press, 1991). He has published numerous articles on drug use, law, and policy in such journals as *Theory and Society,* the *British Journal of Addiction,* the *International Journal of Drug Policy, Addiction Research,* and *Contemporary Drug Problems.*

Marsha Rosenbaum is a research sociologist and associate director of the Lindesmith Center West in San Francisco. For many years, she was senior research scientist at the Institute for Scientific Analysis, where she was principal investigator on a series of research grants from the National Institute on Drug Abuse, for which she also serves as a consultant. Dr. Rosenbaum is the author of *Women on Heroin* (Rutgers University Press, 1981) and co-author of *Pursuit of Ecstasy: The MDMA Experience* (State University of New York Press, 1994). She has also published numerous articles on drug use, drug problems, treatment, and policy in such journals as *Contemporary Drug Problems,* the *Journal of Psychoactive Drugs,* the *Journal of Drug and Alcohol Abuse,* and the *Journal of Drug Issues.*

Patrick J. Ryan is a professor of criminal justice at Long Island University. He is the author of *Contemporary World Issues: Organized Crime in America* (ABC-CLIO, 1995) and a contributor to *The Handbook on Organized Crime* (Greenwood, 1994). From 1991 to 1994, Dr. Ryan was executive director of the International Association for the Study of Organized Crime. He has published numerous articles on the links between drugs and violence and on organized crime in *Justice Quarterly,* the *Journal of Crime and Justice,* and *Crime and Delinquency.*

Loren Siegel is an attorney who is the public education director of the American Civil Liberties Union. She is the author of *The Rights of the Mentally Ill* (Avon Publishing, 1970). Ms. Siegel has monitored the War on Drugs for the ACLU for a decade and has written widely about civil liberties and drug policy issues in such journals as *Physician's Weekly, Drug Law Report, Nova Law Review, Wake Forest Intramural Law Review,* and *Law Enforcement News.*

Dan Waldorf was a senior research associate at the Institute for Scientific Analysis in San Francisco and the principal investigator on a series of research grants from the National Institute of Drug Abuse and the National Institute of Justice until his death in 1996. He is the author of *Careers in Dope* (Prentice Hall, 1973) and co-author of *Cocaine Changes* (Temple University Press, 1991). Mr. Waldorf published numerous scholarly articles on drug use, problems, and policy in such journals as *Social Problems,* the *British Journal of Addiction,* the *International Journal of the Addictions, Contemporary Drug Problems,* the *Journal of Drug Issues,* and *Addiction Research.* In 1995, the Drug Policy Foundation gave Mr. Waldorf its Lindesmith Award for lifetime contributions to drug policy reform in the field of scholarship.

Lynn Zimmer is a professor of sociology at Queens College and the Graduate Center of the City University of New York and a research fellow at the Center for Research on Crime and Justice at New York University Law School. She is the author of *Operation Pressure Point and Disruption of Street-Level Drug Trafficking* (New York University Law School, 1987) and *Women Guarding Men* (University of Chicago Press, 1986). Dr. Zimmer has also published numerous scholarly articles on drug use, drug testing, law enforcement, and prison in such journals as *Behavioral Sciences and the Law, Women and Criminal Justice, Contemporary Drug Problems, Gender and Society,* and the *American Journal of Police.*

ONE

Crack in Context
America's Latest Demon Drug

Craig Reinarman and Harry G. Levine

In the spring of 1986, American politicians and news media began an extraordinary antidrug frenzy that ran until 1992. Newspapers, magazines, and television networks regularly carried lurid stories about a new "epidemic" or "plague" of drug use, especially of crack cocaine. They said this "epidemic" was spreading rapidly from cities to the suburbs and was destroying American society. Politicians from both parties made increasingly strident calls for a "War on Drugs." They even challenged each other to take urine tests to provide chemical proof of their moral purity. In one of the more bizarre episodes, the president and vice president of the United States had their own urine tested for evidence of marijuana, cocaine, and heroin. It is certainly true that the United States has real health and social problems that result from illegal and legal drug use. But it is certainly also true that the period from 1986 through 1992 was characterized by antidrug extremism.

We use the term "drug scare" to designate periods when antidrug crusades have achieved great prominence and legitimacy. Drug scares are phenomena in their own right, quite apart from drug use and drug problems. Drug scares have recurred throughout U.S. history independent of actual increases in drug use or drug problems. During "red scares," like the McCarthy period in the 1950s, leftists were said to be serious threats to the American way of life. Similarly, during drug scares, all kinds of social problems have been blamed on one chemical substance or another.[1] Drug scares typically link a scapegoated substance to a troubling subordinate group—working-class immigrants, racial or ethnic minorities, rebellious youth. The period from 1986 to 1992 was in many ways the most intense drug scare of the twentieth century. With few dissenting voices, politicians and the media embraced the Reagan administration metaphor "War on

Drugs" and pronounced the "drug war" to be good social policy. At dead center of all the hysteria was "crack."

Crack appeared in late 1984 and 1985 primarily in impoverished African-American and Latino inner-city neighborhoods in New York, Los Angeles, and Miami. Crack is smokeable cocaine. It gained its named from the "crackling" sound it makes when heated. It is easily produced in a pot on a kitchen stove by "cooking down" a mixture of powder cocaine, water, and baking soda. Crack is typically sold in tiny vials or envelopes that cost between $5 and $20. Crack was not a new drug; its active ingredient is entirely cocaine. Nor was it a new way of using cocaine; smoking cocaine freebase had been practiced since the 1970s.

Crack was a marketing innovation. It was a way of packaging a relatively expensive and upscale commodity (powder cocaine) in small, inexpensive units. So packaged, this form of smokeable cocaine (crack) was then sold, usually on the street by young African-Americans and Latinos, to a whole new class of customers: residents of impoverished inner-city neighborhoods. The marketing innovation was successful for at least two reasons. First, there was a huge workforce of unemployed young people ready to take jobs in the new, neighborhood-based business of crack preparation and sales. Working in the crack business offered these people better jobs, working conditions, and pay than any "straight" job they could get (and better than other entry-level criminal jobs like burglary or stealing car radios).[2] Second, the marketing innovation succeeded because turning powder cocaine into smokeable "crack" changed the way cocaine was consumed and thereby dramatically strengthened the character of cocaine intoxication. Smoking crack offered a very brief but very intense intoxication. This inexpensive and dramatic "high" was much better suited to the finances and interest in immediate escape of the inner-city poor than the more subtle and expensive effects of powder cocaine.

Cocaine in any form is a stimulant, much like amphetamine or even caffeine. When powder cocaine is sniffed in small doses (as it usually is), it makes the user moderately alert and energized. Thus, the typical psychoactive effects of sniffing powder cocaine are subtle. Users report having to learn to recognize it (see, e.g., Waldorf et al. 1991). In the 1930s, songwriter Cole Porter wrote that he'd "get no kick" from cocaine about powder cocaine.

Cole Porter would have gotten a kick from crack, but he probably would not have liked the experience very much. When cocaine is smoked, it enters the bloodstream quickly, providing a powerful rush. Crack is a strong, even harsh, drug. One experienced cocaine user said that after smoking $10 worth of it, "I was so high I was frightened—and I don't frighten easily. . . . I wouldn't bother with it again."[3] Contrary to the media stories and drug war rhetoric, most of the people who have tried crack or smoked cocaine have *not* continued to use it. From its first appearance, crack has always been used heavily by the same population that has always used heroin heavily: the urban poor. Daily crack smoking, like daily heroin injecting, occurs mainly among the poorest, most marginalized people in American society—and only among a small minority of them. In its most popular year, crack was used heavily by only a small percentage of even the people who used cocaine. Crack never became a popular or widely used drug in the United States, or anywhere else in the world.

This, however, is not the way the mass media and politicians talked about crack from 1986 to 1992. Rather, crack was portrayed as the most contagiously addicting and destructive substance known. Politicians and the media depicted crack and other illicit drugs as virulent diseases that were attacking American society. Beginning in 1986 and continuing into the early 1990s, major American institutions—churches, schools, media, political organizations, voluntary groups, advertisers, foundations—carried on what amounted to a huge national educational campaign about drugs in general and crack in particular. One might expect that, as a result of all this attention, Americans would be among the most knowledgeable people on earth about crack and other illicit drugs. But the campaign did not increase understanding because virtually all these institutions took up the tasks of promoting the policies of the War on Drugs and of single-mindedly and simple-mindedly demonizing illicit drug use. Rather than report the complicated truth, the media joined politicians in producing drug war propaganda. In so doing, reporters found "experts" who provided scary antidrug sound bites and presented frightening, false generalizations as fact.

Consider some of the stories reported in six months in 1986, the first year of the crack scare. On March 17, in a cover story called "Kids and Cocaine," *Newsweek* quoted, without skepticism, a drug expert who announced that "crack is the most addictive drug known to man." He also said that smoking crack produces "instantaneous addiction" (pp. 58–59). As a result, *Newsweek* asserted, crack "has transformed the ghetto" and "is rapidly spreading into the suburbs." On March 20, the *New York Times* explained (in a front-page story) that crack was spreading from the inner city to "the wealthiest suburbs of Westchester county." " 'It's all over the place' " said an official from the New Jersey Health Department. A month later the *Times* printed another front-page story about crack spreading from the city to suburbs. "If we don't stop crack now, it will destroy our young people" said a politician from Westchester (April 27). On June 8, the headline of yet another front-page *Times* story announced that "Crack Addiction Spreads Among the Middle Class." On the same day, another *Times* story reported that on the suburbs of Long Island "the use of crack has reached epidemic proportions (p. 5)." On June 16, *Newsweek* published a full-page editorial titled "The Plague Among Us." It began:

> An epidemic is abroad in America, as pervasive and dangerous in its way as the plagues of medieval times. Its source is the large and growing traffic in illegal drugs . . . a whole pharmacopeia of poisons. . . . [The epidemic] has taken lives, wrecked careers, broken homes, invaded schools, incited crimes, tainted businesses, toppled heroes, corrupted policemen and politicians. . . . [The epidemic] is a national scandal, and . . . we seem powerless to stop it (p. 18).

A week later the *New York Times* (June 29) announced the "growing use of crack" in three suburban and rural counties in New York. With neither evidence nor skepticism, the *Times* reported that in Westchester, Rockland, and Sullivan counties, the "per capita use of cocaine is the heaviest in the state." On July 28, *U.S. News and World Report* told readers that "illicit drugs pervade American life . . . a situation that experts compare to medieval plagues—'the No.1 problem we face' " (p. 49). Two weeks later, *Newsweek* reported that "nearly everyone now concedes that the plague is all but universal" (August 11, p. 19).[4]

On occasion, the same newspaper, magazine, or TV show did a follow-up story that contradicted its earlier accounts. For example, in 1990, after years of reporting that crack is instantly addicting, *Newsweek* wrote: "Don't tell the kids, but there's a dirty little secret about crack; as with most other drugs, a lot of people use it without getting addicted. In their zeal to shield young people from the plague of drugs, the media and many drug educators have hyped instant and total addiction" (February 19, pp. 74–75). *Newsweek* did *not* tell readers that it had been among the first to have "hyped instant and total addiction" and to have quoted, without questioning, the "drug educators" who also did so. Similarly, in 1989, after being a crucial source for the news that in the suburbs crack use was "epidemic" and "all over the place," the *New York Times* quietly noted that just the opposite was true. The *Times* reported that except for a few "urban pockets" in suburban counties, "educators, law enforcement officials, and young people say crack and most other narcotics are rarely seen in the suburbs, whether modest or wealthy." Crack, the *Times* now said, "is confined mainly to poor urban neighborhoods" (October 7, p. 26).

By and large, the media and politicians' pronouncements about drugs spread exaggerations, misinformation, and simplistic theories of cause and effect. They taught bad pharmacology, bad sociology, bad criminology, bad urban anthropology, and even bad history. During this time, some writers, journalists, commentators, TV and radio reports, news articles, and some whole publications provided thoughtful and accurate information about drugs. But such good reports were vastly outnumbered by the misleading and false ones.

This was not the first time the press, politicians, and supposed medical and scientific "experts" in America have blamed an array of social problems on a drug and linked the drug with a "threatening" group. Indeed, American history has had more than its share of drug scares and antidrug crusades.

DEMON DRUGS AND DRUG SCARES IN U.S. HISTORY

The first, largest, and most influential of all antidrug crusades was the American temperance movement's campaign against "demon" alcohol. Indeed, the modern history of concern about "drugs," and of antidrug crusades, begins in America in the late eighteenth century and early nineteenth century with the temperance movement's battle against alcoholic drink. In effect, alcohol was "the first drug." It was the first substance to be regarded as inherently and inevitably addicting (just as heroin and crack are viewed today). It was the first drug to be the focus of a mass movement that sought to eliminate its use and prohibit its production and sale. It was the first drug to be regarded as causing violence and crime. It was the first drug to be blamed—scapegoated—for problems whose complicated origins lay in broader political and economic conditions. Throughout the nineteenth century and into the twentieth, the temperance or antialcohol movement claimed that alcoholic drink was responsible for most of the nation's poverty, crime, violence, mental illness, moral degeneracy, "broken" families, and individual and business failure. Temperance was an eminently respectable, mainstream, middle-class movement—the largest enduring movement of the nineteenth century (Levine, 1984).

In the first two decades of the twentieth century, America's new corporate elite increasingly joined with the middle-class supporters of temperance to create a new single-minded prohibitionist movement. Industrialization brought to America ever growing numbers of working-class and peasant immigrants with different cultural, religious, and drinking practices. The period between 1900 and 1920 was riddled with class, racial, cultural, and political conflict having little to do with drinking problems. As in the nineteenth century, alcohol was offered as a scapegoat; but, more than ever before, prohibition was offered as a panacea. Prohibitionists promised that a constitutional amendment banning alcohol would eliminate social problems, empty prisons and asylums, lower taxes, and ensure permanent prosperity.

Many corporate supporters of prohibition argued that working-class drinking interfered with the rhythms of the modern factory and thus with productivity and profits. To earlier fears of the barroom as a breeding ground of immorality, prohibitionists added the idea of the saloon as alien and subversive. They argued that saloons were where unions organized, where socialists and anarchists found new recruits. For the corporate and political elite, and for much of the old business middle class and the new professional middle class, clamping down on drinking and saloons was part of a much broader strategy of social control—a quest for "order" at a moment when industrialization was transforming American life (Gusfield 1986; Levine, 1984, 1985, 1986; Rumbarger, 1989; Timberlake, 1963). Prohibitionists proudly claimed that the passage of the Eighteenth Amendment to the Constitution in 1919 was a blow against Bolshevism and anarchy and that it would usher in a kind of golden age. On January 16, 1920, the day before constitutional Prohibition went into effect, the evangelical preacher Billy Sunday articulated the utopian dream at the heart of temperance and prohibitionist ideology: "The rein of tears is over. The slums will soon be a memory. We will turn our prisons into factories and our jails into storehouses and corncribs. Men will walk upright now, women will smile and the children will laugh. Hell will be forever for rent" (in Kobler, 1973, p. 12).

Other demon drugs and drug scares have had similar roots and equally outrageous claims. The first law against opium smoking in the U.S. was much more the result of anti-Chinese agitation in California in the 1870s than it was of troublesome opium smoking. Chinese immigrants had been brought in as "coolies" to help build the railroad and work the mines. Some brought the practice of opium smoking with them. But when the railroad was completed and the gold ran out, recession set in. White workers found themselves competing with lower-paid Chinese workers for scarce jobs and viewed the Chinese as an economic threat. The campaign against *smoking* opium (but not against other, non-Chinese uses of opiates) included lurid, fictional newspaper accusations of Chinese men drugging white women into sexual slavery. The law against opium smoking was only one of several repressive laws designed, at least in part, to control the Chinese and thus assuage the economic *cum* xenophobic anxieties of whites (Morgan, 1978; Musto, 1973).

Broader political and racial issues were also factors in the first cocaine scare, which led to the first federal antidrug law, the Harrison Act of 1914. Just as the crack scare blossomed only after the practice of cocaine smoking spread to lower class, inner-city African-Americans and Latinos, so did class and racial fears fuel the first cocaine scare. At the turn of the century, the opiate addict population was shifting from white, middle-class, middle-aged women to younger, working-class men and other "disreputable" groups (Duster, 1970). Sensationalistic press accounts linked drug use with blacks, prostitutes, criminals, and transient workers. There was no evidence that African-Americans used even as much cocaine as whites (Musto, 1973), and the actual number of opiate addicts was probably diminishing when the Harrison Act was being debated. Nonetheless, white politicians used race to incite public reaction against opiates and cocaine, at least in part for political purposes. For example, in an effort to overcome the objections of Southern congressmen to a federal drug law that might infringe on "states' rights," antidrug crusaders spread the myth that cocaine induced African-American men to rape white women (Musto, 1973, pp. 6–10, 67–68). Some Southern sheriffs even switched from .32 to .38 caliber pistols because they claimed that their old guns could not stop the "cocaine-crazed" Negro. As Yale medical historian David Musto has shown, this first cocaine scare was not primarily a response to cocaine use or opiate addiction, or to any drug-related crime wave. Rather, says Musto, it was animated by "white alarm" about "black rebellion" against segregation and oppression (Musto, 1973, p. 7).

Nearly a quarter of a century later, in 1937, Congress passed the Marijuana Tax Act. This first federal law against marijuana was the result of a "reefer madness" scare orchestrated by the quintessential moral entrepreneur, Harry Anslinger, a former Treasury agent who had enforced alcohol Prohibition and who was appointed chief of the Federal Bureau of Narcotics before repeal of Prohibition (Becker, 1963; Himmelstein, 1983). Before Anslinger began to paint marijuana as a great scourge, there was no evidence of widespread marijuana use and almost no coverage of marijuana in the press or public agitation for a clampdown (Becker, 1963; Grinspoon and Bakalar, 1993, p. 9). However, in the midst of the Great Depression, the bureau had endured four straight years of budget cuts, and opiates and cocaine had already been outlawed (Dickson, 1968). Anslinger circulated to newspapers and magazines across the nation alarming propaganda about how marijuana had caused a Texas hitchhiker to murder a motorist, a Florida youth to murder his entire family with an ax, and a West Virginia man to rape a nine-year-old girl. In addition to stirring general fears about crime, Anslinger relied on specific racial fears with his claims that marijuana made Mexicans in particular violent. He then told policy makers and all others who would listen that the use of this "killer weed" was spreading among Anglo youth, who would soon spread violence across society.

In the 1960s and 1970s, a new generation of drug warriors made marijuana the focus of a much broader crusade—not because it made users aggressive and violent but, in a curious way, because it *didn't*. These new crusaders did not view marijuana as the "killer weed," but rather as the "dropout drug" (see Himmelstein, 1983). They claimed that marijuana was "causing" youth to lose the achievement ethic and to become un-American (for example, by opposing the war in Vietnam). In this case, drug crusaders regarded marijuana as a threat not because it was used by a "dangerous class," but because they believed it was turning an entire class of youth in a direction that dominant groups defined as "dangerous." In contrast to Anslinger's crusade thirty years earlier, this time there was substantial evidence of the widespread use of marijuana. However, virtually none of the claims about the horrid consequences of marijuana use were supported by evidence then or now (National Commission on Marijuana and Drug Abuse, 1972; National Research Council, 1982). Nor was evidence of ill effects the real issue. Here, too, a drug provided a useful symbol in an essentially political conflict between cultures and generations.

The anticrack frenzy of 1986 to 1992 was the latest in a long line of drug scares that were about more than drugs. In the next chapter, we lay out the ingredients in the crack scare in more detail. Like other demon drugs, crack became a scapegoat—it was blamed for a range of enduring and intensified urban problems that its use sometimes exacerbated but did *not* cause.

MORE THAN MOLECULES: SET, SETTING, AND THE SOCIOLOGY OF DRUGS

We began this book with a critical historical overview of demon drugs and drug scares to show some of the similarities between the crack scare and its predecessors. In the heat of the crack scare, policy makers, the media, and much of the public seemed to suffer from historical amnesia. For over a hundred years, U.S. drug policy has been forged by symbolic politics and special interests, by moral entrepreneurs and media magnification, and by efforts of dominant groups to control "threatening" others from different races and lower classes. These policies have not saved us from our drug-related problems. They have, however, pushed drug use into deviant subcultures and made users into criminals. They have added drug *policy*-related problems to our drug-related problems by creating a harm-maximizing context for drug use. In this book, we argue that this criminalized context has influenced how illicit drugs are used, by whom, what their effects are taken to mean, and to a significant degree even their behavioral consequences.

The idea that the social context of drug use has helped create our drug problems is heretical, but it is heretical largely because discourse about drugs in American culture is dominated by what we call *pharmacological determinism.* One cumulative consequence of our antidrug crusades and punitive policies has been a thoroughgoing demonization of drugs. This demonization invests the substances themselves with more power than they actually have. Citizens and scientists alike have been inculcated with the notion that illicit drugs are inherently dangerous like contagious diseases. But drugs, unlike viruses, are not active agents; they are inert substances. They do not jump out of their containers and into people's bodies without the people in those bodies actively deciding to ingest them. Many Americans understand that drug abuse is more likely among some types of people and under some conditions than others. Yet, because of our history, American culture lacks a vocabulary with which people can speak about drugs in this more complicated, qualified way.

There is another way of thinking and talking about drugs that reveals more than malevolent molecules "causing" bad behavior. This perspective focuses on the psychological, sociological, and cultural factors shaping users' motives, experiences, and behaviors. Certainly pharmacology matters a great deal; crack is profoundly different than alcohol. But the pharmacological properties of a drug do not by themselves determine even a drug's effects, much less the behaviors that sometimes accompany those effects.

This perspective was most clearly formulated by the late Norman E. Zinberg, professor of psychiatry at Harvard Medical School. The basic premise of this theory of drug effects is that, in addition to the interaction between the molecules of the substance and the cells of the human body, drug effects are shaped by *the psychological mind-set of the user*—his or her expectations, mood, mental health, purposes, and personality—and by *the social setting of use*—the characteristics of the situation of use, the social conditions that shape such situations and impinge upon the users, and the historically and culturally specific meanings and motives used to interpret drug effects. All of us who contributed to this book have found that to understand crack and other drugs, we needed to employ this theoretical perspective.

In his book, *Drug, Set, and Setting,* Zinberg (1984, p. vii) wrote that after years of clinical and historical research on drug abuse and treatment, he had become convinced that "in order to understand how and why certain users had lost control," he "would have to tackle the all-important question of how and why many others had managed to achieve control and maintain it." Zinberg began to develop his theory in 1968 when he was on a Guggenheim Fellowship in Britain observing their heroin maintenance system, in which addicts were prescribed heroin by their doctors or special clinics. He found many addicts who functioned successfully and lived quite normal lives. He also found others who did not function well, but, unlike many American "junkies," even they were not engaging in crime or creating problems for anyone but themselves. Zinberg (1984, p. x) "came to understand that the differences between British and American addicts were attributable to their different social settings—that is, to the differing social and legal attitudes toward heroin in the two countries."

Dr. Zinberg also learned about the importance of set and setting in shaping the nature and consequences of drug use shortly after his return to the U.S. There was a new "terror" about a "heroin epidemic" coming from all the soldiers who used heroin in Vietnam. As a consultant to the U.S. Army, Zinberg visited Vietnam, studied the soldiers, and hypothesized that their heroin use was in part attributable to the social setting of a "destructive war environment" (1984, p. x). The army's generals rejected this understanding, but pathbreaking follow-up research on Vietnam veterans by Dr. Lee Robins demonstrated that nearly nine in ten of those who had been addicted to heroin in Vietnam had *not* become readdicted three years after returning to the U.S. (Robins, 1973; Robins et al., 1974). This was a landmark study because until that time drug researchers and heroin addicts alike had believed "once a junkie, always a junkie." Professor Zinberg went on to do further research on controlled heroin users that supported Robins's finding that heroin use did not inevitably lead to addiction and that showed the significance of psychological set and social setting in explaining why some become addicts while others remain controlled users.

Zinberg deserves credit for articulating the "drug, set, and setting" model, especially at a time when scientists and funding agencies were hostile to it, but he was not the only one to discover the importance of set and setting. Many other scholars also contributed to a more social-scientific understanding of drug use and abuse.[5] In 1947, Alfred R. Lindesmith discovered the crucial cognitive element in heroin addiction. His depth interviews with addicts about their drug careers showed that they became addicted *only after* they experienced withdrawal symptoms, recognized them as such, and then decided to ingest more heroin to relieve them. Without this shift in mind-set, heroin use alone did not always result in addiction.

Another early contributor to this perspective was Howard S. Becker. His classic text on deviant behavior, *Outsiders* (1963), contains two sections on marijuana that call analytic attention to sociohistorical, cultural, and social-psychological variables. "Becoming a Marijuana User," first published in a scholarly journal in 1953, followed Lindesmith's lead. Becker analyzed life history interviews with marijuana users and found that the marijuana high was not merely a reflex response of the human body and mind to the active ingredients in marijuana smoke. Rather, the high was *learned* in interaction with knowledgeable smokers. To be able to experience marijuana intoxication, neophyte users first had to learn how to smoke so they would ingest the active ingredients, then to recognize the initially ambiguous effects, and finally to interpret these as pleasurable. Only after people had taken all three of these steps successfully could they decide to become a "marijuana user." Becker's second piece explained how the construction of new rules and norms creates deviance. He traced how a "moral entrepreneur" orchestrated a crusade to criminalize marijuana in the 1930s. By redefining marijuana as "the killer weed," criminalization changed the broad setting in which marijuana was understood and used thereafter.

A few years later Becker (1967) published a study of LSD-induced "psychotic episodes" that even more powerfully demonstrated the importance of set and setting. He drew upon the history of drugs to predict—accurately—that as more people tried LSD, there would be a lower rather than a higher incidence of "bad trips." Becker theorized that drugs produce a variety of effects, some of which can seem subjectively frightening, but that with experience users learn to focus on the positive or desired effects and not on others. This learning would occur because the number of experienced users would grow over time and a user culture would develop in which positive interpretations of the drug's effects would spread. As users came to learn and to teach each other what to expect from a drug, how to use it so as to minimize risks, and so forth, the drug-induced experience would be interpreted as positive rather than "going crazy." And so it was.[6]

Two years after Becker's article on LSD, the theory that drug effects had to do with learning and culture rather than just pharmacology received a major boost, this time from anthropological research on a legal drug. MacAndrew and Edgerton's (1969) classic study of drunken comportment across different cultures found that alcohol's effects on human behavior are highly independent of its effects on human physiology. Although drinking substantial quantities of alcohol always and everywhere eventually produces altered states of consciousness, the behavior of people in such states varies markedly according to the "limits" specific to each culture. In some cultures, alcohol use leads to aggression and sexual arousal, in other cultures, to one but not the other, and in still different societies, to neither. Americans tend to attribute much violent crime to alcohol use, but many other cultures do not. Despite the strong association between drinking and crime in the U.S., other societies have higher alcohol consumption and far less violent crime. Through MacAndrew and Edgerton's cross-cultural lens, one can see that the link between drinking and crime has more to do with American culture (setting) and character (set) than alcohol's direct chemical effects on the human organism.

The causal significance of set and setting also has since been demonstrated in a variety of laboratory experiments on the effects of alcohol. These showed that the mere *belief* that alcohol has been ingested is sufficient for the experience of altered consciousness and behavior culturally associated with drinking. These experiments have demonstrated that when people believe they have ingested alcohol (even when they have really ingested a placebo), they exhibit higher levels of sociability, aggression, or sexual arousal. Conversely, people who ingest real alcohol believing it to be a placebo often exhibit no behavioral change at all (see Critchlow, 1986, and Reinarman and Leigh, 1987, for reviews of this literature). This point was nicely summarized by Robin Room in his introduction to *Drinking and Disinhibition,* a research monograph published by the National Institute on Alcohol Abuse and Alcoholism:

> In recent years evidence has been building up from a number of disciplinary areas to suggest that the link between alcohol and disinhibition is a matter of cultural belief rather than of pharmacological action. Alcohol is certainly a psychoactive drug; we feel different when drunk than when sober. But how we interpret those feelings, and in particular how we act on them, is largely determined by culture and circumstance; thus what is pharmacologically the same drug can make us aggressive or passive, ebullient or morose, frenetic or immobile. In this view, psychoactivity does not determine whether behavior is disinhibited or controlled: it simply provides an empty vessel of altered consciousness for culture, circumstance, and personality to load with meanings and explanations. (Room and Collins, 1983, pp. v-vi)

One need not resort to rigorous laboratory experiments to understand the influence of set and setting on drug effects. With respect to users' psychological sets, for example, our students report that at their "keggers" or beer parties, everyone gets high on the same beer, but a few people end up dancing on tabletops, one or two others might quietly cry in the corner, and most just dance, talk, and flirt. With respect to the social settings of use, most people have noticed that two drinks at a New Year's Eve party have very different effects than the same two drinks at a relative's wake. Most people understand from their own everyday experience that the felt effects and behavioral consequences of a drug vary according to how users' psychological sets interact with the social settings of their drug use. The mindset and drinking patterns of an office worker joining her colleagues for a beer after work are quite different from those of a bored, alienated, sixteen-year-old high school dropout using malt liquor to get through the day. But because of America's long history of drug demonization and pharmacological determinism, public debate and policy do not usually consider the social and psychological effects of set and setting.

In the case of crack cocaine, the most important psychological sets and social settings are the ones shaped by poverty, racism, and the range of other human troubles that flow from them. We do not mean by this that cocaine smoking has not occurred among the white and the affluent; indeed, the forerunner of crack, freebasing, first became widely known because it was associated with rock stars and Hollywood celebrities. As we note in Chapter 4, there is no doubt that there was considerable experimentation with and even some heavy use of crack and freebase by some white affluent suburbanites in the 1980s. In this book, we emphasize the distinctive mind-sets and settings of the inner-city poor because heavy crack use has been highly concentrated among and most consequential for them. Further, it was the use and sales of crack by young, urban African-Americans and Latinos that animated the crack scare and much of the drug war's imagery.

All forms of licit and illicit drug use, abuse, and addiction can be found in all classes, races, and regions. The sociology of set and setting is just as important for understanding why white youth find LSD a temporary antidote to suburbia's spiritual impoverishment, why stressed-out affluent professionals savor an MDMA or "ecstasy" trip as if it were a chemically induced Club Med weekend, and why so many American men of all classes and races assault or batter women after drinking alcohol. But whatever constellations of sets and settings shape drug use among the broad middle strata of the U.S. population, these people tend to be employed and ensconced in lives that anchor them in the conventional order. Middle-class people whose lives become too difficult often have psychiatrists who prescribe them antidepressants like Prozac. When middle-class Americans become addicted, they have many more resources to use to pull themselves out of trouble and many more opportunities to make a successful life. When some middle-class Americans began having trouble with cocaine freebase in the early 1980s, for example, treatment industry entrepreneurs expanded their services to help them stabilize their lives.

By contrast, the inner-city poor and working class are far less often employed and more often live at the margins of the conventional order. When their lives become too difficult, they rarely have psychiatrists, but they sometimes self-medicate, escape, or seek moments of intense euphoria with what might be called anti*despondents,* such as crack. When some of them become addicted, they have far fewer resources to use to pull themselves out of trouble and far fewer opportunities to make a successful life (Harrell and Peterson, 1992). And when some of the inner-city poor began having trouble with crack, politicians declared a drug war that did *not* help them stabilize their lives.

·   ·   ·   ·   ·   ·   ·

We have sketched this alternative theoretical framework because the drug war rhetoric and scare stories of politicians and the media have consistently attributed devastating consequences to crack, as if these consequences flowed directly from its molecular structure. Such rhetoric squeezes out of public discourse any serious consideration of the social, cultural, economic, and psychological variables that are essential for understanding drug use and its behavioral consequences. If we are to forge more effective and humane responses to our drug problems, then we must move beyond demonization and pharmacological determinism. What we have called the drug, set, and setting perspective is the best theoretical sensibility we have found for this difficult task, and it informs each of the chapters in this book.

From the beginning, we, as editors, conceived of this book as a kind of expert commission report. We asked prominent drug scholars in a variety of fields to write chapters on various dimensions of the crack problem. Understanding all the issues raised by the crack crisis was beyond any one or two individual scientists. There is simply too much to know, too much research to be done. We designed this book to have a thematic and conceptual unity that is uncommon in edited collections. This is in large part because we and so many of our fellow contributors have worked out our ideas together over the years, shared leads and findings, tested hunches, and arrived at the sociological understanding of drugs outlined previously. All the contributors agree about the central role played by poverty and racism in shaping the sets and settings that created the crack crisis, and all believe that American drug policy can be both more effective and more humane.

NOTES

1. Scares have not been limited to drugs and communists. For example, in 1920, there was a ouija board scare of several months duration that shared some characteristics with the crack scare. Newspapers spoke of "a wave of insanity" caused by ouija boards that had grown to "national prominence." A typical front-page article in the *San Francisco Chronicle* read, "Breaking into a house at El Cerrito, . . . police officers yesterday took into custody several persons who had become insane from playing with ouija boards." It seems a fifteen-year-old girl had used the board to "induce unknown power" over the others (March 4, 1920, p. 1). Two days later in another raid, other "victims," including a policeman, were found to have been transformed "from a state of normality to that of madness" under the influence of this parlor game. In a fit of what appeared to be superhuman strength usually attributed to a drug, the policeman had "knocked down two guards," escaped, hijacked a car, and "dashed into the Central National Bank in a nude condition" (*San Francisco Chronicle,* March 6, 1920, p. 1). Before the ouija board scare had run its course, many others had been arrested and jailed or committed to asylums, and "experts" held serious discussions about "abolishing 'seances' " (*San Francisco Examiner,* March 7, 1920, p. 1). For an excellent theoretical analysis of such scares, see Goode and Ben-Yehuda (1994).

2. See, for example, Fagan (1992) for a strong empirical study showing that the youth drawn into crack and other drug sales in "distressed neighborhoods" were not drawn away from legal employment into the crack economy. Rather, most were unemployed and lacked the "human capital" necessary to break into the legal labor market. Thus, for these youth, the drug world provided economic opportunity as well as recreation.

3. From interviews conducted by Pat O'Hare and Peter McDermott, personal communication.

4. When we have pointed out to journalists these sorts of exaggerated and distorted claims, they have often defended their colleagues by saying that such sentiments were merely journalistic hyperbole. But these statements are not hyperbole. Hyerbole is a rhetorical device employing exaggeration that lets the audience in on the joke—for example, saying that the ice cream was "piled a mile high." Statements that the drug "plague is all but universal," that crack is "instantaneously addicting," and that crack is "all over the place" in affluent suburbs earnestly reported as fact what was actually fiction.

5. Although we have drawn in particular on Zinberg's theoretical formulation, we have also benefited greatly from many other scholars whose research on drugs fits within and has contributed to this perspective. They are too numerous to name, but we cite them throughout this book. Deserving of special mention in this regard is Zinberg's Harvard Medical School colleague, Professor Lester Grinspoon, M.D. See especially his book, *Cocaine: A Drug and Its Social Evolution* (1976), co-authored with James Bakalar.

6. Bunce (1982) subsequently tested Becker's prediction with data on the prevalence of "bad trips" on LSD and found it correct. Bunce also added the useful insight that the extraordinarily conflicting accounts of LSD's effects (*e.g.,* insanity producing vs. mind expanding) helped create a cultural setting and psychological sets that increased the likelihood of such "bad trips."

REFERENCES

Becker, Howard S., "Becoming a Marijuana User," *American Journal of Sociology* 59:235–242 (1953).

———, *Outsiders* (New York: Free Press, 1963).

———, "History, Culture, and Subjective Experience: An Exploration of the Social Bases of Drug-Induced Experiences," *Journal of Health and Social Behavior* 8: 162–176 (1967).

Bunce, Richard, "Social and Political Sources of Drug Effects: The Case of Bad Trips on Psychedelics," pp. 105–125 in N. E. Zinberg and W. M. Harding, eds., *Control Over Intoxicant Use: Pharmacological, Psychological, and Social Considerations* (New York: Human Sciences Press, 1982).

Critchlow, Barbara, "The Powers of John Barleycorn: Beliefs About the Effects of Alcohol on Social Behavior," *American Psychologist* 41:751–764 (1986).

Dickson, Donald, "Bureaucracy and Morality," *Social Problems* 16:143–156 (1968).

Duster, Troy, *The Legislation of Morality: Law, Drugs, and Moral Judgment* (New York: Free Press, 1970).

Fagan, Jeffrey, "Drug Selling and Licit Income in Distressed Neighborhoods: The Economic Lives of Street-Level Drug Users and Dealers," pp. 99–142 in A. V. Harrell and G. E. Peterson, eds., *Drugs, Crime, and Social Isolation: Barriers to Urban Opportunity* (Washington, DC: Urban Institute Press, 1992).

Goode, Erich, and Nachman Ben-Yehuda, *Moral Panics: The Social Construction of Deviance* (Cambridge, MA: Blackwell, 1994).

Grinspoon, Lester, and James B. Bakalar, *Cocaine: A Drug and Its Social Evolution* (New York: Basic Books, 1976).

————, *Marijuana: The Forbidden Medicine* (New Haven, CT: Yale University Press, 1993).

Gusfield, Joseph R., *Symbolic Crusade: Status Politics and the American Temperance Movement*, 2nd ed. (Urbana: University of Illinois Press, 1986[1963]).

Harrell, Adele V., and George E. Peterson, eds., *Drugs, Crime, and Social Isolation: Barriers to Urban Opportunity* (Washington, DC: Urban Institute Press, 1992).

Himmelstein, Jerome, *The Strange Career of Marihuana* (Westport, CT: Greenwood, 1983).

Kobler, John, *Ardent Spirits: The Rise and Fall of Prohibition* (New York: Putnam's, 1973).

Levine, Harry G., "The Alcohol Problem in America: From Temperance to Alcoholism," *British Journal of Addiction* 79:109–119 (1984).

————, "The Birth of American Alcohol Control: Prohibition, Repeal, and the Power Elite," *Contemporary Drug Problems* 12:63–115 (1985).

————, "Prohibition, Alcohol Control, and the Problem of Lawlessness," pp. 151–159 in P. Park and W. Matverychuk, eds., *Culture and the Politics of Drugs* (Dubuque, IA: Kendall Hunt, 1986).

Lindesmith, Alfred R., *Opiate Addiction* (Evanston, IL: Principia Press, 1947).

————, *The Addict and the Law* (Bloomington: Indiana University Press, 1965).

MacAndrew, Craig, and Robert Edgerton, *Drunken Comportment: A Social Explanation* (Chicago: Aldine, 1969).

Morgan, Patricia, "The Legislation of Drug Law: Economic Crisis and Social Control," *Journal of Drug Issues* 8:53–62 (1978).

Musto, David, *The American Disease: Origins of Narcotic Control* (New Haven, CT: Yale University Press, 1973).

National Commission on Marijuana and Drug Abuse, *Marijuana: A Signal of Misunderstanding* (Washington, DC: U.S. Government Printing Office, 1972).

National Research Council, *Analysis of Marijuana Policy: Report of the Committee on Substance Abuse and Habitual Behavior on Drug Policy* (Washington, DC: National Academy of Sciences, 1982).

Ostrow, Ronald J., "Casual Drug Users Should Be Shot, Gates Says," *Los Angeles Times* (September 6, 1990, p. A1).

Reinarman, Craig, and Barbara Critchlow Leigh, "Culture, Cognition, and Disinhibition: Notes on Sexuality and Alcohol in the Age of AIDS," *Contemporary Drug Problems* 14:435–460 (1987).

Robins, Lee N., *A Followup of Vietnam Drug Users*. White House Special Action Office Monograph, Series A, #1 (Washington, DC: U.S. Government Printing Office, 1973).

Robins, Lee N., D. H. Davis, and D. W. Goodwin, "Drug Use in U.S. Army Enlisted Men in Vietnam: A Follow-up on Their Return Home," *American Journal of Epidemiology* 99:235–249 (1974).

Room, Robin, and Gary Collins, eds., *Alcohol and Disinhibition*. National Institute on Alcohol Abuse and Alcoholism, Research Monograph 12 (Washington, DC: U.S. Department of Health and Human Services, 1983).

Rumbarger, John, *Profits, Power, and Prohibition* (Albany: State University of New York Press, 1989).

Timberlake, James H., *Prohibition and the Progressive Movement, 1900–1920* (Cambridge, MA: Harvard University Press, 1963).

Waldorf, Dan, Martin Orlick, and Craig Reinarman, *Morphine Maintenance: The Shreveport Clinic, 1919–1923* (Washington, DC: The Drug Abuse Council, 1974).

Waldorf, Dan, Craig Reinarman, and Sheigla B. Murphy, *Cocaine Changes: The Experience of Using and Quitting* (Philadelphia, PA: Temple University Press, 1991).

Zinberg, Norman E., *Drug, Set, and Setting: The Basis for Controlled Intoxicant Use* (New Haven, CT: Yale University Press, 1984).

TWO

The Crack Attack

Politics and Media in the Crack Scare

Craig Reinarman and Harry G. Levine

America discovered crack and overdosed on oratory.
NEW YORK TIMES (EDITORIAL, OCTOBER 4, 1988)

This *New York Times* editorial had a certain unintended irony, for "America's paper of record" itself had long been one of the leading orators, supplying a steady stream of the stuff on which the nation had, as they put it, "overdosed." Irony aside, the editorial hit the mark. The use of powder cocaine by affluent people in music, film, sports, and business had been common since the 1970s. According to surveys by the National Institute on Drug Abuse (NIDA), by 1985, more than twenty-two million Americans in all social classes and occupations had reported at least trying cocaine. Cocaine smoking originated with "freebasing," which began increasing by the late 1970s (see Inciardi, 1987; Siegel, 1982). Then (as now) most cocaine users bought cocaine hydrochloride (powder) for intranasal use (snorting). But by the end of the 1970s, some users had begun to "cook" powder cocaine down to crystalline or "base" form for smoking. All phases of freebasing, from selling to smoking, took place most often in the privacy of homes and offices of middle-class or well-to-do users. They typically purchased cocaine in units of a gram or more costing $80 to $100 a gram. These relatively affluent "basers" had been discovering the intense rush of smoking cocaine, as well as the risks, for a number of years before the term "crack" was coined. But most such users had a stake in conventional life. Therefore, when they felt their cocaine use was too heavy or out of control, they had the incentives and resources to cut down, quit, or get private treatment.

There was no orgy of media and political attention in the late 1970s when the prevalence of cocaine use jumped sharply, or even after middle-class and upper-class users began to use heavily, especially when freebasing. Like the crack users who followed them, basers had found that this mode of ingesting cocaine produced a much more intense and far shorter "high" because it delivered more pure cocaine into the brain far more directly and rapidly than by snorting. Many basers had found that crack's intense, brutally brief rush, combined with the painful "low" or "down" that immediately followed, produced a powerful desire immediately to repeat use—to binge (Waldorf et al., 1991; Chapter 7).

Crack's pharmacological power alone does not explain the attention it received. In 1986, politicians and the media focused on crack—and the drug scare began—when cocaine smoking became visible among a "dangerous" group. Crack attracted the attention of politicians and the media because of its downward mobility to and increased visibility in ghettos and barrios. The new users were a different social class, race, and status (Duster, 1970; Washton and Gold, 1987). Crack was sold in smaller, cheaper, precooked units, on ghetto streets, to poorer, younger buyers who were already seen as a threat (*e.g., New York Times,* August 30, 1987; *Newsweek,* November 23, 1987; *Boston Globe,* May 18, 1988). Crack spread cocaine smoking into poor populations already beset with a cornucopia of troubles (Wilson, 1987). These people tended to have fewer bonds to conventional society, less to lose, and far fewer resources to cope with or shield themselves from drug-related problems.

The earliest mass media reference to the new form of cocaine may have been a *Los Angeles Times* article in late 1984 (November 25, p. cc1) on the use of cocaine "rocks" in ghettos and barrios in Los Angeles. By late 1985, the *New York Times* made the national media's first specific reference to "crack" in a story about three teenagers seeking treatment for cocaine abuse (November 17, p. B12). At the start of 1986, crack was known only in a few impoverished neighborhoods in Los Angeles, New York, Miami, and perhaps a few other large cities.

The news media and politicians played the most important roles in establishing what we have called "the crack scare." In this chapter, first we trace media coverage of the "crack crisis" and some of the core claims made about the destructiveness of the cocaine and crack "plague." Second, we contrast these claims with the primary U.S. government data on which they were purportedly based. We show that a gap existed between the official statistical evidence[1] and the prevalence claims of the media and politicians. We maintain that the media and politicians misrepresented or ignored the evidence and instead provided propaganda for the drug war. The crack scare, in other words, was not merely a rational response to a new threat to public health and public order. It possessed its own causes and logic. Third, we situate the crack scare in the context of the Reagan/Bush era. In this conservative ideological environment, supporting the drug war became extremely useful politically, for Democrats as well as Republicans. The drug war was not effective or wise policy, but politicians promoted it nonetheless because, among other reasons, it provided a convenient scapegoat for enduring and ever growing urban poverty.

THE FRENZY: COCAINE AND CRACK IN THE PUBLIC EYE

When two celebrity athletes died in what news stories called "crack-related deaths" in the spring of 1986, the media seemed to sense a potential bonanza. Coverage skyrocketed and crack became widely known. "Dramatic footage" of black and Latino men being carted off in chains, or of police breaking down crack house doors, became a near nightly news event. In July 1986 alone, the three major TV networks offered seventy-four evening news segments on drugs, half of these about crack (Diamond et al., 1987; Reeves and Campbell, 1994). In the months leading up to the November elections, a handful of national newspapers and magazines produced roughly a thousand stories discussing crack (Inciardi, 1987, p. 481; Trebach, 1987, pp. 6–16). Like the TV networks, leading news magazines such as *Time* and *Newsweek* seemed determined not to be outdone; each devoted five cover stories to crack and the "drug crisis" in 1986 alone.

In the fall of 1986, the CBS news show *48 Hours* aired a heavily promoted documentary called "48 Hours on Crack Street," which Dan Rather previewed on his evening news show: "Tonight, CBS News takes you to the streets, to the war zone, for an unusual two hours of hands on horror." Among many shots from hidden cameras was one of New York Senator Alphonse D'Amato and then-U.S. Attorney Rudolf Guiliani, *in cognito*, purchasing crack to dramatize the brazenness of street corner sales in the ghetto. All this was good business for CBS: the program earned the highest Nielsen rating of any similar news show in the previous five years—fifteen million viewers (Diamond et al., 1987, p. 10). Three years later, after poor ratings nearly killed *48 Hours*, the show kicked off its season with a three-hour special, "Return to Crack Street."

The intense media competition for audience shares and advertising dollars spawned many similar shows. Three days after "48 Hours on Crack Street," NBC ran its own prime-time special, "Cocaine Country," which suggested that cocaine and crack use had become pandemic. This was one of dozens of separate stories on crack and cocaine produced by NBC alone—an unprecedented fifteen hours of air time—in the seven months leading up to the 1986 elections (Diamond et al., 1987; Hoffman, 1987). By mid-1986, *Newsweek* claimed that crack was the biggest story since Vietnam and Watergate (June 15, p. 15), and *Time* soon followed by calling crack "the Issue of the Year" (September 22, 1986, p. 25). The words "plague," "epidemic," and "crisis" had become routine. The *New York Times*, for example, did a three-part, front-page series called "The Crack Plague" (June 24, 1988, p. A1).

The crack scare began in 1986, but it waned somewhat in 1987 (a non-election year). In 1988, drugs returned to the national stage as stories about the "crack epidemic" again appeared regularly on front pages and

TV screens (Reeves and Campbell, 1994). One politician after another reenlisted in the War on Drugs. In that election year, as in 1986, overwhelming majorities of both houses of Congress voted for new antidrug laws with long mandatory prison terms, death sentences, and large increases in funding for police and prisons. The annual federal budget for antidrug efforts surged from less than $2 billion in 1981 to more than $12 billion in 1993. The budget for the Drug Enforcement Administration (DEA) quadrupled between 1981 and 1992 (Massing, 1993). The Bush administration alone spent $45 billion—more than all other presidents since Nixon combined—mostly for law enforcement (Horgan, 1993; Office of National Drug Control Policy, 1992).[2]

Democrats and Republicans, liberals and conservatives alike called repeatedly for an "all-out war on drugs." In 1986, President and Nancy Reagan led a string of prominent politicians in asserting that drugs, especially crack, were "tearing our country apart" and "killing . . . a whole generation [of] . . . our children" (*Time*, September 22, 1986, p. 25). In the 1988 election season, even more politicians claimed that crack was destroying American youth and causing much of the crime, violence, prostitution, and child abuse in the nation.

An April 1988 ABC News special report termed crack "a plague" that was "eating away at the fabric of America." According to this documentary, Americans spend "$20 billion a year on cocaine," American businesses lose "$60 billion" a year in productivity because their workers use drugs, "the educational system is being undermined" by student drug use, and "the family" is "disintegrating" in the face of this "epidemic." This program did not give its millions of viewers any evidence to support such dramatic claims, but it did give them a powerful *vocabulary of attribution:* "drugs," especially crack, threatened all the central institutions in American life—families, communities, schools, businesses, law enforcement, even national sovereignty.

This media frenzy continued into 1989. Between October 1988 and October 1989, for example, the *Washington Post* alone ran 1565 stories—28,476 column inches—about the drug crisis. Even Richard Harwood (1989), the *Post's* own ombudsman, editorialized against what he called the loss of "a proper sense of perspective" due to such a "hyperbole epidemic." He said that "politicians are doing a number on people's heads." In the fall of 1989, another major new federal antidrug bill to further increase drug war funding (S-1233) began winding its way through Congress. In September, President Bush's "drug czar," William Bennett, unveiled his comprehensive battle plan, the *National Drug Control Strategy*. His introduction asks, "What . . . accounts for the intensifying drug-related chaos that we see every day in our newspapers and on television? One word explains much of it. That word is *crack*. . . . Crack is responsible for the fact that vast patches of the American urban landscape are rapidly deteriorating" (The White House, 1989, p. 3, original emphasis).

Bennett's plan proposed yet another $2.2 billion increase in drug war spending, 70% of which was to be allocated to police and prisons, a percentage unchanged since the Nixon administration (*New York Times*, September 6, 1989, p. A11). The funds were to be used nearly to double prison capacity so that even casual users as well as dealers could be incarcerated. The plan also proposed the sale of drug war bonds (reminiscent of World War II) as a means of financing the $7.9 billion first-year costs. President Bush returned to Washington early from summer vacation at his estate on the Maine coast to rehearse with his media advisors the presentation of the plan (*New York Times,* September 6, 1989, p. A1).

On September 5, 1989, President Bush, speaking from the presidential desk in the Oval Office, announced his plan for achieving "victory over drugs" in his first major prime-time address to the nation, broadcast on all three national television networks. We want to focus on this incident as an example of the way politicians and the media systematically misinformed and deceived the public in order to promote the War on Drugs. During the address, Bush held up to the cameras a clear plastic bag of crack labeled "EVIDENCE." He announced that it was "seized a few days ago in a park across the street from the White House" (*Washington Post,* September 22, 1989, p. A1). Its contents, Bush said, were "turning our cities into battle zones and murdering our children." The president proclaimed that, because of crack and other drugs, he would "more than double" federal assistance to state and local law enforcement (*New York Times,* September 6, 1989, p. A11). The next morning the picture of the president holding a bag of crack was on the front pages of newspapers across America.

About two weeks later, the *Washington Post,* and then National Public Radio and other newspapers, discovered how the president of the United States had obtained his bag of crack. According to White House and DEA officials, "the idea of the President holding up crack was [first] included in some drafts" of his speech. Bush enthusiastically approved. A White House aide told the *Post* that the president "liked the prop. . . . It drove the point home." Bush and his advisors also decided that the crack should be seized in Lafayette Park across from the White House so the president could say that crack had become so pervasive that it was being sold "in front of the White House" (Isikoff, 1989).

This decision set up a complex chain of events. White House Communications Director David Demarst asked Cabinet Affairs Secretary David Bates to instruct the Justice Department "to find some crack that fit the description in the speech." Bates called Richard Weatherbee, special assistant to Attorney General Dick Thornburgh, who then called James Millford, executive assistant to the DEA chief. Finally, Milford phoned William

McMullen, special agent in charge of the DEA's Washington office, and told him to arrange an undercover crack buy near the White House because "evidently, the President wants to show it could be bought anywhere" (Isikoff, 1989).

Despite their best efforts, the top federal drug agents were not able to find anyone selling crack (or any other drug) in Lafayette Park, or anywhere else in the vicinity of the White House. Therefore, in order to carry out their assignment, DEA agents had to entice someone to come to the park to make the sale. Apparently, the only person the DEA could convince was Keith Jackson, an eighteen-year-old African-American high school senior. McMullan reported that it was difficult because Jackson "did not even know where the White House was." The DEA's secret tape recording of the conversation revealed that the teenager seemed baffled by the request: "Where the [expletive deleted] is the White House?" he asked. Therefore, McMullan told the *Post,* "we had to manipulate him to get him down there. It wasn't easy" (Isikoff, 1989).

The undesirability of selling crack in Lafayette Park was confirmed by men from Washington, D.C., imprisoned for drug selling, and interviewed by National Public Radio. All agreed that nobody would sell crack there because, among other reasons, there would be no customers. The crack-using population was in Washington's poor African-American neighborhoods some distance from the White House. The *Washington Post* and other papers also reported that the undercover DEA agents had not, after all, actually seized the crack, as Bush had claimed in his speech. Rather, the DEA agents purchased it from Jackson for $2400 and then let him go.[3]

This incident illustrates how a drug scare distorts and perverts public knowledge and policy. The claim that crack was threatening every neighborhood in America was not based on evidence; after three years of the scare, crack remained predominantly in the inner cities where it began. Instead, this claim appears to have been based on the symbolic political value seen by Bush's speech writers. When they sought, after the fact, to purchase their own crack to prove this point, they found that reality did not match their script. Instead of changing the script to reflect reality, a series of high-level officials instructed federal drug agents to *create* a reality that would fit the script. Finally, the president of the United States displayed the procured prop on national television. Yet, when all this was revealed, neither politicians nor the media were led to question the president's policies or his claims about crack's pervasiveness.

As a result of Bush's performance and all the other antidrug publicity and propaganda, in 1988 and 1989, the drug war commanded more public attention than any other issue. The media and politicians' antidrug crusade succeeded in making many Americans even more fearful of crack and other illicit drugs. A *New York Times/CBS News* poll has periodically asked Americans to identify "the most important problem facing this country today." In January 1985, 23% answered war or nuclear war; less than 1% believed the most important problem was drugs. In September 1989, shortly after the president's speech and the blizzard of drug stories that followed, 64% of those polled believed that drugs were now the most important problem, and only 1% thought that war or nuclear war was most important. Even the *New York Times* declared in a lead editorial that this reversal was "incredible" and then gently suggested that problems like war, "homelessness and the need to give poor children a chance in life" should perhaps be given more attention (September 28, 1989, p. A26).

A year later, during a lull in antidrug speeches and coverage, the percentage citing "drugs" as the nation's top problem had dropped to 10%. Noting this "precipitous fall from a remarkable height," the *Times* observed that an "alliance of Presidents and news directors" shaped public opinion about drugs. Indeed, once the White House let it be known that the president would be giving a prime-time address on the subject, all three networks tripled their coverage of drugs in the two weeks prior to his speech and quadrupled it for a week afterward (*New York Times,* September 6, 1990, p. A11; see also Reeves and Campbell, 1994). All this occurred while nearly every index of drug use was dropping.

The crack scare continued in 1990 and 1991, although with somewhat less media and political attention. By the beginning of 1992—the last year of the Bush administration—the War on Drugs in general, and the crack scare in particular, had begun to decline significantly in prominence and importance. However, even as the drug war was receiving less notice from politicians and the media, it remained institutionalized, bureaucratically powerful, and extremely well funded (especially police, military, and education/propaganda activities).

From the opening shots in 1986 to President Bush's national address in 1989, and through all the stories about "crack babies" in 1990 and 1991, politicians and the media depicted crack as supremely evil—*the* most important cause of America's problems. As recently as February of 1994, a prominent *New York Times* journalist repeated the claim that "An entire generation is being sacrificed to [crack]" (Staples, 1994). As in all drug scares since the nineteenth-century crusade against alcohol, a core feature of drug war discourse is the *routinization of caricature*—worst cases framed as typical cases, the episodic rhetorically recrafted into the epidemic.

OFFICIAL GOVERNMENT EVIDENCE

On those rare occasions when politicians and journalists cited statistical evidence to support their claims about the prevalence of crack and other drug use, they usually relied on two basic sources, both funded by the National Institute on Drug Abuse. One was the Drug Abuse Warning Network (DAWN), a monitoring project set up to survey a sample of hospitals, crisis and treatment centers, and coroners across the country about drug-related emergencies and deaths. The other was the National Household Survey on Drug Abuse among general population households and among young people. Other data sources existed, but these usually were either anecdotal, specific to a particular location, or based on a skewed sample.[4] Therefore, we review what these two NIDA data sources had to say about crack because they were the only national data and because they are still considered by experts and claims makers to be the most reliable form of evidence available.[5]

The Drug Abuse Warning Network

DAWN collects data on a whole series of drugs—from amphetamine to aspirin—that might be present in emergencies or fatalities. These data take the form of "mentions." A drug mention is produced when a patient, or someone with a patient, tells attending medical personnel that the patient recently used the drug, or occasionally, if a blood test shows the presence of the drug. These data provided perhaps the only piece of statistical support for the crack scare. They indicated that cocaine was "mentioned" in an increasing number of emergency room episodes in the 1980s. During 1986, as the scare moved into full swing, there were an estimated 51,600 emergency room episodes in which cocaine was mentioned (NIDA, 1993a). In subsequent years, the estimated number of such mentions continued to rise, providing clear cause for concern. By 1989, for example, the estimated number of emergency room episodes in which cocaine was mentioned had more than doubled to 110,000. Although the estimate dropped sharply in 1990 to 80,400, by 1992, it had risen again to 119,800 (NIDA, 1993a).

Unfortunately, the meaning of a mention is ambiguous. In many of these cases, cocaine was probably incidental to the emergency room visit. Such episodes included routine cases in which people went to emergency rooms, for example, after being injured as passengers in auto accidents and in home accidents. Moreover, in most cases, cocaine was only one of the drugs in the person's system; most people had also been drinking alcohol. Finally, the DAWN data do not include information about preexisting medical or mental health conditions that make any drug use, legal or illegal, more risky. For all these reasons, one cannot properly infer direct cause from the estimates of emergency room mentions. Cocaine did play a causal role in many of these emergency cases, but no one knows how many or what proportion of the total they were.

The DAWN data on deaths in which cocaine was mentioned by medical examiners also must be closely examined. When the crack scare got under way in 1986, coroners coded 1092 deaths as "cocaine related" (NIDA, 1986a), and as crack spread, this number, too, increased substantially. In 1989, the secretary of health and human services reported a 20% decline in both deaths and emergency room episodes in which cocaine was mentioned,[6] but both indices rose again in 1991 and 1992. The 1992 DAWN figures showed 3020 deaths in which cocaine was mentioned (NIDA, 1992).

But cocaine *alone* was mentioned in only a fraction of these deaths; in 1986, for example, in less than one in five (NIDA, 1986a). In most of these cases, cocaine had been used with other drugs, again, most often alcohol. Although any death is tragic, cocaine's role in such fatalities remains ambiguous. "Cocaine related" is not the same as "cocaine caused," and "cocaine-related deaths" does not mean "deaths *due to* cocaine." There is little doubt that cocaine contributes to some significant (but unknown) percentage of such deaths. But journalists, politicians, and most of the experts on whom they relied never acknowledged the ambiguities in the data. Nor did they commonly provide any comparative perspective. For example, for every *one* cocaine-related death in the U.S., there have been approximately two hundred tobacco-related deaths and at least fifty alcohol-related deaths. Seen in this light, cocaine's role in mortality and morbidity was substantially less than media accounts and political rhetoric implied.

More serious interpretive and empirical difficulties appeared when the DAWN data were used to support claims about crack. Despite all the attention paid to the crack "plague" in 1986, when crack was allegedly "killing a whole generation," the DAWN data contained *no specific information on crack* as distinct from cocaine. In fact, the DAWN data show that in the vast majority of both emergencies and deaths in which cocaine received a mention, the mode of ingestion of cocaine was *not* "smoking" and therefore could not have been caused by crack. Thus, although it is likely that crack played a role in some of the emergencies and deaths in which cocaine was "mentioned," the data necessary to attribute them accurately to crack did not exist.

NIDA Surveys

The NIDA-sponsored surveys of drug use produce the data that are the statistical basis of all estimates of the prevalence of cocaine and other drug use. One of the core claims in the crack scare was that drug use among teenagers and young adults was already high and that it was growing at an alarming rate. Although politicians and the media often referred to teen drug use as an "epidemic" or "plague," the best official evidence available at the time did not support such claims. The National Household Survey on Drug Abuse surveys over eight thousand randomly selected households each year. These surveys show that the number of Americans who had used any illegal drug in the previous month began to decline in 1979, and in the early years of the crack scare, use of drugs, including cocaine, continued to decline (*New York Times*, September 24, 1989, p. A1; *Newsweek*, February 19, 1990, p. 74). Lifetime prevalence of cocaine use among young people (the percentage of those twelve through twenty-five years old who had "ever" tried it) peaked in 1982, *four years before the scare began*, and continued to decline after that (NIDA, 1991, p. 14). The sharpest rise in lifetime prevalence among young adults had taken place between 1972 and 1979; it produced no claims of an epidemic or plague by politicians and journalists (Johnston et al., 1988; NIDA, 1986b).

In February 1987, NIDA released the results of its 1986 annual survey of high school seniors. The *New York Times* handling of the story shows how even the most respectable media institutions sometimes skew facts about drug use to fit a story line. In the article's "lead," the *Times* announced a rise in the percentage of high school seniors reporting "daily" use of cocaine. Only later did one learn that this had risen very slightly and, more important for evaluating claims of a "plague," that daily use among seniors had now reached 0.4%. Daily crack use, even by this fraction of 1% of high school seniors, is surely troubling, but it hardly constituted a new drug epidemic or plague. Still later in the story, the *Times* presented a table showing other declines in cocaine use by young adults and high school seniors. Indeed, as the *Times* noted toward the end of its piece, virtually all forms of teenage drug use (including marijuana, LSD, and heroin) had declined—as they had in previous years (*New York Times*, February 24, 1987, p. A21; cf. Johnston et al., 1988; NIDA, 1991).

Two leading NIDA scholars, reporting in 1986 on the results of the household survey in *Science* magazine, wrote that "both annual prevalence and current prevalence [of all drug use] among college students and the total sample up to four years after high school has been relatively stable between 1980 and 1985" (Kozel and Adams, 1986, p. 973). The director of NIDA's high school surveys, Dr. Lloyd Johnston, made a similar point in 1987: "To some degree the fad quality of drugs has worn off" (*New York Times*, February 24, 1987, p. A21). When the findings of the high school senior survey for 1987 were released, the survey's director reported that "the most important" finding was that cocaine had again "showed a significant drop in use." He even reported a decline in the use of crack (Johnston et al., 1988).

These reported declines were in keeping with the general downward trend in drug use. In the early 1980s, according to the NIDA surveys, about one in six young Americans had tried cocaine powder. But between 1986 and 1987, the proportion of both high school seniors and young adults who had used cocaine in any form in the previous year dropped by 20% (Johnston et al., 1988). Further, two-thirds of those who had ever tried cocaine had not used it in the previous month. Although a significant minority of young people had tried cocaine powder at some point, the great majority of them did not continue to use it.

There had been a few signs of increasing cocaine use. The proportion of youngsters who reported using cocaine at least once in the previous month had increased slightly over the years, although it never exceeded 2% of all teens in the seven national household surveys between 1972 and 1985. The 1988 NIDA household survey found an increase in the number of adult daily users of cocaine, presumably the group that included crack addicts. But this group constituted only about 1.3% of those adults who had ever used cocaine. NIDA also estimated that about 0.5% of the total U.S. adult population had used cocaine in the week prior to the survey (NIDA, 1988).

But aside from these few slight increases, almost all other measures showed that the trends in official drug use statistics had been down even before the scare began (see Figures 2-1, 2-2, and 2-3). The figures for cocaine use in particular were dropping just as crisis claims were reaching a crescendo, and had dropped still further precisely when the Bush/Bennett battle plan was being announced with such fanfare in 1989. Indeed, as White House officials anonymously admitted a few weeks after the president's "bag of crack" speech, the new plan's "true goals" were far more modest than its rhetoric: the Bush plan was "simply to move the nation 'a little bit' beyond where current trends would put it anyway" (*New York Times,* September 24, 1989, p. A1).

National Survey Data on Crack

Tom Brokaw reported on *NBC Nightly News* in 1986 (May 23) that crack was "flooding America" and that it had become "America's drug of choice." His colleagues at the other networks and in the print media had made similar claims. An ordinarily competent news consumer might well have gathered the impression that crack could be found in the lockers of most high school students. Yet, at the time of these press reports, *there were no prevalence statistics at all on crack* and no evidence of any sort showing that smoking crack had become the preferred mode even of cocaine use, much less of drug use.

When NIDA released the first official data on crack a few months later, they still did not support claims about widespread crack use. On the contrary, the NIDA survey found that most cocaine use could not have been crack because the preferred mode of use for 90% of cocaine users was "sniffing" rather than smoking (NIDA, 1986a; see also Inciardi, 1987). An

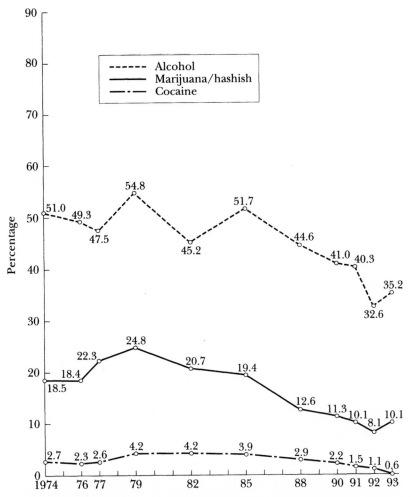

Figure 2-1. Percentage of twelve- to seventeen-year-olds using alcohol, marijuana/hashish, and cocaine once or more in the previous year, selected years, 1974–1993. Source: Substance Abuse and Mental Health Services Administration, *National Household Survey on Drug Abuse: Main Findings 1993* (Washington, D.C.: U.S. Department of Health and Human Services, SAMHSA, Office of Applied Studies, 1994). Data for 1974 from: National Institute on Drug Abuse, *National Household Survey on Drug Abuse: Main Findings 1990* (Washington, D.C.: U.S. Department of Health and Human Services, ADAMHA, 1991).

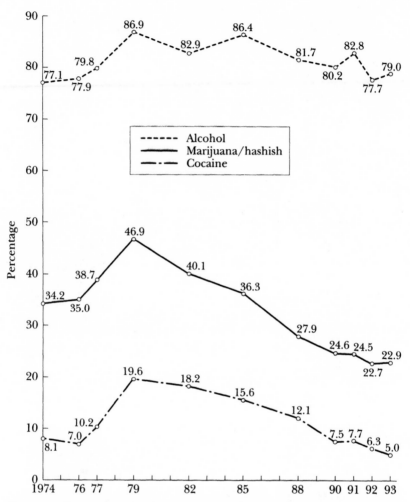

Figure 2-2. Percentage of eighteen- to twenty-five-year-olds using alcohol, marijuana/hashish, and cocaine once or more in the previous year, selected years, 1974–1993. Source: Substance Abuse and Mental Health Services Administration, *National Household Survey on Drug Abuse: Main Findings 1993* (Washington, D.C.: U.S. Department of Health and Human Services, SAMHSA, Office of Applied Studies, 1994). Data for 1974 from: National Institute on Drug Abuse, *National Household Survey on Drug Abuse: Main Findings 1990* (Washington, D.C.: U.S. Department of Health and Human Services, ADAMHA, 1991).

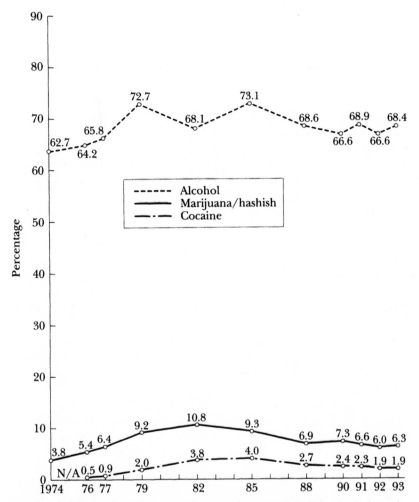

Figure 2-3. Percentage of those twenty-six years and older using alcohol, marijuana/hashish, and cocaine once or more in the previous year, selected years, 1974–1993. Source: Substance Abuse and Mental Health Services Administration, *National Household Survey on Drug Abuse: Main Findings 1993* (Washington, D.C.: U.S. Department of Health and Human Services, SAMHSA, Office of Applied Studies, 1994). Data for 1974 from: National Institute on Drug Abuse, *National Household Survey on Drug Abuse: Main Findings 1990* (Washington, D.C.: U.S. Department of Health and Human Services, ADAMHA, 1991).

all-but-ignored Drug Enforcement Administration press release issued in August 1986, during the first hysterical summer of the crack scare, sought to correct the misperception that crack use was now the major drug problem in America. The DEA said, "Crack is currently the subject of considerable media attention. . . . The result has been a distortion of the public perception of the extent of crack use as compared to the use of other drugs. . . . [Crack] presently appears to be a secondary rather than primary problem in most areas" (Drug Enforcement Administration, cited in Diamond et al., 1987, p. 10; Inciardi, 1987, p. 482).[7]

The first official measures of the prevalence of teenage crack use began with NIDA's 1986 high school survey. It found that 4.1% of high school seniors reported having *tried* crack (at least once) in the previous year. This figure dropped to 3.9% in 1987 and to 3.1% in 1988, a 25% decline (Johnston et al., 1988; *National Report on Substance Abuse*, 1994, p. 3). This means that at the peak of crack use, 96% of America's high school seniors had never tried crack, much less gone on to more regular use, abuse, or addiction. Any drug use among the young is certainly worrisome, particularly when in such an intense form as crack. However, at the start of the crusade to save "a whole generation" of children from death by crack in the spring of 1986, the latest official data showed a national total of eight "cocaine-related" deaths of young people age eighteen and under for the preceding year (Trebach, 1987, p. 11). There was no way to determine whether any of these deaths involved crack use or even if cocaine was in fact the direct cause.

In general, the government's national surveys indicate that a substantial minority of teenagers and young adults experiment with illicit drugs. But as with other forms of youthful deviance, most tend to abandon such behavior as they assume adult roles. Politicians, the media, and antidrug advertisements often claimed that cocaine is inevitably addicting but that crack is still worse because it is "instantaneously addicting." However, according to the official national surveys, two-thirds of Americans of all ages who had ever tried cocaine had not used it in the month prior to the surveys. It is clear that the vast majority of the more than twenty-two million Americans who have tried cocaine do not use it in crack form, do not escalate to regular use, and do not end up addicted.

The 1992 National Household Survey found that even among the age groups in which crack is most widely used (eighteen to thirty-four years old), only about 3% of them had "ever used" it (NIDA, 1993b, p. 37). Moreover, only about one-third of those who had ever used crack reported having used it in the previous year (.9–1.1%), and only about one-third of these (.4%) said they had used it in the past month. In short, the evidence indicated that the lifetime prevalence of crack use began low and declined thereafter. And, despite all the claims that it is "instantaneously addicting," a clear majority of those who do try it do not continue to use it.

The high school surveys similarly showed that the annual prevalence of crack use had declined steadily to 1.5% for 1991, 1992, and 1993. Indeed, when the findings from the 1993 survey of fifty thousand students were announced (February 1, 1994), the six pages of text in the press release did not even *mention* cocaine or crack (University of Michigan, 1994). An appended graph showed that there had been no significant change in the low prevalence of cocaine use, but the prevalence of crack use was apparently too small even to register on the graph. Yet, rather than note that the oft-trumpeted crack "plague" had not materialized after all, the researchers began their report by exclaiming that "Drug use among American young people has been making a clear comeback" (p. 1). They were referring primarily to a "three or four percentage point" rise (p. 2) in the number of students who had used marijuana at least once in the previous year.

In sum, the official evidence on cocaine and crack available during the crack scare gave a rather different picture than Americans received from the media and politicians. The sharp rise in mentions of cocaine in emergency room episodes and coroners' reports did offer cause for concern. But the best official evidence of drug use never supported the claims about an "epidemic" or "plague" throughout America or about "instantaneous addiction." Moreover, as media attention to crack was burgeoning, the actual extent of crack use was virtually unknown, and most other official measures of cocaine use were actually decreasing. Once crack use was actually measured, its prevalence turned out to be low to start with and to have declined throughout the scare (*National Report on Substance Abuse*, 1994, p. 3).

CRACK AS AN EPIDEMIC AND PLAGUE

The empirical evidence on crack use suggests that politicians and journalists have routinely used the words "epidemic" and "plague" imprecisely and rhetorically as words of warning, alarm, and danger. Therefore, on the basis of press reports, it is difficult to determine if there was any legitimacy at all in the description of crack use as an epidemic or plague. Like most other drug researchers and epidemiologists, we have concluded that crack addiction has never been anything but relatively rare across the great middle strata of the U.S. population. If the word "epidemic" is used to mean a disease or diseaselike condition that is "widespread" or "prevalent," then there has never been an epidemic of crack addiction (or even crack use) among the vast majority of Americans. Among the urban poor, however, especially African-American and Latino youth, heavy crack use has been more common. An "epidemic of crack *use*" might be a description of what happened among a distinct minority of teenagers and young adults from impoverished urban neighborhoods in the mid to late 1980s. However, many more people use tobacco and alcohol heavily than use cocaine in any form. Alcohol drinking and tobacco smoking each kills far more people than all forms of cocaine and heroin use combined. Therefore, "epidemic" would be more appropriate to describe tobacco and alcohol use. But politicians and the media have not talked about tobacco and alcohol use as epidemics or plagues. The word "epidemic" also can mean a rapidly spreading disease. In this precise sense as well, in inner-city neighborhoods, crack use may have been epidemic (spreading rapidly) for a few years among impoverished young African-Americans and Latinos. However, crack use was never spreading fast or far enough among the general population to be termed an epidemic there.

"Plague" is even a stronger word than epidemic. Plague can mean a "deadly contagious disease," an epidemic "with great mortality," or it can refer to a "pestilence," an "infestation of a pest, [*e.g.,*] a plague of caterpillars." Crack is a central nervous system stimulant. Continuous and frequent use of crack often burns people out and does them substantial psychological and physical harm. But even very heavy use does not usually directly kill users. In this sense, crack use is not a plague. One could say that drug dealers were "infesting" some blocks of some poor neighborhoods in some cities, that there were pockets of plague in some specific areas; but that was not how "crack plague" was used.

When evaluating whether the extent and dangers of crack use match the claims of politicians and the media, it is instructive to compare how other drug use patterns are discussed. For example, an unusually balanced *New York Times* story (October 7, 1989, p. 26) compared crack and alcohol use among suburban teenagers and focused on the middle class. The *Times* reported that, except for a few "urban pockets" in suburban counties, "crack and other narcotics are rarely seen in the suburbs, whether modest or wealthy." As the *Times* explained:

> Unlike crack, which is confined mainly to poor urban neighborhoods, alcohol seems to cut across Westchester's socio-economic lines. . . . Westchester is not unusual. Across the United States, alcohol eclipses all other drugs tried by high school students. According to a survey by the Institute for Social Research at the University of Michigan, 64 percent of 16,300 high school seniors surveyed in 1988 had drunk alcohol in the last month, compared with 18 percent who had smoked marijuana and 1.6 percent who had smoked crack.

The *Times* also reported that high school seniors were outdrinking the general adult population. Compared to the 64% of teenagers, only 55% of adults had consumed alcohol in the last month. Furthermore, teenagers have been drinking more than adults since at least 1972, when the surveys began. Even more significant is the *kind* of drinking teenagers do—what the *Times* called "excessive 'binge' drinking": "More than a third of the high school seniors had said that in the last two weeks they had had five or more drinks in a row." Drinking is, of course, the most widespread form of illicit drug use among high school students. As the *Times* explained, on the weekend, "practically every town has at least one underage party, indoors or out" and that "fake identification cards, older siblings, friends, and even parents all help teenagers obtain" alcohol.

The point we wish to emphasize is that even though illicit alcohol use was far more prevalent than cocaine or crack use, and even though it held substantial risk for alcohol dependence, addiction, drinking-driving deaths, and other alcohol-related problems, the media and politicians have not campaigned against teen drunkenness. Used as a descriptive term meaning "prevalent," the word "epidemic" fits teenage drinking far better than it does teenage crack use. Although many organizations have campaigned against drinking and driving by teenagers, the politicians and media have not used terms like "epidemic" or "plague" to call attention to illicit teenage drinking and drunkenness. Unlike the *Times* articles on crack, often on the front page, this article on teen drunkenness was placed in the second section on a Saturday.

It is also worth noting the unintentionally ironic mixing of metaphors, or of diagnoses and remedies, when advocates for the War on Drugs described crack use as an epidemic or plague. Although such disease terminology was used to call attention to the consequences of crack use, most of the federal government's domestic responses have centered on using police to arrest users. Treatment and prevention have always received a far smaller proportion of total federal antidrug funding than police and prisons do as a means of handling the "epidemic." If crack use is primarily a crime problem, then terms like "wave" (as in crime wave) would be more fitting. But if this truly is an "epidemic"—a widespread disease—then police and prisons are the wrong remedy, and the victims of the epidemic should be offered treatment, public health programs, and social services.

Finally, we wish to call attention to one particularly flagrant example of a prominent journalist misinforming millions of readers. As we mentioned in Chapter 1, in 1986, the editor in chief of *Newsweek*, Richard M. Smith, began a full-page editorial with the assertion that "An epidemic [of illicit drugs] is abroad in America, as pervasive and dangerous in its way as the plagues of medieval times." The claim that the effect of illicit drug use in America is comparable in destruction to medieval plagues is an easy one to check. Any good encyclopedia explains that the plague is a bacterial disease that kills people, often very quickly. The bubonic plague killed roughly one hundred million people in the Middle East, Europe, and Asia during the sixth century. In the fourteenth century, the so-called "Black Death" killed one-fourth to one-half the entire population of Europe, about seventy-five million people, *in a few years.* In the United States, perhaps seven to ten thousand deaths a year are "related" to all forms of illicit drug use combined. It is simply untrue that in America the effects of illicit drug use are "as pervasive and dangerous" as medieval plagues. *Newsweek's* statement offers falsehoods as facts. Yet it was a high-profile, well-thought-out statement, a model, given by the editor of a top news magazine, of the way reporters should write about drug issues. And reporters and editors certainly seemed to pick up the message. For example, a month later, *U.S. News and World Report* noted that "illicit drugs pervade American life . . . a situation that experts compare to medieval plagues—the No. 1 problem we face" (July 28, 1986, p. 49).

THE POLITICAL CONTEXT OF THE "CRACK CRISIS"

If the many claims about an "epidemic" or "plague" endangering "a whole generation" of youth were at odds with the best official data, then what else was animating the new War on Drugs?[8] In fact, even if all the exaggerated claims about crack had been true, it would not explain all the attention crack received. Poverty, homelessness, auto accidents, handgun deaths, and environmental hazards are also widespread, costly, even deadly, but most politicians and journalists never speak of them in terms of crisis or plague. Indeed, far more people were (and still are) injured and killed every year by domestic violence than by illicit drugs, but one would never know this from media reports or political speeches. The existence of government studies suggesting that crack contributed to the deaths of a small proportion of its users, that an unknown but somewhat larger minority of users became addicted to it, that its use was related to some forms of crime, and so on were neither necessary nor sufficient conditions for all the attention crack received (Spector and Kitsuse, 1977).

Like other sociologists, historians, and students of drug law and public policy, we suggest that understanding antidrug campaigns requires more than evidence of drug abuse and drug-related problems, which can be found in almost any period. It requires analyzing these crusades and scares as phenomena in their own right and understanding the broader social, political, and economic circumstances under which they occur (see, *e.g.,* Bakalar and Grinspoon, 1984; Brecher, 1972; Duster, 1970; Gusfield, 1963, 1981; Lindesmith, 1965; Morgan, 1978; Musto, 1973; Rumbarger, 1989). The crack scare also must be understood in terms of its political context and its appeal to important groups within American society. The mass media and politicians, however, did not talk about drugs this way. Rather, they decontextualized the drama, making it appear as if the story had no authors aside from dealers and addicts. Their writing of the crack drama kept abusers, dealers, crimes, and casualties under spotlights while hiding other important factors in the shadows. We suggest that over and above the very real problems some users suffered with crack, the rise of the New Right and the competition between political parties in a conservative context contributed significantly to the making of the crack scare.

THE NEW RIGHT AND ITS MORAL IDEOLOGY

During the post-Watergate rebuilding of the Republican Party, far right wing political organizations and fundamentalist Christian groups set about to impose what they called "traditional family values" on public policy. This self-proclaimed "New Right" felt increasingly threatened by the diffusion of modernist values, behaviors, and cultural practices—particularly by what they saw as the interconnected forms of 1960s hedonism involved in sex outside (heterosexual) marriage and consciousness alteration with (illicit) drugs. The New Right formed a core constituency for Ronald Reagan, an extreme conservative who had come to prominence as governor of California in part by taking a hard line against the new political movements and cultural practices of the 1960s.

Once he became president in 1981, Reagan and his appointees attempted to restructure public policy according to a radically conservative ideology. Through the lens of this ideology, most social problems appeared to be simply the consequences of *individual moral choices* (Ryan, 1976). Programs and research that had for many years been directed at the social and structural sources of social problems were systematically defunded in budgets and delegitimated in discourse. Unemployment, poverty, urban decay, school crises, crime, and all their attendant forms of human troubles were spoken of and acted upon as if they were the result of *individual* deviance, immorality, or weakness. The most basic premise of social science—that individual choices are influenced by social circumstances—was rejected as left-wing ideology. Reagan and the New Right constricted the aperture of attribution for America's ills so that only the lone deviant came into focus. They conceptualized people *in* trouble as people who *make* trouble (Gusfield, 1985); they made social control rather than social welfare the organizing axis of public policy (Reinarman, 1988).

With regard to drug problems, this conservative ideology is a form of *sociological denial.* For the New Right, people did not so much abuse drugs because they were jobless, homeless, poor, depressed, or alienated; they were jobless, homeless, poor, depressed, or alienated because they were weak, immoral, or foolish enough to use illicit drugs. For the right wing, American business productivity was not lagging because investors spent their capital on mergers and stock speculation instead of on new plants and equipment, or for any number of other economic reasons routinely mentioned in the *Wall Street Journal* or *Business Week*. Rather, conservatives claimed that businesses had difficulty competing partly because many workers were using drugs. In this view, U.S. education was in trouble not because it had suffered demoralizing budget cuts, but because a "generation" of students was "on drugs" and their teachers did not "get tough" with them. The new drug warriors did not see crime plaguing the ghettos and barrios for all the reasons it always has, but because of the influence of a new chemical bogeyman. Crack was a godsend to the Right. They used it and the drug issue as an ideological fig leaf to place over the unsightly urban ills that had increased markedly under Reagan administration social and economic policies. "The drug problem" served conservative politicians as an all-purpose scapegoat. They could blame an array of problems on the deviant individuals and then expand the nets of social control to imprison those people for causing the problems.

The crack crisis had other, more specific political uses. Nancy Reagan was a highly visible antidrug crusader, crisscrossing the nation to urge schoolchildren to "Just Say No" to drugs. Mrs. Reagan's crusade began in 1983 (before crack came into existence) when her "p.r.-conscious operatives," as *Time* magazine called them, convinced her that "serious-minded displays" of "social consciousness" would "make her appear more caring and less frivolous." Such a public relations strategy was important to Mrs. Reagan. The press had often criticized her for spending hundreds of thousands of dollars on new china for the White House, lavish galas for wealthy friends, and high-fashion evening gowns at a time when her husband's economic policies had induced a sharp recession, raised joblessness to near Depression-era levels, and cut funding for virtually all programs for the poor. *Time* explained that "the timing and destinations of her antidrug excursions last year were coordinated with the Reagan-Bush campaign officials to satisfy their particular political needs" (*Time,* January 14, 1985, p. 30).

For the Reagan administration and the Right, America's drug problems functioned as opportunities for the imposition of an old moral agenda in the guise of a new social concern. Moreover, the remedies that followed from this view were in perfect harmony with "traditional family values"—individual moral discipline and abstinence, combined with police and prisons for those who indulged (Reeves and Campbell, 1994). Such remedies avoided all questions about the economic and political sources of and solutions to America's social problems. The Reagan administration preached this ideology from the highest platforms in the land and transformed public policy in its image. It made a most hospitable context for a new drug scare.

POLITICAL PARTY COMPETITION

The primary political task facing liberals in the 1980s was to recapture some of the electorate that had gone over to the Right. Reagan's shrewdness in symbolically colonizing "middle American" fears put Democrats on the defensive. Most Democrats responded by moving to the right and pouncing upon the drug issue. Part of the early energy for the drug scare in the spring and summer of 1986 came from Democratic candidates trading charges with their Republican opponents about being "soft on drugs." Many candidates challenged each other to take urine tests as a symbol of their commitment to a "drug-free America." One Southern politician even proposed that candidates' spouses be tested. A California senatorial candidate charged his opponent with being "a noncombatant in the war on drugs" (*San Francisco Chronicle*, August 12, 1986, p. 9). By the fall of 1986, increasingly strident calls for a drug war became so much a part of candidates' standard stump speeches that even conservative columnist William Safire complained of antidrug "hysteria" and "narcomania" (*New York Times*, September 11, 1986, p. A27). Politicians demanded everything from death penalties in North America to bombing raids in South America.

Crack could not have appeared at a more opportune political moment. After years of dull debates on budget balancing, a "hot" issue had arrived just in time for a crucial election. In an age of fiscal constraint, when most problems were seen as intractable and most solutions costly, the crack crisis was the one "safe" issue on which all politicians could take "tough stands" without losing a single vote or campaign contribution. The legislative results of the competition to "get tough" included a $2 billion law in 1986, the so-called "Drug-Free America Act," which whizzed through the House (392 to 16) just in time for members of Congress to go home and tell their constituents about it. In the heat of the preelection, antidrug hysteria, the symbolic value of such spending seemed to dwarf the deficit worries that had hamstrung other legislation. According to *Newsweek*, what occurred was "a can-you-top-this competition" among "election-bound members of both parties" seeking tough antidrug amendments. The 1986 drug bill, as Representative David McCurdy (D-Okla) put it, was "out of control," adding through a wry smile, "but of course I'm for it" (September 22, 1986, p. 39).[9]

The prominence of the drug issue dropped sharply in both political speeches and media coverage after the 1986 election, but returned during the 1988 primaries. Once again the crack issue had political utility. One common observation about the 1988 presidential election campaigns was that there were no domestic or foreign policy crises looming on which the two parties could differentiate themselves. As a *New York Times* headline put it: "Drugs as 1988 Issue: Filling a Vacuum" (May 24, 1988, p. A14). In the 1988 primary season, candidates of both parties moved to fill this vacuum in part by drug-baiting their opponents and attacking them as "soft on drugs." In the fall, both Democrats Dukakis and Bentsen and Republicans Bush and Quayle claimed that their opponents were soft on drugs while asserting that their side would wage a "*real* War on Drugs." And, just as they did before the 1986 election, members of Congress from both parties overwhelmingly passed a new, even more strict and costly antidrug bill.

The antidrug speeches favoring such expenditures became increasingly transparent as posturing, even to many of the speakers. For example, Senator Christopher Dodd (D-Conn) called the flurry of antidrug amendments a "feeding frenzy" (*New York Times,* May 22, 1988, p. E4). An aide to another senator admitted that "everybody was scrambling to get a piece of the action" (*New York Times,* May 24, 1988, p. A14). Even President Reagan's spokesperson, Marlin Fitzwater, told the White House press corps that "everybody wants to out-drug each other in terms of political rhetoric" (*Boston Globe,* May 18, 1988, p. 4). But however transparent, such election-year posturing—magnified by a media hungry for the readers and ratings that dramatic drug stories bring—enhanced the viability of claims about the menace of crack far more than any available empirical evidence could. In the fall of 1989, Congress finalized yet another major antidrug bill costing more than the other two combined. According to research by the Government Accounting Office, the federal government spent more than $23 billion on the drug war during the Reagan era, three-fourths of it for law enforcement (*Alcoholism and Drug Abuse Week,* 1989, p. 3).

As we mentioned earlier, in opinion polls in 1986, 1988, and 1989, more people picked "drugs" as the "most important problem facing the country" than any other public issue. Politicians and the press frequently cited such poll results as the reason for their speeches and stories. For example, the *New York Times* titled one story "The People's Concern: Illegal Drugs Are an Issue No Politician Can Resist" (May 22, 1988, p. E4). That title got it half right; politicians couldn't resist playing the drug issue, but the drug issue wasn't so much "The People's Concern" until they did. The reporter rightly noted that the 1988 election campaign would "resemble a shoving match" over "who can take a tougher line on drugs" and that "those who counsel reason are vulnerable to accusations of being 'soft.' " But then he falsely attributed this phenomenon to the citizenry: "The politicians were reflecting the concerns of their constituents." He also quoted an aide to then–Vice President Bush saying the same thing: "Voters have made this an issue."

Politicians and the media were *forging,* not following, public opinion. The speeches and stories *led* the oft-cited poll results, not the other way around. In 1987, between elections—when drug problems persisted in the ghettos and barrios but when the drug scare was not so enflamed by election rhetoric and media coverage—only 3 to 5% of those surveyed picked drugs as our most important problem (*New York Times,* May 24, 1988, p. A14). But then again in 1989, immediately following President Bush's speech escalating the drug war, nearly two-thirds of the people polled identified drugs as America's most important problem. When the media and politicians invoked "public opinion" as the driving force behind their actions against crack, they inverted the actual causal sequence (Edelman, 1964, p. 172).

We argued in the previous section that the New Right and other conservatives found ideological utility in the crack scare. In this section, we have suggested that conservatives were not the only political group in America to help foment the scare and to benefit from it. Liberals and Democrats, too, found in crack and drugs a means of recapturing Democratic defectors by appearing more conservative. And they too found drugs to be a convenient scapegoat for the worsening conditions in the inner cities. All this happened at a historical moment when the Right successfully stigmatized the liberals' traditional solutions to the problems of the poor as ineffective and costly. Thus, in addition to the political capital to be gained by waging the war, the new chemical bogeyman afforded politicians across the ideological spectrum both an explanation for pressing public problems and an excuse for not proposing the unpopular taxing, spending, or redistributing needed to do something about them.

THE END OF THE CRACK SCARE

In the 1980s, the conservative drive to reduce social spending exacerbated the enduring problems of impoverished African-American and Latino city residents. Partly in response, a minority of the young urban poor turned either to crack sales as their best shot at the American Dream and/or to the crack high as their best shot at a fleeting moment of pleasure. Inner-city churches, community organizations, and parent groups then tried to defend their children and neighborhoods from drug dealing and use on the one hand and to lobby for services and jobs on the other hand. But the crack scare did not inspire politicians of either party to address the worsening conditions and growing needs of the inner-city poor and working class or to launch a "Marshall Plan for cities." In the meantime, the white middle-class majority viewed with alarm the growing numbers, visibility, and desperation of the urban poor. And for years many Americans believed the central fiction of the crack scare: that drug use was not a symptom of urban decay but one of its most important causes.

All this gave federal and local authorities justification for widening the nets of social control. Of course, the new drug squads did not reduce the dangerousness of impoverished urban neighborhoods. But the crack scare did increase criminal justice system supervision of the underclass. By 1992, one in four young African-American males was in jail or prison or on probation or parole—more than were in higher education (see Chapter 13). During the crack scare, the prison population more than doubled, largely because of the arrests of drug users and small dealers. This gave the U.S. the highest incarceration rate in the world (Currie, 1985; Irwin and Austin, 1994).

By the end of 1992, however, the crack scare seemed spent. There are a number of overlapping reasons for this. Most important was the failure of the War on Drugs itself. Democrats as well as Republicans supported the War on Drugs, but the Reagan and Bush administrations initiated and led it, and the drug war required support from the White House. George Bush appointed William Bennett to be a "tough" and extremely high profile "drug czar" to lead the campaign against drugs. But Bennett, criticized for his bombastic style, quit after only eighteen months (some press accounts referred to it as the "czar's abdication"). After that, the Bush administration downplayed the drug war, and it hardly figured at all in the presidential primaries or campaign in 1992. Bill Clinton said during the campaign that there were no easy solutions to drug problems and that programs that work only on reducing supply were doomed to fail. The Clinton administration eschewed the phrase "War on Drugs," and Lee Brown, Clinton's first top drug official, explicitly rejected the title of drug czar (Reinarman, 1994). After billions of tax dollars had been spent and millions of young Americans had been imprisoned, hard-core drug problems remained. With so little to show for years of drug war, politicians seemed to discover the limits of the drug issue as a political weapon. Moreover, with both parties firmly in favor of the "get tough" approach, there was no longer any partisan political advantage to be had.

The news media probably would have written dramatic stories about the appearance of smokeable cocaine in poor neighborhoods at any time. Television producers have found that drug stories, especially timely, well-advertised, dramatic ones, often receive high ratings. But the context of the Reagan-led drug war encouraged the media to write such pieces. Conservatives had long complained that the media had a liberal bias; in the mid-1980s, drug coverage allowed the media to rebut such criticism and to establish conservative credentials (Reeves and Campbell, 1994). As we have suggested, news coverage of drugs rose and fell with political initiatives, especially those coming from the president. Therefore, as the White House withdrew from the drug issue, so did the press.

After about 1989, it became increasingly difficult to sustain the exaggerated claims of the beginning of the crack scare. The mainstream media began to publish stories critical of earlier news coverage (though usually not their own). As we noted in Chapter 1, *Newsweek* finally admitted in 1990 what it called the "dirty little secret" about crack that it had concealed in all of its earlier scare stories: "A lot of people use it without getting addicted," and that the anonymous "media" had "hyped instant and total addiction" (February 19, 1990, pp. 74–75). As early as 1988, it was clear that crack was not "destroying a whole generation"; it was not even spreading beyond the same poverty context that had long given rise to hard-core heroin addiction. Moreover, because of the obvious destructive effects of heavy use, people in ghettos and barrios had come to view "crack heads" as even lower in status than winos or junkies. Even crack dealers preferred powder cocaine and routinely disparaged crack heads (Williams, 1989). All of this meant that drugs in general, and crack in particular, declined in newsworthiness. Media competition had fueled the crack scare in its early years, and the same scramble for dramatic stories guaranteed that the media would move on to other stories. By 1992, the crack scare had faded beyond the media's horizon of hot new issues.

Finally, the crack scare could recede into the background partly because it had been *institutionalized.* Between 1986 and 1992, Congress passed and two presidents signed a series of increasingly harsh antidrug laws. Federal antidrug funding increased for seven successive years, and an array of prison and police programs was established or expanded. All levels of government, from schools to cities, counties, and states, established agencies to warn about crack and other drug problems. And multimillion-dollar, corporate-sponsored, private organizations such as the Partnership for a Drug-Free America had been established to continue the crusade.

CONCLUSION

Smoking crack *is* a risky way to use an already potent drug. Despite all the exaggerations, heavy use of it *has* made life more difficult for many people—most of them from impoverished urban neighborhoods. If we agree that too many families have been touched by drug-related tragedies, why have we bothered criticizing the crack scare and the War on Drugs? If even a few people are saved from crack addiction, why should anyone care if this latest drug scare was in some measure concocted by the press, politicians, and moral entrepreneurs to serve their other agendas? Given the damage that drug abuse can do, what's the harm in a little hysteria? Much of this book addresses that question, but there are a few points that can be mentioned here.

First, we suspect that drug scares do not work very well to reduce drug problems and that they may well promote the behavior they claim to be preventing. For all the repression successive drug wars have wrought (primarily upon the poor and the powerless), they have yet to make a measurable dent in our drug *problems*. For example, prompted by the crack crisis and inspired by the success of patriotic propaganda in World War II, the Partnership for a Drug-Free America ran a massive advertising campaign to "unsell drugs." From 1987 to 1993, the Partnership placed over $1 billion worth of advertising donated by corporations and the advertising industry. The Partnership claims to have had a "measurable impact" by "accelerating intolerance" to drugs and drug users. The Partnership claims it "can legitimately take some of the credit for the 25% decline in illicit drug usage since our program was launched" (Hedrick, 1990). However, the association between the Partnership's antidrug advertising and the declines in drug use appears to be spurious. Drug use was declining well before the Partnership's founding; taking credit for what was already happening is a bit like jumping in front of a parade and then claiming to have been leading it all along. More important, drug *use* increased in the mid-1990s among precisely those age groups that had been targeted by Partnership ads, while drug *problems* continued throughout their campaign. Furthermore, Partnership ads scrupulously avoided any mention of the two forms of drug use most prevalent among youth: smoking and drinking. This may have something to do with the fact that the Partnership for a Drug-Free America is a partnership between the media and advertising industries, which make millions from alcohol and tobacco advertising each year, and with the fact that alcohol and tobacco companies contribute financially to the Partnership's campaign against illicit drugs. Surely public health education is important, but there is no evidence that selective antidrug propaganda and scare tactics have significantly reduced drug problems.

Indeed, hysterical and exaggerated antidrug campaigns may have increased drug-related harm in the U.S. There is the risk that all of the exaggerated claims made to mobilize the population for war actually arouse interest in drug use. In 1986, the *New England Journal of Medicine* reported that the frequency of teenage suicides increases after lurid news reports and TV shows about them (Gould and Shaffer, 1986; Phillips and Carstensen, 1986). Reports about drugs, especially of new and exotic drugs like crack, may work the same way. In his classic chapter, "How To Launch a Nation Wide Drug Menace," Brecher (1972) shows how exaggerated newspaper reports of dramatic police raids in 1960 functioned as advertising for glue sniffing. The arrests of a handful of sniffers led to anti–glue sniffing hysteria that actually spread this hitherto unknown practice across the U.S. In 1986, the media's desire for dramatic drug stories interacted with politicians' desire for partisan advantage and safe election-year issues, so news about crack spread to every nook and cranny of the nation far faster than dealers could have spread word on the street. When the media and politicians claimed that crack is "the most addictive substance known to man," there was some commonsense obligation to explain why. Therefore, alongside all the statements about "instant addiction," the media also reported some very intriguing things about crack: "whole body orgasm," "better than sex," and "cheaper than cocaine." For TV-raised young people in the inner city, faced with a dismal social environment and little economic opportunity, news about such a substance in their neighborhoods may have functioned as a massive advertising campaign for crack.[10]

Further, advocates of the crack scare and the War on Drugs explicitly rejected public health approaches to drug problems that conflicted with their ideology. The most striking and devastating example of this was the total rejection of syringe distribution programs by the Reagan and Bush administrations and by drug warriors such as Congressman Charles Rangel. People can and do recover from drug addiction, but no one recovers from AIDS. By the end of the 1980s, the fastest growing AIDS population was intravenous drug users. Because syringes were hard to get, or their possession criminalized, injectors shared their syringes and infected each other and their sexual partners with AIDS. In the early 1980s, activists in a number of other Western countries had developed syringe distribution and exchange programs to prevent AIDS, and there is by now an enormous body of evidence that such programs are effective. But the U.S. government has consistently rejected such "harm reduction" programs on the grounds that they conflict with the policy of "zero tolerance" for drug use or "send the wrong message." As a result, cities such as Amsterdam, Liverpool, and Sydney, which have needle exchange programs, have very low or almost no transmission of AIDS by intravenous drug users. In New York City, however, roughly half the hundreds of thousands of injection drug users are HIV positive or already have AIDS. In short, the crack scare and the drug war policies it fueled will ultimately contribute to the deaths of tens of thousands of Americans, including the families, children, and sexual partners of the infected drug users.

Another important harm resulting from American drug scares is they have routinely blamed individual immorality and personal behavior for endemic social and structural problems. In so doing, they diverted attention and resources away from the underlying sources of drug abuse and the array of other social ills of which they are part. One necessary condition for the emergence of the crack scare (as in previous drug scares) was the linking of drug use with the problems faced by racial minorities, the poor, and youth. In the logic of the scare, whatever economic and social troubles these people have suffered were due largely to their drug use. Obscured or forgotten during the crack scare were all the social and economic problems that underlie crack abuse—and that are much more widespread—especially poverty, unemployment, racism, and the prospects of life in the permanent underclass.

Democrats denounced the Reagan and Bush administrations' hypocrisy in proclaiming "War on Drugs" while cutting the budgets for drug treatment, prevention, and research. However, the Democrats often neglected to mention an equally important but more politically popular development: the "Just Say No To Drugs" administrations had, with the help of many Democrats in Congress, also "just said no" to virtually every social program aimed at creating alternatives for and improving the lawful life chances of inner-city youth. These black and Latino young people were and are the group with the highest rate of crack abuse. Although, most inner-city youth have always steered clear of drug abuse, they could not "just say no" to poverty and unemployment. Dealing drugs, after all, was (and still is) accurately perceived by many poor city kids as the highest-paying job—straight or criminal—that they are likely to get.

The crack scare, like previous drug scares and antidrug campaigns, promoted misunderstandings of drug use and abuse, blinded people to the social sources of many social problems (including drug problems), and constrained the social policies that might reduce those problems. It routinely used inflated, misleading rhetoric and falsehoods such as Bush's televised account of how he came into possession of a bag of crack. At best, the crack scare was not good for public health. At worst, by manipulating and misinforming citizens about drug use and effects, it perverted social policy and political democracy.

NOTES

1. We use the word "official" here because (1) we are referring to data produced by federal government agencies whose task is to define and document a particular form of deviance (see Kitsuse and Cicourel, 1963), (2) it is data considered by experts to provide the "best" (*i.e.,* systematically collected from representative national samples) estimates of the prevalence of drug use, and (3) it is explicitly gathered to provide policy makers with a societywide database as a foundation for policy making.

2. These successive increases in drug war funding were so great that the money could not be effectively spent. Even the "drug czar" admitted in 1990 that less than half of the funds for police and prisons from 1987 to 1990 had been spent (*Washington Post,* January 2, 1991, p. A13).

3. Keith Jackson was soon arrested, but his trial for selling drugs to an undercover DEA agent in Lafayette Park ended in a hung jury. A few months later he was convicted of selling drugs and sentenced to ten years in prison.

4. There are several reasons why local police statistics are problematic for assessing the pervasiveness of crack use. Most obviously, they deal with only those users who are apprehended. Police statistics in several major U.S. cities clearly show that cocaine and crack use are pervasive among arrestees. It is also true that crack users now comprise a growing share of those seeking treatment. But just as treatment samples, by definition, tell us little about the much larger population of users who do not seek treatment, arrest figures cannot tell us much about the central question of societal prevalence, even though claims makers routinely use them that way. Perhaps more important, police statistics often *reflect* crisis claims (Kitsuse and Cicourel, 1963). In New York City, for example, then-Mayor Koch, Harlem Congressman Charles Rangel, and the editors of the *New York Times* played leading roles as moral entrepreneurs in drawing attention to crack use. As a consequence, a variety of New York City agencies was politically mobilized, and the number of police assigned to special crack units tripled. This mobilization and vastly expanded law enforcement capacity focused specifically on crack users helps account for why crack users have loomed so large in arrest statistics.

Similarly, crack arrestees were treated far more harshly by the city's criminal justice system than comparable cocaine arrestees, according to studies by the New York City Criminal Justice Agency. In their comparative analysis of 4321 crack arrestees and 9975 earlier cocaine arrestees, the agency found that crack users were twice as likely to be charged with felonies, four times more likely to be detained for arraignment, less likely to be released on recognizance or fined, and more likely to be sentenced to jail terms—even though the crack arrestees had a lower mean number of prior arrests than the cocaine arrestees. The authors concluded "that crack arrests are being treated more seriously than other comparable drug cases" and that this was "apparently [due to] more stringent charging decisions . . . [which] may reflect political pressure" (Belenko and Fagan, 1987, pp. 15–17).

Another difficulty with police data is their apparent unreliability with respect to what substances were involved in such arrests. According to a technical study by the same agency, New York Police Department arrest records coded as "crack arrests" frequently did not specify that crack was indeed the substance that was the basis for the arrest or that crack was confiscated as evidence. Of a sample of 471 so-called crack arrests, 21% mentioned only "cocaine," 31% mentioned only "controlled substance," and 42% mentioned no drug at all (Chin, 1988). It is at best difficult on the basis of such statistics to make accurate estimates of the number of "crack arrests," much less determine how extensive or problematic crack use is.

5. A variety of questions might be raised about this evidence. It is, for example, the product of organizations whose job it is to define and document deviance, and is thus as likely to reflect this organizational mandate as it is accurately to describe some "objective" empirical reality (see Kitsuse and Cicourel, 1963, on the important distinction between "rate-producing processes" and "behavior-producing processes"). Both DAWN and the NIDA surveys were explicitly set up to allow policy makers to make claims about the prevalence—and the dangers presumed to follow from it—of "illicit drug abuse." Mere "yes" responses regarding *use* in the past year or even in one's lifetime are typically taken as indices of *abuse*. However, some critics claim that the NIDA high school surveys miss the very dropouts who are most prone to drug abuse, or that the household surveys sample only one

household member. We focus only on the inferences that have been made on the basis of this "best" "official" evidence. We will assume for the sake of argument that these data are reasonable measures of something "real" and ask (1) how well they support the many claims of mass destruction purportedly based on them and (2) irrespective of evidence, why such claims have achieved such prominence.

6. *New York Times,* "Medical Emergencies for Addicts Are Said To Have Dropped by 20%," May 15, 1990, p. A13; *New York Times,* "Cocaine Epidemic Has Peaked, Some Suggest," July 1, 1990, p. A9; *New York Times,* "U.S. Says Hospital Statistics Show Use of Cocaine May Have Peaked: Cocaine-Related Hospital Visits Drop Again," September 1, 1990, p. 5 L.

7. The DEA later took a very different view, regularly reporting that crack use has spread far and wide with terrible consequences. Our point in citing this early memo is to show that the crack scare has had a momentum of its own, racing ahead of DEA experts and other official evidence upon which it was purportedly based.

8. Even if we accept hyperbole as a "normal" means of attracting readers, viewers, and voters, it is still not possible to explain the character of the crack scare in terms of simple exaggerations of official evidence. Journalists consistently caricatured crack use and users and routinely employed rhetoric that is rare in other types of news stories. They also did not hesitate to make claims for which there was no evidence to "stretch."

9. See "Reagan Call for Cut in Drug Fight Ignites the Anger of Both Parties," *New York Times,* January 8, 1987, p. A1).

10. This advertising effect was probably strongest in 1986, the first year of the crack scare, when crack was new. Antidrug campaigns probably also have different effects on different populations: they may frighten away some middle-class experimenters while increasing interest among those most prone to abuse. In 1986, one student told Arnold Trebach that when he heard that crack was "better than sex and that it was cheaper than cocaine and that it was an epidemic, I wondered what I was missing. I questioned why I seemed to be the only one not doing the drug. The next day I asked some friends if they knew where to get some" (Trebach, 1987, p. 7).

REFERENCES

Alcoholism and Drug Abuse Week, "$23 Billion Spent on Federal Drug Effort Since 1981." July 5, 1989, pp. 3–4.

Anderson, Jack, and Michael Binstein, "Drug Informants Beating the System." *Washington Post,* September 10, 1992, p. D23.

Bakalar, James B., and Lester Grinspoon, *Drug Control in a Free Society.* Cambridge: Cambridge University Press, 1984.

Belenko, Steven, and Jeffrey Fagan, "Crack and the Criminal Justice System." New York: New York City Criminal Justice Agency, 1987.

Brecher, Edward M., *Licit and Illicit Drugs.* Boston: Little, Brown, 1972.

Chin K.-L, "Special Event Codes for Crack Arrests." Internal memorandum, New York City Criminal Justice Agency, 1988.

Currie, Elliott, *Confronting Crime.* New York: Pantheon, 1985.

Diamond, Edwin, Frank Accosta, and Leslie-Jean Thornton, "Is TV News Hyping America's Cocaine Problem?" *TV Guide,* February 7, 1987, pp. 4–10.

Drug Enforcement Administration, "Special Report: The Crack Situation in the U.S." Unpublished, Strategic Intelligence Section. Washington, DC: DEA, August 22, 1986.

Duster, Troy, *The Legislation of Morality.* New York: Free Press, 1970.

Edelman, Murray, *The Symbolic Uses of Politics.* Urbana: University of Illinois Press, 1964.

Gould, Madelyn S., and David Shaffer, "The Impact of Suicide in Television Movies: Evidence of Imitation." *New England Journal of Medicine* 315:690–694 (1986).

Grinspoon, Lester, and James B. Bakalar, *Cocaine: A Drug and Its Social Evolution.* New York: Basic Books, 1976.

Gusfield, Joseph R., *Symbolic Crusade.* Urbana: University of Illinois Press, 1963.

———, *The Culture of Public Problems.* Chicago: University of Chicago Press, 1981.

———, "Alcohol Problems—An Interactionist View," in J. P. von Wartburg et al., eds., *Currents in Alcohol Research and the Prevention of Alcohol Problems.* Berne, Switzerland: Hans Huber, 1985.

Harwood, Richard, "Hyperbole Epidemic." *Washington Post,* October 1, 1989, p. D6.

Hedrick, Thomas A., Jr., "Pro Bono Anti-Drug Ad Campaign Is Working." *Advertising Age,* June 25, 1990, p. 22.

Himmelstein, Jerome, *The Strange Career of Marijuana.* Westport, CT: Greenwood Press, 1983.

Hoffman, Abbie, *Steal This Urine Test: Fighting Drug Hysteria in America.* New York: Penguin Books, 1987.

Horgan, John, "A Kinder War." *Scientific American* , July 25, 1993, p. 6.

Inciardi, James, "Beyond Cocaine: Basuco, Crack, and Other Coca Products." *Contemporary Drug Problems* 14:461–492 (1987).

Irwin, John, and James Austin, *It's About Time: America's Imprisonment Binge.* Belmont, CA: Wadsworth, 1994.

Isikoff, Michael, "Drug Buy Set Up for Bush Speech: DEA Lured Seller to Lafayette Park." *Washington Post,* September 22, 1989, p. A1.

Johnson, Bruce D., et al., *Taking Care of Business: The Economics of Crime by Heroin Abusers.* Lexington, MA: Lexington Books, 1985.

Johnston, Lloyd D., Patrick M. O'Malley, and Jerald G. Bachman, *Illicit Drug Use, Smoking, and Drinking by America's High School Students, College Students, and Young Adults, 1975–1987.* Washington, DC: National Institute on Drug Abuse, 1988.

Kitsuse, John I., and Aaron V. Cicourel, "A Note on the Use of Official Statistics." *Social Problems* 11:131–139 (1963).

Kozel, Nicholas, and Edgar Adams, "Epidemiology of Drug Abuse: An Overview." *Science* 234:970–974 (1986).

Lindesmith, Alfred R., *The Addict and the Law.* Bloomington: Indiana University Press, 1965.

Massing, Michael, Review essay on "Swordfish," *New York Review of Books,* July 15, 1993, pp. 30–32.

Morgan, Patricia, "The Legislation of Drug Law: Economic Crisis and Social Control," *Journal of Drug Issues* 8:53–62 (1978).

Musto, David, *The American Disease: Origins of Narcotic Control.* New Haven, CT: Yale University Press, 1973.

National Institute on Drug Abuse, *Data from the Drug Abuse Warning Network: Annual Data 1985.* Statistical Series I, #5. Washington, DC: National Institute on Drug Abuse, 1986a.

———, *National Household Survey on Drug Abuse, 1985.* Washington, DC: Division of Epidemiology and Statistical Analysis, National Institute on Drug Abuse, 1986b.

———, *National Household Survey on Drug Abuse: 1988 Population Estimates.* Washington, DC: Division of Epidemiology and Prevention Research, National Institute on Drug Abuse, 1988.

———, *National Household Survey on Drug Abuse: Main Findings 1990.* Washington, DC: Epidemiology and Prevention Research, National Institute on Drug Abuse, 1990.

———, *Annual Medical Examiner Data, 1991: Data from the Drug Abuse Warning Network.* Washington, DC: Division of Epidemiology and Prevention Research, National Institute on Drug Abuse, 1992.

———, *Estimates from the Drug Abuse Warning Network: 1992 Estimates of Drug-Related Emergency Room Episodes.* Washington, DC: Substance Abuse and Mental Health Services Administration, U.S. Dept. of Health and Human Services, 1993a.

———, *National Household Survey on Drug Abuse: Population Estimates 1992.* Washington, DC: Substance Abuse and Mental Health Services Administration, U.S. Dept. of Health and Human Services, 1993b.

National Report on Substance Abuse, "Federal Officials Express Alarm at Youth's Rising Illicit Drug Use." February 11, 1994, p. 2.

New York Times, "No Change in Basics: Bush Rejects Any Fundamental Shift, Instead Vowing Unprecedented Vigor." September 6, 1989, p. A11.

Office of National Drug Control Policy, *National Drug Control Strategy: Budget Summary.* Washington, DC: U.S. Government Printing Office, 1992.

Phillips, David P., and Lundie L. Carstensen, "Clustering of Teenage Suicides After Television News Stories About Suicide." *New England Journal of Medicine* 315:685–689 (1986).

Reeves, Jimmie L., and Richard Campbell, *Cracked Coverage: Television News, the Anti-Cocaine Crusade, and the Reagan Legacy.* Durham, NC: Duke University Press, 1994.

Reinarman, Craig, "The Social Construction of an Alcohol Problem: The Case of Mothers Against Drunk Drivers and Social Control in the 1980s." *Theory and Society* 17:91–119 (1988).

———, "Glasnost in U.S. Drug Policy?: Clinton Constrained." *International Journal of Drug Policy* 5:42–49 (1994).

Rogin, Michael Paul, *Ronald Reagan, the Movie: and Other Episodes in Political Demonology.* Berkeley: University of California Press, 1987.

Rumbarger, John, *Profits, Power, and Prohibition.* Albany: State University of New York Press, 1989.

Ryan, William, *Blaming the Victim.* New York: Vintage, 1976.

Schneider, Joseph, and John I. Kitsuse, eds., *Studies in the Sociology of Social Problems.* Norwood, NJ: Ablex, 1984.

Siegel, Ronald, "Cocaine Smoking." *Journal of Psychoactive Drugs* 14:271–359 (1982).

Spector, Malcolm, and John Kitsuse, *Constructing Social Problems*. Menlo Park, CA: Cummings, 1977.

Staples, Brent, "Coke Wars." *New York Times Book Review*, February 6, 1994, p. 11.

Trebach, Arnold, *The Great Drug War*. New York: Macmillan, 1987.

University of Michigan, "Drug Use Rises Among American Teen-Agers." News and Information Services, January 27, 1994.

Waldorf, Dan, Craig Reinarman, and Sheigla Murphy, *Cocaine Changes*. Philadelphia: Temple University Press, 1991.

Washton, Arnold, and Mark Gold, "Recent Trends in Cocaine Abuse," *Advances in Alcohol and Substance Abuse* 6:31–47 (1987).

The White House, *National Drug Control Strategy*. Washington, DC: U.S. Government Printing Office, 1989.

Williams, Terry, *The Cocaine Kids*. Reading, MA: Addison Wesley, 1989.

Wilson, William Julius, *The Truly Disadvantaged*. Chicago: University of Chicago Press, 1987.

Zinberg, Norman E., *Drug, Set, and Setting: The Basis for Controlled Drug Use*. New Haven, CT: Yale University Press, 1984.

PART ONE

Myths and Realities

• • • • • • •

As the introductory chapters have suggested, the crack scare shrouded some complex realities in some rather simple myths. One such myth, now generally recognized as such, was that crack use was spreading rapidly through all communities and social groups. Because smoking crack yields a potent high, the myth held that this potency alone made virtually everyone vulnerable to it. The reality is that crack did not spread very far, but rather remained concentrated among the most impoverished, marginalized, and vulnerable segments of the population. To understand the reality of crack use, it is necessary to see it as much as possible from the points of view of the people who use it.

The first three chapters in this section attempt to do this by employing ethnographic and depth interviewing techniques to render the gritty reality of crack use through the accounts of its users themselves. In Chapter 3, Phillipe Bourgois brings the tools of anthropology to bear upon Spanish Harlem, New York City, where for several years he lived with the people shown on the nightly news being arrested for crack use and sales. His vivid, first-person rendering of crack use and the not-so-underground crack economy puts the lie to the pharmacocentric myth about how crack spread. He shows instead how this dangerous world evolved as an adaptation to the racial and class barriers in the above-ground economy.

In Chapter 4, together with Dan Waldorf and Sheigla Murphy, we report the lived experience of fifty-three freebasers and early crack users (most of whom did not live in the barrio) and the effects they believed crack had on their lives. We use their accounts to give readers a concrete sense of the high, the craving, and the compulsion that have received so much attention. We also use their descriptions of cocaine smoking to distinguish bingeing (an episode of intense use) from addiction (*repeated* heavy use or bingeing) and to develop a new understanding of "compulsive" crack use. Even for those unusual cocaine users who found "the call of the pipe" to be powerful, that call was always contingent upon and constrained by set and setting.

In Chapter 5, Sheigla Murphy and Marsha Rosenbaum further develop this point by comparing the life histories of two very different young women—one from the sort of setting described by Bourgois, the other from the white middle class. Both took risks by getting into cocaine at a tender age, but one ended up selling sex for another hit off the crack pipe while the other went off to college. These close-up case studies illustrate the complex ways in which gender, race, and class interact to shape drug users' career trajectories and their consequences.

Nothing so animated the recent War on Drugs as the alleged causal link between crack and crime. But this link, too, contained a good deal of myth.

Paul Goldstein and his colleagues examined the realities of the crack-crime connection by working with the New York City Police Department and systematically analyzing all the drug-related homicides that occurred during one year at the peak of the crack scare. Their surprising findings, reported in Chapter 6, show that crack-related homicides were almost always the result of dealers going after profits (and each other) rather than users going after victims. In other words, almost none of the crack-related homicides they uncovered had resulted from the pharmacological effects of crack on its users; nearly all were the result of the exigencies of an unregulated, illicit market.

Finally, most of the myths and horror stories about crack as the latest demon drug rested on unexamined claims or twisted inferences from pharmacological research. In Chapter 7, John P. Morgan, MD, a pharmacologist, and Lynn Zimmer, a sociologist, provide an accessible, critical, layperson's guide to the extensive biomedical studies on crack and cocaine and link these studies to the behavioral and sociological questions surrounding crack. They distinguish pharmacological fact from fiction about what crack is, how it interacts with the body and brain, what science knows about crack's role in deaths and hospital emergencies, what the animal experiments on cocaine really show, the so-called "crack baby" issue, and more. As their subtitle suggests, the claims about crack's effects are "not all they're cracked up to be."

THREE

In Search of Horatio Alger

Culture and Ideology
in the Crack Economy

Phillipe Bourgois

The heavyset, white undercover cop pushed me across the ice cream counter, spreading my legs and poking me around the groin. As he came dangerously close to the bulge in my right pocket, I hissed in his ear—"it's a tape recorder." He snapped backwards, releasing his left hand's grip on my neck, and whispered a barely audible "sorry." Apparently he thought he had clumsily intercepted an undercover from another unit instead of an anthropologist, because before I could get a look at his face, he had left the bodega[1] grocery store-*cum*-numbers-joint. Meanwhile the marijuana sellers stationed in front of the bodega that Gato and I had just entered to buy beer saw that the undercover had been rough with me and suddenly felt safe and relieved. They were finally confident that I was a white addict rather than an undercover.[2]

I told Gato to grab the change on my $10 bill from the cashier as I hurried to leave this embarrassing scene. At the doorway, however, I was blocked by Bennie, a thin teenager barging through the door to mug us. Bennie pushed me to the side and lunged at the loose dollar bills in Gato's hand, the change from the beers. "That's my money now Gato—give it to me," he shouted. I started in with a loud "Hey! yo, what are you talking about, that's my money! Get away from it." But one look at the teenager's contorted face and narrowed eyes stopped me halfway through the sentence. Gato's underbreath mutter of "be careful—my man is dusted" was redundant. I was ready to give up the eight bills—and more if necessary—to avoid any out-of-control violence from a mugger high on angel dust.

Cautiously, Gato went through some of the motions of struggling with the angry dust head to whom—I found out later—he really did owe money to cover his share of the supply of marijuana confiscated in a drug bust last week in front of the same bodega. Gato tried two different tacks. One was gentle: staring deeply into his mugger's face—which was two inches from his own—pulling at the fistful of bills, "Yo Bennie, chill out. I know how much I owe you. I'll take care of you tomorrow. This ain't my money. *Please* don't take this money." A second time, a little tougher and louder: "I told you this ain't my money; get off of it! It ain't my money!" Bennie just got tougher; he knew Gato was "pussy" and wrenched at the bills, hissing about the $60 still owed him from last week. They had been selling marijuana together for several weeks on the corner next to the bodega, and he knew that Gato would not fight back. As the bills were about to rip, Gato finally let go, looking back at me helplessly.

As we stepped out the bodega's door, Bennie kept yelling at Gato about the $60 he still owed him, warning him that he better pay up tomorrow. At this point Bennie let out a whistle and a dented Vega came roaring down the block, careening to the curb, cutting us off in the direction we were walking. A young man in the passenger seat tried to open his door and jump skillfully onto the sidewalk before the car stopped, but instead he fell on his face in the gutter. He jumped back to his feet unsteadily, his nose bleeding, and a baseball bat waving in his right hand. The driver, who was steadier, apparently not high on angel dust like his companions, also rushed out of the car and was running at us. Bennie called out that all was "cool," that he already had the money, and they slowed down, walking toward us with puffed backs, one with the baseball bat resting on shoulder.

I ran back to the bodega door, but Gato had to stand firmly because this was the corner he worked, and those were his former partners. They surrounded him, shouting about the money he still owed, and began kicking and hitting him with the baseball bat. Gato still did not turn and run; instead he jumped up and down, prancing sideways along the sidewalk toward the corner on the main avenue in the hopes that the new colleagues he was steering crack customers to at the bogus "botanica"[3] around the corner might be able to catch sight of what was happening to him. He was knocked down two times before reaching the corner; they could have done Gato much more damage but backed away, walking back to the car with deliberate slowness, pretending not to notice me. The two who had driven up in the Vega had not seen the policeman frisk me, and they evidently did not think it wise to pick a fight with an unknown "white boy" who was just the right age to be an undercover. They pulled at Bennie's elbow and hopped into the Vega to drive off. Their attempt at burning rubber merely resulted in whining the car's gears.

By the time I caught up with Gato half a block down the avenue, he had already finished telling the story to a cousin of his who was on her way to the botanica crack house. His cousin was a woman in her late twenties, dressed "butch" in a long-sleeved jean jacket despite the midsummer midnight heat. Her emaciated face and long sleeves left no doubts as to her being a coke mainliner. When I arrived, she was waiving her skinny arms and stamping on the ground, whining hoarsely at Gato, telling him he couldn't just run off like that, that he had to "go down swinging like a man," that he couldn't just let people chase him around like that, that he had to show them who's who, and did he know who he was and where he was? Now what did he expect to do? Where was he going to work? And finally, she needed back right away the money (which he had spent on crack instead) she had lent him yesterday to buy a new supply of marijuana, and she was disgusted with him.

After we finished telling the story at the crack/botanica house where I had been spending most of my evening hours this summer, Chino, who was on duty selling that night with Julio, jumped up, excitedly calling out "What street was that on? Come on, let's go, we can still catch 'em. How many were they?" I quickly stopped this mobilization for a revenge posse, explaining that it was not worth my time and that we should just forget about it. Chino looked at me disgustedly, sat back down on the milk crate in front of the botanica's door, and turned his face away from me, shrugging his shoulders. Julio, whom I had become quite close to, jumped up in front of me to berate me for being "pussy." He also sat back down shortly afterwards, feigning exasperated incredulity with the comment, "Man, you still think like a blanquito." A half dozen spectators—some empty pocketed ("thirsty") crack addicts, most sharply dressed, drug-free teenage girls competing for Chino's and Julio's attentions—giggled and snickered at me.

To recuperate some minimal respect, I turned on Gato, telling him he owed me the $8 Bennie the dust head had stolen, and I ordered him to empty his pockets. Grinning, he pulled out a dollar and promised he would come by tomorrow with seven more. He told me not to worry; he would pay me back first. Of course, I knew he would not because he knew that I was one of the few individuals on the street even more "pussy" than he.

Seeing my feeble attempt, and perhaps hoping to give me a second chance, Julio came up to Gato at this point. Making sure I saw what he was doing, he dropped a vial of crack in Gato's shirt pocket in payment for the half dozen customers he had steered to the crack house that evening. I was supposed to grab the vial—worth $5—from Gato's pocket as partial compensation for the seven he still owed me. But I could not bring myself to rip Gato's shirt pocket open and grab the vial, knowing that Gato was "thirsty" and might get violent with me. He might have been "pussy" in the confrontation with Bennie, but he certainly was not going to be "pussy" with me.

A few minutes later Chino and Julio told everyone it was time to close shop. It had just turned 12:30 a.m, and they had to turn in the evening's receipts to their boss. They hurriedly pulled down the metal gates over the botanica entrance, eager to leave work and get on with an evening of par-tying. As he was walking away, Julio turned around to tell me "good night—I guess you're staying around here tonight, verdad [right]?" For the first time he was not going to invite me up to his girlfriend Jackie's apartment in the nearby projects (which she shared with her adopted grandfather and three children) to drink beer while he and Chino and whoever else was around snorted coke and ate dinner. He had to come home before 10'clock because Jackie was due at "the Candy Store" down the avenue to sell twenties of "rock." Jackie's husband Papito, who used to own the botan-ica crack site that Julio and Chino worked at, was now "upstate" serving two to five years for his second conviction for selling cocaine and pos-sessing firearms. Two nights before Papito was scheduled to go to jail, as he was closing down the botanica, Jackie, who was eight months pregnant at the time, shot him in the stomach right in the doorway of the botanica in front of all his workers and everyone else hanging out that evening. She was furious because, instead of leaving money for her before beginning his jail sentence, Papito had been running around spending thousands of dol-lars on young women and bragging about it at the crack house.

Ten months later Jackie was doing much better, especially following the problem-free birth of her third daughter. Jackie was relieved that the infant had come out "normal" despite the fact that she had been snorting large quantities of cocaine during the final months of her pregnancy. Papito's cousin Big Pete had taken over the crack franchise at the botanica while Papito was serving time. He had witnessed the shoot-out and had been impressed by Jackie's "balls." Consequently, shortly after the birth of her daughter, Big Pete hired Jackie to sell "twenties of rock" at another sales point that he owned in the neighborhood that doubled as a candy store.

Incidentally, not everyone was impressed by Jackie's shooting of her hus-band Papito. After starting up a relationship with Julio shortly after her husband's hospitalization and jailing, Jackie had told Rose, a fifteen-year-old former girlfriend of Julio's, to stop hanging around the crack house or else. I happened to be present one evening when Rose was discussing this threat with the crowd hanging around the crack house. Someone was warn-ing Rose that Jackie meant business and began retelling the story of Jack-ie's shooting Papito when Aida, the seller on shift at the crack house that evening, looked up from the pink baby blanket she was knitting to inter-rupt: "Big deal! Anybody can buy a fucking gun. What's the big deal? You just stay here Rose. You can come visit me any time you want. That wom-an's just a nasty, loud-mouthed bitch. She can't tell me or you or anyone else what to do here. She don't own the place. I'll tell Big Pete to set her straight."

Rose did indeed keep hanging around until another violent complication arose. Another ex-boyfriend of Rose's who claimed he still loved her out of control threatened to kill Julio and commit suicide if she kept hanging out at the crack house. This still did not keep Rose away. Instead, Julio was obliged to call on some friends and have them hang out with him at the crack house for extra protection. Rose's jilted lover did indeed return a few days later with two big friends, but they just kept walking by when they saw the crowd protecting Julio. Julio was exasperated with the whole issue because he had lost all interest in Rose last summer after he had gotten her pregnant (she had been fourteen at the time). She had had a big argument with him when he refused to pay for her abortion.

For the past few weeks we had baby-sat Jackie's children along with her sixty-five-year-old alcoholic grandfather-in-law while Jackie worked selling the twenties of crack. Baby-sitting involved first eating everything in the refrigerator, sending one of the children out for beer, keeping the grandfather from drinking any hard liquor, shouting at the young children if they quarreled, playing tenderly with the nine-month-old, and accompanying Chino and Julio into the bedroom to keep "conversating" with them as they ground up and sniffed cocaine. By daybreak Jackie had usually returned from work with fresh coke for Julio and Chino to sniff and "break night." They would sleep from midmorning until late afternoon, careful to arrive on time for their evening shift (4:00 P.M. to 12:30 A.M.) at the botanica crack house.

CULTURE AND MATERIAL REALITY

The foregoing summary of my fieldwork is merely a personalized glimpse of the day-to-day struggle for survival, *and for meaning*, by the people who comprise the extraordinary statistics on inner-city crack and crime.[4] These are the very same Puerto Rican residents of Spanish Harlem whom Oscar Lewis in *La Vida* declared to be victims of a "culture of poverty," mired in a "self-perpetuating cycle of poverty" (Lewis, 1966:5). The culture-of-poverty concept has been severely critiqued for its internal inconsistencies, its inadequate understanding of culture and ethnicity, its ethnocentric/middle-class bias, and especially its blindness to structural forces and blame-the-victim implications (cf. Eames and Goode, 1980; Leacock, 1971; Stack, 1974; Valentine, 1968; Waxman, 1977). Despite the negative scholarly consensus on Lewis's theory, the alternative discussions either tend toward economic reductionism (Ryan, 1986; Steinberg, 1981; Wilson, 1978) or else ultimately minimize the reality of profound marginalization and destruction—some of it internalized—that envelop a disproportionate share of the inner-city poor (cf. Stack, 1974; Valentine, 1978; see critiques by Harrison, 1988; Maxwell, 1988; Wilson, 1987). More important, the media and a large proportion of the inner-city residents themselves continue to subscribe to a popularized blame-the-victim/culture-of-poverty theory that has not been adequately rebutted by scholars.

The media now refer to the inner-city residents described in my ethnographic vignette as "the underclass," the "hard-core unemployed," and the "unemployables." These pariahs of urban industrial society seek their income, and subsequently their identity and the meaning in their lives, through what they perceive to be high-powered careers "on the street." They partake of ideologies and values and share symbols that, it could be argued, add up to an "inner-city street culture" that is completely excluded from the mainstream economy and society but ultimately derived from it. Most of them have few direct contacts with non-inner-city residents; and when they do, it is usually in a position of domination: teachers in school, bosses, police officers, and later parole or probation officers.

How can the complicated ideological dynamic accompanying inner-city poverty be understood without falling into an idealistic culture-of-poverty and blame-the-victim interpretation? Scholars who offer structural, political-economic reinterpretations of the inner-city dynamic emphasize historical processes of labor migration in the context of institutionalized racism. They dissect the structural transformations in the international economy, which they see as destroying the manufacturing sector in the U. S. while leading to a burgeoning low-wage, low-prestige service sector (cf. Davis, 1987; Sassen-Koob, 1986; Steinberg, 1981; Tabb and Sawers, 1984; Wilson, 1987). These sorts of theories have the virtue of addressing the structural confines of the inner-city dynamic but also a vice: they tend to see the actual actors involved as passive. In my view, such interpretations fail to grasp fully the complex relationship between ideological processes and material reality, and between culture and class.

To explain fully the dynamic I saw day in and day out on New York's mean streets, we have to understand its relationship to the larger structural processes of international labor migration in the world economy. But the inner-city residents I hung out with in Spanish Harlem are more than mere victims of historical transformations or of the institutionalized racism of a perverse political-economic system. They do not passively accept their fourth-class citizen fate. They are struggling determinedly—just as ruthlessly as the corporate robber barons of the nineteenth century and the yuppie investment bankers of today—to earn money, demand dignity, and lead meaningful lives. And in this lies the tragic irony that is at the heart of their existence: their very struggle against—yet within—the system exacerbates the trauma of their community and helps destroy thousands of individual lives (Bourgois, 1992, 1995).

In the day-to-day experience of the street-bound inner-city resident, unemployment and personal anxiety over the impossibility of providing a minimal standard of living for one's family translate into intracommunity crime, intracommunity drug abuse, intracommunity violence. The objective, structural desperation of a population without a viable economy and facing the barriers of systematic discrimination and marginalization gets channeled into self-destructive cultural practices.

Most important, the "personal failure" of those who survive on the street is articulated in the idiom of race. The racism of the larger society becomes internalized on a personal level. Once again, although the individuals in the ethnographic fragment at the beginning of this chapter are the victims of long-term historical and structural transformations, they do not interpret their myriad difficulties in political-economic terms. In their struggle to survive and even to succeed, they daily enforce the details of the trauma and cruelty of their lives on the others who inhabit the excluded margins of urban America.

CULTURAL REPRODUCTION THEORY

Education theorists have developed a literature on the processes by which structures and cultures of privilege and power are made and remade in daily life. They have tried to understand how society is "reproduced" by studying the ideological domination of the poor and the working class in school settings (*e.g.,* Giroux, 1983). Some of these theories of social reproduction tend toward an economic reductionism or a simple, mechanical functionalism (see, *e.g.,* Bowles and Gintis, 1977). More recent variants emphasize the complexity and contradictory nature of the dynamic of ideological domination (Willis, 1983). There are several ethnographies that document how the very process whereby working-class students resist the imposition of middle-class norms in school ends up channeling them into marginal roles in the economy for the rest of their lives (cf. Foley, 1990; Macleod, 1987; Willis, 1977). Other ethnographically based interpretations show that for inner-city African-American students to achieve traditional academic success, they must reject their ethnic identity and cultural dignity; when such students do well in school, they are often seen by their peers as caving in to the demands of white institutions, the educational equivalent of an "Uncle Tom" (Fordham, 1988; Zweigenhaft and Domhoff, 1991).

Beyond school settings, cultural reproduction theory has great potential for shedding light on how structurally induced cultural resistance and self-reinforced marginalization interact at the street level in the inner-city experience. Rather than a culture of poverty, the violence, crime, and substance abuse of the inner city can be understood as manifestations of a "culture of resistance," a culture defined by its stance against mainstream, white, racist, and economically exclusive society. This culture of resistance, however, results in greater oppression and self-destruction. More concretely, resisting the outside society's racism and refusing to accept demeaning, low-wage, entry-level jobs contributes to the sorts of crime, addiction, and intracommunity violence for which crack has become an emblem.

Most of the individuals in my earlier vignette are *proud* that they are not being "exploited" by "the white man," although they also feel "like fucking assholes" for being poor. Contrary to popular images, all of them have previously held numerous jobs in the legal economy. Most of them hit the street in their early teens, working odd jobs as delivery boys and baggers in supermarkets and bodegas. Most have held the jobs that are objectively recognized as among the least desirable in U.S. society. Virtually all of these street participants have had deeply demeaning personal experiences in the minimum-wage labor market due to abusive, exploitative, and often racist bosses or supervisors. They see the illegal, underground economy as offering not only superior wages, but also a more dignified workplace.

Gato, for example, had worked for the ASPCA, cleaning out the gas chambers where stray dogs and cats are killed. Bennie had been fired six months earlier from a night-shift job as security guard on the violent ward for the criminally insane on Wards Island. Chino had been fired a year ago from a job installing high-altitude storm windows on skyscrapers after an accident temporarily blinded him in the right eye. Upon being disabled, he discovered that his contractor had hired him illegally through an arrangement with a corrupt union official who had paid him half the union wage, pocketing the rest, and who had no health insurance for him. Chino also claimed that his foreman was a "Ku Klux Klanner" and had been especially abusive to him because he was a black Puerto Rican. While recovering from the accident, Chino had become addicted to crack and ended up in the hospital as a gunshot victim before landing a job at Big Pete's crack house.

Julio's last legal job before selling crack was as an off-the-books messenger for a magazine catering to New York yuppies. He had gotten addicted to crack, began selling his household possessions, and finally was thrown out by his wife, who had just given birth to his son (the second generation "Julio Junior" to be raised on public assistance). Julio had quit his messenger job in favor of stealing car radios for a couple of hours at night in the very same neighborhoods where he had been delivering messages for ten-hour days at just above minimum wage. After a close encounter with the police, Julio begged his cousin for a job in his crack house. Ironically, the sense of responsibility, success, and prestige that selling crack provided enabled him to kick his crack habit and substitute for it a considerably less expensive powder cocaine and alcohol habit.

The underground economy is the ultimate "equal opportunity employer" for inner-city youth (cf. Kornblum and Williams, 1985). As Mike Davis has noted for Los Angeles, the structural economic incentive to participate in the drug economy is overwhelming: "With 78,000 unemployed youth in the Watts-Willowbrook area, it is not surprising that the jobless resort to the opportunities of the burgeoning 'crack economy' or that there are now 145 branches of the rival Crips and Bloods gangs in south-central L.A." (Davis, 1987:75). In fact, what *is* surprising is how few inner-city youths become active in the underground economy; most still enter the legal economy and accept low-wage jobs.

In contrast, individuals who "successfully" pursue careers in the "crack economy" or any other facet of the underground economy are no longer "exploitable" by legal society. They speak with anger at their former low wages and bad treatment. They make fun of friends and acquaintances—many of whom come to buy drugs from them—who are still employed in factories, in service jobs, or in what they (and most other people) would call "shitwork." Of course, many others are less self-conscious about the reasons for their rejection of entry-level, mainstream employment. Instead, they internalize societal stereotypes and think of themselves as lazy and irresponsible, quitting their jobs to have a good time on the street. Many still pay lip service to the value of a steady, legal job. Still others cycle in and out of legal employment, supplementing their entry-level jobs with part-time crack sales in a paradoxical subsidy of the low wages of the legal economy by the illegal economy.

THE CULTURE OF TERROR IN THE UNDERGROUND ECONOMY

The culture of resistance and the underground economy that have emerged in opposition to demeaning, underpaid employment in the mainstream economy often engender violence. Anthropologist Michael Taussig (1984:492) has shown that in the South American context of extreme political repression and racism against Amerindians and Jews, "cultures of terror" emerge to become "a high-powered tool for domination and a principle medium for political practice." But unlike the Putumayo massacres in the early twentieth century and the Argentine torture chambers of the 1970s, which Taussig writes about, domination in the inner city's culture of terror is self-administered, even if the root causes are generated externally. With the exception of the occasional brutal policeman or the bureaucratized repression of the social welfare and criminal justice institutions, the physical violence and terror of the inner city are carried out largely by inner-city residents themselves.

Regular displays of violence are necessary for success in the underground economy—especially the street-level, drug-dealing world of crack. Violence is essential for maintaining credibility and for preventing rip-offs by colleagues, customers, and holdup artists. Indeed, as I learned the hard way in my fieldwork, upward mobility in the crack sector of the underground economy requires a systematic and effective use of violence against one's colleagues, one's neighbors, and to a certain extent, oneself. Behavior that appears irrationally violent and self-destructive to middle-class (or working-class) outside observers can be more accurately interpreted according to the logic of the underground economy as judicious public relations, advertising, rapport building, and long-term investment in one's "human capital."

This can be seen very clearly in the fieldwork summary at the beginning of this chapter. Gato and I were mugged because Gato had a reputation for being "soft" or "pussy" and because I was publicly unmasked as *not being* an undercover cop and hence safe to attack. Gato had tried to minimize the damage to his future ability to sell on that corner by not turning and running. He had pranced sideways down the street while being beaten with a baseball bat and kicked to the ground twice. Nevertheless, the admonishments of his cousin, the female coke mainliner to whom he told the story, could not have been clearer: where was he going to work after such a public fiasco? Significantly, I found out later that this was the second time this had happened to Gato this year. Gato was not going to be upwardly mobile in the underground economy because of his "pussy" reputation; he was simply not as effectively violent as his "chosen" occupation required. One's "street rep" is as valuable an asset in the world of crack dealers as professional reputations are among stockbrokers, physicians, and business people.

Employers or new entrepreneurs in the underground economy look for people who can demonstrate their capacity for effective violence and thus terror. This is clearly illustrated by Big Pete's hiring of Jackie to sell cocaine at his candy store shortly after he witnessed her shooting Papito, her husband (his cousin). Similarly, Marco, another one of Big Pete's primary street-level sellers, had a "bionic leg." He had been shot through the thigh in a previous crack confrontation ("when I thought I was Superman") by a "dum dum" bullet. His leg had been rebuilt, leaving him with a pronounced limp but quick coordination. He frequently referred to his rebuilt limb in conversation; it was a source of pride and credibility for him. He was considered an effective crack dealer.

For Big Pete, the owner of a string of crack and cocaine franchises, the ability of his employees to hold up under gunpoint was crucial because stickups of dealing dens are not infrequent. In fact, during the first thirteen months of my fieldwork, the botanica was held up twice. Julio happened to be on duty both times. He admitted to me that he had been very nervous when they held the gun to his temple and asked for money and crack. Nevertheless, not only did he withhold some of the money and crack that was hidden behind bogus botanica merchandise, but he also later exaggerated to Big Pete the amount that had been stolen in order to pocket the difference. The possibility of being held up was constantly on Julio's mind. Several times when more than two people walked into the botanica at once, Julio stiffened as if expecting them to pull out weapons. On another occasion, he confided to me that he was nervous about a cousin of his who all of a sudden had started hanging out at the crack house/botanica, feigning friendship. Julio suspected him of casing the joint for a future stickup.

In several long conversations with active criminals (a dealing den stickup artist, several crack dealers, and a former bank robber), I asked them to explain how they were able to trust their partners in crime sufficiently to ensure the longevity and effectiveness of their enterprise. To my surprise, I was not given righteous raps about blood brotherhood trustworthiness or boyhood loyalty. Instead, in each case, in slightly different language, I was told somewhat aggressively, "What do you mean how do I trust him? You should ask, 'How can he trust me?!' " In each case, their point was unmistakable: *their own ruthlessness is their only real security* (*e.g.,* "My support network is me, myself, and I"). The vehemence with which they made these assertions suggests that they felt threatened by the idea that their security and success might depend upon the trustworthiness of a partner or employee. They were claiming—in one case angrily—that they were not dependent upon trust because they were tough enough to command respect, willing to engage in enough violence to enforce all contracts they entered into.

For example, at the end of the summer, Chino was forced to flee out of state to a cousin's because his own cocaine use had gotten sufficiently out of hand that he snorted merchandise he was supposed to sell. When he was unable to turn in the night's receipts to Big Pete, he left town, certain that a violent reprisal was coming. In the same way, my own failure to display a propensity for violence in several instances cost me the respect of the members of the crack scene that I frequented. This was very evident when I turned down Julio and Chino's offer to chase down the three men who mugged Gato and me. Julio despaired that I "still [thought] like a blanquito" and was genuinely disappointed in my lack of common sense and self-respect.

These concrete examples of the need to cultivate a public reputation for violence are extreme but common among the individuals who rely on the underground economy for their income. Their survival and success are dependent upon their capacity for terror. Individuals involved in street crack sales and other sectors of the underground economy cannot turn to lawful means for conflict resolution and so cultivate the culture of terror in order to intimidate competitors, maintain credibility, develop new contacts, cement partnerships, and ultimately have a good time. For the most part, they are not conscious of this process; the culture of terror has become a myth replete with a set of roles, rules, and satisfactions all its own.[5]

Significantly, the pervasiveness of the inner-city culture of terror does not apply solely to crack sellers or to street criminals; to a certain extent, all individuals living in the neighborhood who want to maintain a sense of autonomy (*i.e.*, who do not want to have to rush out of their houses during daylight hours only or quadruple lock their doors at sunset) find it useful to participate to some limited extent in some corner of the culture of terror. In this manner, the culture of terror seeps into the fabric of the inner city, impinging upon its residents—including the majority of the population who work 9 to 5 plus overtime in mainstream jobs just above poverty-level wages.

A powerful ideological dynamic, therefore, poisons interpersonal relations throughout much of the community by legitimizing violence and mandating distrust. On a more obvious level, the culture of terror is experienced physically by anyone who spends time on the street. All who frequent the streets will be exposed to the violence of the underground economy even if they do not participate in it. For example, during just the first thirteen months of my residence in Spanish Harlem, I witnessed a series of violent events: (1) a deadly shooting of the mother of a three-year-old child outside my window by an assailant wielding a sawed-off shotgun (the day before the victim had slashed her future murderer with a razor blade when he complained about the quality of the $5 vials of crack that she sold); (2) a bombing and a machine gunning of a numbers joint by a rival faction of the local "mafia," once again within view of my apartment window; (3) a shoot-out and police car chase scene in front of a pizza parlor where I happened to be eating a snack; (4) the firebombing of a heroin house by an unpaid supplier around the block from where I lived; (5) a dozen screaming, clothes-ripping, punching fights; (6) at least bi-weekly sightings of an intravenous drug-using mother with visible needle "tracks" on her arms walking down the street with a toddler by her side, or a pregnant woman entering and leaving a crack house; (7) almost daily exposure to broken-down human beings, some of them in fits of crack-induced paranoia, some suffering from delirium tremens, and others in unidentifiable pathological fits, screaming and shouting insults to all around them.

Of course, as a street fieldworker, I was looking for these events. They are not, strictly speaking, random samples of inner-city experience. Had I been a typical Spanish Harlem resident intent upon making it on time to my 9 to 5 job every morning, I would not have noticed at least half of these events, and I would not have had the time or the interest to find out the details on most of the other half. I surely would not have paid any attention to the broken-down human beings walking the streets, begging change, and mumbling or shouting to themselves. Nevertheless, these examples do not include the dozens of additional stories of accounts of killings and beatings told to me by eyewitnesses and sometimes even by family members and children of the victims or the perpetrators.

Perhaps the most poignant expression of the pervasiveness of the culture of terror was the comment made to me by a thirteen-year-old boy in the course of an otherwise innocuous, random conversation about how he was doing in school and how his mother's pregnancy was going. He told me he hoped his mother would give birth to a boy "because girls are too easy to rape." He was both sad and bragging when he said this, matter-of-factly asserting his adulthood and "realistic" knowledge of the mythical level of terror on the street where he was growing up.

In order to interact with people on the street, one has to participate at least passively in this culture of destruction and terror. Small children already talk about it in grade school. I overheard the story of a boy whose mother told him never to fight. Not long into the school year a classmate mugged him of his mid-afternoon snack and pocket money. By not fighting back, according to his mother's dictates, the child quickly developed a "pussy" reputation. During the ensuing weeks, he lost his snack and money every single day until finally, when he complained to his mother, she berated him, "What's the matter with you? Can't you fight back?"

THE HORATIO ALGER MYTH REVISITED

It is important to understand that the underground economy and the violence emerging out of it are not propelled by an irrational cultural logic distinct from that of mainstream America. On the contrary, *street participants are frantically pursuing the American Dream.* The assertions of the culture-of-poverty theorists that the poor have been badly socialized and do not share mainstream values is simply wrong. In fact, ambitious, energetic inner-city youths are attracted to the underground economy precisely *because* they believe in Horatio Alger's version of the American Dream. They are, in true American fashion, frantically trying to get their piece of the pie as fast as possible. In fact, they often follow the traditional U.S. model for upward mobility to the letter: aggressively setting themselves up as private entrepreneurs. They are the ultimate "rugged individualists," braving an unpredictable free-market frontier where fortune, fame, and destruction are all just around the corner.

Hence Indio, a particularly enterprising and ambitious young crack dealer who was aggressively carving out a new sales point, shot his brother in the spine and paralyzed him for life while he was high on angel dust in a battle over sales rights. His brother now works for him, selling on crutches.

Meanwhile, the shooting has cemented Indio's street reputation, and his workers are awesomely disciplined: "If he shot his brother, he'll shoot anyone."

For many of the people I met, the underground economy and the culture of terror are seen as the most *realistic* routes to upward mobility. Contrary to the pious preachments of politicians and the privileged, who claim that with hard work anyone can make it in America, they know from their own lived experience that "straight" entry-level jobs are not viable channels to upward mobility, especially for high school dropouts. Drug selling or other illegal activity appears as the most effective and rational option for getting rich within one's lifetime.

Many of the street dealers are strictly utilitarian in their involvement with crack, and they snub their clients despite the fact that they usually ingest considerable amounts of alcohol and powder cocaine themselves. They refer to their merchandise as "this garbage" and often openly make fun of crack heads as they arrive "on a mission" to "see Scotty"[6] with fistfuls of money. Sometimes they even ask their "respectable looking" clients with incredulity, "You don't do this shit do you?" Chino used to chant at his regular customers "Come on, keep on killing yourself; bring me that money; smoke yourself to death; make me rich." On another occasion, I witnessed an argument between a crack seller and two young men who were drug-free and virulently opposed to the underground economy. The crack seller essentially won the argument by deriding the drug-free young men for missing out on a smart, easy opportunity to make good money.

THE SEARCH FOR DIGNITY

Even though the average street seller is employed by the owner of a sales point for whom he has to maintain regular hours, meet sales quotas, and be subject to being fired, the street seller has a great deal of autonomy and power in his daily (or nightly) schedule. His boss comes only once or twice a shift to drop off drugs and pick up money. Frequently, a young messenger is sent instead. Sellers are often surrounded by a bevy of "thirsty" friends and hangers-on—often young teenage women in the case of male sellers— willing to run errands, pay attention to conversations, give support in arguments and fights, and provide sexual favors because of the relatively large amounts of money and drugs passing through their hands. In fact, even youths who do not use drugs will hang out and attempt respectfully to befriend the dealer just to be privy to the excitement of people coming and going, copping and hanging; money flowing, arguments, detectives, and stick-up artists—all around danger and excitement. Other nonusers will hang out to be treated to an occasional round of beer, Bacardi, or on an off night, Thunderbird. Crack dealers attain "status" on the street that they would be hard-pressed to find in any "legit" job open to them.

The channel into the underground economy is by no means strictly economic. Besides wanting to earn "crazy money," people choose "hoodlum" status in order to assert their dignity by refusing to "sling a mop for the white man" for "chump change" (cf. Anderson, 1976:68). Employment—or better yet, self-employment—in the underground economy accords a sense of autonomy, self-worth, and an opportunity for extraordinarily rapid, short-term upward mobility that is only too obviously unavailable in entry-level jobs in the licit economy. To be able to live opulently without "visible means of support"—like, say, the "idle rich" in the Hamptons—is considered the ultimate expression of success for many Americans. For residents of Spanish Harlem, however, this is a viable option only in the underground economy. The proof of this is visible to everyone on the street as they watch teenage crack dealers drive by in convertible Suzuki Samurai jeeps with the stereo blaring, "beam" by in impeccable BMWs, or—in the case of the middle-aged dealers—glide along in well-waxed Lincoln Continentals. Nor are these material achievements unimaginable, for anyone can aspire to be promoted to the level of seller, perched on a twenty-speed mountain bike with a beeper on one's belt. In fact, many youths not particularly active in the drug trade run around with beepers on their belts just pretending to be "big time." It is no coincidence that Julio was able to quit crack only after getting a job selling it.

The feelings of self-actualization and self-respect that the dealer's lifestyle offers cannot be underestimated. A former manager of a coke-shooting gallery who had employed a network of a half-dozen sellers, lookouts, and security guards and who had grossed $7000–$13,000 per week for over a year before being jailed explained to me that the best memories of his drug-dealing days were of the respect he received from people on the street. He described how, when he drove up in one of his cars to pick up the day's receipts, a bevy of attentive men and women would run to open the door for him and engage him in polite small talk, not unlike what happens in many licit businesses when the boss arrives. Others would offer to clean his car. He said that even the children hanging out in the street who were too young to understand what his dealings involved looked up to him in awe. He would invite a half-dozen friends and acquaintances out to dinner in expensive restaurants almost every night.

He also noted that his shooting gallery had enabled his wife and two children to get off welfare. Accepting welfare as an adult head of household had been particularly humiliating for him. Significantly, after coming out of jail, he had been unable to reunite with his wife and children, who were living at his wife's mother's apartment. His mother-in-law would not let him in the house, and his new legit job as a messenger for a Wall Street brokerage firm paid far too little for him to afford an apartment of his own for his family. Consequently, he roomed illegally in the apartment of a woman with two children supported by public assistance who took in boarders to supplement her income off the record. He was determined not to reenter the underground economy for fear of being detected by his parole officer and sent back to jail.

CONJUGATED OPPRESSION

The dynamism of the multibillion-dollar underground economy, the rejection of demeaning exploitation in the mainstream economy, and the dignity offered by illegal entrepreneurial activity explain only a portion of the violence and substance abuse in the inner city. They do not account for the explosive appeal of a drug like crack. It is necessary to examine the structural dynamic of the inner-city experience on a deeper level to explain why so many people would be so attracted to crack today (or heroin only a half-dozen years ago). This involves the conflation of ethnic discrimination with a rigidly segmented labor market, and all the hidden injuries to human dignity that this entails, especially in a place like New York City. It involves, in other words, the experience of many forms of oppression at once, or what I call "conjugated oppression" (cf. Bourgois, 1988, 1989).

A casual, random stroll through Spanish Harlem will expose one to cohorts of emaciated coke and crack addicts. Many will be begging for their next vial; others will be "petro"—crashing from the high and intensely paranoid of everyone around them—shivering, mumbling to themselves in agitated angst with their eyes wide and jaws tense. If the stroller should happen upon a "copping corner," it will look like a street fair, especially late at night—cars driving by, people coming and going, building doors opening and closing, people hanging out all over. Most likely, a hail of whistles and shouts will accompany the stroller's arrival as the lookouts warn the "pitchers" who carry the drugs that a potential undercover has entered the scene.

Conjugated oppression consists of an ideological dynamic of ethnic discrimination that interacts explosively with an economic dynamic of class exploitation to produce an overwhelming experience of oppression that is more than the sum of the parts. It offers insight into why hordes of "petro" crack heads, teenagers and grandparents alike, will continue to fry their brains and burn up their bodies in a hysteria of ecstatic substance abuse. It helps explain why the former heroin mainliners turned coke shooters continue poking their veins into abscesses while sharing HIV-infected needles.

In the Puerto Rican community, there is the added problem of confused and frustrated national identity due to the ambiguous "colonial/commonwealth" status of their homeland (even if they are third generation born on the mainland). When they venture out of El Barrio through the streets of Manhattan, they are confronted everywhere by a rigidly segmented ethnic/occupational hierarchy. In fact, it could be argued that Manhattan sports a de facto apartheid labor market, because a close look at the minute differences in job categories and prestige shows that they generally correlate with ethnicity.

Furthermore, in New York City, the insult of working for entry-level wages amidst extraordinary opulence is especially painful for Spanish Harlem youths who have been raised in abject poverty only a few blocks from all-white neighborhoods commanding some of the highest real estate values in the world. As messengers, security guards, or Xerox machine operators in the corporate headquarters of the Fortune 500 companies, they are brusquely ordered about by young white executives who often make as much in a month as they do in a year and who do not even have the time to notice that they are being rude.

Confronting Manhattan's ethnic/occupational hierarchy drives the inner-city youths depicted in this chapter deeper into the confines of their segregated neighborhood and the underground economy. They prefer to seek out meaning and upward mobility in a context that not only values their skills, but does not constantly oblige them to come into contact with people of a different, hostile ethnicity wielding arbitrary power over them. In the underground economy, especially in the world of substance abuse, they never have to experience the silent, subtle humiliations to which they are routinely subjected in the entry-level labor market or even during a mere subway ride downtown.

In this context, the fleeting relief offered by the crack high and the meaning provided by the rituals and struggles around purchasing and using the drug resemble millenarian religions. Such religious cults have swept colonized peoples attempting to resist oppression in the context of accelerated social trauma—whether it be the Ghost Dance of the Great Plains Amerindians, the "cargo cults" of Melanesia, the Mamachi movement of the Guaymi Amerindians in Panama, or even religions such as Farrakhan's Nation of Islam and the Jehovah's Witnesses in the heart of the inner city (cf. Bourgois, 1986, 1989). Substance abuse in general and crack in particular offer an inverted equivalent to the purification of a millenarian metamorphosis. Users are instantaneously transformed from unemployed, depressed high school dropouts, despised by the world—and secretly convinced that their failure is due to their own inherent stupidity, "racial laziness," and disorganization—into masses of heart-palpitating pleasure, followed only minutes later by a jaw-gnashing crash and wide awake alertness that fills their life with concrete and compelling purpose: get more crack—fast!

NOTES

This is an abbreviated and revised version of an article originally published in *Contemporary Drug Problems* (volume 16, 1989). Another article with a similar theme was published in *Anthropology Today* (volume 5, number 4, 1989).

1. A bodega is a small grocery store.

2. All the names have been changed, as have some of the descriptions of settings, to protect confidentiality. This research was undertaken with the cooperation of the individuals appearing in the chapter. Several of them read—or were read—earlier drafts and provided useful critical comments. I thank them for their help and understanding.

3. A botanica is an herbal pharmacy and utility store for religious objects used in santeria.

4. Fieldwork for this research during the 1985–1990 period was funded by the Wenner-Gren Foundation for Anthropological Research, the U.S. Bureau of the Census, two Washington University junior faculty summer research grants, lottery funds, an Affirmative Action grant from San Francisco State University, the Committees for Research on the Urban Underclass and for Public Policy Research on Contemporary Hispanic Issues, the Harry Frank Guggenheim Foundation, and the National Institute on Drug Abuse. Any errors of interpretation are, of course, my responsibility.

5. For an ethnopsychological perspective on the logic of violence among Chicano youth gang members in Southern California, see Vigil, 1988.

6. A code language around the television series *Star Trek* has emerged among crack users in New York City (as in "Beam me up, Scotty" for getting high).

REFERENCES

Anderson, Elijah. *A Place on the Corner.* Chicago: University of Chicago Press, 1976.

Bourgois, Philippe. "The Miskitu of Nicaragua: Politicized Ethnicity." *Anthropology Today* 2:4–9 (1986).

———. "Conjugated Oppression: Class and Ethnicity Among Guaymi and Kuna Banana Workers." *American Ethnologist* 15:328–348 (1988).

———. *Ethnicity at Work: Divided Labor on a Central American Banana Plantation.* Baltimore: Johns Hopkins University Press, 1989.

———. "From Jibaro to Crack Dealer: Confronting the Restructuring of Capitalism in Spanish Harlem," in Jane Schneider and Rayna Rapp, eds., *Articulating Hidden Histories.* Pp. 125–141. Berkeley: University of California Press, 1992.

———. *In Search of Respect: Selling Crack in El Barrio.* Cambridge, England: Cambridge University Press, 1995.

Bowles, Samuel, and Herbert Gintis. *Schooling in Capitalist America.* New York: Basic Books, 1977.

Davis, Mike. "Chinatown, Part Two? The 'Internationalization' of Downtown Los Angeles." *New Left Review* 164:65–86 (1987).

Eames, Edwin, and Judith Goode. "The Culture of Poverty: A Misapplication of Anthropology to Contemporary Issues," in George Gmelch and Walter Zenner, eds., *Urban Life: Readings in Urban Anthropology*. Pp. 320–333. Prospect Heights, IL: Waveland Press, 1980.

Foley, Doug. *Learning Capitalist Culture*. Philadelphia: University of Pennsylvania Press, 1990.

Fordham, Signithia. "Racelessness as a Factor in Black Students' School Success: Pragmatic Strategy or Pyrrhic Victory?" *Harvard Educational Review* 58:54–84 (1988).

Giroux, Henry. "Theories of Reproduction and Resistance in the New Sociology of Education: A Critical Analysis. *Harvard Educational Review* 53:257–293 (1983).

Harrison, Faye. "Introduction: An African Diaspora Perspective for Urban Anthropology." *Urban Anthropology* 17:111–141 (1988).

Kornblum, William, and Terry Williams. *Growing Up Poor.* Lexington MA: Lexington Books, 1985.

Leacock, Eleanor Burke, ed. *The Culture of Poverty: A Critique*. New York: Simon and Schuster, 1971.

Lewis, Oscar. "The Culture of Poverty," in *Anthropological Essays*. Pp 67–80. New York: Random House, 1966.

Macleod, Jay. *Ain't No Makin' It*. Boulder, CO: Westview Press, 1987.

Maxwell, Andrew. "The Anthropology of Poverty in Black Communities: A Critique and Systems Alternative." *Urban Anthropology* 17:171–191 (1988).

Ryan, William. "Blaming the Victim," in Kurt Finsterbusch and George McKenna, eds., *Taking Sides: Clashing Views on Controversial Social Issues*. Pp. 45–52. Guilford, CT: Dushkin Publishing Group, 1986.

Sassen-Koob, Saskia. "New York City: Economic Restructuring and Immigration." *Development and Change* 17:87–119 (1986).

Stack, Carol. *All Our Kin: Strategies for Survival in a Black Community*. New York: Harper & Row, 1974.

Steinberg, Stephen. *The Ethnic Myth: Race, Ethnicity, and Class in America*. New York: Atheneum, 1981.

Tabb, William, and Larry Sawers, eds. *Marxism and the Metropolis: New Perspectives in Urban Political Economy*. New York: Oxford University Press, 1984.

Taussig, Michael. "Culture of Terror—Space of Death, Roger Casement's Putumayo Report and the Explanation of Torture." *Comparative Studies in Society and History* 26:467–497 (1984).

Valentine, Bettylou. *Hustling and Other Hard Work*. New York: Free Press, 1978.

Valentine, Charles. *Culture and Poverty*. Chicago: University of Chicago Press, 1968.

Vigil, James Diego. "Group Processes and Street Identity: Adolescent Chicano Gang Members." *Ethos* 16:421–445 (1988).

Waxman, Chaim. *The Stigma of Poverty: A Critique of Poverty Theories and Policies*. New York: Pergamon, 1977.

Willis, Paul. *Learning To Labor: How Working Class Kids Get Working Class Jobs*. Aldershot, England: Gower, 1977.

———. "Cultural Production and Theories of Reproduction," in Len Barton and

Stephen Walker, eds., *Race, Class and Education*. Pp 107–138. London: Croom-Helm, 1983.

Wilson, William J. *The Declining Significance of Race*. Chicago: University of Chicago Press, 1978.

———. *The Truly Disadvantaged: The Inner City, the Underclass, and Public Policy*. Chicago: University of Chicago Press, 1987.

Zweigenhaft, Richard L., and G. William Domhoff. *Blacks in the White Establishment: A Study of Race and Class in America*. New Haven, CT: Yale University Press, 1991.

FOUR

The Contingent Call of the Pipe
Bingeing and Addiction
Among Heavy Cocaine Smokers

Craig Reinarman, Dan Waldorf, Sheigla B. Murphy,
and Harry G. Levine

The prevailing image of crack is that it is an instantly addicting drug that inevitably destroys the lives of those who use it. At the start of the crack scare, we explored this claim in depth interviews with over fifty heavy crack users and freebasers. They found cocaine smoking very alluring. They reported compulsive use patterns. They spoke of powerful cravings. Many said they felt addicted, at least at some point. To the extent that the core claims of the crack scare contain truth, it is a truth about these people.

We interviewed these crack and freebase smokers as part of a larger study of heavy cocaine users, most of whom "snorted" the drug intranasally in powder form. The larger sample was comprised of the most extreme 10% of cocaine users in the U.S.; it excluded all users who did not take large amounts of cocaine for a substantial period of time. This eliminated the vast majority of Americans who have ever used cocaine—experimenters, occasional users, light users. The subsample of cocaine smokers we report on here was among the small minority of even heavy cocaine snorters who had both shifted to the most direct mode of cocaine ingestion and used it repeatedly.[1]

These crack users and freebasers were not ordinary illicit drug users. By their own accounts, they were people who repeatedly sought extreme highs. They brought to their use of drugs a relatively rare mind-set: they not only enjoyed drug use and had taken large amounts of licit and illicit drugs over the years; they had also *actively pursued* extreme drug experiences that the vast majority of drug users would actively shun. This does not necessarily mean that their extreme drug use prevented them from functioning in their daily lives; many functioned rather well. Their active pursuit of intense drug experiences does mean that they were in some important ways different—not merely from citizens who drink alcohol or smoke marijuana, but different even from that small subset of citizens who have used a lot of cocaine.

What these heavy cocaine smokers reported to us suggests that there are three related respects in which the prevailing image of crack is false, misleading, or in need of qualification. First, the prevailing image falsely generalizes from these sorts of heavy users to all who might touch this drug, as if these users' experiences were intrinsic properties of the substance itself. As Morgan and Zimmer show in Chapter 7, the psychopharmacology of smoked cocaine lends itself to binge use. But there is no *psychopharmacological* reason why someone who binged once or twice would necessarily do so repeatedly. Indeed, data from the National Household Survey on Drug Abuse show that a clear majority of those who have ever tried crack do not remain regular users, much less go on to addiction and self-destruction (SAMHSA, 1995).

The second aspect of the prevailing image of crack that we need to qualify and complicate has to do with the pattern of heavy crack use—with crack "addiction." Most of our respondents reported periods of compulsively craving and consuming one "hit" after another, and many persisted in "hitting the pipe" even when doing so caused problems in their lives. These behaviors are commonly cited as evidence of addiction. But what we found most striking about such behaviors was that they almost always occurred *within a smoking episode.* For most (although not all) of our heavy crack and freebase smokers, days, weeks, and often a month or more would pass between such episodes, during which time they would go on about their lives neither smoking cocaine nor usually craving it.

What our respondents described, again and again, were *binges,* which is precisely the use pattern that the unique psychopharmacology of smoked cocaine would lead us to expect. Many different kinds of addicts binge, and so bingeing is often confused with addiction. But binges are not the same as addiction and do not by themselves cause addiction. Binges can be long evenings, often whole days, even entire weekends. Binges are not all that rare. Humans have binged on alcohol for thousands of years in many different cultures, alongside more common moderate drinking practices. Many young men in English-speaking societies and in Nordic and other European societies go on drinking binges; indeed, such binges are typically considered a rather normal if sometimes risky rite of passage. Some Americans use the word "binge" to describe their food or drink consumption on New Year's Eve, at big weddings, or other traditional feasts, holidays, and celebrations. Many people even speak of intense periods of shopping, sexual activity, and even housecleaning as binges.

Although various kinds of binges are common enough, relatively few people binge again and again for months or years. In most clinical definitions, addiction must be more than occasionally "losing control" or bingeing; it must be *repetitive*, "out of control" use that has negative consequences and is *sustained over time*. Classic "winos" or heroin "junkies" who remain high nearly all day, nearly everyday, or as much as they can financially and physically tolerate, would fit any definition of addiction. Although many people occasionally binge on shopping, sex, eating, gambling, drinking, or other drug use, most do not engage in these behaviors so heavily and repeatedly that they can be said to be out of control or addicted. And there are very good reasons for this. All these binges are pleasurable for some people some of the time, but binges of any sort constitute a significant disruption of everyday life. Valued relationships and responsibilities are put aside. People on binges tend to be self-absorbed and less aware of other people or things of which they generally wish to be aware. Binges also bring various hangovers in their wakes. Nights of heavy drinking bring nausea and headaches. Shopping sprees bring credit card bills and cash flow problems. Gambling "runs" bring deepening debt and depression. Feasting brings fat and indigestion. Crack binges are invariably followed by a painful "crash." Binges, then, are costly in many ways, and largely for this reason even most people who binge occasionally do not do so repeatedly over sustained periods of time such that they could be said to be addicted.

People who do repeatedly binge on anything are unusual. Our heavy cocaine smokers repeatedly sought out the intense pleasure of the crack or freebase high. But their use pattern followed a distinctive episodic or bingelike shape.[2] As Chapter 7 explains, outside a binge, they were not physiologically "hooked" and were not inexorably propelled by physical withdrawal to smoke more cocaine. Most of their within-binge behavior appeared to them as well as to us as "out of control." However, their pattern of bingeing after days or weeks of no use seemed to be a *choice* over which they did have considerable control. What is called "crack addiction," then—*repeatedly returning to bingeing*—is comprised of volition as well as compulsion and is more a psychological matter than a pharmacological or physiological one.[3]

The third way in which the prevailing image of crack is misleading concerns the claim that crack inevitably destroys the lives of its users. Our respondents describe in this chapter the often substantial price they paid for indulging their desires for crack's extreme highs. Yet what was most telling about their tales is not so much that their extreme use disrupted their lives in various ways, but rather that such disruption almost always remained within the bounds (although in some cases the outer bounds) of their lives. Some of the people we interviewed were poor and some were African-American and Latino, but unlike many of the more common impoverished inner-city crack users, most of our respondents were gainfully employed and had otherwise conventional lives and attachments. Their unusual desire for crack or freebase always cost them money, often disrupted their relationships, and sometimes even caused them problems with their health or their jobs. Ultimately, however, very few of them allowed their craving for crack's intense high to overwhelm their lives. Most eventually cut back or quit precisely because their attachments to conventional life meant more to them than their attachment to the crack high.

Like many other heavy cocaine smokers, our respondents brought to their crack use an unusual mind-set, an extreme desire for intense highs. Whether their love of crack destroyed their lives, however, seemed to depend more on the character of those lives than on the character of the crack high. Unlike impoverished, inner-city crack users who face crushing poverty, discrimination, and despair, most of our respondents smoked crack in settings shaped by gainful employment, steady incomes, opportunities, and hope. They were reasonably well bonded to conventional society. The mind-set with which they approached crack or freebase seemed to lean more toward the pursuit of pleasure and excitement than to self-medicating pain and escaping despair. All this appeared to mediate the power of crack and their desire for extreme highs and thus helped them limit the damage that is often associated with heavy crack use. They would be the first to say that the crack high is powerful and their pursuit of it excessive or foolish. But crack did *not* lead most of them to ruin. As we suggest at the end of this chapter, the powers of the crack pipe did not operate in a vacuum, but rather were constrained by the central feature of the social setting of use—a conventional everyday life in which even these heavy cocaine smokers were invested.

Because the economic status and social circumstances of our respondents were different from those of the more numerous crack users in inner cities, their experiences provide a valuable comparison. Both groups used smokeable cocaine, but aside from sharing the desire for an intense high, their mind-sets and the social settings of their use were very different. By holding the drug constant while varying key aspects of the mind-set of the users and the social setting of use, we were in a better position to see how the latter factors influenced the *consequences* of crack use. In what follows, our respondents provide a glimpse into the lived experience or phenomenology of crack use. We report what they said about the crack high, about their binges, about feeling obsessed, and about how far they were willing—and not willing—to go when they craved more of it.

BECOMING A CRACK USER OR FREEBASER

How does one become a crack user? To judge from crack scare discourse, one can effortlessly become not only a user but an addict merely by putting a crack or freebase pipe to one's lips.[4] Our respondents reported that the process is a good deal more complicated than that. Heating a chunk of white substance in strange-looking pipes and inhaling the vapors in order to achieve a few moments of explosive pleasure is not something just anyone does. As noted, regular cocaine smokers are among the small minority of illicit drug users who seek and enjoy extreme drug experiences. For example, one young man (respondent #433) explained how he started to smoke cocaine in terms of his sensation-seeking tendencies and the forbidden fruit phenomenon: "I have always liked the excitement and have always liked to ride the edge a little bit, and it was like . . . we did it because they told us not to." He and most of the others were, by their own self-descriptions, part of a subset of heavy cocaine users who were interested in "taking it to the max" or getting "more bang for the buck." People ingest drugs because they enjoy the highs. A small subset of them seek different, better, faster, or stronger highs.

To become a crack user or freebaser, one also has to learn how to smoke properly. We began to suspect that the claim of "instant addiction" was too simple when one of our first interview respondents (#616) described his initiation: "It took me a while to figure. I was getting extra instruction and it took me, you know, probably a couple of hours to get like the real good hit. . . . I got some tastes of it, but . . . I probably didn't get real good at it 'til maybe five, six sessions." Two hours of trying by a very experienced drug user to get one effective dose, and five or six sessions to develop proficiency, suggest that real effort is required before one can even experience the crack or freebase high. At first, we thought that reports of such effort implied the need for learning the high (Becker, 1953, 1967), learning to interpret the extreme central nervous system stimulation of this form of cocaine as a euphoric "rush." However, our respondents' accounts of their initiation convinced us that, for smoked cocaine, "learning the high" is less a process of interpreting drug effects than of learning the technical requisites for getting a "real good hit."

For this one needs quite specific knowledge and equipment. Although this varied somewhat from user to user, our respondents generally agreed on the basics: chunks of crack or base that are small enough to burn; the use of screens in the pipe to permit proper "draw"; "a good fire," meaning a steady flame; a subtle touch for "the right burn," meaning close coordination between the smoker and the person lighting the pipe; fine-tuned carburetion or mixing of smoke and air so as not to "miss" the "hit"; and learning to inhale rather than swallow the smoke. Only when they had learned these techniques did they experience the powerful "rush" they were seeking.

THE RUSH, THE HIGH . . . AND THEN THE LOW

Although none of our respondents reported instant addiction, most did say that they found the crack high powerfully attractive, at least for some period in their lives. To learn why, we asked them about the allure of cocaine smoking, what exactly they liked about it. One young man spoke for most others when he exclaimed, "I've never felt nothin' like that!" (#621). Other answers ranged from descriptions of the euphoric boost of self-confidence one gets from directly ingesting such a strong central nervous system stimulant ("the feeling that you're on top of things" [#622]) to statements about how smoking cocaine makes one feel "hyper and smarter, faster and better, you know, sorta' like the $6 million man" (#636). Another respondent exclaimed that, after a hit on the pipe, "You don't care about nothin' else" (#635). This point was echoed by a number of others, including one who noted that, after a couple of hits, "the rest of the world is gone"[5](#616). Thus, in addition to explosive euphoria and heightened self-confidence, respondents often described a carefree, nirvana-like state. Another reported, "It just puts you in a frame of mind that separates you from everybody else. It puts your head on a different level. It's a thousand things. It's a way of coping and it's a way of escape" (#635).

The central theme in their descriptions of the freebase or crack high was the *intensity* of the euphoria. Most of our respondents used this word to distinguish this high from that of most other drugs. They often likened it to sexual orgasm throughout one's whole being. One middle-aged male told us that crack and freebase provide "an orgasmic killer rush . . . really sexual . . . like your whole body is just your cock" (#616). All seemed to agree that smoking crack or freebase was the most intense high one could experience. As one young man put it, "The intensity of it was just so enormous, and I couldn't believe the rush. It was similar if not better than the rush we received from shooting it, but you didn't have to put the holes in your arms. . . . The sensation starts in your head and goes down through your body. . . . It's very similar to an orgasm, the intensity of it"(#613).

We do not want to create the impression that our respondents only raved about this mode of cocaine use. As we show, they had as many negative as positive things to say about their overall experience. Most seemed acutely aware that, ironically, the effects they described so glowingly were precisely what made this form of cocaine use so risky; they seemed to say that basing is so good it's bad. For example, one young man told us, "It's ruined my relationship, put a total strain on my social life, . . . lowered my grades [from an A to a B average], . . . [and] when I'm not high I'm a much better employee. I know all that and yet I get high. I don't understand myself. That tells me how good the drug is" (#621).

Part of this paradox has to do with the extremely fleeting character of the rush. All our respondents noted that the euphoria, escape, and empowerment they got from smoking cocaine was very short-lived. Their reports ranged from "it lasts maybe like for 30 seconds" (#427) when they spoke of the "rush" to a bit longer when they described the "high" and its afterglow ("about fifteen minutes . . . , which is why you use so much" [#636]). But all agreed that the high, which was more intensely pleasurable than other drug highs, also faded more rapidly. As another young man put it, "If we got about $200 worth, okay, I'd be high for about an hour after it's gone. Maybe an hour, but not long. It's just that it doesn't last long, it doesn't last long" (#601).

Because they experienced the rush as intensely pleasurable and yet fleeting, they immediately felt a strong desire to repeat it. In addition, our respondents seemed to agree that there were diminishing returns after the first hit. We heard numerous reports of "chasing that first rush," a chase that our respondents described as invariably futile, a tease: "You're lookin' for something that never gets there, just looking for a high that never comes back" (#635). They reported that they just never got quite as high from the second or twenty-second hit in a smoking episode as they did from the first (see also Siegel, 1982). However, because they so enjoyed and desired it, the knowledge that the first-hit rush was ever elusive or miragelike deterred very few from trying to recapture it: "It was great. I just stepped to the ceiling for like five minutes and immediately wanted more. The first hit I ever did in my life was the best hit I ever did in my life, and from that point on every time you do it you try and get that first high. The more you do the less you get high per hit and the more you want the next hit to come that much faster" (#640).

In addition to their love of an intense rush that fades quickly and the fact that each additional hit yields diminishing returns, their desire to avoid the "low" that followed each high also led them to take repeated hits and, therefore, to binge. Nearly all spoke of sharply negative aftereffects. They described these as "the lows," "the down," "the heebie-jeebies," or the "crash" that rather quickly left them feeling lower than they felt before they began. Although less committed users might well decide that the way to avoid this awful "crash" is to not smoke cocaine in the first place, these users saw another hit as the antidote. One described this "down" as a "blaze depression," a depression accompanied by "burning anxiety" about when he would get another hit. Another spoke of the "jones"[6] and the "extreme nervousness" he felt "between hits" in anticipation of the down, as well as a longer-term "desperation" when supplies ran out:

> As long as I know there's product there, I just get kind of jittery and kind of "waiting for the pipe". . . . But the heebie-jeebies that come when there isn't any more and you can't get it, then it's a real serious thing. I mean, for me and for most of the people I know, you know, it's hell. . . . [The word] "need"

understates it. It's like desperation. It's like you've lost your best friend. There's this big vacuum. It's like, "What am I gonna do?!" I've curled up in bed in the fetal position and just groaned and moaned and [felt] just, just horrible, horrified. (#616)

One respondent described this cycle of extreme highs followed quickly by extreme lows as waves: "You have your waves. . . . You're ridin' high in April and shot down in May, kind of, and you're still chasing that rush" (#E-013). Yet another used a "roller coaster" metaphor: "I started getting to the point where I would just get really high and base like from 5:00 in the afternoon to about midnight and then get depressed. It's like a roller coaster, you get up there and you come down and then you have to take another hit to get back up there. Then when you run out it gets so depressing and strange" (#109).

Contained within all of our respondents' descriptions of the crack high, then, were three elements that together help account for their tendency to keep taking another hit, and therefore to binge. First, the freebaser or crack smoker is rapidly brought way "up" to the "orgasmic rush." Second, this intense euphoria is fleeting; it begins to ebb almost immediately. Third, one proceeds downward almost as quickly as one has just been brought up—and "down" not only to where one was before the rush but seemingly below it because one has just been so high. Thus, by repeatedly taking hits, they were attempting to stave off what they experienced as a very painful "low" and to return to the very pleasurable "rush" they were after. All of our respondents described these same basic elements of the "roller-coaster" ride from orgasmic euphoria to painful dysphoria and back again, so we feel confident these elements are essential to any explanation of crack binges.

But what none of our respondents mentioned—indeed, what they apparently took so much for granted that they felt no need to mention—was the value they placed on maximizing intense, ecstatic highs and "orgasmic rushes." This, too, is a piece of the puzzle. For these heavy users in search of intense highs, the effectiveness of another hit "made sense" in the short-run context of a binge, even though they knew that in the long run their inevitable crash would be more unpleasant.[7] Just as we doubt that most people would find crack's intense rush appealing, we also doubt that the logic of repetition that led to binges would make sense to most people.

TALES OF OBSESSION, COMPULSION, AND CRAVING

Most of our respondents ended up bingeing in ways that some of them described as "obsessive" or "compulsive." *Webster's Dictionary* defines obsession as "a persistent disturbing preoccupation with an often unreasonable idea or feeling" or "a compelling motivation" and compulsion as "an irresistible impulse to perform an irrational act." Although most of our respondents did not use the word "addiction," many did use the terms "obsession" or "compulsion" to describe a relationship with crack that many clinicians would see as addiction. At least at some points in the course of their use careers, most found that when they had a supply of freebase or crack, they did not stop smoking it until it was gone and they could not get any more. These binges typically lasted several hours, sometimes until dawn, and occasionally for more than one day. Some respondents spent several hundred dollars and a few even spent a thousand dollars in a single binge, depending on how many people were partaking and for how long. Interestingly, there was no clear line where their descriptions of the rush or high ended and their tales of obsession began. In fact, in the open-ended portions of our interviews, they spoke as often and with as much amazement about being "obsessed" as they did about the high or rush:

> I can't think of any other way to describe it other than a total obsession. I did absolutely nothing but sit cross-legged on the floor, cooking it, cleaning the pipe and smoking it, you know, constantly doing that. The only time I would get up would be to go bang on some dealer's door. (#121)

> My body no longer had the ability to just comfortably stop at any point, no matter how much or how little [was smoked]. . . . There was a physical craving that overcame me *when I was basing* that I couldn't control. (#432) [emphasis added]

> Snorting is more controllable and basing seems to be an obsession. Once you start you don't want to stop. . . . Snorting you can take a hit and not think about it until like a day or so or maybe even a month. But with base, it's there and when it's gone . . . I've never felt so angry about something being gone. That's crazy, it really is. It's sick. (#642)

Virtually all our heavy cocaine smokers reported that other interests and activities tended to fall by the wayside during a smoking session. One respondent captured the point succinctly when we asked what he liked to do when freebasing. "Just base some more" was all he said (#635). Other activities, including socializing with friends and, for many, even sex, all seemed to pale next to the pipe, which became the sole *objet du desir.* In the early stages of their crack careers, sessions tended to be rather social. Friends would plan elaborate evenings together that were focused on cocaine smoking, but also included conversation, music, movies, and sometimes sex. And for many, in the beginning, smoking was a ritual that often did enhance sociability. One man spoke of the "amazing camaraderie" he experienced while freebasing with friends; others described an "opening up." Yet, in the course of a binge, most quickly came to push aside such other activities in favor of smoking cocaine. Unlike drinkers or users of other drugs, these crack users and freebasers did not get high and then go out to dinner or a party. Many said they simply could not "deal with it"—"it" meaning anything that required them to manage the normal exigencies of interaction in their overamped state or anything that came between them and their next hit. As one experienced male baser put it, "If you have to go out to the store, you can, but it's kind of gruesome. You'd rather just stay at home. . . . You certainly don't want to deal with anything besides the pipe. . . . [Y]ou don't want to deal with anyone, so it becomes completely introverted. So you really feel kind of . . . I don't know, I feel kind of isolated, kind of weird, you know, 'cause I can't relate to anyone else once I get really high" (#616). Another respondent made a similar point when he told us that cocaine smoking is "an indoor sport," during which he tends to "forget about everybody" and to end up "in some room or some corner somewhere just hittin' the pipe" (#635). Again, to "forget about everybody," not to want to "deal with anything but the pipe," to feel "isolated" or "weird," and to be unable to "relate to anyone else" are not states of mind most people desire.

Some made a related observation about the strangeness of the crack or freebase experience compared to that of other drugs such as marijuana, which is ritually passed around, and even cocaine powder, which friends regularly snort with each other. According to many of the cocaine smokers we interviewed, a different ethic tends to hold sway around crack or freebase. One called freebasing "a completely selfish disease": "You take one hit and you don't stop thinking about taking another hit until it's all gone. Four, five, six hours will pass and nothing will take your mind off of it unless someone's gonna give you more. It's like you can't even think about anything else. . . . You find yourself staring at the ground a lot. . . . You stare at the floor and look for extra pieces of coke that might have fallen onto the floor. You pick through the carpet" (#640). A half-dozen different respondents recounted some version of this obsessive carpet-picking scenario; some even had a name for it—"the carpet crusade." As any given binge came to a close, most found it psychologically hard to accept the fact that their supply was gone and they could neither feel the rush again nor prolong the crash. Of course, no one ever reported *finding* any "extra pieces" of crack on the carpet, but that did not dissuade any of them from looking.

The same craving that led many to crawl around on the floor looking for nonexistent crumbs also led many to suspect their own friends and family of taking more than their share. People who were dearly loved when crack or base was not around were sometimes neglected, lied to, and even stolen from in order to continue smoking. One thirty-two-year-old woman, for example, noted that her feelings about freebasing sometimes overpowered her feelings for family members: "We cut-throat each other a lot, me and my brother . . . he used to steal [crack] from me and I used to steal from him" (#118). Many of these cocaine smokers were apparently so drawn to the rush and so desired to repeat it that they felt a narcissistic greed rather than the ethic of sharing or "turning on" others that has long held sway in illicit drug subcultures. During the course of a binge, some longtime friends and even spouses and lovers ended up "arguing over what's on the plate" (#642). Others were turned off to freebasing and crack use precisely because they observed others "getting greedy" and anxious about their "share" or their turn at the pipe. This was one reason why isolation often supplanted sociability during crack use: when alone, they not only did not have to "deal" with anyone else; they didn't have to share precious supplies. One respondent told us that he had sometimes tried to "find an empty hole somewhere" in which to freebase, once even renting a hotel room to be alone with his pipe. He called crack "a selfish drug," as if his behavior while smoking it was built into its molecules:

> It's a selfish drug and no one is interested in getting the other guy high. When you smoke pot, somebody will come in who hasn't had any pot. . . . "Here, you need to get high." With [crack] you are sitting there and you're not interested. . . . For one thing you don't think the hit that the guy gives you is big enough. Or you don't think that the hit you got was as big as the guy who took a hit before you. There's always something you don't like about the fact you're not getting enough or whatever. . . . You're always working for your own shit all the time and no one gives a goddamn about anybody else. . . .
>
> It tends to get worse and worse. Your outside attention dwindles. . . . The first couple of times it's still kind of social and people are still able to hold a conversation. That goes on for about 15 or 20 minutes. But the longer the night goes the more people are definitely into the coke and don't talk or think about anything else. . . . Snorting it is usually a social situation and the coke usually sits on a mirror and everybody does a line and then they're all talking about it and it's like a half an hour before another line gets done. I don't think it's nearly as intense. . . . [Freebase is] an addictive drug and psychologically you do feel that you need it and you can feel it in the palms of your hands that you want that. But when you're snorting [cocaine] you can also drink and think about other things and talk and smoke pot and party. Whereas with freebase, you don't think about anything else, which is why people who [initially] do it in social situations, I think, end up doing it by themselves. . . . You don't go to "freebase parties." It's more like, "I've got a gram of coke, where can I go? What closet can I sit in?" (#640)

Another measure of their "obsession" was what they were willing to sacrifice financially in order to continue smoking cocaine. By sacrifice, we mean more than the $50 to $500 our respondents typically spent in a binge—expenditures that even they would have seen as absurdly extravagant for anything else. One college student told us of watching a friend offer to trade his Rolex watch, worth several thousand dollars, for a few grams of crack. Another respondent eventually quit in part because of what he saw as the drug's power over people's purses: "I'd go to a couple of dealer's houses and I would notice, seeing these guys behind freebasing selling like their brand new Mercedes for like 2 or 3 thousand dollars. They would lose their house and everything! That was the main reason why I quit, because I realized that it could break you financially more than anything else, and that scared me. I said, 'I don't need that'" (#622).

Perhaps the clearest sign of obsessive use during a binge was the extent to which many of our respondents continued to smoke crack or freebase in the face of physical harm. Several told us of seeing basers and crack users take hit after hit in a given smoking session until they felt their lungs would collapse or until they experienced heart palpitations. Some of them were surprised by this. One long-term baser, for example, told us about helping a friend who was "freaked" by chest pains during a binge: "About an hour later the sucker was back on the pipe. I couldn't believe it" (#616). Such instances of what even they saw as "going too far" *within* a binge are not by themselves evidence of addiction any more than nausea and passing out among students who "chug" beer are evidence of alcoholism. But just as those who *repeatedly* binge drink despite nausea and blackouts can be said to have a "drinking problem," so did our cocaine smokers who kept bingeing in the face of, say, chest pains, have what they saw as a "crack problem."

THE LIMITS ON CRAVING AND COMPULSION

At least at some point in their careers, most of our heavy cocaine smokers engaged in the sort of repetitive, out of control bingeing that clinicians define as addiction. And yet in nearly every case, their crack use remained "within limits," albeit limits that some of them sometimes stretched. As we have noted, even most of those who smoked cocaine continuously within a binge often went days and weeks without using and without serious craving. Just as a respondent was prompted to quit when he saw another baser sell his Mercedes, so did the experience of physical harm or disrupted daily lives prompt others to cut back or stop. Models of addiction that are overly pharmacological or physiological tend to miss the paradox here. For many users, the experience of the *possibility* of losing control was a spur to exert control.[8] Although they knew or soon learned that they were taking risks with this mode of cocaine ingestion, for surprising periods of time, most managed such risks so they could enjoy those highs a while longer. Virtually all of the problems reported by many of the heavy cocaine powder snorters we interviewed—problems with mental and physical health, families, finances, and functioning in daily life—tended to appear more often and more quickly, and to be more profound, among these heavy cocaine smokers.[9] Despite such signs of "trouble," as several of them called these problems, many others managed to limit their use over time. All of our respondents were extreme users who employed an extreme mode of ingestion, but such problems were neither universal nor an inexorable part of continued crack use.

Although most of our respondents left little doubt about their abuse of this drug, most also managed to continue to work productively, progress in their careers, and maintain their daily lives. We heard many anecdotes about embarrassing or deviant behavior, and even a couple of instances of criminal behavior, which they attributed to their desire for crack or freebase (see Davies, 1992). Most told of feeling unable to control their use, within a binge, during some portion of their heavy use periods. Two of the fifty-three sold their cars and more than a few slowly drained their savings accounts in order to continue smoking. Yet many others always paid their bills before spending any money on crack or freebase, and many managed for months to restrict their use to weekends. Perhaps most telling was the fact that even those who sometimes sat smoking their pipes all day did not do so day after day. Nearly all used in what even they felt was a compulsive manner *during a binge*, but few of them remolded their lives into one long binge. In short, not even these extreme crack and freebase smokers were driven—or willing—to "do anything" to keep using. Even though most of our respondents loved the rush enough to persist in the face of problems or disruptions in their lives, almost all of them eventually drew lines that they did not allow themselves to cross.

CRACK, CRIME, AND CONTEXT: AN EPILOGUE

Over the course of our research, the media reported hundreds of frightening stories claiming that crack use spurs all manner of violence, robbery, theft, and prostitution. Such stories implied that it is the peculiarly potent and addictive psychopharmacology of this form of cocaine use that is the direct cause of the crime and other problems plaguing our inner cities. As noted in Chapters 1 and 2, these stories were the *raison d'être* invoked by the Reagan and Bush administrations for launching and escalating their War on Drugs. However, the fact that even the obsessive use patterns described by our users remained episodic and constrained within their daily lives suggests that crack's criminogenic image is in need of revision.

First, if media reports are read carefully, it becomes clear that the bulk of what are called "crack-related homicides" are not cases of people who kill because they are somehow "crazed" on or desperately craving crack. As Goldstein and his colleagues show in Chapter 6, most so-called crack-related homicides stem from the illicit market; they do not entail a crack addict and an innocent victim. There are enormous profits to be made when a desired product has been criminalized, and illicit dealers have no recourse to legal forms of dispute resolution. Thus, as Bourgois noted in the previous chapter, suppliers who are in fierce competition for lucrative sales frequently resort to their own, often brutal forms of social control (Black, 1983). The War on Drugs prompted by crack only added to a long line of laws and policies specifically designed to make drug dealing as dangerous and hair-raising as possible. We should not be surprised, therefore, when the illicit drug industry attracts people who are (or quickly learn to be) callous and vicious. With huge sums at stake, in a market without lawful regulation, and with guns widely available, some dealers shoot at each other. Innocent bystanders in several cities have been killed or wounded by stray bullets from such individuals, but these tragedies should not obscure the fact that shootings between dealers in a black market context reveal nothing about the relationship between crack's *psychopharmacological effects* and crime.

Some readers might point to our own respondents' reports of compulsive use and sometimes desperate behaviors to support the notion that crack could "cause crime." Many of our respondents believed that the call of the pipe was powerful enough to lead them to do things they would not have done otherwise. But almost none engaged in any criminal behavior other than using or sharing illicit drugs. Their behavior shows again that the alleged causal connection between crack and crime has far more to do with the social context of crack use than with its effects on individual users.

But this is not the way crack is usually discussed. The dominant discourse about crack and freebase consistently implies that this form of cocaine use is so overwhelmingly pleasurable that it is not only "instantly" but *universally* addictive. One could study every TV, billboard, magazine, or newspaper ad ever produced by the Partnership for a Drug-Free America, for example, and not hear a word about the links between poverty and hard-drug use. Yet the fallacy of pharmacological determinism on which this view rests is exposed by the very unequal susceptibility to crack abuse across middle-class and impoverished communities. Historically, from the so-called "gin epidemic" in the slums of eighteenth-century London to the "heroin epidemic" of urban America in the early 1970s, the worst drug problems have always been concentrated amid profound and preexisting human suffering.

The evidence for such a contextual theory of crack problems exists in dozens of U.S. cities, where heavy crack use arose among the most impoverished and troubled segments of the population. Indeed, if we wanted to design a rigorous experiment to test the hypothesis that it is the myriad of human troubles associated with poverty rather than the mere presence of crack that leads to crack problems, we would want to compare the susceptibility of two groups of young people, one upper middle class and the other poor. Ideally, we would want these two groups to live close to one another, with one street primarily upper middle class and another primarily poor, where both groups had access to crack, where sales are common, relatively open, and well known. And we would want such conditions to hold for a period of years so that we could see what happened over time. Precisely such an experiment has been going on of its own accord in part of the Upper West Side of New York City since at least 1987.[10] Along many blocks of upper Columbus Avenue, on various stretches of Amsterdam Avenue, and on numerous streets linking the two, crack can be purchased day or night. *New York Times* articles listing the heaviest crack-dealing areas in the city have often included this neighborhood, and many affluent residents there complain about the crack sales and use they see when they venture out from their co-op apartments.

The media have made all of America aware of the crack use and crack-related problems in the African-American and Latino blocks in this part of Manhattan. But how many Americans have heard about similar use and problems four or five blocks away among the affluent? Has there ever been a *New York Times* story about crack use at any of the prestigious private schools—like Dalton, Trinity, and Horace Mann—that service the professional-managerial-class families on the Upper West Side? There are also bright, adventurous middle-class kids in this neighborhood who go to elite public high schools—Hunter, Stuyvesant, and Bronx Science—and who ride the subways to get around. Has any significant number of them developed crack problems? Has there been a significant crack problem among the thousands of Columbia University students who live all over this area? The answer to each of these questions is "no." Contrary to all the stories during the crack scare asserting that this "plague" permeated all class boundaries, was spreading rapidly into the suburbs, and was "killing a whole generation" of youth, *none of this has happened.*

Ironically, such scare stories put into bold relief the centrality of social context, which has been treated as a nonstory. Any reporter in the U.S. could get nationwide coverage and a major career boost with a story about a white, upper-middle-class high school with a large group of crack users. The story would almost write itself. The headline would read, "The School Called 'Crack High.' " In the six years of the crack scare and since, there have been no such stories for one simple reason: such schools don't exist. If one did, dozens of journalists would have camped out there and produced a blizzard of such stories.

We are not saying that affluent people are immune from serious drug abuse and drug problems. Before there was crack in the ghettos, there was freebasing in Hollywood, on Wall Street, and elsewhere among some members of the well-to-do. Even today some part of the customer base for

streetside crack dealers drive in from the suburbs. And many of these people, like many of our respondents, find themselves bingeing, craving, and
using compulsively; some of them come to feel addicted and enter treatment. But as earlier chapters have suggested, middle-class status and sta-
bility do tend to make people less vulnerable to all forms of long-term,
hard-drug abuse and addiction and its most disruptive consequences. Conversely, permanent unemployment, horrible living conditions, and no reasonable hope for a better future make the poor more vulnerable to them.
This latter point was made well by Jefferson Morley of the *Washington Post*,
perhaps the only American journalist who ever actually tried crack before
reporting on it: "If all you have in life is bad choices, crack may not be the
most unpleasant of them" (1989:12). As Morley implies, and as the natural
experiment on the Upper West Side suggests, very few people who have
good choices available have opted for crack very often or for very long (cf.
Jencks, 1995:41–43).

The relatively few economically secure people who do develop crack or
freebase problems have health insurance that gives them fast, mostly free
access to treatment. When they come out of treatment, their prognosis is
good because they return to skills, educational credentials, networks, jobs,
businesses, homes, families, and life chances. In short, they have a stake in
conventional life that they want to protect and the resources with which
they can protect it. Much the same point is made in Part II of this book, in
which Canadian, Dutch, and Australian drug scholars show that whatever
crack problems exist in their societies are overwhelmingly concentrated
among the most impoverished and vulnerable segments of their populations.

Most of the crack users and freebasers we interviewed were gainfully
employed, some were middle class, and a few were even affluent. Many of
them behaved in ways they were not proud of, but virtually none engaged
in the sort of street crime, violence, or prostitution that media reports
imply are inevitable consequences of this form of cocaine use. Despite
their extraordinary candor about their compulsive crack use and embarrassing behavior, they reported almost no criminal acts, and they had the
same low levels of criminal convictions as the larger sample of cocaine
snorters. When we have reported this finding at scientific conferences,
someone always asked, "Yes, but aren't many of your respondents middle
class?" Our answer was always, "Yes, and that is precisely the point." If heavy
freebasers and crack users who have resources almost never committed
crimes or became violent, then the putative causal connection between
crack and crime has far more to do with finances than pharmacology.

No users, including our respondents, condone their heavy crack use any
more than the misdeeds they attribute to it. Their love of crack's intense
rush was strong enough to influence them to engage in behaviors that they

might not have engaged in otherwise, but it was not so strong as to push them beyond all constraints. The two most criminal of our freebasers and crack users were a lawyer who embezzled and a payroll clerk who filed a false insurance claim. They spent their proceeds smoking cocaine. They committed crimes that they knew how to do; they did not become burglars. They engaged in forms of deviant behavior that seemed, in the context of their lives, conceivable and available. Pursuit of the crack high led many of our respondents to violate norms and in a few instances even laws, but it did not make them muggers.

Many impoverished street "junkies" and "crack heads" steal or rob and spend the proceeds on drugs. But more affluent addicts, or those who happen to be doctors, nurses, or pharmacists with alternative supplies, do not. A majority of violent crimes involves alcohol, but only a tiny proportion of drinking incidents involves crime or violence. The criminal behaviors so often attributed to one drug or another are not in any direct, mechanistic sense "caused" by the psychopharmacological properties of those substances. As criminologists have repeatedly shown, crime and violence are learned responses to situational exigencies, and they are more likely to be learned by people who live under certain conditions (*e.g.*, Sutherland and Cressey, 1978). Just as ghetto youth do not engage in stock swindles, affluent professionals do not steal cars. Thus, almost none of our freebasers and crack users ever resorted to anything like the kinds of street crime we have been led to believe are inevitably "caused" by this form of drug use. Many blew paychecks and drained savings accounts; a few even sold treasured belongings. But once they began to experience fiscal exhaustion on top of physical exhaustion, many simply stopped. When we asked why, their typical responses were simple: "I just couldn't afford it anymore" (#641). For our respondents, the idea that they could solve their money problems and get more crack or base through street crime simply did not occur to them. In the culture of most working- and middle-class people, serious crime is not a thinkable option, not part of their behavioral repertoire. Even those who believed they were addicted to crack or freebase rarely found it powerful enough to push them beyond the normative constraints of their social world.

One middle-class respondent illustrated the force of such constraints while explaining to us why he gave up crack: "I could no longer afford the habit . . . and I'm too chicken to steal" (#419). We see important insight (as well as appropriate modesty) in this remark, for it suggests that what these users believed was the extraordinary power of the pipe was mediated by the social circumstances under which they used it (Zinberg, 1984). Although many of our heavy freebasers and crack users loved the high enough to break norms and even on a few occasion laws, they always did so within bounds that were set by their socialization, their social location, and their sense of self. Yes, the intense craving for the crack rush and the desire to avoid the low that follows it surely can encourage crime and other unwanted behaviors in some heavy users. But to judge from our respondents, this mode of cocaine ingestion is most likely to "cause" crime among those who have no alternative means of financing their use, few bonds to society, little stake in conventional life, not much to lose by throwing off normative constraints, and the capacity to conceive of and conduct criminal acts.

We believe this helps explain why the consequences of crack use are most serious in impoverished inner-city areas like the one described by Bourgois in Chapter 3. Our respondents' experiences make it clear that the alleged causal connection between crack and crime is contingent on class and culture. Freebasers and crack users who are not already involved in criminal activities, who have legal means of getting money for their drug, and who have a stake in conventional life will be far less likely to engage in criminal behavior than users who do not share such characteristics. This suggests that those who blame America's crime and other urban problems on crack or some other chemical bogeyman, and then peddle ever-harsher laws as the cure, are closer to modern-day snake oil salesmen than they like to think. If there is any direct connection between crack and crime, it is largely a product of social inequality.

NOTES

1. These crack users and freebasers were identified via chain-referral or "snowball" sampling techniques (Biernacki and Waldorf, 1981; Watters and Biernacki, 1989) as part of a larger study of 267 heavy cocaine users (Waldorf et al., 1991), about one in five (53 or 19.8%) of whom had been primarily crack or freebase smokers during the peak use period of their careers. Those who simply experimented with this mode of ingestion were excluded from the smokers subsample. The mean age in both groups was thirty-one; one in five of both groups were women. Crack users and freebasers used slightly higher amounts of cocaine on average than snorters (the mean was five vs. four grams per week) and tended to report that cocaine-related problems with health, work, and personal relationships occurred earlier and more intensely. Both snorters and smokers averaged less than one lifetime criminal conviction. The smoker subsample was more often African-American or Latino, tended to have less education (*e.g.,* 17% of smokers vs. 8% of snorters had dropped out of high school), and were more often employed in lower-income occupations (see Waldorf et al., 1991, for more details on this sample). Although our snowball sampling strategy allowed us to interview in-depth a diverse range of people who could not otherwise be studied, we have no way of knowing how representative they are of the larger population of crack or freebase users. However, we do know that interviewing them *in situ,* in the San Francisco Bay Area

communities where they lived and worked, allowed us to see a broader range of users than seen in most samples. Most research on illicit drug users, especially heavy users, takes place in prisons, jails, or treatment facilities where they are captive and easy for scientists to locate and study. However, those in treatment or jail tend to be, almost by definition, the heaviest and most troubled users and are therefore likely to be far less representative of the much larger population of users who are not in treatment or incarcerated (Reinarman et al., 1994). Thus, although we cannot say how representative these subjects are, we can say that, by studying them in the more natural contexts of their own lives, we increased our chances of seeing what this form of drug use looks like among the majority of users who never appear in treatment or prison.

2. This bingeing pattern is much like the one described by Bill Wilson and other alcoholics in the first editions of *Alcoholics Anonymous* (1939). A pattern of binges interspersed with periods (sometimes lengthy) of little or no alcohol use was called "gamma alcoholism" by E. M. Jellinek, who saw it as a major form of alcoholism in the U.S. It is said to be a common middle-class alcoholism pattern; it is also found in cultures (e.g., Nordic countries) where people drink much of their alcohol in the form of distilled liquor (Jellinek, 1960; Levine, 1978).

3. What Kaplan (1983:33–34) has called "the inevitability of addiction myth" about heroin is likely even more applicable to cocaine and all other illicit drugs. See also Peele (1985) and Fingarette (1988).

4. For example, on September 8, 1989, *ABC World News Tonight* anchorman Peter Jennings told millions of American TV viewers that "Using [crack] even once can make a person crave cocaine for as long as they live."

5. Although escape from worldly concerns has been a valued effect of all drugs for centuries, researchers have tended to neglect such concerns and to focus on the drug use alone.

6. The noun "jones," from heroin addict argot, means an addiction or a strong craving characteristic of addiction.

7. The authors are grateful to Douglas McDonnell for his insights on this point.

8. The cessation process for the entire sample, smokers and snorters alike, is described in Waldorf et al. (1991: pt. 4).

9. The one exception was nasal irritations, which most snorters reported experiencing at one time or another, but which did not affect freebasers and crack users. In fact, both snorters and shooters remarked that one advantage of smoking was that it did not "fuck up your nose" or leave you with "holes in your arms." For a more detailed comparison of problems experienced by snorters vs. smokers, see Waldorf et al. (1991:159–186).

10. This "natural experiment" was first reported in Levine (1992).

REFERENCES

Alcoholics Anonymous, *Alcoholics Anonymous* (New York: AA World Services, 1939).
Becker, Howard S., "Becoming a Marijuana User," *American Journal of Sociology* 59:235–242 (1953).

————, "History, Culture, and Subjective Experience: An Exploration of the Social Bases of Drug-Induced Experiences," *Journal of Health & Social Behavior* 8:162–176 (1967).

Biernacki, Patrick, and Dan Waldorf, "Snowball Sampling: Problems and Techniques of Chain Referral Sampling," *Sociological Methods and Research* 10:141–161 (1981).

Black, Donald J., "Crime as Social Control," *American Sociological Review* 48:34–45 (1983).

Cheung, Yuet W., Patricia Erickson, and Tammy Landau, "Experience of Crack Use: Findings from a Community-Based Sample in Toronto," *Journal of Drug Issues* 21:121–140 (1991).

Davies, John Booth, *The Myth of Addiction: An Application of the Psychological Theory of Attribution to Illicit Drug Use* (Chur, Switzerland: Harwood Publishers, 1992).

Fingarette, Herbert, *Heavy Drinking: The Myth of Alcoholism as a Disease* (Berkeley: University of California Press, 1988).

Jellinek, E. M., *The Disease Concept of Alcoholism* (Highland Park, NJ: Hillhouse, 1960).

Jencks, Christopher, *The Homeless* (Cambridge, MA: Harvard University Press, 1995).

Kaplan, John, *The Hardest Drug: Heroin and Public Policy* (Chicago: University of Chicago Press, 1983).

Levine, Harry G., "The Discovery of Addiction: Changing Conceptions of Habitual Drunkenness in America," *Journal of Studies on Alcohol* 39:143–174 (1978).

————, "Just Say Poverty," pp. 40–46 in Arnold Trebach and Kevin Zeese, eds., *Strategies for Change: New Directions in Drug Policy* (Washington, DC: Drug Policy Foundation, 1992).

MacAndrew, Craig, and Robert Edgerton, *Drunken Comportment* (Chicago: Aldine, 1969).

McDonnell, Douglas, Jeanette Irwin, and Marsha Rosenbaum, "Hop and Hubbas, a Tough New Mix," *Contemporary Drug Problems* 17:145–156 (1989).

Morley, Jefferson, "What Crack Is Like," *New Republic* (October 2, 1989, pp. 12–13).

Peele, Stanton, *The Meaning of Addiction: Compulsive Experience and Its Interpretation* (Lexington, MA: D.C. Heath, 1985).

Reinarman, Craig, Sheigla Murphy, and Dan Waldorf, "Pharmacology Is Not Destiny: The Contingent Character of Cocaine Abuse and Addiction," *Addiction Research* 2:21–36 (1994).

SAMHSA, *Preliminary Estimates from the 1994 National Household Survey on Drug Abuse,* Advance Report #10 (Rockville, MD: U.S. Dept. of Health and Human Services; Substance Abuse and Mental Health Services Adm., Office of Applied Studies, 1995).

Siegel, Ronald K., "Cocaine Smoking," *Journal of Psychoactive Drugs* 14:277–359 (1982).

Sutherland, Edwin H., and Donald R. Cressey, *Criminology* (Philadelphia: Lippincott, 1978).

Waldorf, Dan, Craig Reinarman, and Sheigla Murphy, *Cocaine Changes: The Experience of Using and Quitting* (Philadelphia: Temple University Press, 1991).

Watters, John K., and Patrick Biernacki, "Targeted Sampling: Options for the Study of Hidden Populations," *Social Problems* 36:416–430 (1989).

Wilson, William Julius, *The Truly Disadvantaged: The Inner City, the Underclass, and Public Policy* (Chicago: University of Chicago Press, 1987).

Zinberg, Norman E., *Drug, Set, and Setting: The Basis for Controlled Intoxicant Use* (New Haven, CT: Yale University Press, 1984).

FIVE

Two Women
Who Used Cocaine Too Much
Class, Race, Gender, Crack, and Coke

Sheigla B. Murphy and Marsha Rosenbaum

"Monique" felt her whole head throb with the pounding headache that sometimes followed numerous hits on the pipe. Her mouth was dry and her stomach growled loudly. She thought to herself, "When was the last time I ate something? I just spent my last $20 on a rock and I'm so hungry." Her eyes filled with tears, but her crying did not make a sound.

A few moments later she looked around the dark, smoky room where she had spent the last several hours. It was an abandoned apartment in a dilapidated public housing complex. The last tenant was a crack dealer who repeatedly sold gaffle (fake or "bunk" crack). Disgruntled customers had firebombed the apartment, and now crack users had turned it into a rock house, a place where people go to smoke in relative privacy. There were no doors or windows—people just stepped through the fire hole near the former door. The place smelled of feces and urine because smokers had kept using the toilet after the housing authority turned off the water months before.

Monique sat on the only piece of furniture, a filthy mattress off in the corner of what once was a bedroom. She waited. Soon a man approached. She knew him vaguely. They had lived in the same project for a few months. He made the usual offer: a rock for some head. Monique asked him to show her the rock. He answered, "Bitch, you know I'll do right by you," as he unzipped his pants. Monique lit a cigarette and placed it on a ledge by the bed and began to perform fellatio, checking the progress of the burning cigarette every few minutes.[1] When Monique's cigarette was burned down to the filter, the man had still not achieved orgasm.

Monique stopped and said, "Now wasn't that nice, honey? Give me a hit now and maybe we can finish this later." The man replied, "Bitch, I didn't come. I'm not giving you no hit till I come." Monique pleaded, "Baby, the

cigarette burned down and you know how that goes. You owe me a rock."
He slapped her, muttering, "Fucking tossup bitch," and walked away. Again
Monique began crying silent tears while her stomach growled.

"Becky" arrived for work at about 8:30 on a Saturday night. The band
was setting up in the quiet-before-the-storm atmosphere of a rock and roll
nightclub about to open for business. Bartenders, waitresses, and security
guards hustled around arranging tables and chairs and setting out bottles
of alcohol for the coming onslaught of customers. In the coat check room,
Becky and her two teenage coat check coworkers each pooled their eight
dollars and change to buy the night's first quarter-gram of cocaine. Becky
asked matter-of-factly, "Okay, girls, who is going to buy and who are we
gonna buy from?" One of her friends replied, "We'll get the coat racks
ready. You go buy the quart from Bobby. He likes you and you'll get a good
deal."

Becky left the coat check room in search of the connection. In a few
minutes, her mission accomplished, she hurried to the back room to cut
the lines (match stick–sized amounts of powder cocaine snorted into the
nose) with a razor blade on the makeup mirror they always used for this
purpose. Throughout the next couple of hours, the girls would go back
and snort small lines until they had used up all the cocaine. After the first
rush of coats at about 10:30, the girls bought another quarter from another seller, a woman bartender. They vowed after the second purchase
they were *not* going to buy any more. Becky complained, "We're supposed
to be making money here, girls, not just buying drugs."

By closing time, they had used all their cocaine. As they were getting
ready to leave, Bobby came by and offered to sell them a big fat quarter
for only $20. The girls found his offer too good to pass up and, once again
laughing at themselves, they all chipped in. This brought their individual
totals in drug expenditures for the evening to $22 each. They had gotten
high throughout their shift and still went home with almost $15 apiece in
remaining tips.

The girls all went back to Becky's downstairs bedroom in her mother's
house. They drank some beer, smoked some marijuana, and finished off
the last quarter. They laughed and talked and played dominoes until they
heard the chirping of early morning birds. They all giggled as they tried
to be quiet when Becky's mom left for her 6:30 a.m. racquetball game.
Soon afterwards they fell asleep, waking up around 3:00 that afternoon.
The other two girls left for their respective homes. Becky got up, ate a
quick breakfast, and began to prepare for the week ahead by washing her
high school uniform. The next day was Monday and she had a big day at
school.

These two anecdotes were among dozens reported by "Monique" and
"Becky" during depth interviews we conducted with them in 1990, when

both were in their late teens. Monique is an African-American member of the so-called underclass who lives in a public housing project. Becky is white, middle class, and lives in her mother's four-bedroom home. We interviewed both in the course of a larger study of women and cocaine funded by the National Institute on Drug Abuse.[2] They are real women[3] who, although not necessarily "typical" of their socioeconomic or ethnic groups, illustrate some of the differences between women cocaine users. They were close to the same age and used the same substance, albeit in different forms. But the patterns of their drug use, and especially the *consequences* of these patterns, were very different. We argue in this chapter that class, race, and gender are more important in shaping these different experiences with and consequences of cocaine use than the cocaine itself. We use the life histories of Monique and Becky to illustrate the different processes through which each came to try, to continue using, and ultimately to quit using cocaine.

As we listened to these two and the one hundred other women in our study tell of their experiences, it occurred to us that, if they had never used crack or cocaine, the differences between them would still loom large. Monique grew up in poverty and began prostituting before she ever tried crack in order to get the things her family could not provide. While attempting to stop using crack, Monique still lived in poverty, although an even deeper sort. Becky grew up in relative privilege, her life full of promise and opportunity before she tried cocaine. She continued to enjoy her middle-class lifestyle during her period of cocaine use and after she quit using.

In our interviews, such differences brought us again and again to the notion that to understand the consequences of cocaine and crack, we had to understand differences in the setting of use. As we show, gender is an important aspect of setting in that women gain access to cocaine and crack principally through men. Men generally have or sell the drugs, and women users attempt to manipulate this uneven power relationship to their best advantage. Race, too, is an important part of the context of use in that racial minorities are disproportionately poor and more often live in segregated areas where certain drugs are more available. To a significant degree, race is the modality in which class is lived in the U.S. African-Americans, Native Americans, Latinos, and some Asian groups are predominantly working class or poor. On virtually every measure of socioeconomic status (occupation, income, wealth, education, housing), they are located below the white population (Hurtado, 1989). But even among people of color who have managed to move up to the middle and upper classes, racism still forms the contours of their lives. Race also interacts with gender in that women of color are oppressed not only by whites of both genders, but by men of color (Hill-Collins, 1989; hooks, 1981; Hurtado, 1989). Class is a crucial aspect of the context or setting of drug use in that middle-class women have more resources to dissipate before they "hit bottom," whereas poor women with fewer such resources are more easily coerced into trading sex for drugs when whatever resources they do have are depleted. Class interacts with race and gender such that, in the sexual marketplace, white women's sexual favors typically command a higher price than those of women of color (Hurtado, 1989).

A simple mental experiment will show the centrality of class in shaping the context of crack use. If Becky were a young middle- or upper-class black woman who used drugs in a protected and privileged context, then when she decided to quit, she could have returned to her conventional cocoon (Rosenbaum, 1981). Conversely, if Monique were a young underclass white woman in an impoverished inner-city neighborhood, she would have found the most dangerous forms of drugs abundant, economic opportunities scarce, and little help with quitting.

No doubt some readers were shocked and dismayed by the stigmatizing image of a young black woman in our opening narrative. We chose such a worst-case scenario precisely to be able to show the importance of class and racism in shaping the setting, mind-sets, and consequences or drug use. We were inspired to do this in part by the distinguished African-American sociologist William Julius Wilson's discussion of different approaches to depicting thorny public problems associated with race:

> One approach is to avoid describing any behavior that might be construed as unflattering or stigmatizing to ghetto residents, either because of a fear of providing fuel for racist arguments or because of a concern of being charged with "racism" or with "blaming the victim." Indeed, ... liberal social scientists, social workers, journalists, policymakers, and civil rights leaders have been, until very recently, reluctant to make any reference to race at all when discussing issues such as the increase of violent crime, teenage pregnancy, and out-of-wedlock births [and, we think he would agree, drug abuse]. The more liberals have avoided writing about or researching these problems, the more conservatives have rushed headlong to fill the void. (1987:6)

Our opening narrative on Monique is an accurate rendering of her lived experience as she described it to us. We present her situation as a case study in order to show that her experience with drugs (and those of women like her) was profoundly affected by the poverty, racism, and sexism that shaped her life.

LIFE BEFORE CRACK AND COCAINE

Monique's mother was seventeen when Monique was born. She already had a two-year-old son. Monique was raised in the public housing projects of San Francisco. She has never met her father. Her mother let Monique come and go as she pleased, not really paying much attention to her. At about fifteen, when she began high school, Monique began smoking marijuana. About the same time, she began performing sexual acts for money. Initially, she was not using this money to purchase drugs. Her family did not have much money, and occasional "tricks" allowed her to get the things she wanted, things other kids had. Ultimately, she was arrested for prostitution. Because she had no previous record, the juvenile authorities called her mother to pick her up. Her mother refused to come for her, telling the authorities to keep her in custody. Because her mother was unable to supervise her, she was removed from her mother's care by the juvenile court. Monique was placed in a "group home" for troubled teenagers because:

> [I was] not going to school and I got picked up. I don't really remember, they just took me out of my [Mother's] home. They said I was "out of control" at home; my mom didn't care if I went to school or not. My attendance was real bad.
>
> *Q:* What was your mother into that she wasn't paying attention about you going to school?
>
> *A:* Nothing. Well, she had a best friend from Fresno, and she was also on welfare and it's like she [the friend] had three girls. I don't know, I just, I saw them laying up there every day. I'm like, "Well, I don't have to go to school. I want to watch stories [television soap operas] too," and stuff like that. I played hooky and was with my friends, too.

Monique was very hurt and upset by all this. Although she felt that living in the group home had positive effects on her life, she also came to believe that her mother did not want her: "It hurt me because I sat there in court with my Mom and I thought she really didn't want me, like to ever see me again. It was my first time ever in a group and it was hard."

For most of her twenty-one years, Becky has lived in a four-bedroom, family-owned home in a tree-lined, middle-class neighborhood along one of San Francisco's hills. When she was in the second grade, her parents divorced, and her father moved to a nearby city to begin his first job as a practicing attorney. By the time Becky was ten, her mother had also begun her soon-to-be successful private law practice in downtown San Francisco. From kindergarten through eighth grade, Becky attended private Catholic schools. She did well in high school, although she felt somewhat shy about making friends. Becky graduated from high school while holding a fairly well paying part-time job in a trendy South of Market rock and roll nightclub managed by her aunt. She began smoking marijuana when she was in the seventh grade, at the age of twelve (three years before Monique):

> *Q:* Who gave you pot when you were 12?
>
> *A:* I stole it from my mother. And actually, it was leaf; I didn't know there

was such a thing as bud until I was in the eighth grade. . . . About a year and a half later I smoked some bud and I got so high!

Q: How often would you smoke it?

A: Just about every day after school. Sometimes we wouldn't have it, but the deal was if you were cool you smoked.

Becky and her friends also experimented with alcohol in the seventh and eighth grades. In her school, the popular girls played on the basketball team: "We would have little parties on the weekend. And the basketball coach, actually, we went to her house and she'd make us strawberry daiquiris and stuff like that. . . . I think she'd do that so we wouldn't go out and drink alcohol."

Long before either tried cocaine, there were some important similarities and differences in Monique's and Becky's life experiences. Both girls were raised in single-parent homes. However, Becky's parents were able to pay for a private school education. Monique's mother's limited resources allowed her to do very little for her daughter. A teenage mother herself, she was burdened with all the problems of single parenthood (Card and Wise, 1987; Furstenberg and Morgan, 1987; National Research Council, 1987) and may well have been overwhelmed by the situation. Becky's family used their connections to get her a conventional job to earn her own spending money. Middle-class privileges like private schools, access to job opportunities, and safe housing protected Becky.

By the time both girls were fifteen, Monique had been through the court system, her drug use had been discovered, and as a result, her mother had rejected her. At the same time in Becky's career, neither her family nor the justice system had discovered her drug use, although she was the more experienced user.

LIFE DURING CRACK AND COCAINE USE

Initiation into drug use is a social process in which friends (rather than the proverbial "pushers") turn each other on to a new experience (Becker, 1953; Morningstar and Chitwood, 1987; Reinarman, 1979; Stephens and MacBride, 1976). Women typically use for the first time with a group of friends or with a man (Rosenbaum, 1981; Waldorf, 1973; Waldorf et al., 1991). Monique began using cocaine with two girlfriends when she was fifteen years old. One of the girls had a boyfriend who had supplied them with marijuana and alcohol. One day he asked them if they would like to try some cocaine. Monique refused the first offer, but the next time she accepted, snorting the cocaine through a straw. She explained that, after seeing him do it, she felt comfortable trying it herself. Monique enjoyed the high, reporting that it made her feel energized and euphoric. Although she expected enhanced sexual feelings, the cocaine did not stimulate her sexual desire. She continued to snort cocaine occasionally throughout the school year.

Monique's first crack experience was arranged by another man while she was living in the group home and going back to her mother's home every other weekend:

> So I did go back and, I don't know, that's when I started. He took me in the back. He had a little room back there and he gave me the pipe and put the cocaine and stuff on there and I just smoked it. . . . My first time when I did it I laid down and went to sleep. So I don't really—that's weird, 'cause when I do it now it's like I can't sleep at all. My first time, after a couple of hits I just sat there and maybe I was into space [staring off into nowhere, oblivious to surroundings] and I fell asleep or something, but I did go to sleep. And he was still back there doing his thing. . . . I liked it. It gave me a real, real heavy head rush, real heavy head rush. . . .

It was several weeks before Monique went back to the man's place, and when she did, he provided her with more crack to smoke. The next morning she had intercourse with him. This continued for several weeks, until he stopped offering her crack when she visited. Soon she began to buy crack for herself whenever she had money. When she left the group home (at almost nineteen years of age), she quickly spent all the money she saved from the clerk typist job the staff at the group home had helped her find. She described her use pattern this way:

> *A:* I would wait till my check came and that would be on the weekend.
> *Q:* So you just did it on the weekend?
> *A:* No, during the week sometimes I would go outside. I would go in the house and roll my hair or something, then go back outside and see if I seen someone who had some and wanted to give me some until I could pay. And that was never, hardly, so I'd just go in the house and go to sleep. But when I got money I couldn't go in the house. It was like the drug just had me out, so I'd stay out.

Monique's crack use escalated rapidly, particularly after she lost her job for absenteeism. At this point, she would spend whatever money she could scrape together for crack. When her funds were depleted, she began to exchange sex for money and/or drugs, often in the very places where the crack was being sold. Paradoxically, while Monique was using crack, she was not interested in sex at all. However, her craving for crack, coupled with her lack of economic resources, led her to become what is known in the scene as a "rock house toss-up," a woman who trades sex for crack. Monique cried as she told us what it was like to be a toss-up. She explained that under the influence of crack, men were sexually aroused but often could not achieve orgasm. And when they did not, they would often refuse to pay her.

When Becky was approximately fourteen years old, she snorted her first line of cocaine with a group of friends at a relative's wedding. Becky recalled the almost trivial nature of her first experiments with cocaine:

> [O]ne of my friends' mother just got married, and the daughter of the groom was probably a senior in high school. I was a freshman and my brother was a junior. . . . And she said, "Have you done it?" And I said I hadn't done it before, but everybody else was gonna do it, so I wanted to do it. So I said, "Yes". . . . It had no effect as far as I was concerned. . . . There were a few [other] times I just tried it, then never did it for awhile after. There was always no effect. I didn't know what to expect.

It wasn't until two years later, when one of Becky's coworkers at the nightclub gave her a few lines of cocaine, that she began to appreciate the high. While still in high school, Becky began using a few lines of cocaine every Saturday night, the only night she worked. After graduating from high school, Becky began to work more steadily at the club and to use cocaine more often. She told us how she got it:

> I was just sixteen years old and I'd just started working in the nightclub, probably about four months after I started. . . . And I got to know one of the guys and . . . he would always try to get it for people so he could have a line. He would be the go-between, and he had a crush on me. . . . The whole time from 16 till now he's always been trying to get me to go out with him and I would say, "Give me a break!" 'cause it's just not there. . . . And then T. [her best girlfriend] got a job at the nightclub. . . . And slowly after a couple months I finally realized that I could get a connection—I knew the connections and I could do it for myself rather than him doing it for me and him knowing that I had it.

Becky chose her suppliers from the one man and several women who sold it to fellow employees. She and her girlfriends who worked in the coat check room would buy and share a quarter-gram or two over an evening. The young women paid for their cocaine with their tips from club customers. Concurrently, Becky's marijuana and alcohol use increased. The marijuana and alcohol highs served to level out the "wired" or edgy feeling that comes with repeated cocaine use, and at the end of a night's indulgence, they helped her sleep. Some nights, however, nothing helped her get to sleep:

> *Q:* What didn't you like about cocaine?
> *A:* The birds! [laughter] Trying to get to sleep is the only thing that bugged me. . . . But the birds chirping [at dawn] were so horrible . . . and trying to get to sleep was just the worst thing. Or just not being able, period, to get to sleep. You know, we would smoke joint after joint after joint and it was like . . . [no sleep].

Both Monique and Becky snorted their first lines of cocaine in a mixed-gender group with close friends. Neither was terribly impressed with her first powder cocaine highs. It was only after several experiments that they each began to appreciate the subtle effects. Many women (regardless of racial or class backgrounds) who snort or smoke cocaine continue their experimentation despite what for many are rather unimpressive initial effects. As in both her and Becky's initial powder experiences, Monique was not overwhelmed by her first crack experience. In fact, she went to sleep almost immediately. Each of these young women, like her male counterparts, seemed to continue to use not because she was immediately thrilled by the high, but because her experience was not negative and because she was part of a *social scene*[4] or accepted within a trusted group of friends who were using drugs. One major difference between these two drug careers is that while crack had become a prominent part of the underclass drug scene, the less direct and less potent practice of snorting powder cocaine remained the most readily available and preferred form of use in middle-class scenes.

Race and social class, particularly as they influence geographic location and access to drugs, sort women into one scene or another. In San Francisco, most crack sellers are black men without better economic options, and they work the turf they know best—the areas around public housing projects inhabited disproportionately by poor people of color. This sort of social geography places poor women of color in greater physical and cultural proximity to crack (often a few steps from their front doors) than middle-class women, black or white. While growing up in the projects, Monique was exposed to powder cocaine in early 1985; by the end of the year, she was shown how to smoke crack. By then, crack had become plentiful in her neighborhood while less risky drugs such as powder cocaine and marijuana were difficult to find. Monique's crack use escalated steadily, beginning as a weekend activity and quickly becoming an everyday occurrence. Many of Monique's friends either used or sold crack.

Becky, living in a white, middle-class neighborhood, found her first cocaine source at a downtown rock and roll club that catered to affluent whites. Cocaine was an integral part of the bar and club scene, where young people used it for "partying." For the first two years, Becky's cocaine use was limited to the one Saturday night she worked. Like Monique, many of her friends used powder cocaine, and Becky's own cocaine snorting increased. The key difference was that no one in Becky's social scene smoked crack, and few even knew where to buy it.

Another major factor differentiating Monique and Becky is the relationship between sex and drugs in their respective scenes. In the crack scene, men play a more central role in the initiation and continued use of women. Recall that Monique was initiated to crack use by a man interested in having sex with her. He supplied the drugs, at first. This is not to say that women of all races and ethnicities have not engaged in sexual activity while high on powder cocaine (to say nothing of alcohol) or that women powder users have not in direct and indirect ways traded sexual favors for cocaine (Morningstar and Chitwood, 1987). But our respondents suggest that especially in crack using circles, men use their power—their control over the supply of crack, in addition to more traditional forms of power like physical prowess—to manipulate sexual access to women.

Of course, some women, in turn, attempt to manipulate men for drugs and money. When Monique began to buy crack herself, she turned to the men who sold it in her neighborhood; and when she ran out of money, she, like many of her cohorts, found herself in the less powerful position of having only her body to sell. Monique's experience was not a rare one, unfortunately; women crack users are routinely expected to get men "off" via fellatio for as little as a single hit off the crack pipe. Thus, the web of gender and power relations in which they are enmeshed is even more asymmetrical than usual.

This is not to suggest that gender equality has been realized in white, middle-class circles. But white, middle-class women who use cocaine have many more resources to deplete before making any compromises, much less selling their bodies. Becky bought her first cocaine from an older man on the job. He, too, was interested in her sexually, but Becky never really was interested in him. Once she found she could buy cocaine with her own resources without his assistance, she had a more egalitarian choice of sellers of both genders. Having both the money and the connections to get cocaine on her own terms made a concrete difference in Becky's cocaine experience. She never felt any need to exchange sexual favors for cocaine or money. She had more power than Monique to make choices regarding her sexual partners. Monique, without money or resources with which to acquire it, used what was available to her—her body—at considerable social and psychological cost.

A final important difference between the two young women was Becky's ability to conceal her drug use, thereby escaping parental or institutional detection. Becky had her own private room, both at work and at home, in which to use drugs in secrecy. But using crack kept Monique outside of her house and literally on the streets. Monique suffered stigma, maternal rejection, and state punishment because of the discovery of her drug use. In this way, too, the very different material conditions wrought by their race and class memberships shaped Monique's and Becky's differential ability to camouflage their drug use. This in turn helped Becky maintain a "normal," nondeviant identity despite her rising drug use, while similar behavior brought Monique both formal and familial stigma and the attendant loss of self-esteem.

LIFE AFTER CRACK AND COCAINE

At the time of our final interviews, Monique lived in a homeless shelter, her only possessions the clothes on her back. She had not used crack for about six weeks, but described herself as depressed and craving it continuously. Monique told us that her crack use had damaged her relationship with her boyfriend because she had stolen from him and prostituted herself: "And he puts me down. He don't trust me from all the stuff that I did." She was having a dreadful time—totally impoverished, no immediate prospect of employment. Her mother was moving to another state with her current boyfriend and had refused to give Monique her new address. Monique was ashamed, stigmatized, and in great emotional pain: ". . . 'cause a lot of times when I was doing it—and I know it wasn't me, it was the drug. . . . It just hurt. . . . It hurt to even be thinking, even wanting to do something like that [robbing] your friends. . . . It [crack] kills you and it will mess up your life. Stay away from it."

Just after she turned twenty, Becky and her father moved to Hawaii. She saw this as an opportunity to get away from the nightclub lifestyle and her escalating drug and alcohol use. We asked Becky about her strategies for quitting:

> Q: And so when you went to Hawaii, you said, 'OK, that's it. I'm not doing any more?'
> A: Well, it was very available in Hawaii. . . . But I never asked about it, because I knew I could get it very easily. I mean, just everybody—it was so available over there, and I could tell. But I never asked any questions and I never found out where. . . . I got offered, but only a few times. . . . I told them, "I don't do it and please don't offer me because I don't want to. I did it before and I don't like it." I tried it after I came back from Hawaii a couple times, you know, did a line here and there, and I didn't like it.
> Q: Why didn't you like it? What didn't you like?
> A: Dealing with this feeling of like, like it used to be when you did too much coke, but I had only done a little. It used to be satisfying, but it was just like irritating. . . . It wasn't like it used to be.

What had once been for Becky a fun, satisfying experience became an unsatisfying, irritating experience.[5] When we last interviewed her, Becky had not used cocaine at all in nearly a year and expressed no desire to do so. She had also stopped drinking alcohol and used only small amounts of marijuana (two or three "hits") once or twice a week. Becky appeared to us a very confident, cheerful young woman. She went back to school to pursue her career goals and had just finished her second semester of college. Her mother was supporting her financially while she went to school. Becky said her relationship with her mother had "never been better," and her mother was very pleased with her because she was getting good grades. Becky described her future plans concerning both drug use and career this way: "I have a feeling that I'll be smoking pot for the rest of my life. . . . No coke. . . . I want to try to get it together. You know, get a good job in business accounting. But . . . then when I think about it, I'd rather open my own business."

CONCLUSION

The pharmacological potency of any given drug is surely an important factor in drug problems. But our two case studies as well as the many other interviews we conducted suggest that nonpharmacological factors such as social class are at least as important in understanding how people develop drug problems. Being a member of the middle class means having material possessions and/or the resources with which to acquire them (*e.g.*, family help, education, job connections, etc.). Although virtually anyone from any background can get into trouble with drugs, individuals who possess life options (Rosenbaum, 1989) or have a stake in conventional life (Waldorf et al., 1991) tend to have a greater capacity for controlling their drug use or for getting out of trouble if they don't. For middle-class people like Becky who enjoy using illicit drugs, controlling expenditures and avoiding drug-related problems serve as important constraints. Moreover, among white, middle-class drug users, smoking cocaine in crack or freebase form acquired a reputation as much more difficult to control than snorting and thus a mode of ingestion to avoid (Waldorf et al., 1991). This is one reason why crack has not become the predominant mode of cocaine use in middle-class drug scenes and one reason why in her years of cocaine use Becky never encountered crack.

Being a member of the underclass, by contrast, means having few if any possessions, no resources with which to acquire them, and no reasonable expectation that circumstances will improve. Stakes in a conventional life or compelling reasons to "just say no" are harder to come by. Monique lived intermittently in run-down public housing and later homeless shelters where the future looked bleak, privacy was nonexistent, and crack was sold a few feet from her door. Because she is black and poor, she has had less access to opportunities for developing a conventional life in which to build a stake, and more access to more dangerous forms of cocaine. Being in the underclass placed her in closer geographical proximity to where rocks are sold and closer psychological proximity to where smoking them is thinkable.

In Becky's case, the protective power of race and class privilege helped make her period of heavy cocaine use a mere detour on the road to a solid future. In Monique's case, the weight of class and race oppression meant that she started out in worse shape, got introduced to a more dangerous form of cocaine, experienced more deeply disturbing consequences, and had fewer resources with which to deal with them. Her period of heavy crack use exacerbated her existing impoverishment and left her emotionally devastated.

No drug experts or drug users would claim that snorting cocaine and smoking crack have exactly the same effects. The consensus is that smoking crack is a more direct mode of ingestion that gets more cocaine to the brain more quickly and that it is therefore more likely to have destructive consequences. In calling attention to the importance of class and race, we do not wish to imply otherwise or to leave the impression that our two case studies are identical in all ways save class and race. Our point is that class and race profoundly shaped the context in which these different types of cocaine use became differentially available to these two women in the first place, and then conditioned their use patterns and the consequences that flowed from them.

NOTES

The research on which this chapter was based was supported by a two-year grant from the National Institute on Drug Abuse (#1-R01 DAO4535), Dr. Jag Khalsa, project officer. The authors gratefully acknowledge their support. Our interpretations of the data, of course, do not necessarily reflect the opinions or policies of NIDA. The authors also acknowledge the contributions of Brandy Britton, Adele Clark, Jeanette Irwin, Diane Lewis, Deidre Murphy, Craig Reinarman, and Lynne Watson. An earlier version of this chapter was presented at the annual meeting of the American Society of Criminology, Baltimore, Maryland, November 1990.

1. It is customary in crack houses to use a burning cigarette as a yardstick for how long a woman—typically trading sex for crack—should be expected to continue fellating a man, whether or not he achieves orgasm.

2. This two-year study began in June of 1989. We completed 125 in-depth, life history interviews, 100 with crack smokers and 25 with powder cocaine snorters.

3. The names of the two women have been changed to preserve their anonymity.

4. John Irwin (1977), writing about urban life in the late twentieth century, developed the concept of "scenes" to describe unifying interests and activities (*i.e.,* jazz music, nudism, surfing, etc.) that bring people together. Such scenes are replete with special languages, modes of dress, and often ideologies. Cocaine users speak about a "crack scene" that is very separate from snorter scenes.

5. Becky's characterization dovetails with what Waldorf et al. (1991) found in their study of heavy, long-term cocaine (powder and crack) users: over time, such users often undergo a "transformation of experience," for example, a change from euphoria to dysphoria.

REFERENCES

Becker, Howard S., "Becoming a Marijuana User," *American Journal of Sociology* 59:235–242, 1953.

Biernacki, Patrick, and Waldorf, Dan, "Snowball Sampling: Problems, Techniques and Chain-Referral Sampling," *Sociological Methods and Research* 10:141–163, 1981.

Card, J., and Wise, L., "Teenage Mothers and Teenage Fathers: The Impact of Early Childbearing on Parents' Personal and Professional Lives," *Family Planning Perspectives* 10:199–205, 1987.

Davis, Angela, *Women, Race, and Class* (New York: Random House, 1981).

Furstenberg, F., and Morgan, S., "Adolescent Mothers and Their Children in Later Life," *Family Planning Perspectives* 19:142–151, 1987.

Hill-Collins, P., "Learning from the Outsider Within: The Sociological Significance of Black Feminist Thought," *Social Problems* 33:14–32, 1986.

———, "The Social Construction of Black Feminist Thought," *Signs: Journal of Women in Culture and Society* 14:745–773, 1989.

hooks, bell, *Ain't I a Woman? Black Women and Feminism* (Boston: South End Press, 1981).

Hurtado, Aida, "Relating to Privilege: Seduction and Rejection in the Subordination of White Women and Women of Color," *Signs: Journal of Women in Culture and Society* 14:833–855, 1989.

Irwin, John K., *Scenes* (Beverly Hills, CA: Sage, 1977).

Krieger, N., and Bassett, M., "The Health of Black Folk: Disease, Class, and Ideology in Science," *Monthly Review* 38:74–85, 1986.

Morningstar, Patricia, and Chitwood, Dale, "How Women and Men Get Cocaine: Sex-role Stereotypes and Acquisition Patterns," *Journal of Psychoactive Drugs* 19:135–142, 1987.

National Research Council, *Risking the Future: Adolescent Sexuality, Pregnancy and Child Bearing* (Washington, DC: National Academy Press, 1987).

Reinarman, Craig, "Moral Entrepreneurs and Political Economy: Historical and Ethnographic Notes on the Construction of the Cocaine Menace," *Contemporary Crises: Crime, Law, and Social Policy* 3:225–254, 1979.

Rosenbaum, Marsha, *Women on Heroin* (New Brunswick, NJ: Rutgers University Press, 1981).

———, *Getting Off Methadone*. Final Report, Grant #R01 DA-02242 (Rockville, MD: National Institute on Drug Abuse, 1985).

———, *Just Say What?* (San Francisco: National Council on Crime and Delinquency, 1989).

Salvo, J., and MacNeil, J., *Lifetime Workforce Experience and Its Effect on Earnings: Retrospective Data from 1979 Income Survey Development Program*. U.S. Department of Commerce, Bureau of Census, Current Population Reports, Series P-23, No. 136 (Washington, DC: Government Printing Office, 1984).

Stephens, Richard, and MacBride, Dwayne, "Becoming a Street Addict," *Human Organization* 35:87–93, 1976.

Taeuber, C., and Baldisera, V., *Women in the American Economy*. U.S. Bureau of the

Census, Current Population Reports, Series P-23, No. 146 (Washington, DC: U.S. Government Printing Office, 1986).

Waldorf, Dan, *Careers in Dope* (Englewood Cliffs, NJ: Prentice Hall, 1973).

Waldorf, Dan, Reinarman, Craig, and Murphy, Sheigla, *Cocaine Changes: The Experience of Using and Quitting* (Philadelphia: Temple University Press, 1991).

Wilson, William J., *The Truly Disadvantaged: The Inner City, the Underclass and Public Policy* (Chicago: University of Chicago Press, 1987).

SIX

Crack and Homicide in New York City

A Case Study in the Epidemiology of Violence

Paul J. Goldstein, Henry H. Brownstein, Patrick J. Ryan, and Patricia A. Bellucci

If an opinion poll were to ask Americans whether they believe that crack causes violence, surely all but a few would say "yes." Criminal justice researchers,[1] practitioners,[2] and private citizens[3] have all argued that, compared to other drugs, the consequences of crack are measurably worse. But there also has been considerable confusion in interpreting the evidence linking crack to rising rates of violent crime. For example, the number of homicides nationally reached a high of 21,860 in 1980 and then declined, remaining fairly level throughout most of the 1980s (Jamieson and Flanagan, 1987). New York City paralleled the nation in this regard. Then, in 1988, the number of homicides in many American cities surpassed the peak years of 1979–1981. In New York City, the total number of homicides committed in 1988 reached 1896—an increase of more than 13% over the 1987 total and an apparent single-year record for New York City. The number of homicides increased to record or near record levels that year in other American cities as well.[4]

Even before the observed rise in the number of homicides in 1988, policy makers were expressing concern about the extent to which homicides were drug related (Graham, 1987; Gropper, 1985). Law enforcement officials had begun to suggest that much of the homicide rate could be explained by the relationship between drugs and violence.[5] Some argued that crack specifically was responsible for increases in the homicide count.[6]

In this chapter, we examine the relationship between homicide and the use of and trafficking in crack in New York City. We collected our data directly from the New York City Police Department (NYPD) during the peak year of 1988 (see the appendix to this chapter).[7] The case illustrations in what follows are often gruesome, shocking, and saddening. But we offer them to put human flesh on the statistical bones of homicide rates in the hope of illuminating the very different causal processes at work beneath the catchall phrase "crack-related murder."

BACKGROUND

Despite the popular belief that drugs and violence are closely linked, social scientists are only beginning to generate theory and data that will contribute to a better understanding of the relationship between drug abuse and violent crime.[8] The variables needed to study the drugs-violence nexus have never been adequately specified in major national databases such as Uniform Crime Reports, Supplementary Homicide Reports, and the National Crime Survey (Goldstein, 1989; Harwood et al., 1984). Consequently, the study of drug-related violence or homicide has remained largely dependent on local studies for data.

Most local studies have provided support for the argument that the relationship between drugs and violence is strong. Stephens and Ellis (1975) argued that criminal patterns of heroin users were shifting in the direction of greater amounts of violence. McBride (1981) found the same increasing trend of violent behavior among Miami narcotic users. Ball et al. (1983) studied heroin addicts in Baltimore and found that the number of days in which they engaged in violent crime was eighteen times higher during their initial addiction periods than it was during their initial days off opiates.

In terms of homicide specifically, Zahn and Bencivengo (1974) reported that, in Philadelphia in 1972, homicide was the leading cause of death among drug users, higher even than deaths due to the adverse effects of drugs, and accounted for approximately 31% of the homicides in Philadelphia that year. Monteforte and Spitz (1975) studied autopsy and police reports in Detroit and suggested that drug use and distribution may be more strongly related to homicide than to property crime. Preble (1980) conducted an ethnographic study of heroin addicts in East Harlem between 1965 and 1967. About fifteen years later, in 1979 and 1980, he followed up the seventy-eight participants and obtained detailed information about what had happened to them. He found that twenty-eight had died, eleven of whom (40%) had been the victims of homicide.

Heffernan and his associates (1982) studied homicide in a New York City police precinct and concluded that drug-related murders were a major subtype of homicide. Felson and Steadman (1983) studied 159 homicides and concluded that homicide victims were significantly more likely than assault victims to have used alcohol or drugs. Gary (1986) examined data from various U.S. cities and concluded that, at least for African-American males, the relationship between drinking and homicidal violence remained consistently strong. Goodman et al. (1986) conducted a study of blood alcohol levels in persons killed in Los Angeles between 1970 and 1979 and concluded that alcohol consumption was common among victims. Abel (1987) studied toxicological data for homicide victims in Erie County, New York, and found alcohol present in almost half of the victims and other drugs in a few others.

The state of the art with regard to the relationship between drugs and violence, particularly homicide, may be summarized as follows. The issue is not specified in major national data collection efforts. Local studies suggest a strong association between the two phenomena, but investigators have been unable to explain either the nature or the causal direction of this observed association. The lack of consensus and standardization in concepts, operational definitions, and empirical indicators seriously hampers any efforts to do comparative research over time or between different localities.

THREE TYPES OF DRUG-RELATED HOMICIDE

Our own fieldwork over a decade (Goldstein, 1979; Johnson et al., 1985) not surprisingly found a strong association between drugs and homicide or other types of violence. However, there were no studies that distinguished among drug-related homicides in terms of the different ways that drugs and violence can be related. The research in this area generally has tended to depend on medical examiner data and to focus primarily on the drug use of the victim (Abel, 1987; Felson and Steadman, 1983; Haberman and Baden, 1978; Zahn, 1975). Therefore, we formulated a new conceptual framework (Goldstein, 1985) comprised of three different models of drug-related homicide: psychopharmacological (homicide related to drug effects), economic compulsion (homicide related to addict crime), and systemic (homicide related to trade in an illicit market).

The *psychopharmacological model* suggests that, after ingesting a drug, some persons may become excitable and/or irrational and may act out in a violent fashion. Psychopharmacological violence may also result from the irritability associated with withdrawal syndromes from addictive substances. Psychopharmacological violence may involve substance use by *either* victims or perpetrators of violent events; drug use may contribute to a person behaving violently, or it may alter a person's behavior in such a manner as to bring about that person's violent victimization. Finally, some persons may ingest substances purposely in order to reduce nervousness or boost courage and thereby facilitate the commission of previously intended violent crimes.

The *economic compulsion* model suggests that some persons, due to craving certain drugs, feel compelled to engage in economic crimes in order to finance costly drug use. Sometimes these economic crimes are inherently violent, as in the case of robbery, and sometimes the violence results from an unintended or extraneous factor in the social context in which an otherwise nonviolent economic crime is perpetrated. Such factors include the perpetrator's nervousness, the victim's reaction, the presence or absence of weapons carried by either, the intercession of bystanders, and so on.

The *systemic model* suggests that violence arises from the exigencies of working or doing business in an illicit market—a context in which the monetary stakes can be enormous but where the economic actors have no recourse to the legal system to resolve disputes. Examples of systemic violence include territorial disputes between rival dealers, assaults and homicides committed within particular drug-dealing operations in order to enforce normative codes, robberies of drug dealers, elimination of informers, punishment for selling adulterated or bogus drugs, or assaults to collect drug-related debts. Systemic violence may also occur between users, as in cases of disputes over drugs or drug paraphernalia.

CRACK-RELATED HOMICIDES
OF THE PSYCHOPHARMACOLOGICAL TYPE

In sharp contrast to media images, a total of only 31 (7.5%) of the 414 homicides in our sample (Table 6-1) were caused by the effects of drugs and were, therefore, classified as psychopharmacological. Most of these involved alcohol, with only 5 (1.2%) involving the use of crack. Of these 5, 1 involved crack and alcohol in combination and 1 involved crack, cocaine, and alcohol. The other 3 involved crack only. Two of the 3 crack-only psychopharmacological homicides were classified as victim precipitated. For example, in case #60, the perpetrator was a twenty-two-year-old male. Police did not have evidence as to whether he was a drug dealer or a drug user. The victim was an eighteen-year-old male who was reportedly high on crack and acting irrationally, annoying the perpetrator and failing to stop. A dispute developed and culminated in the perpetrator shooting the victim in the head. We classified this as a psychopharmacological homicide because it stemmed from the effects of crack, but note that it was the victim rather than the perpetrator who was high on crack.

CRACK-RELATED HOMICIDES
OF THE ECONOMIC COMPULSION TYPE

Given popular conceptions about drug-related homicide, we were surprised to find that only about 2% of the homicides in our sample were motivated by economic compulsion (Table 6-1). However, all eight of these murders were classified as crack related. Tragically, six of the eight involved

TABLE 6-1   Primary Drug-Related
Classifications of Homicide Events

Classification	N	%
Psychopharmacological	31	7.5
Economic compulsive	8	1.9
Systemic	162	39.1
Multidimensional	17	4.1
Not drug related	196	47.3
Total	414	99.9

the murder of elderly persons during robberies or burglaries by crack users seeking money to finance their crack use. Victims included four females: three African-Americans, and one white. The two male victims were a sixty-four-year-old African-American and an eighty-six-year-old white. In case #73, for example, the victim was a seventy-one-year-old African-American female. The victim's granddaughter was reported to be a heavy crack user. She and a boyfriend entered the victim's home in order to steal money with which to buy crack. In the process, the boyfriend hit the grandmother in the head with a blunt instrument, killing her. After the murder, the granddaughter attempted suicide with an overdose of drugs, but survived.

The two crack-related, economic compulsion type homicides that did not involve elderly victims involved crack users. In case #70, the perpetrator was a twenty-three- year-old male. The victim was a thirty-one-year-old male. The victim was found in his auto, shot twice in the head. Police report the perpetrator knew the victim possessed drugs and money and killed him during a robbery undertaken to finance his drug use. One of the eight crack-related, economic compulsion type homicides appears to have been victim precipitated. In this case, #197, the victim was a thirty-two-year-old male crack user. He was found lying in a park with his head smashed by an automobile jack handle. Police report that the victim was known in the neighborhood to "rip off" automobile parts in order to finance his crack use. The police believe that an automobile owner surprised the victim while he was committing a theft, chased him into the park, and hit him with the jack handle. No perpetrator has been apprehended. This homicide is classified as economic compulsive because the event occurred in the apparent context of a crime to obtain money for drugs. This classification is not altered by the fact that the *victim* of the homicide appeared to be the *perpetrator* of the economic crime.

CRACK-RELATED HOMICIDES STEMMING
FROM THE ILLICIT MARKET SYSTEM

The most striking finding in our study was that about two-fifths of all the homicide events we studied (162 or 39%) and nearly three-fourths of all the drug-related homicides (162 or 74.3%) had to do with the exigencies of the illicit market system (Tables 6-1 and 6-2). Of these systemic homicides, nearly two-thirds (106 or 65%) were classified as being primarily crack related (Table 6-2). This suggests that however severe the psychopharmacological consequences of crack use and however strongly crack addicts may feel economic compulsion to support their use, *the vast bulk of crack-related homicides occurred between dealers or dealers and users.* They did not involve the murder of strangers outside the crack world.

Table 6-3 compares crack, cocaine, and other drug-related systemic homicides with regard to their specific characteristics having to do with the illicit market. Because 3 of the "other drug" cases involve unknown drugs, and there are only 11 cases in this category to start with, our findings on "other drugs" should be viewed with caution. Several systemic homicides were sufficiently complex to be coded in more than one category. Table

TABLE 6-2   Primary Drugs Involved in Drug-Related Homicides

Drug	Psychophar- macological	Economic Compulsive	Systemic	Multi- dimensional	Total
Crack	3 (3%)	8 (7%)	100 (85%)	7 (6%)	118
Cocaine	1 (2)	0	44 (92)	3 (6)	48
Alcohol	21 (100)	0	0	0	21
Marijuana	1 (14)	0	6 (86)	0	7
Heroin	0	0	2 (67)	1 (33)	3
Cocaine/crack	0	0	4 (80)	1 (20)	5
Cocaine/alcohol	2 (67)	0	0	1 (33)	3
Cocaine/ marijuana	1 (50)	0	1 (50)	0	2
Crack/alcohol	1 (33)	0	0	2 (67)	3
Crack/ marijuana	0	0	2 (100)	0	2
Crack/cocaine/ alcohol	1 (50)	0	0	1 (50)	2
Crack/cocaine/ alcohol/ marijuana	0	0	0	1 (100)	1
Unknown	0	0	3 (100)	0	3
Total	31 (14.2%)	8 (3.7%)	162 (74.3%)	17 (7.8%)	218 (100%)

TABLE 6-3   Circumstances of Systemic Homicides*

Circumstance	Crack (N= 106)	Cocaine (N= 45)	Other Drug (N= 11)
Territorial dispute	44%	22%	18%
Robbery of drug dealer	18	29	9
Assault to collect debt	11	16	27
Punishment of worker	9	11	9
Dispute over drug theft	9	4	9
Dealer sold bad drugs	6	2	—
Other	12	20	18
Unknown	2	—	18

*Percentages total more than 100 because some cases were too complex to place in a single circumstance category.

6-3 shows 116 circumstances for the 106 crack-related cases, 47 circumstances are reported for the 45 cocaine-related cases, and 10 circumstances are reported for the 11 other drug-related cases.

Case #8 is an example of a multiple-circumstance, crack-related systemic homicide. The victim was a twenty-four-year-old male. He was standing with a female at a street telephone booth in a drug sales location. He was approached by a thirty-year-old male who shot him in the head three times. The victim was a low-level crack dealer. He worked for a higher level dealer, but was trying to "freelance" by taking over a portion of the big dealer's territory. He was reportedly financing the start of his independent operation by selling the big dealer's wares but not returning the sales receipts to the big dealer. Police report that his killing was ordered by the big dealer. This homicide was therefore classified as having four systemic circumstances: a territorial dispute, a dispute over theft of drugs, an assault over a drug-related debt, and punishment of a worker by a dealer.

It was often difficult to identify the exact circumstances of systemic homicides. For example, the two most common circumstances were territorial fights between rival dealers and homicides occurring during robberies of drug dealers. However, the distinction between these two forms of systemic homicide was often blurred because certain homicides contained elements of both phenomena. For example, a drug dealer may steal a rival's cash and drugs in the course of eliminating him for some other reason. In some cases where a dealer is murdered and robbed, especially when the perpetrators are unknown, it is difficult to ascertain a single, discrete, primary motive. In coding the circumstances of such homicides, we relied heavily on the police investigators' knowledge of the neighborhood and informed assessment of available evidence.

The forty-seven crack-related systemic homicides that included territorial disputes between rival dealers constituted about 11% of our total homicides and over a third (36%) of all crack-related homicides. As Table 6-3 shows, territorial disputes were at least twice as likely to be the cause in crack-related systemic homicides than in systemic homicides related to other drugs. Only 22% of the cocaine-related and 18% of the other drug-related systemic homicides, as compared to 44% of the crack-related systemic homicides, included territorial disputes.

Our category of "territorial disputes" conceals a number of variations on a theme. Some cases involved low-level dealers operating as individuals in conflict with one another. Other cases involved organized gangs, frequently established along ethnic lines, in ongoing wars with each other. In many of these cases, the participants in the homicide were not the actual dealers. Rather, they were hired "enforcers" or "shooters." Still other cases involved individuals who were seen as infringing on a gang's "turf" or workers in a drug-dealing gang trying to "freelance," that is, attempting to sell crack for personal profit in territory claimed by their gang. Finally, some cases labeled as territorial disputes were revenge killings for prior homicides connected to territorial disputes. For example, the victim in case #31 was a thirty-year-old male. He had been previously ousted from his drug sales location and had returned in an attempt to reassert his claim to the area. He was shot by a twenty-four-year-old male. Police report that this was not an isolated event, but part of a continuing turf war between two gangs. The perpetrator fled to Washington, D.C., where he, in turn, was killed by associates of the victim.

In many cases, it was difficult to determine whether participants in territorial disputes were acting as independent operators or were part of larger organizations. But it was clear that the driving force behind homicides of this type was illicit drug market disputes rather than the psychopharmacological effects of crack or the economic compulsion of crack addicts. Case #42, for example, was a revenge killing stemming from a "turf war" between rival dealers. One perpetrator was a twenty-year-old male, who was apprehended; the other was identified only as a male who was not apprehended. This case was an assassination that was made to look like a robbery. The victim was accosted with several other persons in the lobby of an apartment building known to house a drug sales spot and a shooting gallery. The perpetrators asked all present for their valuables. Before even collecting them, they shot the victim five times. The case was first considered a robbery-homicide, but detectives subsequently developed information that the victim and perpetrators were in rival drug gangs and the homicide was actually a revenge murder that was part of an ongoing turf war.

Nearly one in five of the crack-related systemic homicides (nineteen or 18%) occurred during the attempted robbery of a dealer. In some of these cases, the drug dealer was killed. In case #136, for example, a low-level crack dealer was killed in the street during a robbery.[9] In others, the robbery attempt failed, and the robber was killed by the dealer.

Just over one in ten of the crack-related systemic homicides (twelve or 11%) involved drug-related debts. In case #369, for example, the victim was a twenty-seven-year-old female crack user. The perpetrator was a twenty-two-year-old male who was both a crack user and a low-level crack dealer. He had lent her both money and crack, but she was not able to repay the debts. They engaged in an argument at a street crack sales location, which culminated in the woman being stabbed once in the chest.

About one in ten of the crack-related systemic homicides (ten or 9%) involved the "punishment" of a worker by a dealer. In case #105, for example, the victim was a thirty-seven-year-old Puerto Rican woman who was a crack user and low-level crack dealer. She worked for a number of different higher-level dealers and was said to be "messing up the money." According to reports that the police obtained from the victim's family, she was using the income from crack supplied by one dealer to pay for crack supplied by another dealer. She was falling further and further behind because she was ingesting some of the crack that she was supposed to be selling. Eventually, her "game" collapsed. She was stabbed and beaten by an "enforcer" for one of the dealers.

Nearly another one in ten of the crack-related systemic cases involved disputes over the theft of drugs. In case #277, the victim was a thirty-two-year-old male. The perpetrator was a seventeen-year-old male. On a prior occasion, the victim had robbed the perpetrator of money and crack. The perpetrator subsequently shot the victim once in the abdomen in retaliation. In 6% ($N=6$) of the crack-related systemic homicides, a dealer was killed for selling "bogus," adulterated, or tainted drugs. In case #94, for instance, the victim was a twenty-nine-year-old white male Dominican. He was reported to be a high-level crack dealer who sold from his house. He was found shot multiple times in the head and body. Crack and other drug paraphernalia were found in his residence. No perpetrators were apprehended. Information developed by the police indicated that the victim had sold "bad" drugs and was killed for this reason.

Nearly one in eight of the crack-related systemic homicides (thirteen or 12%) occurred for such a wide variety of reasons that we included them in an "other" category. Case #266 involved the shooting of a thirty-nine-year-old African-American woman by a seventeen-year-old Puerto Rican male. Both were crack users. He was a low-level crack dealer. She was purchasing crack from him at the time of the killing. For some reason, he suspected that she was an undercover police officer. According to him, he challenged her with a .38 caliber revolver and the gun discharged accidentally.

MULTIDIMENSIONAL CRACK-RELATED HOMICIDES

Twelve of the crack-related homicides contained two or more of the three dimensions of drug relatedness in sufficiently equal weights that it was impossible to say that one dimension was more responsible than any other. We classified these as "multidimensional" crack-related cases. These included seven homicides that involved crack only and five that involved crack along with alcohol and other drugs in combination. Six of these homicides combined psychopharmacological and systemic elements. All occurred between persons in the drug scene and involved disputes over drugs where at least one of the participants was high at the time. Four of these six disputes occurred between users. One homicide in this category (case #265) involved a dispute between low-level dealers. A thirty-year-old crack dealer was shot to death by another crack dealer in an apparent "turf battle" over a sales spot. The dispute began in one location and continued to another. Shots were fired in both locations. The victim was reported to be high on cocaine at the time, and the police reported finding crack on or near the victim. We classified this case as multidimensional because it seemed to involve both the exigencies of the illicit distribution system and the psychopharmacological effects of crack.

Five of the multidimensional crack-related homicides combined elements of psychopharmacological effects and economic compulsion. Four of these involved robberies in which at least one of the participants was high, and in three of these homicides, the context was a drug "party" or a crack house. One of the multidimensional crack-related homicides was classified as containing all three dimensions of drug relatedness. In case #398, a twenty-year-old male stabbed a twenty-nine-year-old male to death in the street. Both were reported to have used crack at the time, but only the perpetrator was reported to be high. The perpetrator was also considered to be a low-level crack dealer. The victim attempted to rob the dealer. He apparently wanted crack for his own use and may have believed that, because the dealer was high, he could be "taken." However, the dealer resisted the robbery. As in many other homicides reported in this chapter, this case involved victim precipitation.

DISCUSSION

Crack-related homicides are a topic that has been the subject of more speculation than empirical inquiry. Whether rendered in political speeches, sensational reporting, or talk on the street, "crack-related murders" are taken to be a discrete "thing." Our data suggest, however, that this is oversimplified. This "thing" is not all of a piece; the phrase "crack-related murders" tends to lump together behaviors and events that are all tragic but that should, at least analytically, be separate. In fact, even the more general term "drug-related murder" is in need of elaboration. We have shown that there are at least three major types of drug relatedness and numerous subtypes and combinations.

Several findings emerged rather clearly. First, just over half (52.7%) of the homicides in our 1988 sample were in some way drug related. Second, our three-part conceptual framework proved to be a useful tool for classifying these drug-related homicides into different types with different primary causal mechanisms. Third, there is a sizeable kernel of truth in the popular images of crack and cocaine associated with violence. A majority of the drug-related homicides we studied did involve crack or cocaine.[10] Fourth, contrary to popular images, most crack-related homicides were *not* caused directly by the psychopharmacological effects of the drug on its users or even the economic compulsion that we have been led to believe drives crack addicts to commit crimes to support their use or addiction.[11] Rather, a large majority of all the drug-related homicides (alcohol-related cases excepted) had to do with the intensely risk-laden characteristics of the illicit drug market *system.* This was most true for crack-related homicides. On the basis of our data, we conclude that about one-fourth (26%) of the drug-related homicides in New York City in 1988 involved illicit crack sales, the most common subtype being those caused by territorial disputes between rival crack dealers.

The fact that crack can be made relatively easily has meant that a large number of predominantly poor people with few if any licit economic opportunities were drawn into small-scale entrepreneurial roles in this illicit marketplace. Some of these small dealers are independent of established organizations and the normative controls evident in more traditional dealing hierarchies. The entry of many small dealers into a new, unstable crack marketplace created a number of boundary disputes that led to violence. In an area as small as an apartment house, a tenement stoop, or a street corner, two or more crack dealers may be competing for the same customers and the same profits. Dealers and customers thus interact in a highly volatile illicit environment in which disputes and conflicts cannot be settled legally and so are routinely settled by resort to physical force. In this sort of commercial context, entrepreneurs learn early on that their success, often their very survival, depends upon carrying firearms. And, of course, firearms only beget more firearms in an escalating, self-fulfilling prophecy.[12] Unlike virtually any other commercial or professional arena, however, crack sales offered these people a chance to begin their own, potentially lucrative businesses. All that is required is a small amount of capital to purchase an initial inventory of cocaine. Although the case illustrations we gave clearly show that the risks are high, it is clear that the rewards are also likely to seem high relative to the legal alternatives.

APPENDIX: METHODOLOGY AND SAMPLE

The New York City Police Department divides the city into patrol zones, or divisions. Each zone generally includes between three and six police precincts. For purposes of this study, we selected one zone in each of four boroughs: the Fifth Zone (Manhattan), Ninth Zone (Bronx), Thirteenth Zone (Brooklyn), and Eighteenth Zone (Queens). Staten Island (Richmond), which is the smallest and least populated of the city's five boroughs, was not included. The selected zones comprise seventeen (23%) of the NYPD's seventy-five precincts.

The primary considerations in choosing zones were threefold. First, we wanted to survey about 25% of all homocides that were likely to occur in 1988. Second, we wished to utilize the existing police administrative structure, with its hierarchal controls, in order to assure a high degree of compliance with our research protocol, facilitate training and dissemination of materials, and maintain liaison with the top of the command structure. Finally, we wanted the sample of precincts to represent a cross-section of New York City with regard to high and low homocide rates, social and ethnic composition of neighborhoods, and geographical locale. Except for a somewhat higher concentration of lower socioeconomic areas in the Brooklyn precincts, the zones selected represent the best demographic mix possible when utilizing the existing NYPD zone structure.

Throughout New York City, all detectives are required to follow the same procedures in recording the progress of a homocide investigation. They routinely use a checklist of forms prepared, notifications made, interviews conducted, evidence vouchered, reports prepared, and so forth. Our data collection form was included as part of the "routine" paperwork in each detective's case folders in the selected precincts. That is, during active case investigation, detectives were required to record and then provide to us detailed information on the presence/absence and role of drugs in each homicide case. This unique inclusion of a research instrument in an investigative protocol could not have been accomplished without full support of the study by the NYPD.

We established initial contact with the police commissioner and then with the office of the chief of detectives. Prior to the start of our data collection, we held a training session at NYPD headquarters for all detective squads. We presented the purposes of the study, explained the data collection form, and discussed procedures for implementation. Each commander was given a manual with definitions and procedures for use in his or her squad. In all of this, we paid particular attention to the meaning of "drug relatedness" and to our three types of drug-related homicides. We visited each squad as often as necessary both to provide technical assistance and to ask clarifying and elaborative questions about forms already returned.

The data collection form was designed to gather a wide variety of information about the drug relatedness of homicides that is not typically gathered by police departments. Heretofore, when such information was known to the police, it was seledom recorded in a systematic fashion. Our data collection instrument included queries about specific drugs used by victims and perpetrators at the time of each homicide, potential drug-related circumstances of events, location (*e.g.*, drug sale site or "shooting gallery"), involvement of victims and perpetrators in trafficking, and so on. The homicide detectives also provided a narrative account of "what happened" on the instrument. For each question about the drug relatedness of the case, an additional question was asked about the source of that information. When the instrument was completed and coded, we had sufficient detail about each homicide to determine drug relatedness. The data collection form remained in the active case file until the case was closed or until two months after the close of data collection. This allowed new evidence to be entered whenever it became available.

To assure some level of standardization and to obtain as much information as possible about each case, we reviewed each case with every squad commander or his or her representative. We paid particular attention to the issue of drug relatedness and to the classification of cases into one of the three types in our conceptual framework. Whenever there was a question about a classification, we asked detectives about the information used to classify the case and the source of that information.

The final coding of cases into one of our three types was done by two members of our research team. First, each case was coded by the researcher who conducted the interview with the squad commander. Then all completed forms were given to the second researcher, who independently reviewed the data on each case and classified them. The two researchers then met and reviewed all the cases together. Whenever they were in agreement about a classification, it remained as coded. In those cases where they disagreed, they reviewed the case data and then jointly decided on the appropriate classification. In many of the cases where there was disagreement, we reinterviewed the detective to clarify confusing incidents and achieve consensus.

Sample

The data set that resulted from these procedures included 414 homicide events that occurred in the selected precincts at the peak of the crack scare between March 1, 1988, and October 31, 1988. These 414 homicide events involved 490 perpetrators and 434 victims. The perpetrators included 250 who were arrested, 39 for whom names were provided despite the fact that no arrest had yet been made, and 201 who could not be identified by the police. In many of the cases where a specific perpetrator had not been identified, the police were still able to provide important information about the circumstances of the homicide and the activities of the victim. The 434 homicides represent about 23% of the 1896 homicides that were reported in New York City in 1988.

The homicides were fairly evenly distributed across the city, with the Ninth Zone (Bronx) reporting the fewest (19.8%) and the Thirteenth Zone (Brooklyn) reporting the most (33.3%). There was, however, variation between precincts within zones. For example, the Thirteenth Zone includes the seventy-fifth precinct—encompassing Bedford-Stuyvesant, a predominantly poor, minority neighborhood—where there were 70 homicides during the study period, more than any other single precinct and about 17% of the study total. By contrast, the Thirteenth Zone also includes the eighty-first precinct, a more middle-class neighborhood that recorded only 27 (7%) of the total 414 homicide events.

About 45% of the 414 homicide events occurred in the street. An additional 35% occurred in residences, primarily the home of the victim. The remainder occurred in bars, abandoned buildings, the transit system, and commercial or other public sites. Most of the homicides (68%) involved the use of firearms. The vast majority of these were handguns, with .38 caliber and 9 mm weapons the most prevalent. About 20% of the homicides were committed with knives or other cutting instruments. Physical force, such as beating, was used in 7% of the homicide events.

In those homicides where data were available, perpetrators tended to be male (95%) and black[13] (83%); their mean age was twenty-seven years. About 23% of the perpetrators were also identified as Hispanic. The victims tended to be male (84%) and black (78%) as well, but to have a slightly higher mean age (thirty). About 31% of the victims were identified as Hispanic. Where known, the predominant nationality among both Hispanic perpetrators and victims was Dominican.

The police identified a total of 140 perpetrators (29%) as drug sellers. They classified a somewhat higher proportion (34%) of the victims as sellers ($N=148$). Detectives who completed the forms were asked to distinguish high- and low-level dealers. They were instructed to define low-level dealers as persons involved in drug buying and selling mainly to support a personal habit. High-level dealers were defined as persons who bought and sold drugs as a business to make a profit. Almost all perpetrators and victims were low-level sellers. Only sixteen perpetrators and fifteen victims were considered high-level sellers.

These data suggest that the majority of the homicide events in our sample involved perpetrators and victims who were relatively young, minority males from the so-called underclass.

Classifying Drug-Related Homicides

Table 6-1 shows the distribution of all the homicides across our three basic types. Over half the homicides in our sample (218 or 52.7%) were classified as primarily drug related. We defined a case as "drug related" only when both our staff and the police had sufficient information to determine that drugs contributed to the outcome in an important and causal manner. Many of the cases classified as "not drug related" had insufficient information for any classification to be made, for example, when the police discovered a dead body and had no idea who did it or why. Hence, our finding that 52.7% of the homicides were drug related must be viewed as conservative.

Table 6-1 shows only the *primary* classifications of homicides. It was possible for homicides to contain dimensions of the other types in our framework, without those dimensions being considered the main reason for the homicide. For example, a cocaine dealer who planned to murder a rival in a territorial dispute might ingest alcohol prior to the killing in order to boost his courage. We would classify such a homicide as systemic (*i.e.*, deriving from the system of illicit sales) but as also having a psychopharmacological *dimension*.

Perhaps the most striking finding in Table 6-1 is that about *three-fourths (74%) of the drug-related homicides were systemic in nature,* that is, had to do with the inherently criminal and often violent exigencies of the illicit market. This contrasts rather sharply with the "commonsense" views found in the media and public discourse that "drug-related murder" means that a person is directly "driven" to violence by virtue of a drug's effects or that an addict commits homicide in the course of an economic crime to "support a habit."

Within each of our three primary types of drug-related homicide, we recorded the specific drug or drugs in use. In three-fifths (60%) of all drug-related homicides (about one-third of all our homicides [131 or 32%]), that drug was crack. In 118 of these cases, crack was the sole drug involved. In the remaining 13 cases, crack was present in combination with other drugs. There were 87 additional homicides that were drug related but dod not involve crack.

Table 6-2 presents data on the specific drug related to each of the primary classifications. Table 6-2 reiterates the core finding in Table 6-1: the overwhelming majority of drug-related murders were systemic, that is, stemmed from the nature of illicit markets rather the psychopharmacological effects of a drug or the need to commit crime to "support a habit." This was true for every drug except alcohol; all twenty-one alcohol-related homicides were psychopharmacological. Alcohol-related murders constituted two-thirds (68%) of the thirty-one homicides that were psychopharmacological.

NOTES

The research on which this chapter was based was supported by a National Institute of Justice grant (#87-IJ-CX-0046). The points of view expressed herein do not necessarily reflect those of the U.S. government, the New York State government, or Narcotic and Drug Research, Inc., where the study was conducted. The authors gratefully acknowledge the guidance and support of Dr. Bernard A. Gropper of the National Institute of Justice, Dr. Jeffrey Fagan of the Columbia University School of Public Health, and two anonymous reviewers whose comments contributed much wisdom to the preparation of this chapter.

1. See Belenko and Fagan, 1987; Governor's Office of Employee Relations, 1986; and Kolata, 1988.

2. See James, 1988; Kerr, 1987, 1988; Krajicek, 1988; Pitt, 1988; and Wines, 1988.

3. See, *e.g.,* Pooley, 1989.

4. See Johnson, 1989; Molotsky, 1988; and Wolff, 1988.

5. See Johnson, 1989; Martz et al., 1989; Molotsky, 1988; and Wolff, 1988.

6. *e.g.,* Krajicek, 1988; and Morganthau et al., 1989.

7. See Goldstein, 1985, 1986, 1987, 1989.

8. See, *e.g.,* Watters et al., 1985.

9. All robbery/homicides involving dealers were classified as systemic, though in some cases, economic compulsion may also have been a motivation. It was not always possible empirically to ascertain the precise, full motivation for robbery/homicides involving dealers.

10. A reviewer rightly expressed surprise that we found so few alcohol-related homicides. Alcohol-related homicides may well have been undercounted by the NYPD. Some inebriated perpetrators, for example, may not have been apprehended until sobering up. Signs of drinking by either perpetrators or victims may well have gone unnoticed by witnesses or police, and we were unable to collect systematic data from the toxicology reports of medical examiners. Moreover, alcohol figures very heavily in "domestic" homicides, but only 6% of our sample cases were of this type.

11. This finding supports earlier research showing that drug users are more likely to finance their drug use by working in the drug distribution system than by engaging in violent, predatory theft (e.g., Goldstein, 1981).

12. Although the crack distribution system is indeed violent, the crack-related homicides that stemmed from the exigencies of the illicit market do not appear to have increased the overall homicide rate in New York City as reported in the FBI's *Uniform Crime Reports*. This rate did rise sharply in 1988, our sample year. But crack first appeared in late 1984, and the homicide rates between 1984 and 1987 were still below the precrack peak years of 1979 to 1981. It is possible that crack-related homicides have replaced other types of homicides rather than added to the existing rate. For example, the fact that only 3 of our 414 homicides were primarily related to the use or sales of heroin indicates a decline in heroin-related homicides.

13. We have chosen to use the generic racial category "black" instead of "African-American" because we had numerous cases in our sample of mixed race/ethnicity for whom the latter term would be inaccurate (*e.g.*, Puerto Ricans who were racially black but did not identify ethnically as African-Americans).

REFERENCES

Abel, E. L., 1987. "Drugs and homicide in Erie County, New York," *The International Journal of the Addictions* 22:195–200.

Ball, J. C., J. W. Schaeffer, and D. N. Nurco, 1983. "The day-to-day criminality of heroin addicts in Baltimore—a study in the continuity of offense rates," *Drug and Alcohol Dependence* 12:119–142.

Belenko, S., and J. Fagan, 1987. "Crack and the Criminal Justice System," New York City Criminal Justice Agency.

Browne, A., 1987. *When Battered Women Kill* (New York: Free Press).

Felson, R. B., and H. J. Steadman, 1983. "Situational factors in disputes leading to criminal violence," *Criminology* 21:59–74.

Gary, L. E., 1986. "Drinking, homicide, and the black male," *Journal of Black Studies* 17:15–31.

Goldstein, P. J., 1979. *Prostitution and Drugs* (Lexington, MA: Lexington Books).

———, 1981. "Getting over: Economic alternatives to predatory crime among street drug users," in J. A. Inciardi (ed.), *The Drugs/Crime Connection* (Beverly Hills, CA: Sage Publications), pp. 67–84.

———, 1985. "The drugs/violence nexus: A tripartite conceptual framework," *Journal of Drug Issues* 14:493–506.

———, 1986. "Homicide related to drug traffic," *Bulletin of the New York Academy of Medicine* 62:509–516.

————, 1987. "The impact of drug related violence," *Public Health Reports* 102:625–627.

————, 1989. "Drugs and violent crime," in N. A. Weiner and M. E. Wolfgang (eds.), *Pathways to Criminal Violence* (Newbury Park, CA: Sage Publications), pp. 16–48.

Goldstein, P. J., D. S. Lipton, B. J. Spunt, P. A. Bellucci, T. Miller, N. Cortez, M. Khan, and A. Kale, 1987. "Drug Related Involvement in Violent Episodes [DRIVE]." Interim final report to the National Institute on Drug Abuse, Washington, DC. July.

Goldstein, P. J., P. A. Bellucci, B. J. Spunt, T. Miller, N. Cortez, M. Kahn, R. Durrance, and A. Vega, 1988. "Female Drug Related Involvement in Violent Episodes [FEMDRIVE]." Final report to the National Institute on Drug Abuse, Washington, DC. March.

Goodman, R. A., J. A. Mercy, F. Loya, M. L. Rosenberg, J. C. Smith, N. H. Allen, L. Vargas, and R. Kolts, 1986. "Alcohol use and interpersonal violence: Alcohol detected in homicide victims," *American Journal of Public Health* 76:144–149.

Governor's Office of Employee Relations, 1986. "Crack—the deadliest cocaine of all," *Office of Employee Relations News*, New York State, vol. 2, September, pp. 4–5, 12.

Graham, M. C., 1987. "Controlling drug abuse and crime: A research update," U.S. Department of Justice, *NIJ Reports* SNI 202, March/April.

Gropper, B. A., 1985. "Probing the links between drugs and crime," U.S. Department of Justice, *Research in Brief*, February.

Haberman, P. W., and M. M. Baden, 1978. *Alcohol, Other Drugs, and Violent Death* (New York: Oxford University Press).

Harwood, H., D. Napolitano, P. Kristiansen, and J. Collins, 1984. "Economic Costs to Society of Alcohol and Drug Abuse." Final report to the Alcohol, Drug Abuse and Mental Health Administration, Washington, DC.

Heffernan, R., J. M. Martin, and A. T. Romano, 1982. "Homicide related to drug trafficking," *Federal Probation* 46:3–7.

Hewitt, J. D., 1988. "The victim-offender relationship in convicted homicide cases: 1960–1984," *Journal of Criminal Justice* 16:25–33.

James, G., 1988. "Murders in Queens rise by 25%; crack described as a major factor," *New York Times*, April 20, pp. A1, B4.

Jamieson, K. M., and T. Flanagan (eds.), 1987. *Sourcebook of Criminal Justice Statistics, 1986* (Washington, DC: U.S. Department of Justice, Bureau of Justice Statistics, NCJ-105287).

Johnson, B. D., P. J. Goldstein, E. Preble, J. Schmeidler, D. S. Lipton, B. Spunt, and T. Miller, 1985. *Taking Care of Business: The Economics of Crime by Heroin Abusers* (Lexington, MA: Lexington Books).

Johnson, C., 1989. "Homicide linked to drug use in the District of Columbia," *CJSA Forum*, Criminal Justice Statistics Association, January, vol. 7, no. 1, pp. 4–6.

Kerr, P., 1987. "A crack plague in Queens brings violence and fear," *New York Times*, October 19, pp. A1, B5.

————, 1988. "Addiction's hidden toll: Poor families in turmoil," *New York Times*, June 23, pp. A1, B4.

Kolata, G., 1988. "Drug researchers try to treat a nearly unbreakable habit," *New York Times,* June 25, pp. 1, 30.

Krajicek, D. J., 1988. "Crack whips killing toll," *New York Daily News,* December 30, p. C13.

Martz, L., M. Miller, S. Hutchinson, T. Emerson, and F. Washington, 1989. "A tide of drug killing," *Newsweek,* January 16, pp.44–45.

McBride, D. C., 1981. "Drug and violence," in J. A. Inciardi (ed.), *The Drugs-Crime Connection* (Beverly Hills, CA: Sage Publications), pp. 105–124.

Mercy, J. A., and L. E. Saltzman, 1989. "Fatal violence among spouses in the United States, 1976–1985," *American Journal of Public Health* 79:595–599.

Molotsky, I., 1988. "Capital's homicide rate is at a record," *New York Times,* October 30, p. 14.

Monteforte, J. R., and W. U. Spitz, 1975. "Narcotic abuse among homicides in Detroit," *Journal of Forensic Sciences* 20: 186–190.

Morganthau, T., M. Miller, R. Sandza, and P. Wingert, 1989. "Murder wave in the Capital," *Newsweek,* March 13, pp. 16–19.

Pitt, D. E., 1988a. "Battle for crack trade in Queens may hold key to officer's killing," *New York Times,* February 28, pp. 1, 35.

———, 1988b. "New York City nears record for slayings," *New York Times,* November 22, pp. B1, B2.

Pooley, E., 1989. "Fighting back against crack," *New York Magazine,* January 23, pp. 31–39.

Preble, E., 1980. "El Barrio revisited," paper presented at the annual meeting of the Society of Applied Anthropology.

Stephens, R. C., and R. D. Ellis, 1975. "Narcotic addicts and crime: Analysis of recent trends," *Criminology* 12:474–488.

Tardiff, K., and E. M. Gross, 1986. "Homicide in New York City," *Bulletin of the New York Academy of Medicine* 62:413–426.

Watters, J. K., C. Reinarman, and J. Fagan, 1985. "Causality, context, and contingency: Relationships between drug abuse and delinquency," *Contemporary Drug Problems* 12:351–373.

Wines, M., 1988. "Against drug tide, police holding action," *New York Times,* June 24, pp. A1, B4.

Wolff, C., 1988. "As drug trade rises in Hartford, so does violent crime," *New York Times,* December 16, pp. B1, B2.

Zahn, M. A., 1975. "The female homicide victim," *Criminology* 13:400–415.

Zahn, M. A., and M. Bencivengo, 1974. "Violent death: A comparison between drug users and nondrug users," *Addictive Diseases* 1:283–296.

SEVEN

The Social Pharmacology of Smokeable Cocaine

Not All It's Cracked Up to Be

John P. Morgan and Lynn Zimmer

This chapter introduces the pharmacology of crack cocaine to help readers evaluate the claims that have been made regarding its danger to individual users and society. Because, materially and pharmacologically, *crack is cocaine,* most of what is known about cocaine applies to crack as well. The fact that crack is smoked—rather than sniffed, swallowed, or injected—is significant. Our review of the evidence indicates, however, that its importance has been exaggerated. Clearly, using either cocaine powder or crack entails risks, but both can also be used in less or more risky ways. In fact, among the things we will show is that the amount of harm resulting from the use of powder cocaine and crack has less to do with their pharmacological properties than with the social circumstances of their use.

FROM COCA LEAVES TO CRACK

For centuries, people have consumed cocaine to enhance work performance, forestall drowsiness, lift mood, and produce feelings of elation and euphoria.[1] In the South American Andes, for over a thousand years people have ingested cocaine by chewing coca leaves or brewing them into a tea. This form of consumption seems not to be associated with significant biological harm or social dysfunction (Aldrich and Barker, 1976; Antonil, 1978; Forno et al., 1981; Weil, 1986) and has not, by and large, been subjected to repressive government control (Henman, 1990; Morales, 1989).

There was little use of coca in the United States or Europe until the mid-nineteenth century, when the plant's principal active ingredient was extracted and made available as a water-soluble powder—cocaine hydrochloride. Western physicians soon discovered that cocaine was an effective local anesthetic; they also used it, although less effectively, as an antidepressant, asthma remedy, and a treatment for opiate addiction. About the same time, cocaine was added to numerous patent medicines and tonics that people purchased without prescription to combat a variety of common ailments, including chronic fatigue.

During the late nineteenth century, Americans also consumed cocaine recreationally, often in beverage form. Vin-Mariani wine and Coca-Cola, for example, were popular cocaine-based drinks—and the latter was even marketed as a "temperance beverage" to people wishing to avoid alcohol (Pendergrast, 1993). There is less information available about the recreational use of cocaine *powder* during the nineteenth century, but it seems to have been most common among members of the "criminal underworld" (Grinspoon and Bakalar, 1985; Inciardi, 1992; Musto, 1987)—a fact that helped fuel public support for increased government controls. Also precipitating anticocaine legislation around the turn of the twentieth century were growing concern about cocaine's potentially harmful physical effects (Alexander, 1990; Courtwright, 1982; Grinspoon and Bakalar, 1985) and fear, especially in the South, that the drug caused blacks to behave violently (Morgan, 1981; Musto, 1987; Pendergrast, 1993). However, because this was an era of increasing government control over most available intoxicants—including alcohol—the laws regulating cocaine may have had little to do with this drug's *particular* characteristics and effects.

As early as 1887, states began passing anticocaine laws (Ashley, 1976); and in 1906, with enactment of the first Pure Food and Drug Act, the federal government began requiring that products with cocaine (and some other drugs) be labeled as to content. Then, in 1914, Congress passed the Harrison Act, which originally only imposed tax and registration requirements on the legitimate providers of certain drugs, including cocaine. However, courts soon interpreted this law as giving federal drug enforcement officials the power to decide what constituted "legitimate" use of these drugs; and, through this power, they quickly transformed the Harrison Act into a law prohibiting all recreational use of cocaine.

One immediate consequence of cocaine prohibition was the elimination of cocaine tonics and beverages. Another was the emergence of an organized black market in cocaine hydrochloride, which was smuggled into the country from South America. Almost certainly, the purity of the product available to users declined, the price rose far above the $2 an ounce that had been common during the previous century (Courtwright, 1991), and use became even more concentrated in deviant subcultures (Ashley, 1976; Grinspoon and Bakalar, 1985; Inciardi, 1992).

After 1930, when a number of synthetic stimulants (particularly amphetamine) became available, cocaine use may have decreased further, although it continued to be used by some artists and entertainers,[2] who generally sniffed it, and by intravenous heroin users, who employed it either as an occasional alternative to heroin or mixed with heroin to form a "speed-ball" (Grinspoon and Bakalar, 1985). During the 1960s, as part of the more general increase in the use of illegal drugs among more "main-stream" Americans, the use of cocaine probably increased as well, although in 1972, still less than 3% of the population (aged twelve and over) said they had tried it (Johnson and Muffler, 1992).

During the remainder of the 1970s and into the early 1980s, cocaine use increased steadily, especially among young adults aged eighteen to twenty-five (NIDA, 1991a). Probably contributing to cocaine's appeal was the government's success, first, in curtailing diverted medicinal amphetamine (Brecher, 1972; Inciardi, 1987; Morgan and Kagan, 1978) and, second, in interdicting enough marijuana substantially to decrease its availability and increase its price (Cowan, 1986; Hamid, 1992; Lazare, 1990). As the demand for cocaine increased, supplies increased as well,[3] and by 1982, approximately 28% of eighteen- to twenty-five-year-olds had at least tried it (NIDA, 1991a). However, because of cocaine's relatively high price—up to $100 for a gram of powder in the early 1980s—use was most prevalent among the middle and upper classes (Grinspoon and Bakalar, 1985). The typical mode of ingestion was to sniff cocaine hydrochloride powder into the nose, which permits absorption through the nasal mucosa.

Today, essentially all cocaine enters the U.S. in the form of hydrochloride powder. This powder is extracted in a process that begins by mixing pulverized coca leaves with a solvent (such as ether or gasoline) and partially drying it. Then, to make the product water-soluble, this "coca paste" is treated with hydrochloric acid and dried to a white powder. In this form, cocaine can be sniffed, swallowed, or dissolved in water for injection, but it cannot be smoked because igniting it degrades the cocaine before it will volatilize. However, through a series of fairly simple chemical procedures, cocaine can be turned into "freebase"—a product that resembles the smokeable coca paste. To produce freebase, cocaine hydrochloride is mixed in water with a liquid base (such as ammonia, baking soda, or sodium hydroxide) to remove the hydrochloric acid. The resulting alkaloidal cocaine is then dissolved in a solvent (such as ether) and gently heated, causing most of the liquid to evaporate.[4] The product created, when placed in a glass pipe and ignited, produces vapors of relatively pure cocaine.

Inhaling cocaine vapor into the lungs delivers the drug more rapidly to the bloodstream—and therefore to the brain—than does sniffing the powder; as a consequence, it produces quicker, more intense effects. Most cocaine users do not want this more dramatic experience—especially because it means, as well, a more rapid diminishing of the drug's effects. Also reducing freebase's attractiveness is the somewhat complicated conversion process—which occasionally can be dangerous because some of the solvent used in the preparation may remain in the product being ignited. Nonetheless, freebasing did increase in popularity in the early 1980s (Hamid, 1992; Inciardi, 1987; Siegel, 1984), mainly attracting people who were already fairly heavy users of powder cocaine (Siegel, 1984; Waldorf et al., 1991; Washton et al., 1986).

Around 1985, another form of smokeable cocaine—called "rock" or "crack"—became available. Its production resembles that of freebase, but without the final purification process: cocaine hydrochloride is dissolved in water, sodium bicarbonate (baking soda) is added, and the mixture is heated and then dried into hard, smokeable pellets. These pellets contain not only alkaloidal cocaine, but sodium bicarbonate and whatever other fillers and adulterants had been added earlier to the powder; thus, crack is not as highly purified as freebase, and street samples tend to range from 10 to 40% cocaine by weight (Inciardi, 1987). Still, igniting crack produces a vapor that is largely pure cocaine (Snyder et al., 1988), making the experience of smoking crack quite similar to that of smoking freebase. However, unlike freebase, which users generally produced themselves from the powder, crack was usually cooked (or "cracked up") by drug dealers who then sold it in ready-to-smoke form (Hamid, 1990).

Crack quickly gained in popularity, although it never became as popular as cocaine powder. For example, in 1991, nearly twenty-four million Americans (aged twelve and over) said they had tried cocaine, compared to less than four million for crack (NIDA, 1991b). Although the price of cocaine had been decreasing and its quality increasing during the early 1980s, it was still, in 1985, too expensive to be used very much by the poor. What crack did was to lower dramatically the cost of the "cocaine high." Simply because smoking delivers a drug more efficiently to the brain than does snorting, an amount of cocaine too small to produce an effect in powder form becomes an effective dose when converted to crack.[5] In 1986, a single dose of crack could be purchased for as little as $5 or $10; and, over the next few years as the price of cocaine powder fell even further, the price of a pellet of crack fell as low as $2 in some parts of the country (Cohn, 1986). Thus, by the late 1980s, what had once been called "the champagne of drugs"[6] had become available to the poor—and its use spread especially quickly in impoverished urban areas where enterprising youth turned powder cocaine into crack and sold it on the streets (Fagan and Chin, 1989; Hamid, 1990; Williams, 1992).

As Chapter 2 showed, once crack had been introduced to the inner-city poor, the "crack epidemic" became a major media event—with literally thousands of articles appearing in newspapers and magazines in 1986 alone. At the time, no scientific studies of the drug had been conducted, but journalists found and quoted a handful of "experts"—mostly law enforcement officials and drug treatment providers—who had decided that crack was "the most dangerous drug known to man." They claimed that crack was highly potent and highly toxic, causing record numbers of heart attacks, seizures, and strokes. They blamed crack for recent increases in crime, family violence, and child abandonment. They claimed that crack was "instantly addicting," making moderate and controlled use impossible. And when used by pregnant women, crack was said to produce babies so severely damaged that they would never fully recover.

Before long, articles supporting these claims appeared in the drug abuse and medical literatures. Although clothed in scientific garb, most of these "studies" were simply "case reports" of crack and cocaine users enrolled in drug abuse treatment programs—a self-selected and nonrepresentative sample (Gold et al., 1986; Honer et al., 1987; Isaacs et al., 1987; Miller et al., 1989; Mody et al., 1988; Spitz and Rosecan, 1987; Washton et al., 1986; Weiss and Mirin, 1987). Even today, few of the "facts" that are "well known" about cocaine and crack come from careful scientific studies.[7] Nonetheless, they have made their way into government documents,[8] drug education materials, and antidrug public service announcements—particularly those of the Partnership for a Drug-Free America. In addition, although a number of journalists have been critical of the media's handling of the crack story (Gladwell, 1986; Martz, 1990; Morley, 1989; Weisman, 1986), exaggerated tales of cocaine- and crack-caused horror still appear regularly in the popular press.

The faulty assumption on which such drug horror stories are based is that a drug's pharmacology holds the key to understanding the patterns of its use and the behavior of its users.[9] One of our goals in this chapter is to demonstrate that this "pharmacocentrism" is misleading. In doing so, we are not suggesting that a drug's pharmacology is unimportant. After all, for a drug to be used recreationally, people have to like how it makes them feel, and how a drug makes people feel is a product of its "pharmacological fit" with the human organism. However, a description of this "fit" cannot explain why only some people use a particular drug, why only some of them become regular users, or why fewer still use it in a volume and frequency that disrupts their lives.[10] In short, to explain how a drug *works in the brain* reveals no more about why and how people use it than explaining how a specific food is *processed by the body* reveals why and how people eat it. Like food consumption, drug consumption must be understood, primarily, as a social-psychological phenomenon. In fact, one of the things we hope to show in the following overview of crack cocaine's pharmacology is how little it reveals about the drug's popularity or the social consequences of its use.

PHARMACODYNAMICS: COCAINE'S INTERACTION
WITH THE HUMAN ORGANISM

Like all stimulant drugs, those prescribed by physicians as well as those taken recreationally, cocaine produces a psychoactive effect by interacting with the central nervous system, stimulating it to perform its ordinary functions more intensely. This system operates through the release of various neurochemical transmitters (from the nerve cells in which they are produced) and their binding to receptor sites on neighboring cells. The constant release and binding of these neurotransmitters forms a pathway of "messages" that travel throughout the body, sustaining life and making possible the organism's response to environmental stimuli.

Cocaine also has an impact in the autonomic (or involuntary) division of the central nervous system, which helps regulate a variety of bodily functions that are generally free of volitional impact, including respiration, circulation, digestion, and body temperature. Ordinarily, these functions are maintained at relatively stable levels throughout the day. But they are slowed down during periods of rest through diminished production, release, and binding of neurotransmitters and can be speeded up, as needed, through increased neurotransmitter activity.[11] Cocaine operates in this system by increasing the concentration and binding activity of the body's own neurotransmitters—particularly dopamine.[12] Thus, what people experience as cocaine's stimulant effect is an intensification of the body's normal stimulatory mechanisms.[13]

Cocaine is both a *quick*-acting and a *short*-acting drug.[14] When cocaine enters the bloodstream directly, via injection, it reaches the brain quickly, and users feel its effects within minutes. Inhalation also delivers cocaine quickly to the brain because air passages in the lungs are positioned close to capillary accesses to the bloodstream.[15] When cocaine is sniffed, the onset of effect is slower because the drug must pass through the nasal mucosa before entering the bloodstream. Swallowing cocaine delays delivery to the brain even more because most of the drug is passed through the gastrointestinal tract before it crosses through cell membranes into the bloodstream.

Controlling for dose, sniffing and swallowing also produce *less intense effects*. This is not only because these routes of administration cause active cocaine molecules to reach the brain more gradually, and therefore in lower concentrations, but also because the additional passage of time allows more of the cocaine molecules to be transformed into inactive byproducts (or metabolites) before they reach the brain.[16] Both injection and inhalation deliver a greater number of *active cocaine molecules* per dose to the brain than snorting.

Whatever the route of administration, within thirty to sixty minutes, the processes of biotransformation and excretion cut in half cocaine's concentration in the blood[17]—which is one reason its effects are of relatively short duration. However, even before this decline, cocaine's effects are diminished through other "protective mechanisms." The most important is the rapid distribution of the drug from the bloodstream to the rest of the body, including to sites with no cocaine receptors. Thus, the same activity that delivers cocaine rapidly to active sites in the brain and heart also removes it from these sites, thereby reducing the drug's effects. At the same time, cocaine's effects are also diminished through homeostatic mechanisms that reduce neurotransmitter activity at receptor sites—the same mechanisms that operate when factors other than drugs cause an increase in neurotransmitter activity.[18] It is this diminishing of effects—prior even to the decline in the drug's concentration in the blood—that cocaine users experience as "acute tolerance."[19] That is, to maintain a stable effect over time, users must follow each dose of the drug with a larger subsequent dose. However, acute tolerance also can be viewed as a preexisting protective mechanism because it diminishes cocaine's potentially harmful effects on the cardiovascular and central nervous systems.

Cocaine's Psychostimulant Effects

The intensity of cocaine's impact on the central nervous system depends largely on dose. At low doses, cocaine's effects are fairly similar to those of caffeine: it combats drowsiness and fatigue, increases energy and alertness, and enhances mental acuity.[20] With increasing doses, most users begin to experience negative effects—such as nervousness, jitteriness, sleeplessness, and agitation—and at very high doses, feelings of suspicion, hypervigilance, and paranoia are common (Cohen, 1989; Erickson et al., 1987; Spotts and Shontz, 1980; Waldorf et al., 1991).

Extremely high does of cocaine—like extremely high doses of many stimulant drugs—can produce a toxic psychosis, with symptoms similar to the delirium of high fever. However, toxic psychoses appear to be rare among cocaine users, probably because of the body's protective mechanisms referred to previously. In addition, because cocaine is relatively short acting, when psychosis does occur, it tends to be short-lived (Weil, 1986). Permanent psychosis is found occasionally among cocaine users (Washton, 1989; Weiss and Mirin, 1987), but there is no evidence of a causal link, and, for most people, even heavy and prolonged use appears to have no permanent impact on mental health, personality, mood, cognition, memory, or perception.

Among people predisposed to behave violently, cocaine may increase the likelihood of their involvement in violent episodes, but there is no evidence that cocaine *causes* generally nonviolent people to behave violently. Some researchers have identified crack as more violence producing than cocaine powder (Peterson, 1991; Washton, 1989), and journalists have been prone to attribute increases in violent crime to the pharmacological properties of crack.[21] However, a growing number of social scientists refute these claims.[22]

Crack use by women has also been blamed for rising rates of child abuse (Peterson, 1991). However, to the extent that crack users seem to "lose their mothering instinct" and begin abusing or neglecting their children, it is probably due less to the pharmacology of the drug than to the lifestyle that accompanies heavy involvement in the street drug scene—regardless of the drug (Rosenbaum et al., 1990). In fact, research on a variety of drugs shows that the same drug is associated with very different behaviors in different cultures, which indicates that there is no *direct link* between any specific drug and any specific behavior (see, *e.g.*, MacAndrew and Edgerton, 1969; Zinberg, 1984). In this culture, crack—like alcohol—is associated with violence primarily because it is often used by people already at high risk for behaving violently and because it is often used in social settings in which violence is already common (Williams, 1992). No drug *directly causes* violence simply through its pharmacological action.

Cocaine's Physiological Effects

Because it constricts blood vessels and speeds up the heart, cocaine has the potential to produce cardiovascular disease. However, at low doses, the increases in blood pressure and heart rate caused by cocaine are fairly similar to those associated with over-the-counter appetite suppressants—and are less dramatic than those experienced by most people during aerobic exercise, urban driving, or sex. With larger doses, cocaine's cardiovascular effects become more pronounced, and users face an increased risk of harm to the heart through coronary artery constriction or arrhythmia. High-dose users also face an increased risk of adverse stimulant effects in the central nervous system, including seizures, convulsions, and strokes (Cregler and Mark, 1986).

Because intravenous injection allows the rapid delivery of a large dose of cocaine, injectors are more likely to experience adverse physiological effects. Rapid consumption of multiple doses increases the risk associated with other routes of administration, but the body's capacity quickly to diminish cocaine's effects protects even most high-dose smokers, sniffers, and swallowers from serious harm. Oral ingestion clearly has the greatest safety margin, although an extremely large dose swallowed can be dangerous, as indicated by the death of "body packers"—people who swallow balloons or condoms filled with cocaine to smuggle it across borders (Amon et al., 1986; Suarez et al., 1977).

Although most people can consume a fairly high dose of cocaine without serious harm, even a low dose can be dangerous for people with pre-existing central nervous system or cardiac abnormalities (Isner et al., 1986; Mittleman and Wetli, 1987). People with enzyme deficiencies that interfere with cocaine's biotransformation may also be at higher risk (Devenyi, 1989). There is recent evidence that consuming alcohol with cocaine may be risky, especially for persons with heightened sensitivity to cocaine's effects (Karch, 1992).[23]

Cocaine Toxicity as a Cause of Death

Cocaine's lethal potential has been demonstrated through the administration of high doses to animals (Finkle and McCloskey, 1978; Smart and Anglin, 1987), but until fairly recently, death was regarded as a rare occurrence among human cocaine users (Lundberg et al., 1977). Then, in 1979, in the *Journal of the American Medical Association*, the coroner from Dade County Florida reported that during the previous decade there had been sixty-eight deaths from "recreational use of cocaine" (Wetli and Wright, 1979). This article is still widely cited as evidence of cocaine's dangers, even though the "study" actually involved little more than attributing to cocaine all deaths in which evidence of cocaine had been detected by post-mortem examination.

Examining the sixty-eight cases used by Wetli and Wright, Bruce Alexander (1990) found that fifteen of the deaths had actually been caused by trauma (automobile accidents, drownings, gunshot wounds) and that another had been a suicide. Drugs other than cocaine were found in the bodies of *all sixty-eight* victims; and, in fact, at the time of the autopsy, twenty-nine deaths had been officially attributed to "multiple drug intoxication." In none of these cases was there an attempt to determine each drug's contribution to the death or to identify the presence of any physical abnormalities that might have played a contributory role. Alexander estimates that in only seventeen of the sixty-eight cases was it likely that cocaine had made a pharmacological contribution to the death—and five of these seventeen deaths were of "body packers" who had smuggled extremely large quantities internally in balloons or condoms that broke. The remaining twelve victims may have died after using cocaine "recreationally," although because the records contained no information regarding dose or frequency of use, there is no way of knowing how much cocaine these people had used or by what mode of ingestion.

Also widely cited as evidence of cocaine's deadly potential are data from a national sample of hospitals and coroners' offices compiled in association with the federally funded Drug Abuse Warning Network (DAWN) project. These data, which show steadily increasing numbers of cocaine-related deaths during the second half of the 1980s when crack use was spreading, are no better for determining cause of death than those used by Wetli and Wright. According to DAWN guidelines, any death that "involves" drug abuse—defined as any use of a controlled substance for its psychic effects, without medical approval—can be counted as *drug related,* without proof that drugs actually *caused* the death. In fact, in some cases, deaths are attributed to drugs solely on the basis of circumstantial evidence of drug abuse, without even toxicological verification of their presence at the time of death (Benowitz, 1992). In 1990, nearly twenty-five hundred deaths nationwide were estimated by DAWN to be cocaine related, but in about three-quarters of those, one or more additional drugs were mentioned—most commonly alcohol.

Casting further doubt on the validity of DAWN's fatality data is Tardiff et al.'s (1989) review of the coroner's reports from 935 New York City deaths that had been officially labeled cocaine related. They found that about half these deaths had been due to trauma (caused by accidents, homicides, and suicides) and that less than 12% were even *possibly* related to the pharmacological effects of cocaine. If these 935 cases are at all representative of the coroners' reports used by DAWN, the number of deaths caused by cocaine nationwide in 1990 may have been more in the neighborhood of 250 than the 2500 estimated by DAWN (NIDA, 1991c). *In fact, a finding from this NIDA report that has not been widely publicized is that in only 172 cases (less than 7% of the 2483 officially identified as cocaine related) was cocaine identified as the single, direct cause of death.*

Cocaine-Related Medical Emergencies

DAWN also compiles data on drug-related hospital emergency room visits and, since the mid-1980s, has reported steadily increasing numbers of emergencies related to cocaine—with increases in some years as much as 100%. However, like the data for drug-related deaths, the data for drug-related emergency room visits are problematic because DAWN compilers count as a "drug-related episode" any emergency room visit that "involves" drug abuse. And, if more than one drug is identified in an episode, each is reported as a separate drug "mention," whether or not it contributed substantially to the condition prompting the visit. In 1990, for example, cocaine was mentioned in an estimated eighty thousand emergency episodes, but in only about one-quarter of those was it the only drug mentioned; the drug most often mentioned in combination with cocaine was alcohol (NIDA, 1991d).

The DAWN data cannot be used to estimate the incidence of *medical complications* associated with the use of cocaine or other drugs because there is not, among the six possible "reasons" for emergency room contacts recognized by DAWN, one for *physical symptoms related to drug use.* Surely some of the visits included in the category "unexpected drug reactions" (*e.g.*, 22.9% of the cocaine-related episodes reported in 1990) involved physical symptoms, but even many of those may not have required medical attention.[24] In fact, given the recent publicity regarding cocaine's dangers, it is possible that some users became frightened by fairly mild cardiovascular symptoms and were prompted to seek medical attention they did not actually need.[25]

Despite these (and other) problems with the research methodology— most of which inflate the incidence of cocaine-related toxicity[26]—the DAWN data are routinely offered as proof that cocaine users face grave risks of physiological harm. At the same time, the fact that cocaine-related emergency room mentions have continued to rise, even as overall rates of *cocaine use* have declined, is used as evidence that *hard-core cocaine abuse* has risen (Millman, 1991; White House, 1989).[27] Increases in both cocaine abuse and cocaine-related emergency room visits are, in turn, often attributed to the increased use of crack (Kandel, 1991; Schuster, 1990).

There is little direct evidence that crack users suffer more physiological harm than do those who use comparable amounts of powder cocaine. It is difficult to know if crack users are overrepresented among DAWN's cocaine mentions,[28] but if they are, it may be because people who use crack are more likely than cocaine powder users to *go to* emergency rooms. After crack first appeared in the mid-1980s, politicians, clinicians, journalists, and drug czars all predicted that its use would quickly spread to all communities and all socioeconomic groups. However, as earlier chapters have shown, crack has remained a drug used primarily by the urban poor, who are most likely to seek treatment for their medical problems, drug related or not, at hospital emergency rooms (Wishner et al., 1991).

Such a socioeconomic explanation for the overrepresentation of crack users in the DAWN reports[29] is supported by Waldorf et al.'s (1991) study of heavy cocaine users. Within their sample of predominantly middle-class cocaine snorters and smokers, they found that smokers (who used freebase and/or crack) developed no more drug-related health problems than did cocaine sniffers—although the smokers did, as a group, develop health problems earlier (see Chapter 4). In addition, although most of the predominantly middle-class cocaine users in their sample did attribute some health problems to cocaine, there is no evidence that they visited hospital emergency rooms. Indeed, like most of the twenty-five million Americans who have used cocaine, very few ever sought medical help for the physiological problems they believed were related to their use of the drug. Clearly, both cocaine and crack have the *potential* to produce serious harm, even death; but the evidence is—despite government reports showing ever-increasing harm—that *most* people consume these drugs in a way that does not cause them lasting or even temporary harm.

CRACK AS AN ADDICTIVE DRUG

Evaluating the addictive potential of cocaine—or any drug—is compli-cated by the fact that addiction is, as Bakalar and Grinspoon (1984) put it, "an essentially contested concept." In fact, the term "drug addiction" sel-dom appears in the substance abuse literature anymore, having been re-placed by "drug dependence" or "substance abuse disorder"—conditions diagnosed largely on the basis of behavior. Definitions vary, but most in-clude as a core criterion the continued use of a drug despite the appear-ance of negative consequences for the user's health, work, financial stabil-ity, relationships, and the like. The key element is "compulsion" or "loss of control," which suggest an inability to alter drug-taking behavior (see, *e.g.,* Jaffe, 1990).

There is no question that some people use crack or cocaine in other forms despite its negative impact on their lives. Furthermore, as the crack users and freebasers in Chapter 4 suggest, in virtually every sample of co-caine users, some people identify themselves as "addicts" or describe their relationship to cocaine as "obsessive," "compulsive," or "out of control" (Cohen, 1989; Erickson et al., 1987; Siegel, 1980; Waldorf et al., 1991). Thus, among drug users as well as drug experts, cocaine, especially in the form of crack, is generally accepted as having substantial *addictive potential.* Because cocaine does not produce physical dependence and withdrawal of the sort associated with opiates (Gawin and Kleber, 1986), cocaine addic-tion was once thought to be primarily psychological in nature. Increasingly, however, it is being described in *physiological* terms. In fact, some drug treat-ment entrepreneurs maintain that cocaine addiction *must be physical* be-cause "no drug can become psychologically compelling *without* there being physical (indeed cellular) changes in brain activity that both result from and contribute to its continued use" (Washton, 1989:36–37).

A Biochemical Theory of Cocaine Addiction

Cocaine produces psychoactive effects by increasing the neural activity of dopamine and other neurotransmitters[30]—in effect, stimulating the "plea-sure system" that is activated when humans have pleasurable real-life expe-riences. This "chemical reward" is the pharmacological basis for cocaine's use as a recreational drug—and for cocaine users' descriptions of its ef-fects as "intensely pleasurable," "euphoric," or, in the case of crack, even "orgasmic." Because people tend to use frequently only drugs that produce pleasurable effects, cocaine's stimulation of the brain's "pleasure system" is also what gives it addictive potential.[31]

However, this is far from a *sufficient explanation* of cocaine addiction. After all, the government's own data show that most people who try cocaine do not even become regular users, much less "addicts" (NIDA, 1991a). What Washton (1989) and others[32] who have attempted to prove cocaine's inherent addictiveness suggest is that, with *continued use*, cocaine alters the chemical structure and functioning of cells in the brain's "pleasure system," to the point where the cells themselves begin to "crave cocaine." In fact, Washton claims that it is this new understanding of cocaine's ability physically to alter brain cells that has made the old distinction between psychological and physical addiction meaningless.

The physiological mechanisms of cocaine addiction are presumed to operate more intensely when the drug is smoked, and many early media reports went so far as to identify crack as "the most addictive drug known to man."[33] Before long, similar claims also began to appear in the drug abuse literature, most of them attributing crack's unique addictiveness to the intensity of its high, the rapid onset and short duration of its effects, and the severe "crash" that accompanies its decline (Miller et al., 1989; Spitz and Rosecan, 1987; Washton, 1989; Washton et al., 1986). In fact, Washton maintained that crack so quickly altered the brain's functioning that it was often "instantaneously addicting." Today, many doubt that crack causes instant addiction, but it continues to be widely accepted—even among scholars who challenge most other unproven "drug truths"—that crack is much more addictive than powder cocaine (Inciardi, 1987; Kleiman, 1992; Musto, 1987; Trebach, 1987).

Comparing the Addictiveness of Crack and Cocaine

The hypothesis that smoked cocaine is more likely to lead to addiction than is an equal dose used intranasally has never been tested on either animals or humans. Nor is it likely to be because animals cannot be easily trained to use either of these drug administration techniques and fortunately ethical reasons prevent the random assignment of human subjects to an experimental condition (smoking) that is believed to be more dangerous. However, NIDA data can be used to calculate and compare the "continuation rates" for crack and cocaine: the proportion of people who, after trying each drug, continue to use it regularly. Of course, even regular users of crack and cocaine are not *necessarily* addicts, but if crack is, indeed, more addictive than cocaine, the continuation rates for crack should be markedly higher.

The best data available for this comparison are the population estimates from the National Household Survey on Drug Abuse sponsored by the National Institute on Drug Abuse (NIDA, 1991b). Readers reared on the frightening claims of clinicians, politicians, and the media may be surprised to learn from the NIDA survey that only about one in twelve (8%) of Americans aged twelve and over who have ever tried cocaine had used it at all in the month prior to the survey. This figure was somewhat higher for crack, but still *only about one in eight (12.3%) of those who have ever tried crack had used it in the month prior to the survey.* The fraction of these "past-month" users who go on to daily use and therefore, arguably, to "addiction" is far smaller. In interpreting these data, it is also important to recognize that precisely because smoking is a more direct mode of ingestion offering a much more intense high, the fraction of cocaine users who are drawn to crack is very likely to be among the heaviest users to begin with. Further, crack was introduced and systematically marketed in impoverished inner-city communities where powder cocaine was less affordable and less available (Hamid, 1992; Inciardi, 1987), which means that crack has been disproportionately available to just those parts of the population who are most vulnerable to the abuse of any drug (Anthony, 1991; Kandel, 1991). Thus, the different continuation rates for crack and powder cocaine may be explained in part by differences in the social circumstances of users themselves.

Data from NIDA's High School Senior Survey make much the same point. For example, in 1991, among students who reported having ever tried crack, only one in thirty-five reported daily or near daily use—rates virtually identical to those for powder cocaine. In fact, among high school seniors, the continuation rates for alcohol, marijuana, cigarettes, and LSD were all higher than for *either* powder cocaine or crack (Johnston et al., 1991). Regular use of any drug, licit or illicit, is not something anyone wants to see among high school students. But when the best available evidence shows that the vast majority of young people who try crack do not go on to use it regularly, and when only a small fraction of even these go on to daily use, it is clear that the claim that crack is "instantaneously addicting" is false.

These data indicate not only that relatively few cocaine users become "dependent"—whatever their route of administration—but that smoking cocaine by itself does not increase markedly the likelihood of dependence. This latter finding is important because it means that the claim that cocaine is much more addictive when smoked (Gold, 1984; Inciardi, 1987; Jekel et al., 1986; Jeri et al., 1978; Siegel, 1982, 1984; Washton et al., 1986) must be reexamined. We think that a more accurate interpretation of existing evidence is that *already abuse-prone* cocaine users are most likely to move toward a more efficient mode of ingestion as they escalate their use. The claims of Washton, Gold, and others about crack's extreme dependence liability are based on treatment populations and those who call help hotlines—people who are, by definition, among the most problematic users. Thus, claims made on the basis of their reports cannot be safely generalized to all who have experimented with crack or freebase.

The Pharmacology of Cocaine Bingeing

A cocaine binge is an episode of continuous drug taking, lasting several hours or more, in which additional doses of the drug are consumed in an effort to forestall diminution of the effects. People binge on drugs other than cocaine, and, in fact, occasional alcohol bingeing seems almost a "rite of passage" for American youth. Still, bingeing seems to be particularly prevalent among cocaine users—a fact that may be related to cocaine's specific pharmacological action. As discussed earlier, soon after cocaine produces its effects, the body's mechanisms of homeostasis respond to diminish them. This is why, for example, cocaine's cardiovascular effects diminish more quickly than does its concentration in the blood (Fischman et al., 1985). By and large, the more dramatic the cocaine effect, the more dramatic the homeostatic response; and, following a large dose, blood pressure, heart rate, and the like may actually go below normal before returning to normal.

Similar mechanisms operate to diminish cocaine's psychoactive effects, and the bigger the dose, the more dramatic the neural system's homeostatic response. Thus, a dose large enough to produce feelings of *euphoria* may, a short time later, produce feelings of *dysphoria* as neurotransmitter activity declines to below normal levels (Waldorf et al., 1991:223–226). Not all cocaine users experience a dramatic shift from euphoria to dysphoria (Van Dyke et al., 1976), but it is common among cocaine users who engage in binges. In fact, it is during this "crash phase" that they report an intense craving for the drug—especially once they have learned that consuming an additional dose restores the euphoria, if only temporarily. Of course, each restoration of effect is followed by another "crash" in which users will have to decide, again, whether to continue or stop.

Cocaine bingeing is reported with all routes of administration (Cohen, 1989; Erickson et al., 1987; Siegel, 1982; Waldorf et al., 1991), but appears to be more common among cocaine smokers than sniffers. This makes sense because, even if the dose consumed through smoking is smaller than the dose sniffed—and it often is—smoking delivers the drug to the brain in a more concentrated form, producing first a more dramatic high and then a more dramatic "low" as the neural system responds to cocaine's presence. In a sense, smoking almost "tricks" the organism into responding to a relatively small dose of cocaine as if it were a large dose; as a consequence, the "crash" following the smoking of crack is likely to be more intense. Thus, as the accounts in Chapter 4 suggest, when using the drug, crack smokers may indeed experience more intense "craving" to continue bingeing than do cocaine sniffers and may, as a result, find it harder to resist the urge to binge, especially if the drug is readily available. In addition, because the duration of effect is shorter with smoking than sniffing, crack users are likely to consume more doses during a similar time period. This doesn't mean necessarily that they will consume *more cocaine* than sniffers do during a typical binge. What makes the crack binge more dramatic is that the transitions from euphoria to dysphoria are more frequent and more intense.

Whatever the association between bingeing and route of administration, bingeing per se is not evidence of *drug dependence.* Most people who meet the diagnostic criteria for cocaine dependence probably *do* engage in episodes of bingeing. However, both cocaine and crack users may binge occasionally—and experience "craving" and "compulsion" during the binge—*without becoming dependent* (see Cohen, 1989; Waldorf et al., 1991). Of course, during periods of temporary abstinence, many regular cocaine users also report "craving" the drug. But these feelings probably have little to do with cocaine's pharmacological properties because they occur even long after cocaine's impact on the central nervous system has disappeared and are similar to what people describe when they give up other drugs (and even other activities) they enjoy. Indeed, we suspect that the craving linked to cocaine's pharmacological activity is short-lived, making it harder for cocaine users to resist bingeing, but not harder for them—after a drug-taking episode is over—to resist using the drug again. The desire to use cocaine again is probably not pharmacologically linked to whether or not the preceding episode of drug taking was a binge or whether the drug was smoked or sniffed. To become "cocaine dependent," users must repeatedly decide—during periods of diminished or absent pharmacological effect— to use the drug again.

Pharmacology Is Not Destiny

All the data gathered by NIDA since the 1970s show *lower* continuation rates for cocaine than for most other drugs. Among high school seniors who have tried cocaine, only 5.2% report having tried unsuccessfully to stop using it—a lower percentage than for most other drugs (Bachman et al., 1991a). Most cocaine users take the drug occasionally and recreationally—without experiencing compulsion, without bingeing, and without developing symptoms of drug dependence.

The likelihood that cocaine will be used in a dysfunctional way seems to be greater when the drug is smoked, sniffed, or injected than when it is swallowed. In this culture, the most common routes of administration are sniffing and smoking; and, controlling for other variables, smoking appears to be marginally riskier—probably increasing the incidence of bingeing, but not dramatically affecting whether current users decide to continue or cease taking the drug. Some people who use cocaine do become "dependent" on it, but many also, at some point, stop or reduce their use, often without obtaining drug treatment (Cohen, 1989; Erickson et al., 1987; Kandel et al., 1985; Shaffer and Jones, 1989; Siegel, 1980; Waldorf et al., 1991). No route of administration makes it easier (or harder) for "addicts" to overcome their "addiction," although there is evidence that crack smokers begin the process sooner (Millman, 1991; Washton et al., 1986)—probably because their greater propensity to binge creates more of the problems that motivate drug users to change their behavior.

There is no evidence to support the claim made by Washton and others that continuous use of cocaine permanently alters brain cells in a way that "compels" people to keep using it—or that smoking crack cocaine is markedly more addictive than sniffing cocaine powder. Instead, the literature shows that, even with direct modes of cocaine ingestion like crack smoking, use patterns and consequences vary widely. This evidence supports the theoretical perspective outlined in the beginning of this book: that abusive use patterns and addiction are more a function of the characteristics of certain users and certain social circumstances of use than of the drugs themselves (see Peele, 1985; Szasz, 1974; Zinberg, 1984). This is why all drugs, including cocaine and crack, show such enormous variation in patterns of use. In fact, as the following section discusses in more detail, research with animals shows that the more the conditions under which drugs are administered resemble the conditions under which humans take drugs, the more variation in their drug-taking behavior.

Animal Self-Administration of Cocaine

Laboratory scientists sometimes joke that the definition of a drug is any substance that, when injected into a rat, produces a journal article. Hundreds of studies have proven that laboratory animals can be taught to self-administer cocaine, even to the point of causing their own death. The earliest such studies, conducted in the late 1960s (Deneau et al., 1969; Pickens and Thompson, 1968) are important because they show that even drugs that do not produce physical dependence and withdrawal can be highly "reinforcing"; that is, after being administered the drug, lab animals can be made to self-administer more of it. Deneau et al., for example, demonstrated that monkeys would push a lever for cocaine over twelve thousand times—nearly as many times as physically dependent monkeys push it for heroin.[34] By the late 1980s, over five hundred articles describing the reinforcing properties of cocaine had been published (Johanson and Fischman, 1989).

The assumption on which animal research is justified—and repeatedly funded—is that much can be learned about human cocaine use from studying cocaine self-administration in caged animals (Bozarth, 1988; Brady and Griffiths, 1976; Fischman, 1988; Washton, 1989). However, to provoke animals to self-administer cocaine (and most other drugs), they must be "trained" to do so. In order to maximize the dose and frequency of use, researchers tether animals to the cage and surgically implant a permanent injection apparatus in their backs. This unreachable catheter injects cocaine intravenously following operant behavior (such as depressing a lever). Many researchers starve the rats before training begins because this increases the likelihood that animals will repeatedly inject cocaine.

But just as humans are typically distracted from drug use by other pleasures and life commitments, so are animals. Simply giving a cocaine-injecting rat a solution of water sweetened with glucose and saccharin decreases the injection rate (Carroll et al., 1989); so does maintaining rats on an adequate diet (Carroll et al., 1979). In addition, if instead of unlimited access, animals are given cocaine (or heroin) under conditions of limited access, they tend to arrive at a controlled daily dose and do not "choose drugs over life." In fact, in these settings, if the concentration of the drug is increased, the animals tend to administer *fewer* injections, holding constant their total daily doses (*e.g.,* Wilson et al., 1971).

When animals are allowed to interact socially, their drug consumption also tends to decrease. In one series of studies, rats were trained to drink a morphine solution but then permitted access to an open area populated with other rats and scattered with objects for inspection and play. These opportunities for exercise, play, and socializing markedly decreased their consumption of morphine (Alexander et al., 1981).[35] Environmental factors also affect the trainability of rats for cocaine injection; for example, Schenk et al. (1987) found that rats reared in groups were less likely to self-administer cocaine than were rats reared in isolation.

Studies of drug self-administration by rodents, dogs, and even primates have garnered much attention but have not contributed much to understanding cocaine use in humans. This is true because the conditions used in most animal studies are so extreme, so *unlike* the conditions of ordinary human life. In fact, experimental conditions are *expressly designed* to maximize animals' self-injection of cocaine. For example, test animals are raised in isolation or removed from social interaction with others of their kind. They are outfitted for solitary life and implanted with an IV injection apparatus. They are often starved to prepare them for their lives as cocaine "addicts" and almost always denied all opposing reinforcers—even sweetened water. And experimenters make unlimited supplies of cocaine constantly available. Thus, it is not surprising that researchers can train "nine out of ten laboratory rats" to inject themselves with lethal doses of cocaine (Bozarth and Wise, 1985). Such studies are then cited as scientific "proof" of cocaine's extreme addictiveness—implying that what is true for rats is also true for humans. This is the clear message in the Partnership for a

Drug-Free America's "Dead Rat" video, which has been shown frequently on television.[36]

The National Institute on Drug Abuse has paid for much of this animal research and continues to do so—now defining as a prime objective the discovery of a cocaine "antagonist" that will block or counter cocaine's effects and be useful for "treating" cocaine and crack addiction in humans (Leary, 1993; McNeil, 1992). This effort is premised on the idea that current "cocaine addicts" cannot stop using the drug—an idea that is continuously reinforced by the animal self-administration studies. However, the accumulated data on human cocaine use show that most users do not become addicted to the drug, and, of those who do, most eventually stop or greatly reduce their use.

CRACK, COCAINE, AND PREGNANCY

Another core claim in the most recent War on Drugs concerns so-called crack babies. Among the earliest reports of possible fetal damage associated with cocaine was a study by a group of clinical investigators that appeared in the *New England Journal of Medicine* in 1985. Chasnoff and his colleagues found a higher than normal incidence of certain abnormalities among babies who had been exposed prenatally to cocaine and suggested that cocaine might be more harmful to fetuses than previously believed. Prior to this, cocaine had been largely ignored by researchers interested in drugs and pregnancy[37] and, in fact, was not even discussed in either of the research monographs on fetal drug effects published by NIDA in 1985 (Chiang and Lee, 1985; Pinkert, 1985). However, interest in the topic grew quickly; and within a few years, dozens of articles on fetal exposure to cocaine had appeared, most of them reporting evidence of harm. However, few of the studies using human subjects used rigorous standards of scientific investigation, and those using animals (as we explain later) provide little insight into cocaine's effects in humans.

When pregnant laboratory animals (usually rats) are given cocaine, among the abnormalities noted in their offspring are low birth weight, eye and skeletal defects, cardiovascular malformation, delayed social development, impaired reflexes, increased shock sensitivity, and heightened reaction to painful stimuli (Fantel and Macphail, 1982; Finnell et al., 1990; Mahalik et al., 1980, 1984; Smith et al., 1989; Webster and Brown-Woodman, 1990). However, some of these effects have been found in only a single study; and, in some cases, researchers following similar experimental protocols have been unable to replicate earlier findings (Mayes, 1992; Neuspiel and Hamel, 1991). Thus, although taken as a whole, these studies indicate some vulnerability to cocaine among fetal rats, they do not constitute a "settled" body of research. The value of this research is limited by the fact that the animals are generally given extremely large doses of cocaine—sometimes twenty-five or more times (per kilogram of body weight) those typically consumed by humans.[38] This is a serious methodological flaw because the effects of high-dose drug use are often not only *quantitatively* different from low-dose effects, but *qualitatively* different. In fact, if these animals had been given doses comparable to those consumed by humans, there might have been no adverse effects at all.

Even if adverse effects occur in fetal rats following doses of cocaine comparable to those consumed by humans, it does not necessarily mean human fetuses will be similarly affected. As shown in the literature on prenatal exposure to other drugs, fetal structure, function, and development are quite different in rats and humans (Juchau, 1976, 1985; Miller and Kellogg, 1985; Rudolph, 1985; Wang et al., 1985). For one thing, the human placenta—unlike that of the rat—has some capacity to metabolize drugs; thus, although some active cocaine molecules are transferred from the pregnant woman to the fetus, they tend to be a lower proportion of those consumed than occurs in rats (Spear et al., 1989). In addition, human fetuses themselves have more drug-metabolizing enzymes than rats—giving human fetuses a shorter period of exposure to whatever active cocaine they receive. Finally, because fetal development is more rapid in rats than humans, the impact of a single drug episode is likely to be more pronounced in rats than in humans. Because of these differences, effects found in rats exposed prenatally to cocaine might never occur in exposed human offspring.

To study cocaine's fetal effects in humans, researchers compare the babies of women who used cocaine during pregnancy to the babies of women who did not. However, only if the women in the two groups are otherwise similar can adverse pregnancy outcomes—prematurity, low birth weight, physical deformities, and the like—be attributed to prenatal cocaine exposure. In most comparative studies, women in the drug-exposed and control groups differ substantially. In fact, although cocaine use is well distributed across class and racial groups, the cocaine users selected for fetal impact studies are overwhelmingly poor and minority—which means they are *less likely* to have had adequate nutrition and medical care during their pregnancies and *less likely* to have healthy babies, whether they use cocaine or not. Further complicating the results of these studies is the fact that poor pregnant women who use cocaine are more likely than pregnant women generally to have an infectious disease and to use other drugs, particularly alcohol and tobacco—conditions known to contribute to fetal harm (Graham and Koren, 1991; Koren et al., 1990). Even the best designed of the cocaine and pregnancy studies control for only a few of these confounding variables, and many studies control for none (Neuspiel and Hamel, 1991).

As a consequence, researchers have been unable to determine the magnitude of cocaine's impact on pregnancy—or, indeed, whether cocaine has an independent impact at all.

Had this research been published at any other time, it might have gone unnoticed outside the scientific community. However, its appearance in the late 1980s—at the height of the crack scare—practically guaranteed the attention of the popular press. In fact, although the studies themselves generally made no mention of the route through which pregnant women had consumed cocaine, journalists almost uniformly identified *crack* as the drug causing extensive fetal harm. By ignoring the methodological limitations in the scientific research, they presented preliminary data as fact.

THE CRACK BABY: A MEDIA-CREATED CRISIS

Virtually every adverse outcome found in every fetal study involving cocaine—whether the subjects were humans or rats—was reported in the mass media as evidence that crack *causes* damage in babies. Journalists described "crack babies" as permanently impaired—physically, intellectually, and emotionally. Some of these babies, it was claimed, so lacked "normal human feelings" and "impulse control" that, as they matured, they were certain to pose a danger to others. Continually, Americans were told about the financial cost to taxpayers of the growing number of crack babies—many of whom would need extensive medical treatment, special education, and long-term institutional care. Estimates of the magnitude of the "crisis" varied, but the media often quoted a Department of Health and Human Services report predicting one hundred thousand crack-damaged babies per year, at an annual cost to society of about $20 billion (Kusserow, 1990).

Journalists also continually portrayed crack babies as having been born "addicted" to cocaine. For example, one television news broadcast depicted a tiny African-American baby in an incubator waving his arms in apparently futile gestures as a voice-over described the horror of watching such babies "craving cocaine." In numerous magazine and newspaper articles as well, journalists described "tiny addicts" who were "poisoned in the womb" and then forced, at birth, into a "world of nightmarish withdrawal." [39]

Of all the drug horror stories ever told, perhaps none has provoked as much public concern as that of the crack baby. In response, various remedial programs were implemented, particularly in the public schools, with the goal of helping crack babies compensate for their handicaps (Chira, 1990; Toufexis, 1991), but more commonly, a punitive approach has been taken. For example, hospitals now regularly test the urine of babies whose mothers they suspect of having used drugs, and babies are often taken away on the basis of a positive drug test alone (Siegel, 1991). In some parts of the country, women are prosecuted and imprisoned for using drugs during pregnancy (see Chapter 12 of this volume; Paltrow, 1992; Siegel, 1991), and state legislatures are searching for new ways to control pregnant drug users—for example, laws that would force them, once detected, to choose between drug treatment and sterilization (Berrien, 1990; Chavkin, 1991). A recent survey of college students found widespread support for such policies—particularly when the drug being used by pregnant women was cocaine (Vener et al., 1992)—and probably most Americans would agree. Indeed, among defenders of drug prohibition, the goal of "saving crack babies" is now often offered as the primary justification for escalating the entire War on Drugs.[40]

The "crack baby" on which drug policy is increasingly based does not exist. Crack babies are like Max Headroom and reincarnations of Elvis—a media creation. Cocaine does not produce physical dependence, and babies exposed to it prenatally do not exhibit symptoms of drug withdrawal. Other symptoms of drug dependence—such as "craving" and "compulsion"—cannot be detected in babies. In fact, without knowing that cocaine was used by their mothers, clinicians cannot distinguish so-called crack-addicted babies from babies born to comparable mothers who had never used cocaine or crack (Hadeed and Siegel, 1989; Parker et al., 1990).

In the scientific literature itself, the issue of *fetal damage* related to cocaine is more complicated, but journalists have blatantly misrepresented that literature by reporting only studies that found evidence of harm[41] and then minimizing, if not ignoring, the limitations in their research design. The mass media have consistently portrayed crack as a direct *cause* of adverse pregnancy outcomes even though no study has convincingly shown that to be so. In fact, there is now evidence that cocaine actually contributes little to the abnormalities detected in the babies of women who use cocaine during pregnancy.

A number of people have criticized the cocaine and pregnancy studies, pointing out how biased sample selection and the lack of control over other variables prevent their being used as evidence that cocaine causes fetal harm (Alexander, 1990; Kandall, 1991; Mayes, 1992; Mayes et al., 1992; Neuspiel and Hamel, 1991). In addition, the few studies that have monitored cocaine-exposed babies during the first few years of life have found that the differences detected at birth almost disappear by age two (Chasnoff et al., 1992; Graham et al., 1992). However, the study we find most persuasive was done by a group of Canadian researchers who combined data from the twenty best-designed studies published prior to 1989 and performed a "meta-analysis" that challenges most of their findings (Lutiger et al., 1991). A meta-analysis is particularly useful when the results of similarly designed studies are inconsistent, as they are in this case. It also reduces the impact of selection bias, increases control over potentially confounding variables, and eliminates some of the problems of small sample size—thus permitting the use of more sophisticated statistical measures.

After combining the data from both drug users and controls, Lutiger et al. compared the reproductive risks associated with (1) polydrug use, including cocaine; (2) polydrug use, excluding cocaine; (3) cocaine use only; and (4) no drug use. Analyzing the data as a whole, they discovered that most of the fetal effects associated with cocaine disappeared.[42] They did find significant differences between the offspring of women who had used drugs during pregnancy and those who had not—but both the type and rate of fetal abnormalities were similar regardless of the drugs consumed.

This latter finding is important because it calls into question the alleged harmful consequences of cocaine's vasoconstrictive impact on the umbilical cord and placenta. In sufficient doses, cocaine probably does restrict the flow of blood from mother to fetus, but because infants exposed prenatally to cocaine tend to be indistinguishable from those exposed to drugs that do not cause vasoconstriction, we cannot conclude that cocaine's slowing of the blood flow compromises fetal development. In fact, there is evidence that, in response to cocaine's presence, receptors in the placenta "down-regulate" fairly quickly, reducing vasoconstriction even before serum levels decline substantially—thus shortening the period of time in which blood from the mother is restricted (Wang and Schnoll, 1987).[43]

We still know almost nothing about cocaine's interaction with the fetal brain, although the incidence of cardiovascular and central nervous system damage seems to be quite low (Neuspiel and Hamel, 1991). It has been suggested that the fetal neural system is more sensitive than that of adults and therefore more easily damaged by cocaine. But it is just as possible that the opposite is true. We know that fetal anatomy and function differ from those of adults—so much so that inferences about a drug's fetal effects can never be made on the basis of detected effects in adults (Miller and Kellogg, 1985; Rudolph, 1985; Wang et al., 1985). Some drugs are *less harmful* to fetuses than adults and some are *more harmful;* however, overall, human fetuses have proven to be remarkably *resistant* to the drugs consumed by their mothers (Alexander et al., 1985).

Given the recent increases in cocaine use and our failure to persuade some pregnant women not to take it, it is fortunate that the evidence to date does not suggest that cocaine is among the drugs that are particularly damaging to the fetus. This does not mean that cocaine use by pregnant women poses *no risk.* However, it is now clear that the high rate of abnormalities found in babies exposed prenatally to cocaine has less to do with the pharmacological effects of the drug than with other factors of high-risk pregnancy that "cluster" in drug users—particularly impoverished drug users who more often have poor diets and no prenatal care and who are more frequent victims of violence against women and other crimes.[44]

The route through which cocaine is administered probably makes little difference,[45] although the greater use of crack by the inner-city poor means that crack users are more likely than powder cocaine users to have unhealthy babies. In addition, impoverished drug users are more likely than their wealthier counterparts to be enmeshed in a deviant lifestyle that carries with it many additional pregnancy risks. This *association* between crack use and adverse pregnancy outcomes will continue to exist as long as poor women are overrepresented among crack users and as long as socioeconomic status remains a critical determinant of many non-drug-related pregnancy risks. Again, there is no evidence that crack is a direct cause of fetal harm, so reductions in crack use will not lead automatically to a reduction in the number of unhealthy babies being born.

CONCLUSION

Popular beliefs and attitudes about cocaine and crack have been shaped by journalists. Because the media are businesses seeking ever-larger markets of readers and audiences, they generally frame stories in ways that resonate with the sympathies and antipathies that make up conventional wisdom regarding drugs. In this sense, the crack story is simply the most recent installment in a series of morality tales that simultaneously construct and confirm Americans' belief in the power of drugs to disinhibit and harm users. However, there is something new—or at least refined—in crack journalism: the emergence of a group of "drug experts" who use pharmacological language and concepts to support existing drug myths while ignoring pharmacological principles and evidence that challenge those myths. Some of the articles published in drug abuse and medical journals appear scientific but are not because the taken-for-granted premise of their authors—like that of most journalists—is simply that any crack use is highly destructive.

Our review of the available literature indicates that most of the claims that have been made about crack's hazards are either exaggerated or unfounded. In both powder and crack form, cocaine *can be* toxic, especially when consumed in large doses, and even small doses may produce harm in some users. However, most users experience no serious adverse health consequences related to their use. Cocaine also appears to be weak as a fetal toxin, and no physical or developmental abnormalities in infants can be attributed causally and specifically to maternal use of cocaine or crack. In both fetuses and adults, the relatively large safety margin associated with cocaine is probably linked to humans' extensive homeostatic responses to stimulant drugs—protective mechanisms confirmed by pharmacological science but rarely even mentioned by those interested in publicizing cocaine's harms.

Cocaine does not produce physical dependence, and babies are not born addicted to this drug. Numerous studies have shown that laboratory animals can be manipulated to self-administer cocaine repeatedly, but such studies provide very little insight into cocaine's addictive potential in humans. Among humans, cocaine addiction is relatively rare as a proportion of the total number of people who have tried it, regardless of the form in which the drug is employed. Early claims that smokeable cocaine caused instant addiction were clearly wrong. In fact, there is no evidence that the rapid onset/rapid decline of effect associated with smoking makes addiction or even escalated use inevitable. As Reinarman et al. suggest in Chapter 4, smoking may increase the likelihood that cocaine users will engage in bingeing. But it may also turn out that the problems associated with such bingeing may move crack users—"drug dependent" or not—more quickly toward quitting or curtailing their use. Because the excessive use of a drug over a short period of time is likely to cause more individual and social dysfunction than moderate use over a long period of time, the tendency of crack users to binge means that crack can be viewed as more risky than powder cocaine. However, it is important keep in mind that many crack users take the drug occasionally, do not engage in prolonged binges, and do not become dysfunctional.

We have argued that the route of cocaine administration matters less than the public has been led to believe—a conclusion based on comparing smoking and sniffing, the two modes of ingestion most prevalent in American society. The practice of swallowing cocaine, although not free from abuse potential, almost certainly provides users with a substantially wider safety margin. Of course, swallowing is also a more "inefficient" way to consume a drug, and under a system of drug prohibition, such milder (and more "expensive") modes of ingestion tend to disappear. In this sense, the emergence of crack is part of a general trend that has been operating since cocaine prohibition was put into place early in the twentieth century. Fortunately, this more efficient mode of ingesting cocaine has not dramatically increased the risks associated with its use. Although there *are* risks involved in using crack, they have been consistently exaggerated. As the other chapters in Part I of this book demonstrate, most of the problems associated with crack are products of the social context in which it arose and is used, not its pharmacological powers or "efficient" route of administration.

NOTES

The authors acknowledge the valuable help of Lester Grinspoon, M.D., and Michael R. Aldrich, Ph.D.

1. For a more complete history of cocaine in the U.S. prior to the introduction of crack, see Grinspoon and Bakalar (1985).

2. Some artists included cocaine in their work. For example, in the 1930s film classic *Modern Times,* Charlie Chaplin's "little tramp" accidentally consumed cocaine and became a hero when, energized by the substance, he single-handedly stopped a jailbreak.

3. Inciardi (1992) notes that without the building of new highways in Peru, making transport across the Andes Mountains easier, cocaine supplies to the U.S. could not have grown as they did. See also Morales (1989).

4. For a more detailed description of freebase production, see Raye (1980).

5. Injecting cocaine also produces "more effect for the money," but generally only highly committed users inject. Because crack is "smokeable," it appealed to users who are reluctant to inject any drug.

6. For example, in July 1981, *Time* magazine ran a story identifying cocaine as a drug of the "rich and famous."

7. Only recently have medical scientists become more interested in cocaine. In 1984, only 89 articles on cocaine were listed in the *Cumulated Index Medicus.* In 1989, the number was 426 and in 1992, 842. "Crack" was added as a separate category in 1992 and 45 articles were listed.

8. See, for example, documents published by the National Institute on Drug Abuse (NIDA, 1990, 1991e, 1991f, 1991g, 1991h). All focus on the hazards of cocaine, none reports the drug's margin of safety, and none discusses the possibility of controlled use.

9. Drug tales take on the character of folkloric horror narratives that can be told either with or without the drug theme. They usually focus on the drug user as crazed, dangerous, possessed of superhuman strength, sexually rapacious, and from a different social class or race than the teller of the tale (Brecher et al., 1988; Morgan and Kagan, 1980).

10. We would make the same argument for nonpsychoactive drugs. For example, pharmacology can describe *how* aspirin works to reduce pain, but it cannot explain why some people choose to endure pain and avoid its use; why some people take aspirin at the first sign of pain, while others wait for pain to escalate; or why others take aspirin when they are not experiencing pain at all.

11. An extreme example of the autonomic nervous system's capacity quickly to increase the release of neurotransmitters is when the organism is faced with danger and survival requires it to "fight" or "flee." Increased neurotransmitter activity stimulates the heart to beat faster and more forcefully and heightens the nervous system's responses to stimuli.

12. Two other neurotransmitters that are known to play a role in operation of the autonomic nervous system are serotonin and norepinephrine. Less is known about their activity, but cocaine probably interacts with them, too, to produce or modulate its stimulant effects.

13. All stimulant drugs work by interacting with this system, although in somewhat different ways. For example, the drug bromocriptine, which is used to treat Parkinson's disease, produces an effect by binding directly to and activating the nerve cell's receptors for dopamine. Other stimulants (*e.g.,* amphetamine) work by entering the nerve cell and "displacing" the body's own neurotransmitters—forcing their release at a faster pace and making more available for binding to receptor sites on neighboring cells. Cocaine works more indirectly, blocking the nerve cell's ordinary "reuptake" of neurotransmitters once they have performed their function and are released from the receptor site; these neurotransmitters thus remain in the space between cells (the synapse) and are available for additional activation of receptors.

14. Drug molecules diffuse into cells based, in part, on their lipid solubility. The cell membrane is largely lipid (fatty) in character, and drugs behave as if they were dissolving in the membrane to pass through it. Thus, the likelihood that a drug molecule will enter cells is reflected in its likelihood to dissolve in lipid, nonhydrous solvents (ether, toluene, carbon tetrachloride). Plant alkaloids (compounds containing a nitrogen, including cocaine, mescaline, morphine, ibogaine, ephedrine, and atropine) generally have rapid cell penetration, making possible rapid psychopharmacological activity.

15. Both *time to onset* of effect and *peak concentration* of effect are quite similar for inhalation and injection (Jones, 1984). Some cocaine users report a slightly quicker onset of effect with inhalation (Inciardi, 1992; Miller et al., 1989; Weil, 1986), but if this is the case , it is a difference of only a few seconds.

16. Laboratory detection of the by-product benzoylecognine allows identification of cocaine users, through urinalysis, for up to seventy-two hours following use—even longer for heavy users (Weiss, 1988).

17. Pharmacologists identify the time it takes for blood concentrations to decline to half a previous concentration as a drug's "half-life." Cocaine's half-life is thirty to sixty minutes, which also approximates its duration of effect.

18. Among the known mechanisms of "acute tolerance" to cocaine—in the neural system—are "down-regulation" of dopamine receptors (leaving fewer available for binding) and "autoinhibition" of the nerve cell's dopamine excretion process. Outside the brain, other homeostatic adjustments occur; for example, a "baroreceptor" in the neck senses the rise in blood pressure caused by cocaine, as it does for other reasons, and relays a message to the brain to diminish cardiovascular activity. These mechanisms are effective enough so that, in experiments in which cocaine is continuously injected to maintain a constant blood concentration, both mood elevation and increased heart rate disappear within four hours (Ambre et al., 1988).

19. Acute tolerance to a drug may develop during a single episode of use and occurs in the presence of bodily mechanisms that counter or compensate for the drug's effects. Cocaine produces an acute rather than a chronic tolerance. Therefore, when people stop using it, for even a few hours, responsiveness begins to return. However, the impact of additional doses of cocaine, consumed while the body is actively countering the effects of the earlier dose, will be diminished. By consuming continuously larger subsequent doses of cocaine, users might come

close to re-creating the effects of the original dose, but at some point, acute tolerance may be so nearly complete that even extremely high doses produce little effect.

20. Under the influence of cocaine, people may perform various cognitive and motor tasks more quickly and effectively. There is no research on cocaine's impacts on performance, and it is unlikely that it would be funded by NIDA or other government bodies. There is evidence that amphetamine and caffeine can enhance performance in athletics and other endeavors (Laties and Weiss, 1982; Weiss and Laties, 1962).

21. See, for example, "Users of Crack Cocaine Link Violence to Drug's Influence," *Washington Post,* March 24, 1989, p. A11; "Capital Offers a Rare Market to Drug Dealers," *New York Times,* March 28, 1989, p. A1; "Crack Murder: A Detective Story," *New York Times Magazine,* February 15, 1987, p. 29; "Crack and Crime," *Newsweek,* June 16, 1986, pp. 16–22.

22. For example, Fagan and Chin (1990) found few differences in the criminal histories of crack and cocaine powder users. Corman et al. (1991) found no evidence of an increase in homicide rates specifically related to the introduction of crack. And Goldstein and his colleagues in Chapter 6 of this volume show that almost none of the homicides identified by the police as crack related were due to its pharmacological effects; in fact, most were due to the unregulated (thus often violent) illicit crack market.

23. Taken together, alcohol and cocaine generate production of cocaethylene, a toxic condensation product that, like cocaine, prevents the reuptake of dopamine and norepinephrine, thereby increasing their synaptic concentrations. That cocaethylene biodegrades more slowly than cocaine makes it potentially more dangerous than cocaine (Bailey, 1993; Jatlow et al., 1991).

24. In a study of 137 cocaine users seeking admittance to an emergency room, Derlet and Albertson (1989) found that the most common complaint (29%) was an "altered mental state." Most remaining patients reported at least one physical symptom commonly associated with cocaine, but this does not necessarily mean that they suffered physical harm or really needed medical treatment.

25. This may be why nearly 60% of the cocaine users who entered emergency rooms in 1990 left without being admitted to the hospital (NIDA, 1991d). Because cocaine's effects wear off quickly, the symptoms that bring users to emergency rooms may disappear before they can be officially admitted.

26. The additional problems include frequent changes in the panel of reporting hospitals; only recently has NIDA decided that the sampling adequately reflects national trends. In addition, we believe that the training of those who collect the data bias the process toward inflating drug mentions, as does the failure to confirm drug mentions toxicologically. We know, for example, that the availability of amphetamine look-alikes makes self-reports of amphetamine use unreliable (Morgan et al., 1987).

27. For a more in-depth examination of possible reasons for the incongruence between the DAWN data and the national drug use data, see Harrison (1992).

28. Using the DAWN data, Adams et al. (1990) and Gampel (1992) found that crack users were overrepresented, but this finding is questionable because, for a

large majority of the emergency room visits attributed to cocaine, there was no evidence of route of administration in the record (NIDA, 1991d).

29. This race/class difference can also be seen in the DAWN statistics: in 1988, although accounting for only 37% of past-month crack users and 15% of past-month cocaine users, blacks made up 48% of cocaine-related emergency room episodes (Gampel, 1992).

30. Olds and Milner (1954), who first identified a structural substrate for "reward," showed that animals will repeatedly self-administer electrical shocks if electrodes are planted in certain areas of the brain. Because giving animals some stimulant drugs (including cocaine) causes a reduction in the voltage required to maintain self-administered shocks, it is assumed these drugs operate within the same system. For more recent research in this area, see Gardner (1992).

31. Drugs that people do not experience as pleasurable have little "abuse potential." For example, antipsychotic drugs, such as chlorpromazine, are almost never used recreationally, and people who take them under medical supervision do not "crave" them when use is discontinued, even in the face of a withdrawal syndrome (Jaffe, 1990). In fact, it is often patients' unwillingness to sustain use of nonpleasurable psychoactive drugs, rather than patients' overuse, that is defined as a problem (Weintraub, 1975).

32. For variations on this biochemical determinism theme, see Dackis and Gold (1985), Gawin and Ellinwood (1988), Gold et al. (1985), Nahas (1989), Spitz and Rosecan (1987), Washton and Gold (1984).

33. For example, an article from *Newsweek* (June 16, 1986, p. 17) announces that "when smoked, cocaine molecules reach the brain in less than 10 seconds; the resulting euphoric high is followed by a crushing depression. The cycle of ups and downs reinforces the craving and, according to many experts, can produce a chemical dependency within two weeks."

34. Other studies have confirmed these findings for cocaine and other stimulants (Johanson et al., 1976; Yanagita et al., 1973). To our knowledge, no later study has reproduced the twelve thousand lever pushes, and some studies of "extinction" have reported many fewer pushes prior to cessation (Griffith et al., 1979).

35. This interaction experiment highlights the need for isolation in IV injection studies. The apparatus customarily employed will be inspected, bitten, and disrupted by another animal placed in the cage.

36. The Partnership ad corrupts the animal study even further by depicting a rat just prior to death drinking water "laced with cocaine." Again, to cause rats to die from cocaine, researchers must limit their food, tether them to an injection apparatus, provide unlimited access to cocaine, and eliminate all alternative stimuli and activities—conditions virtually never present in human life.

37. There had, however, been some research on cocaine's fetal impacts in rats and mice (*e.g.,* Fantel and Macphail 1982; Mahalik et al., 1980, 1984).

38. Giving animals a dose comparable to that consumed by humans decreases substantially the probability that researchers will find a drug effect. Thus, they escalate doses to whatever level is necessary to achieve an effect—which is one reason why they so often find effects.

39. This quote comes from the *Readers' Digest.* See Yeager (1991).

40. See, for example, the importance of the crack baby story in the remarks of antireform participants at the Hoover Institution's Conference on U.S. Drug Policy held at Stanford University in 1990 (see Hay, 1991; Peterson, 1991; Rosenthal, 1991).

41. This may be typical of journalists. For example, Koren and Klein (1991) searched major newspapers for coverage of two radiation damage studies published in the same issue of the *Journal of the American Medical Association*—one with positive and one with negative findings. The study finding harm was given considerably more attention.

42. This result is all the more remarkable given that studies failing to find any adverse cocaine effects had been systematically excluded from the medical science literature (Koren et al., 1989). Thus, if Lutiger et al.'s findings contain any bias, it is probably in the direction of exaggerating—not minimizing—cocaine's effects.

43. Although vasoconstriction is generally thought to be detrimental, it may be cocaine's *initial* vasoconstrictive action in the umbilical cord and placenta that protects the fetus from receiving an even larger dose of active cocaine from the mother. Thus, even if cocaine is potentially teratogenic, the actual occurrence of cellular damage, resulting in malformation, may be quite rare. Clearly, the incidence of congenital abnormality is much lower in humans than in rats—which suggests that the capacity of the human placenta to metabolize drugs also plays a role in protecting human fetuses from harm. In fact, the only physical defect consistently found in cocaine-exposed babies is genitourinary malformation (Chasnoff et al., 1988; Chavez et al., 1989; Rosenstein et al., 1990)—and even this relationship may be spurious because these studies do not adequately control for the use of other drugs.

44. A similar conclusion has been reached regarding fetal abnormalities found in offspring of heroin users: the cumulative effects of the addict's lifestyle are more detrimental than heroin itself (Alexander et al., 1985; Forfar and Nelson, 1973; Neumann, 1973).

45. Most of the research does not distinguish between crack and powder users. Wang et al. (1985) suggest that absorption of drugs through inhalation may be enhanced during pregnancy, but there is as yet no evidence that this alters a drug's impact on the fetus.

REFERENCES

Adams, E. H. Blanken, A. J. Ferguson, L. D. Kopstein, A. 1990. *Overview of Selected Drug Trends.* Rockville, MD: National Institute on Drug Abuse. Pp. 1–7.

Aldrich, M. R. Barker, R. W. 1976. Historical aspects of cocaine use and abuse. In: Mule, S. J. (ed.). *Cocaine: Chemical and Treatment Aspects.* Cleveland: CRC Press. Pp. 3–11.

Alexander, B. K. 1990. *Peaceful Measures: Canada's Way Out of the "War on Drugs."* Toronto: University of Toronto Press.

Alexander, B. K. Beyerstein, B. L. Hadaway, P. R. 1981. Effects of early and later colony housing on oral ingestion of morphine in rats. *Pharmacology Biochemistry and Behavior* 15:571–576.

Alexander, B. K. Peele, S. Hadaway, P. F. Morse, S. J. Brodsky, A. Beyerstein, B. L. 1985. Adult, infant, and animal addiction. In: Peele, S. (ed.). *The Meaning of Addiction.* Lexington, MA: Lexington Books. Pp. 73–96.

Ambre, J. J. Belknap, S. M. Nelson, J. Tsuen, I. R. Shin, S. G. Atkinson, A. J. 1988. Acute tolerance to cocaine in humans. *Clinical Pharmacology and Therapeutics* 44:1–8.

Amon, C. A. Tate, L. G. Wright, R. K. Matusiak, W. 1986. Sudden death due to ingestion of cocaine. *Journal of Analytical Toxicology* 10:217–218.

Anthony, J. C. 1991. Epidemiology of drug addiction. In: Miller, N. S. (ed.). *Comprehensive Handbook of Drug and Alcohol Addiction.* New York: Marcel Dekker. Pp. 55–73.

Antonil (Henman, A.). 1978. *Mama Coca.* London: Hassle Free Press.

Ashley, R. 1976. *Cocaine: Its History, Uses and Effects.* New York: Warner Books.

Bachman, J. G. Wallace, J. M. O'Malley, P. M. Johnston, L. D. Kurth, C. L. Neighbors, H. W. 1991a. Racial/ethnic differences in smoking, drinking, and illicit drug use among high school seniors. *American Journal of Public Health* 81:372–377.

Bachman, J. G. Johnston, L. D. O'Malley, P. M. 1991b. *Monitoring the Future: Questionnaire Responses from the Nation's High School Seniors, 1988.* Ann Arbor: Institute for Social Research, University of Michigan.

Bailey, D. N. 1993. Serial plasma concentrations of cocaethylene, cocaine and ethanol in trauma victims. *Journal of Analytical Toxicology* 17:79–83.

Bakalar, J. B. Grinspoon, L. 1984. *Drug Control in a Free Society.* Cambridge, England: Cambridge University Press.

Benowitz, N. 1992. How toxic is cocaine? In: Edwards, G. (ed.). *Cocaine: Scientific and Social Dimensions.* Chichester, England: Wiley. Pp. 125–148.

Berrien, J. 1990. Pregnancy and drug use: The dangerous and unequal use of punitive measures. *Yale Journal of Law and Feminism* 2:239–250.

Bozarth, M. A. 1988. New perspectives on cocaine addiction: Recent findings from animal research. *Canadian Journal of Physiology and Pharmacology* 67:1158–1167.

Bozarth, M. A. Wise, R. A. 1985. Toxicity associated with long-term intravenous heroin and cocaine self-administration in the rat. *Journal of the American Medical Association* 254:81–83.

Brady, J. V. Griffiths, R. R. 1976. Behavioral procedures for evaluating the relative abuse potential of CNS drugs in primates. *Federation Proceedings* 35:2245–2253.

Brecher, E. M. 1972. *Licit and Illicit Drugs.* Boston: Little, Brown.

Brecher, M. Wang, B. W. Wong, H. Morgan, J. P. 1988. Phencyclidine and violence: Clinical and legal issues. *Journal of Clinical Psychopharmacology* 8:397–401.

Carroll, M. E. France, C. P. Meisch, R. A. 1979. Food deprivation increases oral and intravenous drug intake in rats. *Science* 205:319–321.

Carroll, M. E. Lac, S. T. Nygaard, S. T. 1989. A concurrently available nondrug reinforcer prevents the acquisition or decreases the maintenance of cocaine-reinforced behavior. *Psychopharmacology* 97:23–29.

Chasnoff, I. J. Burns, W. J. Schnoll, S. H. Burns, K. A. 1985. Cocaine use in pregnancy. *New England Journal of Medicine* 313:666–669.

Chasnoff, I. J. Chisum, G. M. Kaplan, W. E. 1988. Maternal cocaine use and genitourinary tract malformations. *Teratology* 37:201–204.

Chasnoff, I. J. Griffith, D. R. Freier, C. Murray, J. 1992. Cocaine/polydrug use in pregnancy: Two-year follow up. *Pediatrics* 89:284–289.

Chavez, G. F. Mulinare, J. Cordero, J. F. 1989. Maternal cocaine use during early pregnancy as a risk factor for congenital urogenital anomalies. *Journal of the American Medical Association* 262:795–798.

Chavkin, W. 1991. Mandatory treatment for drug use during pregnancy. *Journal of the American Medical Association* 266:1556–1561.

Chiang, C. N. Lee, C. (eds.). 1985. *Prenatal Drug Exposure: Kinetics and Dynamics.* Rockville, MD: National Institute on Drug Abuse.

Chira, S. 1990. Crack babies turn 5, schools brace. *New York Times,* May 25, p. A1.

Cohen, P. D. A. 1989. *Cocaine Use in Amsterdam in Non-Deviant Subcultures.* Amsterdam, Netherlands: University of Amsterdam Press.

Cohn, V. 1986. Crack use. *NIDA Notes* 4:6–7.

Corman, H. Joyce, T. Mocan, N. 1991. Homicide and crack in New York City. In: Krauss, M. B. Lazear, E. P. (eds.). *Searching for Alternatives: Drug-Control Policy in the United States.* Stanford, CA: Hoover Institute Press. Pp. 112–137.

Courtwright, D. 1982. *Dark Paradise: Opiate Addiction in America before 1940.* Cambridge, MA: Harvard University Press.

———. 1991. The first American cocaine epidemic. *Crack-Cocaine Research Working Group Newsletter* 1:3–5.

Cowan, R. C. 1986. How the narcs created crack. *National Review,* December 5, pp. 26–31.

Cregler, T. J. Mark, H. 1986. Medical complications of cocaine abuse. *New England Journal of Medicine* 315:1495–1500.

Dackis, C. A. Gold, M. S. 1985. New concepts in cocaine addiction: The dopamine depletion hypothesis. *Neurosciences Biobehavioral Review* 9:469–477.

Deneau, G. Yanagita, T. Seevers, M. H. 1969. Self-administration of psychoactive substances by the monkey: A measure of psychological dependence. *Psychopharmalogia* 16:30–48.

Derlet, R. W. Albertson, T. E. 1989. Emergency department presentation of cocaine intoxication. *Annals of Emergency Medicine* 18:182–186.

Devenyi, P. 1989. Cocaine complications and pseudocholinesterase. *Annals of Internal Medicine* 110:167–168.

Edwards, C. N. 1974. *Drug Dependence: Social Regulation and Treatment Alternatives.* New York. Jason Aronson.

Erickson, P. G. Adlaf, E. M. Murray, G. F. Smart, R. G. 1987. *The Steel Drug: Cocaine in Perspective.* Lexington, MA: Lexington Books.

Fagan, J. A. Chin, K. 1989. Initiation into crack and cocaine: A tale of two epidemics. *Contemporary Drug Problems* 16: 579–617.

———. 1990. Violence as regulation and social control in the distribution of crack. In: de la Roza, M. Gropper, B. Lambert, E. C. (eds.). *Drugs and Violence.* Rockville, MD: National Institute on Drug Abuse. Pp. 8–39.

Fantel, A. G. Macphail, B. J. 1982. The teratogenicity of cocaine. *Teratology* 26:17–19.

Finkle, B. S. McCloskey, K. L. 1978. The forensic toxicology of cocaine (1971–1976). *Journal of Forensic Science* 23:173–189.

Finnell, R. H. Toloyan, S. VanWaes, M. 1990. Preliminary evidence for a cocaine-induced embryopathy in mice. *Toxicology and Applied Pharmacology* 103:228–237.

Fischman, M. W. 1988. Behavioral pharmacology of cocaine. *Journal of Clinical Psychiatry* 49:7–10.

Fischman, M. W. Schuster, C. R. Hatano, Y. 1983. A comparison of the subjective and cardiovascular effects of cocaine and lidocaine in humans. *Pharmacology Biochemistry and Behavior* 18:123–127.

Fischman, M. W. Schuster, C. R. Javaid, J. I. Hatano, Y. Davis, J. 1985. Acute tolerance development to the cardiovascular and subjective effects of cocaine. *Journal of Pharmacology and Experimental Therapeutics* 235:677–682.

Forfar, J. O. Nelson, M. M. 1973. Epidemiology of drugs taken by pregnant women: Drugs that may affect the fetus adversely. *Clinical Pharmacology and Therapeutics* 14:632–642.

Forno, J. J. Young, R. T. Levitt, C. 1981. Cocaine abuse: the evolution from coca leaves to freebase. *Journal of Drug Education* 11:311–315.

Gampel, J. C. 1992. Trends in drug-related emergency room mentions in DAWN: 1988–1991. Paper presented at the Drugs, Medicine & Health Conference. Drug Policy Foundation. Washington, DC, November.

Gardner, E. L. 1992. Brain reward mechanisms. In: Lowinson, J. H. Ruiz, P. Millman, R. B. Langrod, J. G. (eds.). *Substance Abuse: A Comprehensive Textbook*. Baltimore: Williams & Wilkins. Pp. 70–99.

Gawin, F. H. Ellinwood, E. 1988. Cocaine and other stimulants: Actions, abuse, and treatment. *New England Journal of Medicine* 318: 1173–1183.

Gawin, F. H. Kleber, H. D. 1986. Abstinence symptomatology and psychiatric diagnosis in cocaine abusers. *Archives of General Psychiatry* 43:107–113.

Gladwell, M. 1986. A new addiction to an old story. *Washington Times Insight* 2(43):8–12.

Gold, M. S. 1984. *800-Cocaine*. New York: Bantam Books.

Gold, M. S. Dackis, C. A. Pottash, A. L. Extein, I. Washton, A. R. 1986. Cocaine update: From bench to bedside. *Advances in Alcohol and Substance Abuse* 5:35–60.

Gold, M. S. Washton, A. M. Dackis, C. A. 1985. Cocaine abuse: Neurochemistry, phenomenology, and treatment. In: Kozel, N. J. Adams, E. H. (eds.). *Cocaine Use in America: Epidemiologic and Clinical Perspectives*. Rockville, MD: National Institute on Drug Abuse. Pp. 130–150.

Goldstein, P. F. Brownstein, H. H. Ryan, P. J. Bellucci, P. A. 1989. Crack and homicide in New York City: A conceptually-based event analysis. *Contemporary Drug Problems* 16:651–687.

Graham, K. Feigenbaum, A. Pastuszak, A. Nulman, I. Weksberg, R. Einarson, T. Goldberg, S. Ashley, S. Koren, G. 1992. Pregnancy outcome and infant development following gestational cocaine use by social cocaine users in Toronto, Canada. *Clinical Investigations and Medicine* 15:384–394.

Graham, K. Koren, G. 1991. Characteristics of pregnant women exposed to cocaine in Toronto between 1985 and 1990. *Canadian Medical Association Journal* 144: 563–588.

Griffiths, R. R. Bradford, L. D. Brady, J. V. 1979. Progressive ratios and fixed ratio schedules of cocaine-maintained responding in baboons. *Psychopharmacology* 65:125–136.

Grinspoon, L. Bakalar, J. B. 1985. *Cocaine: A Drug and Its Social Evolution* (rev. ed.). New York: Basic Books.

Hadeed, A. J. Siegel, S. R. 1989. Maternal cocaine use during pregnancy: Effect on the newborn infant. *Pediatrics* 84:205–210.

Hamid, A. 1990. The political economy of crack-related violence. *Contemporary Drug Problems* 17:31–78.

———. 1992. Drugs and patterns of opportunity in the inner city: The case of middle-aged, middle-income cocaine smokers. In: Harrell, A. V. Peterson, G. E. (eds.). *Drugs, Crime, and Social Isolation.* New York: The Urban Institute Press. Pp. 209–240.

Harrison, L. O. 1992. Trends in illicit drug use in the United States: Conflicting results from national surveys. *International Journal of the Addictions* 27:817–847.

Hay, J. W. 1991. The harm they do to others: A primer on the external costs of drug abuse. In: Kraus, M. B. Lazear, E. P. (eds.). *Searching for Alternatives: Drug-Control Policy in the United States.* Stanford, CA: Hoover Institution Press. Pp. 200–225.

Henman, A. R. 1990. Coca and cocaine: Their role in "traditional" cultures in South America. *Journal of Drug Issues* 20: 577–588.

Honer, W. G. Gewirtz, G. Turey, M. 1987. Psychosis and violence in cocaine smokers. *Lancet* 2(8556):451.

Inciardi, J. A. 1987. Beyond cocaine: Basuco, crack, and coca products. *Contemporary Drug Problems* 14: 461–493.

———. 1992. *The War on Drugs II.* Mountain View, CA: Mayfield.

Isaacs, S. O. Martin, P. Willoughby, J. H. 1987. Crack (an extra potent form of cocaine) abuse; a problem of the eighties. *Oral Surgery, Oral Medicine, and Oral Pathology.* 63:12–16.

Isner, J. M. Ester, N.A. M. Thompson, P. D. Costanzo-Nordin, M. R. Subramanian, R. Miller, G. Katsas, G. Sweeney, K. Sturner, W. Q. 1986. Acute cardiac events temporally related to cocaine abuse. *New England Journal of Medicine* 315:1438–1443.

Jaffe, J. H. 1990. Drug addiction and drug abuse. In: Gilman, H. G. Rall, T. W. Nies, A. S. Taylor, P. (eds.). *Goodman and Gilman's The Pharmacological Basis of Therapeutics* (8th ed.). New York: Pergamon Press. Pp. 522–573.

Jatlow, P. Elsworth, J. D. Bradberry, C. W. Winger, G. Taylor, J. R. Russell, R. Roth, R. H. 1991. Cocaethylene: A neuropharmacologically active metabolite associated with concurrent cocaine-ethanol ingestion. *Life Sciences* 48:1787–1794.

Jekel, J. F. Allen, D. F. Podlewski, H. 1986. Epidemic freebase cocaine abuse: Case study from the Bahamas. *Lancet* 8479:459–462.

Jeri, F. R. Sanchez, C. C. DelPozo, T. D. Fernandez, M. 1978. The syndrome of coca paste. *Journal of Psychedelic Drugs.* 10:361–370.

Johanson, C. E. Balster, R. L. Bonese, K. 1976. Self-administration of psychomotor stimulant drugs: The effects of unlimited access. *Pharmacology Biochemistry and Behavior* 4:45–51.

Johanson, C. E. Fischman, M. W. 1989. The pharmacology of cocaine related to its abuse. *Pharmacological Reviews* 41:3–52.

Johnson, B. Muffler, J. 1992. Sociocultural aspects of drug use and abuse in the

1990's. In: Lowinson, J. Ruiz, P. Millman, R. B. Langrod, J. A. (eds.). *Substance Abuse: A Comprehensive Textbook.* Baltimore, Williams & Wilkins. Pp. 118–137.

Johnston, L. D. O'Malley, P. M. Bachman, J. G. 1991. *Drug Use, Drinking and Smoking: National Survey Results from High School, College and Young Adult Population 1975–1990.* Rockville, MD: National Institute on Drug Abuse.

Jones, R. T. 1984. The pharmacology of cocaine. In: Grabowski, J. (ed.). *Cocaine: Pharmacology, Effects, and Treatment of Abuse.* Rockville, MD: National Institute on Drug Abuse. Pp. 34–53.

Juchau, M. R. 1976. Drug biotransformation reactions in the placenta. In: Mirkin, B. L. (ed.). *Perinatal Pharmacology and Therapeutics.* New York: Academic Press. Pp. 71–118.

———. 1985. Biotransformation of drugs and foreign chemicals in the human fetal-placenta unit. In: Chiang, C. N. Lee, C. C. (eds.). *Prenatal Drug Exposure: Kinetics and Dynamics.* Rockville, MD: National Institute on Drug Abuse. Pp. 17–24.

Kandall, S. R. 1991. Physician dispels myths about drug-exposed infants. *Crack-Cocaine Research Working Group Newsletter* 2:7–8.

Kandel, D. B. 1991. The social demography of drug use. *Milbank Quarterly* 69:365–414.

Kandel, D. B. Murphy, D. Karus, D. 1985. Cocaine use in young adulthood: Patterns of use and psychosocial correlates. In: Kozel, N. J. Adams, E. H. *Cocaine Use in America: Epidemiologic and Clinical Perspectives.* Rockville, MD: National Institute on Drug Abuse. Pp. 76–110.

Karch, S. 1992. More on cocaethylene. *Forensic Drug Abuse Advisor* 4:35–36.

Kleiman, M. 1992. *Against Excess: Drug Policy for Results.* New York: Basic Books.

Koren, G. Feldman, Y. MacLeod, S. M. 1990. Motherisk II: Analysis of the first year of counseling women on drug, chemical and radiation exposure in pregnancy. In: Koren, G. (ed.). *Maternal Fetal Toxicology.* New York: Marcel Dekker. Pp. 383–402.

Koren, G. Graham, K. Shear, H. Einarson, T. 1989. Bias against the null hypothesis: The reproductive hazards of cocaine. *Lancet* 2:1440–1442.

Koren, G. Klein, N. 1991. Bias against negative studies in newspaper reports of medical research. *Journal of the American Medical Association* 266:1824–1826.

Kusserow, R. 1990. *Crack Babies: Report of the Office of the Inspector General.* Washington, DC: Department of Health and Human Services.

Laties, V. G. Weiss, B. 1982. Performance enhancement by the amphetamines. *Proceedings of the 5th Congress of the Collegium International Neuro-psychopharmacology.* Reprinted: Excerpta Medica International Congress Series 129.

Lazare, D. 1990. How the drug war created crack. *Village Voice,* January 23, pp. 22–28.

Leary, W. E. 1993. Scientists create an enzyme that may curb addiction to cocaine. *New York Times,* March 16, p. A18.

Lundberg, G. D. Garriott, J. C. Reynolds, P. C. Cravey, R. H. Shaw, R. F. 1977. Cocaine-related death. *Journal of Forensic Sciences* 22:402–408.

Lutiger, B. Graham, K. Einarson, T. R. Koren, G. 1991. Relationship between gestational cocaine use and pregnancy outcome: A meta-analysis. *Teratology* 44:405–414.

MacAndrew, C. Edgerton, R. 1969. *Drunken Comportment.* Chicago: Aldine.

Mahalik, M. P. Gautieri, R. F. Mann, D. E. 1980. Teratogenic potential of cocaine hydocholoride in CF-1 mice. *Journal of Pharmaceutical Sciences* 69:703–706.

———. 1984. Mechanisms of cocaine-induced teratogenesis. *Research Communications in Substance Abuse* 5:279–302.

Martz, L. 1990. A dirty drug secret. *Newsweek,* February 19, pp. 74–77.

Mayes, L. C. 1992. Prenatal cocaine exposure and young children's development. *Annals of the American Academy of Political and Social Sciences* 521:11–27.

Mayes, L. C. Granger, R. Bornstein, M. Zuckerman, B. 1992. The problem of prenatal cocaine exposure: A rush to judgement. *Journal of the American Medical Association* 267:406–408.

McNeil, D. 1992. Why there's no methadone for crack. *New York Times,* June 14, p. E7.

Miller, N. S. Gold, M. S. Millman, R. L. 1989. Cocaine. *American Family Physician* 39:115–120.

Miller, R. K. Kellogg, C. K. 1985. The pharmacology of prenatal chemical exposure. In: Chiang, C. N. Lee, C. C. (eds.). *Prenatal Drug Exposure: Kinetics and Dynamics.* Rockville, MD: National Institute on Drug Abuse. Pp. 39–57.

Millman, R. B. 1991. Comment. In: Krauss, M. B. Lazear, E. P. (eds.). *Searching for Alternatives: Drug Control Policy in the United States.* Stanford, CA: Hoover Institution Press. Pp. 435–440.

Mittleman, R. E. Wetli, C. V. 1987. Cocaine and sudden "natural" death. *Journal of Forensic Sciences* 32:11–19.

Mody, C. K. Miller, H. B. McIntyre, S. K. Cobb, S. K. Goldberg, M. A. 1988. Neurological complications of cocaine use. *Neurology* 38:1189–1193.

Morales, E. 1989. *Cocaine: White Gold Rush in Peru.* Tucson: University of Arizona Press.

Morgan, H. W. 1981. *Drugs in America: A Social History, 1800–1980.* Syracuse, NY: Syracuse University Press.

Morgan, J. P. Kagan, D. 1978. Street amphetamine quality and the Controlled Substances Act of 1970. *Journal of Psychedelic Drugs* 10:303–317.

———. 1980. The dusting of America: The image of phencyclidine (PCP) in popular media. *Journal of Psychoactive Drugs* 41:583–586.

Morgan, J. P. Wesson, D. R. Puder, K. S. Smith, D. E. 1987. Duplicitous drugs: The history and recent status of look-alike drugs. *Journal of Psychoactive Drugs* 19:21–31.

Morgan, J. P. Zimmer, L. In press. Animal self-administration of cocaine: Misinterpretation, misrepresentation, and invalid extrapolation to humans. In Erickson, P. G. et al. (eds.). *New Public Health Policies and Programs for the Reduction of Drug-Related Harm.* Toronto, Canada: University of Toronto Press.

Morley, J. 1989. Aftermath of a crack article. *The Nation,* November 20, p. 592.

Musto, D. F. 1987. *The American Disease: Origins of Narcotic Control* (exp. ed.). New Haven, CT: Yale University Press.

Nahas, G. G. 1989. *Cocaine: The Great White Plague.* Middlebury, VT: Paul S. Eriksson.

Neumann, L. L. 1973. Drug abuse in pregnancy: Its effects on the fetus and newborn infant. In: Harms, E. (ed.). *Drugs and Youth: The Challenge of Today.* New York: Pergamon Press. Pp. 1–32.

Neuspiel, D. R. Hamel, S. C. 1991. Cocaine and infant behavior. *Journal of Developmental Behavior and Pediatrics* 12:55–64.

NIDA. 1990. *Drugs and Violence: Causes, Correlates, and Consequences.* Rockville, MD: National Institute on Drug Abuse.

———. 1991a. *National Household Survey on Drug Abuse: Highlights 1990.* Rockville, MD: National Institute on Drug Abuse.

———. 1991b. *National Household Survey on Drug Abuse: Population Estimates 1991.* Rockville, MD: National Institute on Drug Abuse.

———. 1991c. *Annual Medical Examiner Data 1990: Data from the Drug Abuse Warning Network.* Rockville, MD: National Institute on Drug Abuse.

———. 1991d. *Annual Emergency Room Data 1990: Data from the Drug Abuse Warning Network.* Rockville, MD: National Institute on Drug Abuse.

———. 1991e. *Crack/Cocaine: The Big Lie.* Rockville, MD: National Institute on Drug Abuse.

———. 1991f. *Drugs and the Brain.* Rockville, MD: National Institute on Drug Abuse.

———. 1991g. *Crack/Cocaine: A Challenge for Prevention.* Rockville, MD: National Institute on Drug Abuse.

———. 1991h. *The Epidemiology of Cocaine Use and Abuse.* Rockville, MD: National Institute on Drug Abuse.

Olds, J. Milner, P. 1954. Positive reinforcement produced by electrical stimulation of septal area and other regions of rat brain. *Journal of Comprehensive Physiology and Psychology* 47:419–427.

Paltrow, L. M. 1992. Criminal prosecutions against pregnant women. *Reproductive Freedom Project of the American Civil Liberties Union.* New York: American Civil Liberties Union.

Parker, S. Zuckerman, B. Bauchner, H. Frank, D. Vinci, R. Cabral, H. 1990. Jitteriness in full-term neonates: Prevalence and correlates. *Pediatrics* 85:17–23.

Peele, S. 1985. *The Meaning of Addiction: Compulsive Experience and Its Interpretation.* Lexington, MA: Lexington Books.

Pendergrast, M. 1993. *For God, Country and Coca-Cola: The Unauthorized History of the Great American Soft Drink and the Company.* New York: Charles Scribner's Sons.

Peterson, R. E. 1991. Legalization: The myth exposed. In: Krauss, M. B. Lazear, E. P. (eds.). *Searching for Alternatives: Drug-Control Policy in the United States.* Stanford, CA: Hoover Institution Press. Pp. 324–355.

Pickens, R. Thompson, T. 1968. Cocaine-reinforced behavior in rats: Effects of reinforcement magnitude and fixed-ratio size. *Journal of Pharmacology and Experimental Therapeutics* 161:122–129.

Pinkert, T. M. (ed.). 1985. *Current Research on the Consequences of Maternal Drug Abuse.* Rockville, MD: National Institute on Drug Abuse.

Prendergast, M. L. Austin, G. A. Maton, K. I. Baker, R. 1989. *Substance Abuse Among Black Youth.* Madison: Wisconsin Clearinghouse, University of Wisconsin.

Raye, D. 1980. *Pipe Dreams: An Inside Look at Free-Base Cocaine.* Cotati, CA: The Family Publishing Company.

Reinarman, C. Levine, H. G. 1989. Crack in context: Politics and media in the making of a drug scare. *Contemporary Drug Problems* 16:535–577.

Rosenbaum, M. Murphy, S. Irwin, J. Watson, L. 1990. Women and crack: What's the real story? *The Drug Policy Letter,* March/April, p. 2.

Rosenstein, B. J. Wheeler, J. S. Heid, P. L. 1990. Congenital renal abnormalities in infants with in utero cocaine exposure. *Journal of Urology* 144:110–112.

Rosenthal, M. S. 1991. The logic of legalization: A matter of perspective. In: Krauss, M. B. Lazear, E. P. (eds.). *Searching for Alternatives: Drug-Control Policy in the United States.* Stanford, CA: Hoover Institution Press. Pp. 226–238.

Rudolph, A. M. 1985. Animal models for study of fetal drug exposure. In: Chiang, C. N. Lee, C. C. (eds.). *Prenatal Drug Exposure: Kinetics and Dynamics.* Rockville, MD: National Institute on Drug Abuse. Pp. 5–16.

Schenk, S. Lacelle, G. Gorman, K. Amit, Z. 1987. Cocaine self-administration in rats influenced by environmental conditions: Implications for the etiology of drug abuse. *Neuroscience Letters* 81:227–231.

Schuster, C. R. 1990. Statement before the Committee on the Judiciary, Subcommittee on Criminal Justice, U.S. House of Representatives. March 27.

Shaffer, H. Jones, S. 1989. *Quitting Cocaine: The Struggle Against Impulse.* Lexington, MA: Lexington Books.

Siegel, L. 1991. The criminalization of pregnant and child rearing users: An example of the American "harm maximization" program. Paper presented at the First International Conference on the Reduction of Drug Related Harm, April 1990.

Siegel, R. K. 1980. Long term effects of recreational cocaine use: A four year study. In: Jeri, F. (ed.). *Cocaine.* Lima, Peru: Pacific Press. Pp. 11–16.

———. 1982. Cocaine smoking. *Journal of Psychoactive Drugs* 14:271–359.

———. 1984. Cocaine smoking disorders. *Psychiatric Annals* 14:728–732.

Smart, R. G. Anglin, L. 1987. Do we know the lethal dose of cocaine? *Journal of Forensic Sciences* 32:303–312.

Smith, R. F. Mattran, K. M. Kurkjuan, M. F. 1989. Alterations in offspring behavior induced by chronic prenatal cocaine dosing. *Neurotoxicology and Teratology* 11:35–38.

Snyder, C. A. Wood, R. W. Graefe, J. F. Bowers, A. Magar, K. 1988. "Crack" smoke is a respirable aerosol of cocaine base. *Pharmacology Biochemistry and Behavior* 29:93–95.

Spear, L. P. Frambes, N. A. Kirstein, C. L. 1989. Determination of gestational cocaine exposure by hair analysis. *Journal of the American Medical Association* 97:427–431.

Spitz, H. R. Rosecan, J. J. 1987. *Cocaine Abuse: New Directions in Treatment and Research.* New York: Bruner/Mazel.

Spotts, J. V. Shontz, F. C. 1980. *Cocaine Users: A Representative Case Approach.* New York: Free Press.

Suarez, C. A. Arango, A. Lancelot, J. 1977. Cocaine-condom ingestion. *Journal of the American Medical Association* 238:1391–1392.

Szasz, T. 1974. *Ceremonial Chemistry: The Ritual Persecution of Drugs, Addicts, and Pushers.* Garden City, NJ: Anchor Press.

Tardiff, K. Gross, E. M. Wu, J. Stajic, M. Millman, R. 1989. Analysis of cocaine-positive fatalities. *Journal of Forensic Sciences* 34:53–63.

Toufexis, A. 1991. Innocent victims. *Time*, May 13, pp. 56–63.

Trebach, A. 1987. *The Great Drug War.* New York: Macmillan.

Van Dyke, C. Barash, P. G. Jatlow, P. Byke, R. 1976. Cocaine plasma concentrations after intranasal applications in man. *Science* 191:859–861.

Vener, A. M. Krupka, L. R. Engelmann, M. D. 1992. Drugs in the womb: College student perceptions of maternal v. fetal rights. *Journal of Drug Education* 22:15–24.

Waldorf, D. Reinarman, C. Murphy, S. 1991. *Cocaine Changes: The Experience of Using and Quitting.* Philadelphia: Temple University Press.

Wang, C. H. Schnoll, S. H. 1987. Prenatal cocaine use associated with down regulation of receptors in human placenta. *Neurotoxicology and Teratology* 9:301–330.

Wang, C. N. Rudolph, A. M. Benet, L. Z. 1985. Pharmacokinetics of drugs and metabolites in the maternal-placenta-fetal unit. In: Chiang, C. N. Lee, C. C. (eds.). *Prenatal Drug Exposure.* Rockville, MD: National Institute on Drug Abuse. Pp. 25–28.

Washton, A. M. 1989. *Cocaine Addiction: Treatment, Recovery, and Relapse Prevention.* New York: W. W. Norton.

Washton, A. M. Gold, M. S. 1984. Chronic cocaine abuse: Evidence for adverse effects on health and functioning. *Psychiatric Annals* 14:733–743.

Washton, A. M. Gold, M. S. Pottash, A. C. 1986. "Crack," an early report on a new drug epidemic. *Postgraduate Medicine* 80:52–58.

Webster, W. S. Brown-Woodman, P. D. C. 1990. Cocaine as a cause of congenital malformations of vascular origin: Experimental evidence in the rat. *Teratology* 41:689–697.

Weil, A. T. 1986. *The Natural Mind.* Boston: Houghton Mifflin.

Weintraub, M. 1975. Promoting patient compliance. *New York State Journal of Medicine* 75:2263–2266.

Weisman, A. P. 1986. I was a drug-hype junkie. *The New Republic*, October 6, pp. 14–17.

Weiss, B. Laties, V. G. 1962. Enhancement of human performance by caffeine and the amphetamines. *Pharmacological Reviews* 14:1–32.

Weiss, R. D. 1988. Protracted elimination of cocaine metabolites in long-term, high-dose cocaine abusers. *American Journal of Medicine* 85:879–880.

Weiss, R. D., Mirin, S. M. 1987. *Cocaine: The Human Danger, the Social Costs.* New York: Ballantine.

Wetli, C. V. Wright, R. K. 1979. Death caused by recreational cocaine use. *Journal of the American Medical Association* 241:2519–2522.

White House. 1989. *National Drug Control Strategy.* Washington, DC: U.S. Government Printing Office.

Williams, T. 1992. *Crack House.* Reading, MA: Addison-Wesley.

Wilson, M. C. Hitomi, M. Schuster, C. R. 1971. Psychomotor stimulant self-administration as a function of dosage per injection in the rhesus monkey. *Psychopharmacologia* 22:271–281.

Wishner, A. R. Schwarz, D. F. Grisso, J. A. Holmes, J. H. Sutton, R. L. 1991. Interpersonal violence-related injuries in an African-American community in Philadelphia. *American Journal of Public Health* 81:1474–1476.

Yanagita, T. 1973. An experimental framework for evaluation of dependence liability in various types of drugs in monkeys. *Bulletin of Narcotics* 25:57–64.

Yeager, R. 1991. Kids who can't say no. *Reader's Digest* 138 (826):66–71.

Zinberg, N. E. 1984. *Drug Set and Setting: The Basis for Controlled Intoxicant Use.* New Haven, CT: Yale University Press.

PART TWO

Crack in Comparable Societies

. . . .

If the claims of the crack scare are to be believed, it is the pernicious effects of the drug itself that lay behind its spread and its consequences, not the characteristics of users or the conditions under which they live and use it. If this were the case, then crack would have become widespread not only across the U.S., but across other countries as well. However, this has generally not been the case. In Part II, the thematic issues addressed in earlier chapters are explored by leading drug scholars from three other cultures, all advanced industrial democracies comparable to the U.S. They describe the nature and extent of crack use and its consequences in their countries and how crack and other drugs are thought of and dealt with there.

Starting closest to home, Canadian drug researchers Patricia Erickson and Yuet Cheung show in Chapter 8 that, despite Canada's proximity to the U.S., its parallel cultural trends, and the spillover of media and politics that brought them predictions of a crack epidemic, Canada has not experienced the levels of crack use found in the U.S. Nor has the little crack use that does exist been associated with the dire consequences associated with crack use in the U.S. In Chapter 9, Stephen Mugford discusses crack and other drug use in Australia. He shows that, despite the many reasons crack might have spread "down under," this has not happened. His analysis of why highlights how Australia's more just social welfare policies combined with less repressive drug control policies have created drug use contexts that are different from those in the U.S.

The final comparison society, the Netherlands, has the least punitive, most tolerant drug policies in the industrialized world. If the claims of drug warriors and other prohibitionists are even half right, then an "instantly addictive" drug like crack should have spread fastest and farthest there. Instead, as Peter Cohen shows in Chapter 10, crack use remains rare in the Netherlands, far less prevalent than in the U.S. He interprets this in the context of the history of drug use and broad social policy in the Netherlands and shows how effective income distribution policies and social services mitigate against all forms of drug abuse.

Each of these cross-cultural comparisons approaches crack issues from a slightly different angle and offers unique insights. One common theme is that in each of these similar societies crack and other hard drug abuse is less prevalent and less problematic because national policies are based on greater commitment to social justice, human services, and public health than are policies in the U.S. Taken together, these comparative cases suggest that the devastation attributed to crack use in the U.S. is largely a consequence of U.S. social and economic policies and how these shape the social settings of use and the mind-sets of users.

EIGHT

Crack Use in Canada
A Distant American Cousin

Yuet W. Cheung and Patricia G. Erickson

> *. . . the drug habit in Toronto is on the increase, but the increase has not been very remarkable. It is not an alarming increase. Canadians do not take to the habit like their American cousins. . . .*
>
> TORONTO STAR, JUNE 3, 1905 (REPRINTED IN THE TORONTO STAR, FEBRUARY 24, 1992, P. A2)

To many Canadians, their much larger American "relative" in the south is a crystal ball for forecasting forthcoming drug problems in Canada. When large American cities are reported to be plagued with a certain drug "epidemic," Canadians expect a similar epidemic to strike Canada any day. This kind of convenient referencing is not totally illusionary. Illicit drugs and their dealers recognize no geographical boundaries, and their tentacles tend to stretch as far as possible in all directions. The histories of illicit drug use and misuse in the two countries have also shown a more or less similar pattern of drug waves: heroin misuse increased in both countries in the 1950s, followed by cannabis in the 1960s and 1970s, and cocaine in the 1980s.

However, what Canadians get from the American crystal ball are mainly caricatured images of crime and drug problems in the U.S., and these images shape, or misshape, the perception of these social problems in Canada. Such a "misplacement" of images of social problems is often facilitated by the American media, especially television, to which Canadians are heavily exposed. Research has shown that Canadians tend to overestimate both the extent and seriousness of crime in Canada, perceiving that their problems are similar to those in the U.S. (Griffiths and Verdun-Jones, 1989:25), when actual crime rates and levels of violence in Canada are substantially lower than in the U.S. (Currie, 1985; Hagan, 1991:46–54). The same is true for drug abuse and drug-related crime. For example, with few exceptions, the annual rate of arrests for drug-related offenses per one hundred thousand population aged eighteen and over has always been less than two-thirds of that in the U.S.[1] Epidemiological surveys of student and adult populations in the U.S. and Canada show rates of cocaine use in the U.S. three or four times higher than in Canada (Erickson et al., 1987:43–52).

Canada's lower rates of drug abuse and crime can be attributed in part to Canada's more extensive welfare system, including universal medical care, and in part to a national race relations policy of multiculturalism. Together, these social policies minimize the formation of a large, poverty-stricken underclass in inner-city ghettos in which certain racial groups (such as African-Americans and Latinos in the U.S.) are overrepresented. The low level of criminality and the relative lack of inner-city problems mitigate against drug abuse in Canada (Smart, 1983:171).

Despite the substantial differences in actual drug abuse, drug-related crime, and sociocultural conditions, Canada's response to illicit drug problems has been similar to that of the U.S. (Blackwell and Erickson, 1988; Erickson, 1980; Inciardi and Chambers, 1974; King, 1980; Trebach, 1987). In Canada, there have been open debates over drug policies since the 1960s, and since the late 1980s, there has been more emphasis on treatment and prevention measures than in the U.S. But Canada's response to substance abuse problems remains rooted in law enforcement and punitive sanctions (Erickson, 1990b; Smart, 1983:171; Solomon, 1988b).[2] It came as no surprise, therefore, that strong warning signals were hoisted by the Canadian police and media when the U.S. was reported to be devastated by crack in the mid-1980s. Beginning in 1987, when crack began to appear in Canada, the Canadian media and police reports quickly alerted Canadians to the arrival of a "crack epidemic."

The *Toronto Star* (1989b) told its readers that the "crack problem" was "the greatest threat to society in general, of any single development over the past 15 years." It also claimed (1989c) that crack was "a one-way ticket to hell for the user." The *Globe and Mail* (1989) reported that crack use had reached "crisis proportions," having its most devastating effects in poorer neighborhoods; it characterized users as "a very, very paranoid, psychotic group." *Maclean's* (1989), a popular Canadian weekly magazine, devoted a number of pages to describing the "deadly plague of drugs" in Toronto and other Canadian cities. Even a municipal newspaper in Metro Toronto warned that the "nightmare" of epidemic crack use, like that found in poor enclaves in U.S. cities, is "now taking a foothold in Metro" (*Mirror,* 1989).

Police reported that "much" of the 73.7 kilograms of cocaine seized in Metro Toronto in 1989 was crack (*Toronto Star,* 1990). The Royal Canadian Mounted Police described crack as "the drug of choice of a new sector in the cocaine-user population, primarily in Toronto," and said crack was at least partly responsible for the threefold increase in cocaine-related deaths from 1986 to 1988 (RCMP, 1988). As in the U.S., the media linked crack use to crime, asserting that its extraordinary addictiveness led users to do "anything" for another hit (*Globe and Mail,* 1989; RCMP, 1989).

Despite the abundance of anecdotal accounts by the media and police about crack's powerful addictive properties and their devastating effects on individuals and society, such reportage provided little concrete information about the prevalence of crack use in Canada and about the many crack users who are not identified in the media or by law enforcement agencies. In this chapter, therefore, we try to redress this imbalance. We have three objectives: (1) to review existing data about the extent of crack use in Canada that are so often neglected in media accounts; (2) to present findings from a community-based study of crack users in Toronto as a basis for empirically comparing real crack users with media images; and (3) to discuss the policy implications of our findings.

THE EXTENT OF CRACK USE IN CANADA

Contrary to all the public fervor about the danger of crack, very little data on the extent of crack use are available for Canada thus far. Police reports have indicated increases in seizures of crack since 1986–1987, but the exact amounts of crack seized were seldom given. For example, the RCMP reported that crack comprised "a very modest proportion" of all cocaine seizures in Canada in 1986–1987 (RCMP, 1987), whereas in 1988, the number of crack seizures made by Metro Toronto police jumped from 117 to 726 (RCMP, 1989). No figures on the amount of crack seized have been provided in such reports. But even if they were, it still would be difficult to determine the exact amount of crack being *used*. That is because there is no way of knowing how much crack has been *successfully* smuggled into the country. Moreover, no one knows how much powder cocaine gets made into and used as crack. Data on such seizures are always used to infer a growing rate of crack use, but they really say very little about that.

Since 1987, hospital and treatment centers have experienced large increases in cocaine cases. But the inference of crack use from cocaine use is also made in such statistics. For example, in a treatment center in Toronto, the growth of crack abuse was said to be reflected in the two- or threefold increases in patients treated for *cocaine* (*Toronto Star*, 1989c). Some center officials estimated that a quarter of addicts in Toronto were crack users; others even suggested that the "majority" of cocaine addicts were young adult crack smokers (*Toronto Star*, 1989c). But the only real data they had were on the general category of cocaine.

In addition to the limitations stemming from collapsing crack cases into cocaine cases, these statistics are beset with biases. Crack users who are not identified as such by the police would not enter into police statistics. Also, because of the perception of a crack menace, law enforcement agencies have the tendency to "target" cocaine and crack over other illicit drugs, leading to more cocaine and crack seizures and more arrests of crack and cocaine users. Thus, more crack seizures and arrests are in some part an artifact of more police attention, but they nonetheless reinforce perceptions of a crack epidemic.

That seizures are a flimsy indicator of rising crack abuse can be seen even in police reports. For example, in their annual publication for 1988–1989, the RCMP on one hand described crack as "almost instantly addictive," reported that crack seizures in Toronto grew by 310% in 1988, and noted that the price of cocaine has been deflated. On the other hand, however, the very same document notes that "the use of crack is not widespread in Canada at this point [1988–1989]" (RCMP, 1989:42). The latter suggests that crack use had *not* reached an "epidemic" level by 1989 as the police and the media had claimed.

Treatment center statistics are not much better, for they include only heavy users under treatment. Most addicts never come to official attention, to say nothing of the far more numerous lighter users.[3] Also, the rise in the number of cocaine users admitted for treatment does not necessarily indicate a corresponding increase of cocaine (and hence crack) users because larger admission figures may mean cocaine users are now more eager for treatment than before. Moreover, the number of cocaine users admitted for treatment appeared to have tapered off by 1989 (Single et al., 1992).

Most of the scanty information available on the prevalence of crack use in Canada came from a few surveys. In the U.S., surveys of adult and student populations have generally indicated low prevalence levels of crack use (*e.g.*, Johnston et al., 1988; NIDA, 1989; SAMHSA, 1995). In Canada, surveys show similarly low prevalence figures. For example, in their survey of 1040 Ontario adults aged eighteen and over during 1987, Smart and Adlaf (1987a) found that less than 1% ($N=8$ or .7%) reported ever using crack. Two years later Smart and Adlaf conducted another survey of 1101 Ontario adults and found that the percentage who reported ever using crack was still less than 1% (Adlaf and Smart, 1989). Their 1991 survey of 1041 adults also found that lifetime users of crack remained less than 1% (Adlaf et al., 1991).

The same researchers also conducted surveys of high school students in Ontario. In their 1987 study involving 4267 students, only 1.4% of the students reported crack use in the last year (Smart and Adlaf, 1987b). This percentage dropped to 1% in their 1989 study of 4500 students (Smart and Adlaf, 1989) and stayed at 1% in their 1991 study of 3945 students (Smart et al., 1991). A 1990 study of 479 high school students in Metro Toronto indicated similarly that only 0.8% of the students had used crack in the last year (Leonard, 1990). The small percentages of student and adult crack users in these studies fail to confirm the presence of what the media have limned a "crack epidemic" in Canada—not only for 1987 (Smart, 1988) but for each year since.[4]

The greatest limitation of student surveys is that they miss school dropouts in their samples. In order to remedy this, Smart and associates conducted a study of "street youths" in Toronto in early 1990 (Smart et al., 1990). Altogether they interviewed 145 youths aged twenty-four or under. Among them, 108 were randomly selected from youth agencies, and the other 37 were approached in the street. Their results showed that 46% had used crack at least once in their lifetimes, 39% had used crack in the past year, and 6% were using crack daily. These figures show that crack use in this segment of youth is much more prevalent than that among ordinary students.

A third source of information about crack use is community-based studies that generate self-selected samples from the community through advertising or other campaigns and/or the snowball technique. Although recruiting subjects this way inevitably misses users currently in treatment or other institutions, this type of study has the advantage of including subjects at various levels and patterns of use, so that samples are more typical of users in the community than are those in police or treatment records. Moreover, such studies can also collect more in-depth information on different patterns of use and characteristics of users (Erickson et al., 1987). Findings of community-based studies in the U.S. have found the level of crack use to be somewhat between two extremes, one extreme represented by police/treatment data and the other by survey findings (*e.g.*, Inciardi, 1987; Waldorf et al., 1991).

Our 1989 study of crack use in Toronto offered the first findings about crack use in a community-based sample in Canada (Cheung et al., 1991). We interviewed seventy-nine subjects who were eighteen or older and had used crack. Results showed an *infrequent* pattern of use even though this was a group of "crack users" (Table 8-1).

In the past *month*, 67% had not used crack, 19% had used it fewer than ten times, 5% had used it between ten and nineteen times, 6% had used it twenty to thirty-nine times, and only 3% had used it forty times or more. If we treat twenty times or more in the past month as "heavy use," then 9% (*N* = 7) of respondents were currently "heavy users." Their use in the *past year* and in their *lifetimes* was lower. In the *past year,* 14% had not used crack at all, and 38% had used it fewer than twenty times. Half had not used crack twenty times or more. As to *lifetime* use, 40% had not used it forty times or more, 23% had used it between forty and ninety-nine times, and 37% had used it one hundred times or more.

In sum, because each type of study or source of information has its limitations, the exact extent of crack use is difficult to determine. However,

TABLE 8-1   Frequency of Crack Use (*N*= 79)

Frequency	Use in Lifetime		Use in Past Year		Use in Past Month	
	%	N	%	N	%	N
Never	0.0	0	13.9	11	67.1	53
1–2 times	11.4	9	13.9	11	13.9	11
3–5 times	11.4	9	10.1	8	5.0	4
6–9 times	3.8	3	3.8	3	0.0	0
10–19 times	8.8	7	10.1	8	5.1	4
20–39 times	5.1	4	6.3	5	6.3	5
40–99 times	22.8	18	12.7	10	1.3	1
100 times or more	36.7	29	29.1	23	1.3	1

SOURCE: Cheung et al., 1991.

on the basis of findings from surveys and a community-based study, there is no strong evidence for media and police claims that crack use has reached an "epidemic" level in Canada. Even if increases in police seizures of cocaine and crack and the deflation of the price of street cocaine do indicate increased *distribution* of crack, there is little evidence of increased *consumption* in the general student and adult populations. However, increases in the use of crack may have occurred among impoverished segments of the population such as street youths and the economic underclass.

THE CRACK EXPERIENCE
AMONG A GROUP OF USERS IN TORONTO

A core premise of media and law enforcement claims of an epidemic is that crack's rapid and intense high quickly leads to compulsive use and a powerful addiction. Once addicted, users would soon ruin their lives by draining income, destroying family relationships, suffering physical and psychological problems, and losing their jobs. By the same logic, crack addicts would then pose a threat to society because they would engage in whatever level of crime or violence was needed to obtain the money for maintaining uncontrollable use. Anecdotal accounts of this sort abound in the media, and they have gained support from studies of known addicts, usually in clinical samples, which generally show that crack abuse entails serious physical, psychological, and social consequences (*e.g.*, Golbe and Merkin, 1986; Kissner et al., 1987; Washton et al., 1986; see also Smart, 1991).

However, because the samples in most such studies were heavy users requiring treatment, results of such studies cannot be generalized to the much larger number of low-level users in the community. In order to capture the phenomenon of crack use within the broader spectrum of crack users who exist *in the community,* and to test the popular image of crack as powerfully addicting, we present more of our findings from a community-based study of crack users in Toronto (Cheung et al., 1991).

The Study and the Sample

Through advertisements in the media and in public places, we recruited for interviews one hundred subjects aged eighteen or older who had used cocaine and/or crack.[5] Among these respondents, seventy-nine had used crack, and the remaining twenty-one had used only cocaine powder. Of the seventy-nine who had ever used crack, seventy-four had also used powder, twenty-one had injected cocaine, and five had not used forms of cocaine other than crack. Most of the respondents had experience with a wide range of licit and illicit drugs (Erickson et al., 1991).

Three-quarters of the seventy-nine crack users were male. Over half were between twenty-one and thirty years old, and 70% were never married. Forty percent had finished only grades nine through thirteen. Over half were employed full-time, mostly in semi-, low- or unskilled jobs. About 40% were earning $20,000 (Canadian) or less a year, and another 38% were earning between $21,000 and $40,000. Thus, the majority of the crack users in the sample were young, single males, with relatively low-level educations, occupations, and incomes. These crack users did not differ significantly from the twenty-one other respondents in the sample who only snorted powder cocaine with respect to the previous sociodemographic characteristics or with respect to self-rated physical health and psychological well-being. Moreover, most of the crack users were current or past powder users as well. Thus, these crack users were not a distinct group of cocaine users. They used crack *in addition to* powder, rather than as a substitute for it.

The Experience of Crack Use

We asked these respondents a number of questions concerning various aspects of their crack use. Results are shown in Table 8-2.

Over three-quarters of the respondents had not tried crack until three years prior to our interviews (about 1986), when crack began to enter the Canadian illicit drug scene. Most were introduced to crack by males, and over 75% of introducers were friends, coworkers, or intimates of the respondents. The most common situation for crack use was taking it with friends in either one's own home or a friend's home (67%). Thirty percent of respondents reported that "about half" or "almost all" of their friends

TABLE 8-2   Experience of Crack Use (N = 78 unless otherwise stated) *

Aspects of Crack Use	%	N
Years ago first used crack (N = 77)		
1 year	23.4	18
2 years	41.5	32
3 years	13.0	10
4 years	11.7	9
5 years	2.6	2
6 years	5.2	4
7 years	2.6	2
Sex of introducer		
Male	74.4	58
Female	19.2	15
More than on person	6.4	5
Introducer's relationship to respondent		
Spouse/commonlaw/intimate friend	10.3	8
Other friends	61.5	48
Coworker	6.4	5
Dealer	11.5	9
Other	10.3	8
Most common situation for use (N = 73)		
Club/bar	2.7	2
Parties	5.5	4
Own home alone	9.6	7
Own home with others living there	9.6	7
Own home with friends	19.2	14
Friend's home	38.4	28
Other situation	10.9	8
Varies a lot	4.1	3
Availability of crack		
Very difficult	6.4	5
Difficult	1.3	1
Sometimes difficult	9.0	7
Easy	11.5	9
Very easy	71.8	56
Friends who sometimes use crack		
None	19.2	15
Only a few	48.7	38
About half	11.5	9
Almost all	19.2	15
Don't know	1.3	1
Effects of crack liked most (selected responses)		
"Rush"	43.6	34
Euphoric feeling	16.7	13

TABLE 8-2   *(continued)*

Aspects of Crack Use	%	N
Effects of crack liked least (selected responses)		
"Coming down"	17.9	14
Short "high"	11.5	9
Craving to use more	21.8	17
Financial cost	15.4	12
Various adverse physical effects	43.6	34
Frequency of craving for crack		
Never	35.9	28
Rarely	17.9	14
Sometimes	15.4	12
Most times	14.1	11
Always	16.7	13
Perceived risk of harm in trying crack once or twice		
No risk	10.3	8
Slight risk	15.4	12
Moderate risk	19.2	15
Great risk	55.1	43
Perceived risk of harm in using crack occasionally		
No risk	2.6	2
Slight risk	12.8	10
Moderate risk	17.9	14
Great risk	66.7	52
Perceived risk of harm in using crack regularly		
No risk	1.3	1
Slight risk	0.0	0
Moderate risk	7.7	6
Great risk	91.0	71
Ever concerned about becoming addicted		
No	68.7	38
Yes	48.7	38
No answer	2.6	2
Preferred form of cocaine		
Powder	47.4	37
Crack	46.2	36
No preference/don't know	5.1	4
No answer	1.3	1

* N was reduced from 79 to 78 because of one missing case.
SOURCE: Cheung et al., 1991.

sometimes used crack. Compared to peer use of cocaine and cannabis, this figure indicates low peer use of crack.[6] The majority of these respondents (83%) reported that it was "easy" or "very easy" to get crack.

We asked respondents to name up to three things they liked most about crack. Almost half mentioned "the rapid, intense reaction" (the "rush") as one of their three. About one-fifth mentioned "the really good or euphoric feeling." Some other pleasurable effects were also reported, including "boost in energy," "sexual arousal," improvement in sociability," "escape from worries or tensions," "new experience," and "the taste of it."

We also asked them to name up to three effects they liked least about crack. Over 40% disliked the adverse physical effects of crack such as "nausea," "faster heart rate," "sweating," and "burnt lungs." Eighteen percent mentioned "coming down," and 12% mentioned the related "short high" as things they liked least. Also, 15% complained about the "financial cost" of use, whereas a larger percentage (22%) considered "the urge/craving to use more" to be what they liked least about crack. This craving problem became more apparent when nearly a third (31%) reported that they "always" or "most of the time" experienced this urge; another 15% admitted that they had "sometimes" experienced such an urge.

It is noteworthy that less than half of these subjects reported any problem with craving. This suggests that crack may not be as overwhelmingly reinforcing as one might guess from examining the minority of users who experience sufficient problems to end up in jail or treatment. However, based on their experience of negative effects and craving, our respondents showed a healthy respect for the risks; a majority thought that people would be at least in danger of harming themselves if they used crack. More than half said there would be great risk if people "try crack once or twice," two-thirds mentioned great risk if people "use crack occasionally," and nine-tenths perceived great risk if people "use crack regularly." But when asked about their own use, less than half our respondents felt concerned about becoming addicted to crack. In fact, less than half (46%) considered crack their preferred form of cocaine.

In sum, crack users were likely to have first tried crack less than three years ago, to have been introduced to crack by a male friend, and to use crack at their own or a friend's home. Although crack was easily available to these respondents, it was used less commonly in their circles of friends than cocaine or cannabis. The rush and euphoria were what users liked most about crack. The short high, the "coming down," adverse physical effects, and the craving to use more were what users liked least. About half of respondents had experienced the craving, felt concerned about becoming addicted, and preferred crack over other forms of cocaine. Most perceived that people in general would run real risks with regular and even occasional use of crack.

Types of Crack Users and Variation in the Crack Experience

In order further to capture individual differences in use between two time periods, we constructed a typology of users, based on use in the past year and the past month (Cheung et al., 1991). We identified three types: *continuous users*, who had used crack in the past year *and* in the past month (32% of the sample); *inactive users*, who had used crack in the past year but *not* in the past month (54%); and *abstainers*, who had *stopped* use for one year (14%).

The facts that only 32% of the sample were currently continuous users and that among them only 28% were "heavy" users (twenty times or more per month) suggest that crack use is not necessarily compulsive, even well after the first use. Most people in our sample had refrained from use for either a month or a year at the time of the interview. Thus, it is not unreasonable to predict that, in the future, many, perhaps most, of the inactive users and abstainers will continue to avoid at least compulsive or addictive use.

We compared the three types of users with respect to most of the experience items discussed previously (Cheung et al., 1991). Our statistical tests (not reported here) indicated that the three groups did *not* differ significantly in friends' use of crack, what was liked most and least about crack, frequency of craving, concern about addiction, and preferred form of cocaine. They also did not differ substantially in their assessment that *regular* crack use entails serious risks (100% of abstainers, 93% of inactive users, and 84% of continuous users).

The three types of users differed significantly only in their perception of the risk of harm in "trying crack once or twice" and in "occasional use of crack." Many more abstainers and inactive users perceived great or moderate risk in trying crack (90% and 80%, respectively) than did continuous users (56%). Conversely, many more continuous users (44%) than inactive users (19%) or abstainers (9%) saw no risk or only slight risk in trying crack. Similarly, nearly a third (32%) of continuous users perceived no risk or only slight risks in occasional use, whereas only 10% of inactive users and none of the abstainers held the same view.[7] All three groups perceived great risk in regular use, which may be why not even the continuous users ingested crack on a daily or even regular basis (see Table 8-1). This apparent capacity of users to recognize the risks of crack and to modulate their use accordingly is at variance with media and police accounts.

CONCLUSION: USERS MAKE CHOICES, SO CAN POLICY MAKERS

Like other drug problems, crack in Canada must be understood in the context of (1) the great American influence in the formation of popular images about the crack problem in Canada and (2) Canada's traditionally punitive, law enforcement–centered approach to dealing with drug problems. The anticipation of the "crack epidemic," the portrayal of its arrival by the media and police reports, and government responses to such an "epidemic" all neatly resembled the typical U.S. "War on Drugs" approach. Crack was introduced to the public as extremely dangerous because its quick and intense high made it so powerfully addictive that serious health and financial consequences were inevitable. In the short span of time since its appearance, crack use was said to have reached "crisis levels" in Canada. According to available evidence about the scope and nature of crack use in Canada, however, virtually all of these claims are seriously misleading.

A review of different sources of evidence about the extent of crack use in Canada has shown that publicly available police and treatment center data are flawed and hence could not demonstrate the presence of "crisis" levels of crack use. Yet, more representative surveys of students and adults have shown low prevalence rates of crack use between 1987 and 1989–1990. Low frequencies of use were also reported in a community-based study of crack users in Toronto in 1989. Only an exploratory study of street youth in Toronto in 1990 showed a substantially higher rate of crack use. As earlier chapters have shown, it is thus likely that rapid increases in crack use have occurred largely in socially and economically devastated segments of the population. However, there is little evidence that serious levels of crack use exist in the general Canadian population.

Findings from our community-based study of crack users in Toronto allowed us to illustrate some of the major aspects of crack use among a self-selected group of crack users from the Canadian city said to be most seriously plagued with the drug. These results lend support to only a small part of the popular images of crack. The "rush" and euphoria from smoking crack were, indeed, what the respondents were attracted to. However, there was little evidence to support the view that the use of crack is necessarily compulsive. Over half of the respondents had rarely or never experienced a craving to take crack. Less than half preferred crack to powder cocaine. At the time of the interview, two-thirds of the respondents had not used crack for a month, and 14% had even stopped use for a year. Only 30% had used it continuously in the past year, and daily users comprised only 9% of the sample. For a majority of respondents, crack was *not* the "drug of choice." The data do not show whether or not a respondent's use of crack had been uncontrollable in the initial period. But even if compulsive use had occurred before, reduction to infrequent use or abstinence was the pattern for the majority of crack users over time.

The Toronto study suggests that users' knowledge of the possible dangerous physical, social, and financial consequences of crack addiction helped keep most of them away from regular use. The more users *perceived risks of harm* in crack use, the less they used crack. This sort of *user* rationality is precisely what is ignored in claims that crack's pharmacological powers are omnipotent. Crack users in this study were not sociodemographically different from other cocaine users. For most, crack was used in addition to powder, not as a substitute. Therefore, crack use and its consequences should be understood within the context of cocaine use in general. In a detailed review of animal studies, clinical studies, population surveys, and studies of community samples of cocaine users, Erickson and Alexander (1989) showed that the "addictive liability" of cocaine has been overstated because only 5% to 10% of those who try cocaine would progress to more intensive use, such as weekly or more often. Data from the Toronto study revealed a similar pattern. At most, only 9% of the crack users in the sample were in the "heavy use" category. Others either maintained a very low level of continuous use or simply abstained from use for various lengths of time.

The discrepancies between popular beliefs about crack and the findings of our Toronto study result from two different perspectives on drug use, the pharmacocentric and the sociological. The popular perspective, derived from media images and police claims, is a pharmacocentric one. It focuses only on the pharmacological properties of a drug and assumes that users are vulnerable biological organisms who can only passively and mechanically behave according to what the drug dictates. Such a view is supported by cases of addicts who have become victims of compulsive use. Some users do, indeed, become compulsive users. However, many more users do not. Even many of those whose initial use was compulsive were later able to regain control, with or without therapeutic intervention. Thus, the power of this perspective to help us understand the nature of the crack problem and what to do about it is quite limited.

The second perspective, a sociological one, views the user as an active human subject capable of making choices. This approach does not downplay the pharmacological powers of drugs, but it does not consider them the only important factor. Drug use does not occur in a social vacuum; psychological, social, economic, and cultural factors all play important roles in shaping a person's drug use behavior. For example, social policies that reduce inequality, ensure that basic human needs like health care are met, and do not marginalize racial or ethnic groups shape a social context in which the harms that drugs *can* do are reduced. In such a context, more users of potentially highly addictive drugs are able to weigh the pleasure derived from the use of the drug against perceived risk and undesirable consequences. Many of them maintain a level of ongoing use that their physical, social, and financial conditions allow. Others may simply quit because either the risk is too high for continuous use or the excitement of experimentation has faded. Data from the Toronto crack users study suggest that this perspective is a more accurate description of actual crack use patterns.

These two perspectives paint different pictures of the drug problem and have radically different implications for drug policy. Overemphasizing the extraordinary pharmacological powers of crack could dilute the effects of prevention efforts. The worst-case scenarios of crack addiction that the media have depicted as typical are not likely to match the experience of most current users. For potential users, the credibility of prevention information is likely to be eroded once they learn from current users that the worst-case scenario is an exception rather than a rule. The real risks of crack addiction are scary enough and should be spelled out so that the public can have an accurate perception of the risks involved if they start use. The importance of accurate information about risks in prevention efforts has been noted in recent studies showing that users' perceived health risks in illicit drug use has contributed to reductions in use (*e.g.,* Bachman et al., 1990; Erickson and Murray, 1989).

The sociological approach to prevention does not stop at providing accurate information about risks. It also points to the need to understand the psychological, social, and economic factors that affect a person's *decisions* to use or to continue using a drug. As Waldorf et al. (1991) have shown in their book on heavy cocaine users, the user's "stake in conventional life"—job, career, family, community responsibilities, and so forth—is a crucial determinant of his or her capacity for controlling use. Although they show that this may be more difficult with crack than with powder cocaine, the principle still holds. People with jobs, homes, and families to protect and who have the life chances that make this protection possible are less likely to be overwhelmed by their drug use. Again, this is why social and economic policies that shape the distribution of such "stakes" and life chances are crucial parts of the context of drug use.

Wallace's analysis of a U.S. treatment sample of 245 crack addicts showed similarly that crack addiction is affected not only by the neurochemistry of crack, but also by a range of social and psychological factors such as childhood development in troubled families. She concluded, "The reinforcement or rewards associated with a good salary, spouse, or home may compete effectively with the reinforcement associated with the crack euphoria and deter a crack smoker from exclusive focus upon and pursuit of the crack high" (Wallace, 1990:113). Conversely, people who have not fared well in employment, family relationships, or social circles are much more vulnerable. Therefore, there is a need for prevention work to move beyond imploring people to "just say no"—an approach predicated on the pharmacology-based mechanistic perspective. Instead, a prevention policy rooted in the more accurate, sociological perspective on drug problems would focus on the *social sources of vulnerability* and the social support programs that could raise people's capacities for resisting crack and other drugs.

NOTES

Some of the material used in this chapter appeared earlier in *The Steel Drug: Cocaine and Crack in Perspective,* by Erickson et al. (2nd ed., 1994). The authors thank Valerie Watson, Tim Weber, Tammy Landau, Christine Leonard, and Joan Moreau for their research assistance on this chapter. The views expressed are those of the authors and do not necessarily reflect those of the Addiction Research Foundation or the University of Toronto.

1. For example, rates of arrests for drug-related offenses per 100,000 population aged eighteen and over in Canada and the U.S. were 96.3 and 314.6, respectively, in 1970; 257.3 and 402.6, respectively, in 1982; and 221.5 and 409.2, respectively, in 1984. (These figures were calculated from these sources: Statistics Canada, *Canadian Crime Statistics,* 1970, 1982–1984; Statistics Canada, *Estimates of the Population by Sex and Age for Canada and the Provinces;* and Federal Bureau of Investigation, *Uniform Crime Reports,* 1970, 1982–1984.)

2. Narcotic drug legislation in Canada dates back to the first anti-opium statutes enacted in 1908. The addition of other drugs defined as narcotics (*e.g.,* cocaine, cannabis, heroin, morphine, and phencyclidine) and greater measures for controlling illicit drug use culminated in the Narcotic Control Act of 1961 and the Food and Drugs Act of 1970, which control the nonmedical distribution of amphetamines, barbiturates, and hallucinogens (Smart, 1983:129–145; Solomon, 1988a; Solomon and Green, 1988). Until struck down by the Charter of Rights and Freedoms in the mid-1980s, Canada's drug law provided for (1) a mandatory minimum penalty of seven years for importing narcotics, (2) "writs of assistance," which allow warrantless search of dwellings in drug cases by the police, and (3) the placing of the burden of proof of innocence on the person accused of trafficking rather than the prosecutor. Since the late 1960s, there have been challenges to this crime control approach. In 1969, as a response to the excessive number of "cannabis criminals" (Erickson, 1980) who flooded the courts in the late 1960s, the Le Dain Commission was set up to provide a forum for public debate about Canada's drug problems and policies, resulting in a penalty reduction for simple possession of cannabis (Erickson and Smart, 1980). In 1982, the Charter of Rights and Freedoms was proclaimed in Ottawa. The charter provides some previously unavailable protections for individual rights, although it does not in effect change the power of law enforcement agencies in handling drug cases (Solomon, 1988b). In 1987, an approach that emphasizes education, prevention, and treatment, *apart from* enforcement and control, began to take shape when Health and Welfare announced "Action on Drug Abuse" as a "new strategy" (Erickson, 1990b). Whether this new approach will signify a commitment to the search for, and the test of, alternative means of controlling drug use remains to be seen.

3. For a discussion of the limitations of official statistics and some of the

cultural and social-structural factors in the underutilization of addiction treatment and other health care facilities by ethnic minorities, see, for example, Cheung (1989, 1990–1991).

4. In 1989, Health and Welfare Canada conducted a "National Alcohol and Other Drugs Survey," the first national survey that focused exclusively on alcohol and other drugs in Canada, which included 11,364 adult Canadians aged fifteen and over. Unfortunately, among questions regarding illicit drug use, cocaine and crack were lumped into one category as "cocaine or crack," making it impossible to separate cocaine use from crack use (Health and Welfare Canada, 1990). The use level in the past year for this combined category was 1.4%. This figure is not much higher than the 0.9% reporting past year use of cocaine alone in the 1985 national health survey (Erickson et al., 1987: 63).

5. The study, entitled "A Longitudinal Study of Cocaine Users: The Natural History of Cocaine Use and Its Consequences Among Canadian Adults," was funded by the National Health and Research Development Program, Health and Welfare Canada.

6. For example, a study of 111 cocaine users in 1983–1984 found that about 50% of the subjects had half or more of their friends using cocaine, and about 90% had at least half of their friends using cannabis (Erickson and Murray, 1989).

7. The associations between level of use (user type) and perceived risk of harm in trying and occasional use do not by themselves suggest any causality between use and risk perception. However, there is reason to believe that perceived risk influenced level of use rather than vice versa. If increases in use could reduce perceptions of risk, then the percentage of continuous users perceiving "great risk" in "regular crack use" should have been much smaller than percentages for the other two groups. However, as reported earlier, as many as 84% of continuous users perceived great risk, which is not substantially smaller than the 93% for inactive users.

REFERENCES

Adlaf, E. M., and R. G. Smart. 1989. *The Ontario Adult Alcohol & Other Drug Survey 1977–1989.* Toronto: Addiction Research Foundation.

Adlaf, E. M., R. G. Smart, and M. D. Canale. 1991. *Drug Use Among Ontario Adults 1977–1991.* Toronto: Addiction Research Foundation.

Alexander, B. K. 1990. *Peaceful Measures: Canada's Way Out of the "War on Drugs."* Toronto: University of Toronto Press.

Bachman, J. G., L. D. Johnston, and P. M. O'Malley. 1990. "Explaining the recent decline in cocaine use among young adults: Further evidence that perceived risks and disapproval lead to reduced drug use." *Journal of Health and Social Behavior* 31:173–184.

Blackwell, J. C., and P. G. Erickson (eds.). 1988. *Illicit Drugs in Canada: A Risky Business.* Scarborough, Ontario: Nelson.

Cheung, Y. W. 1989. "Making sense of ethnicity and drug use: A review and suggestions for future research." *Social Pharmacology* 3:55–82.

———. 1990–1991. "Ethnicity and alcohol/drug use revisited: A framework for future research." *International Journal of the Addictions* 25 (5A&6A):581–605.

Cheung, Y. W., P. G. Erickson, and T. C. Landau. 1991. "Experience of crack use: Findings from a community-based sample in Toronto." *Journal of Drug Issues* 21(1):121–141.

Currie, Elliott. 1985. *Confronting Crime: An American Challenge.* New York: Pantheon.

Erickson, P. G. 1980. *Cannabis Criminals: The Social Effects of Punishment on Drug Users.* Toronto: Addiction Research Foundation Books.

———. 1989. "The law in addictions: Principles, practicalities and prospects." Prepared for the 40th Anniversary Scientific Lecture Series, November 8. Toronto: Addiction Research Foundation.

———. 1990a. "A public health approach to demand reduction." *Journal of Drug Issues* 20:563–575.

———. 1990b. "Past, current and future directions in Canadian drug policy." *International Journal of the Addictions* 25:981–1000.

Erickson, P. G., E. M. Adlaf, G. F. Murray, and R. G. Smart. 1987. *The Steel Drug: Cocaine and Crack in Perspective* (2nd ed. 1994). Lexington, MA: Lexington Books.

Erickson, P. G., and B. K. Alexander. 1989. "Cocaine and addictive liability." *Social Pharmacology* 3:249–270.

Erickson, P. G., and G. F. Murray. 1989. "The undeterred cocaine user: Intention to quit and its relationship to perceived legal and health threats." *Contemporary Drug Problems* 16:141–156.

Erickson, P. G., and R. G. Smart. 1980. "Canada." Pp. 91–129 in S. Einstein (ed.), *The Community's Response to Drug Use.* New York: Pergamon.

Erickson, P. G., V. Watson, and T. Weber. 1991. "Cocaine users' perception of their health status and the risks of drug use." Pp. 82–89 in P. A. O'Hare, R. Newcombe, A. Mattews, E. C. Buning, and E. Drucker (eds.), *The Reduction of Drug Related Harm.* London: Routledge.

Globe and Mail [Toronto]. 1989. "Crack use near epidemic, Toronto police warn." February 11.

Golbe, L. I., and M. D. Merkin. 1986. "Cerebral infarction in a user of free-base cocaine (crack)." *Neurology* 36:1602–1604.

Goodstadt, M. S. 1990. "The future of substance abuse prevention: Etiology, public health, and health promotion." Unpublished manuscript, Center of Alcohol Studies, Rutgers University.

Griffiths, C. T., and S. N. Verdun-Jones. 1989. *Canadian Criminal Justice.* Toronto: Butterworths.

Hagan, J. L. 1991. *The Disreputable Pleasures*, 3rd ed. Toronto: McGraw-Hill Ryerson.

Health and Welfare Canada. 1990. *National Alcohol and Other Drugs Survey: Highlights Report.* Ottawa, Ontario: Minister of Supply and Services Canada.

Inciardi, J. A. 1987. "Beyond cocaine: Basuco, crack, and other coca products." *Contemporary Drug Problems* 14:461–492.

Inciardi, J. A., and C. D. Chambers (eds.). 1974. *Drugs and the Criminal Justice System.* Beverly Hills, CA: Sage.

Johnston, D. L., P. M. O'Mally, and J. G. Bachman. 1988. *Illicit Drug Use, Smoking and Drinking by America's High School Students and Young Adults, 1975–1987.* Rockville, MD: National Institute on Drug Abuse.

Jonas, S. 1990. "Solving the drug problem: A public health approach to the reduction of the use and abuse of both the legal and the illegal recreational drugs." *Hofstra Law Review* 18: 751–794.

King, R. 1980. "United States." Pp. 130–145 in S. Einstein (ed.), *The Community's Response to Drug Use.* New York: Pergamon.

Kissner, D. G., W. D. Lawrence, J. E. Selis, and A. Flint. 1987. "Crack lung: Pulmonary disease caused by cocaine abuse." *American Review of Respiratory Disease* 136:1250–1252.

Leonard, C. A. 1990. "Alcohol and drug use among students in a high school in North York, Metropolitan Toronto." Unpublished report, Addiction Research Foundation, Toronto.

Maclean's. 1989. "A deadly plague of drugs." April 3.

Mirror. 1989. "Creating a social nightmare." March 15.

Mitchell, C. N. 1990. *The Drug Solution: Regulating Drugs According to Principles of Justice, Efficiency and Democracy.* Ottawa: Carlton University Press.

Morgan, P., L. Wallack, and D. Buchanan. 1988. "Waging drug wars: Prevention strategy or politics as usual." *Drugs and Society* 3:99–124.

National Institute on Drug Abuse (NIDA). 1989. *National Household Survey on Drug Use: Population Estimates 1988.* Rockville, MD: National Institute on Drug Abuse.

Royal Canadian Mounted Police (RCMP). 1987. *National Drug Intelligence Estimates 1986/1987.* Ottawa, Ontario: Minister of Supply and Services Canada.

———. 1988. *National Drug Intelligence Estimate 1987/1988.* Ottawa, Ontario: Minister of Supply and Services Canada.

———. 1989. *National Drug Intelligence Estimates 1988/1989.* Ottawa, Ontario: Minister of Supply and Services Canada.

SAMHSA. 1995. *Preliminary Estimates from the 1994 National Household Survey on Drug Abuse.* Advance Report #10. Rockville, MD: U.S. Department of Health and Human Services, Substance Abuse and Mental Health Services Administration, Office of Applied Studies.

Single, E., P. Erickson, J. Skirrow, and R. Solomon. 1992. "Drug and public policy in Canada." *National Drug Policy Project.* Washington, DC: Rand Institute Drug Policy Research Center.

Smart, R. G. 1983. *Forbidden Highs.* Toronto: Addiction Research Foundation Books.

———. 1988. " 'Crack' cocaine use in Canada: A new epidemic?" *American Journal of Epidemiology* 127:1315–1317.

———. 1991. "Crack cocaine use: A review of prevalence and adverse effects." *American Journal of Drug & Alcohol Abuse* 17:13–26.

Smart, R. G., and E. M. Adlaf. 1987a. *Alcohol and Other Drug Use Among Ontario Adults 1977–1987.* Toronto: Addiction Research Foundation.

———. 1987b. *Alcohol and Other Drug Use Among Ontario Students in 1987, and Trends Since 1977.* Toronto: Addiction research Foundation.

———. 1989. *The Ontario Student Drug Use Survey: Trends Between 1977–1989.* Toronto: Addiction Research Foundation.

Smart, R. G., E. M. Adlaf, K. M. Porterfield, and M. D. Canale. 1990. *Drugs, Youth and the Street.* Toronto: Addiction Research Foundation.

Smart, R. G., E. M. Adlaf, and G. W. Walsh. 1991. *The Ontario Student Drug Use Survey: Trends Between 1977–1991.* Toronto: Addiction Research Foundation.

Solomon, R. 1988a. "Canada's federal drug legislation." Pp. 117–130 in J. C. Blackwell and P. G. Erickson (eds.), *Illicit Drugs in Canada: A Risky Business.* Scarborough, Ontario: Nelson.

———. 1988b. "The noble pursuit of evil: Arrest, search, and seizure in Canadian drug law." Pp. 263–290 in J. C. Blackwell and P. G. Erickson (eds.), *Illicit Drugs in Canada: A Risky Business.* Scarborough, Ontario: Nelson.

Solomon, R., and M. Green. 1988. "The first century: The history of non-medical opiate use and control policies in Canada, 1870–1970." Pp. 88–116. In J. C. Blackwell and P. G. Erickson (eds.), *Illicit Drugs in Canada: A Risky Business.* Scarborough, Ontario: Nelson.

Toronto Star. 1989a. "New group joins fight to curb cocaine trade." February 24.

———. 1989b. " 'Aroused' public needed to fight drugs, mayor says." June 16.

———. 1989c. "Sharp increase reported in cocaine addiction." November 27.

———. 1990. "Drug seizures double as charges jump 36%." February 1.

Trebach, A. S. 1987. *The Great Drug War.* New York: Macmillan.

Waldorf, D., C. Reinarman, and S. Murphy. 1991. *Cocaine Changes.* Philadelphia: Temple University Press..

Wallace, B. C. 1990. "Crack addiction: Treatment and recovery issues." *Contemporary Drug Problems* 17:79–119.

Washton, A. M., M. G. Gold, and A. C. Pottash. 1986. "Crack: Early report on a new epidemic." *Postgraduate Medicine* 80 (5):52–58.

NINE

Crack in Australia
Why is There No Problem?

Stephen K. Mugford

Preceding chapters have described various facets of the recent cocaine "epidemic" in the U.S., which started with widespread snorting of powder cocaine and had by the latter 1980s developed into a crack "crisis." This smokeable freebase rapidly caught on in many American cities. Supply and distribution organizations sprang up, especially in poorer areas. Fortunes were made and lost, ugly "turf wars" broke out, and drug-related violence was said to be common. Politicians and the media hyped all this, and hysteria seemed to spread faster than crack itself.

During the same time period in Australia, no comparable pattern of crack use occurred. Why not? America and Australia share many features. Both are modern, urban, industrial, capitalist democracies (with all the things that all this implies). They share a common language and a similar Anglo-Christian, multicultural tradition. Their polities are remarkably similar—a federation of states with a national bicameral parliament. Travel between the two nations is common, and Australia both imports American cultural material (from *CNN News* to *The Cosby Show*) and exports some back (*Crocodile Dundee*, etc.). What features, then, account for this marked difference where a recent trend—crack use—is concerned?

In this chapter, I set out to answer this question. I begin by reviewing schematically the available evidence on cocaine imports, seizures, use, and price in order to establish the very important empirical claim upon which the chapter rests, that is, that Australia has not experienced a cocaine epidemic nor, more importantly, any hint of a crack epidemic. Available data show a definite rise in supply and use of cocaine that looks substantial if expressed only in percentage growth but remains small in absolute terms—to put it crudely, ten times nothing is still nothing. These same data show hardly any evidence of crack use in Australia. I then turn to examine various possible explanations for why Australian experience differs from that in the U.S. These explanations fall into two broad groups—those that emphasize contingent factors and those that emphasize social-structural factors. Contingent explanations examine differences in geography and time frame, suggesting that Australia either would have had the same problem had it been closer to Latin America or yet will have the problem. I argue that these explanations have limited utility in understanding the difference. This suggests that social-structural explanations may be more important. In the third section, I suggest that there are a number of key social-structural differences between the two countries that lead to the U.S. having a greater demand for crack, a greater supply of individuals willing to sell crack, and a greater public concern about the immorality of drug use, which leads to harsher penalties that exacerbate the problem.

COCAINE IN AUSTRALIA

To document my assertion that there is some cocaine use in Australia yet virtually no crack use, I draw on material from the Second National Drug Indicators Conference of 1990, where representatives from the eight jurisdictions (six states and two territories) of Australia presented data on drug-related mortality and morbidity, arrests, price, purity, and so forth. The eight reports (collected in Wardlaw, 1991) contain a few fragments about cocaine, which I summarize:

New South Wales: In the period July 1987 to December 1988, 2184 deaths were referred to the coroner as possibly drug related. Of these, less than 1% were cocaine related. Of calls to the Alcohol and Drug Information Service in the period 1984–1989, those relating to cocaine rose from 0.9% to 1.3%. In the years 1980–1988, police seizures of cocaine rose from seven to eighty. The bulk of the increase was by 1985 (sixty-seven seizures). In comparison, heroin seizures in the same period rose from 163 to 779, with a peak of 812 in 1985. In the years 1987–1988 and 1988–1989, the police made 7037 drug seizures; only 188 (2.7%) involved cocaine. In the years 1986–1987 and 1987–1988, the police recorded 37,646 drug offenses; but only 275 (less than 1%) involved cocaine.

South Australia: "Offenses are few. Price has remained static."

Victoria: This state listed virtually no information, except that when examining client admissions to funded nongovernment treatment agencies in the eight health regions, overall admissions ranged from 56 to 74.3 per 10,000 of the population, of which cocaine accounted for between 0.1 and 0.9 per 10,000.

West Australia: "The amount of cocaine use in this State appears negligible according to data from the drug indicators. Between 1981 and 1986 there was only one death, eight hospital stays between 1981 and 1988, very few drug charges and approximately one percent of calls . . . [to the Alcohol and Drug Information Service concerned] . . . cocaine."

Tasmania: No real indication of any measurable use.

Queensland: Between 1981–1982 and 1987–1988, the number of drug offenses involving cocaine rose from 10 to 30. In the same period, heroin offenses rose from 123 to 272 and cannabis offenses from 4072 to 4989, with a peak in 1984–1985 of 7423.

Australian Capital Territory: In 1988, cocaine accounted for 0.6% of admissions to drug treatment agencies and about 0.3% of drug offenses.

Northern Territory: Of 570 drug-related offenses in 1988–1989, 5 were shown as "other," of which some may have been cocaine.

From these statistics, two conclusions might be drawn. The first, which is direct and correct, is that Australia cannot be said to have a cocaine problem in any sense comparable to the U.S. Yet, as I have shown in earlier research (Mugford and Cohen, 1989), there is an established network of cocaine users who use powder cocaine, which they snort for leisure purposes, similar to much middle-class cocaine use in the U.S. Nonetheless, overall use levels are relatively low, and crack is effectively absent. Thus, there are both similarities and differences in overall cocaine use between the two countries that need to be explained.

The second conclusion one might infer from these statistics is that Australia has no drug problem to speak of. The latter is hard to support. Take, for example, the Northern Territory (NT). Centered around the city of Darwin (population 64,000), the NT is a massive land area of 525,000 square miles, about one-sixth (16%) of the area of the continental U.S. The NT—famous overseas as the site for the film *Crocodile Dundee*—has a population of 157,000, 22% of whom are aboriginal Australians. This is a land of "frontier" (for the white population) and of very mixed fortunes for the Aborigines—some of whom now profit from mining royalties, others of whom live in extremely poor conditions with heavy alcohol use. Table 9-1 shows the death statistics for the NT for the years 1981 through 1986.

As this table shows, drug-related deaths make up over half of all male deaths in the period and about one-third of female deaths. These staggering statistics relate, however, to the licit drugs tobacco and alcohol. Per capita alcohol intake in the Northern Territory is the highest in the country and one of the highest in the world. Illicit drug use barely figures in

TABLE 9-1   Drug-Related Deaths as a Percentage of Total Deaths,
Northern Territory, 1981–1986

Year	Sex	Drug-Related Deaths	Total Deaths	% Deaths Drug Related
1981	M	300	582	51.5
	F	98	272	36.0
1982	M	190	373	50.9
	F	72	200	36.0
1983	M	255	472	54.0
	F	81	266	30.5
1984	M	176	327	54.4
	F	81	223	36.3
1985	M	228	414	55.0
	F	81	237	34.2
1986	M	238	437	54.5
	F	81	234	34.6

SOURCE: Based on d'Abbs, 1989:4.

the area. More typical of the whole country, the figures for Victoria tell a similar tale. In 1988, there were 30,726 deaths in Victoria. Of these, 5768 (18.8%) were listed as drug related. Of those, 5569 (96.5%) were due to alcohol and tobacco. With respect to illicit drug use, substantial markets exist for cannabis, and there is also a sizeable market for heroin. Nonetheless, the deleterious health and social consequences from these drugs pale to insignificance when compared to those of the legal drugs, a point well documented in recent government inquiries:

> [I]llegal drugs are only a small part of the total picture of drug use in Australia. Legal drugs—alcohol, tobacco, caffeine and pharmaceutical drugs—are for obvious reasons the most widely used. Over eighty per cent of the adult population drink alcohol and around thirty per cent smoke tobacco products. By contrast a recent nationwide survey found that only 6.2 per cent of the population over the age of 14 had used cannabis in the last 12 months. The figures for heroin, cocaine and "pills" . . . were too low to have any statistical significance. (Cleeland Report, 1989:3; cf. Collins and Lapsley, 1991)

In short, Australia clearly has a drug problem, but equally clearly, it does not involve cocaine, less still crack. Insofar as cocaine is used, it is snorted in powder form, not smoked as crack. Thus, we need an explanation that identifies continuities between Australia and the U.S. that might account for the similar patterns of powder cocaine use while also identifying discontinuities that account for the difference in crack use.

CONTINGENT EXPLANATIONS FOR THE DIFFERENCE
BETWEEN THE U.S. AND AUSTRALIA

If Australia is socially a very similar country to the United States—and in terms of global comparisons, the similarities are much more obvious than the differences—why does Australia not have a cocaine or crack epidemic? The question is not merely academic. It has concerned senior government officials and elected politicians over the last six to seven years, based upon the belief that, in many areas of life, a new fashion or trend in the U.S. often appears soon after in Australia. Indeed, in the mid-1980s, some people were so convinced that this would happen that research projects on cocaine were started, police precautions were instituted, and so forth. Yet the epidemic has not occurred.

Two contingent explanations for this nonoccurrence have been advanced, centering on time and space, which must be scrutinized briefly. First, many still think the epidemic will come and read signs of increased cocaine trafficking as its portent. They may turn out to be right, but to sustain the argument, one must assume a very slow rate of contagion or imitation. "Imitation" of central countries by peripheral countries certainly occurs in the modern world, but with the speed and frequency of travel as well as instant media coverage and telecommunications, the time lags continually shorten—for example, "rap" music was popular in Australia within months of its commercial appearance in the U.S. Moreover, Australians are as ready to acquire new ideas, gadgets, and routines as Americans. In short, time lag has no real bite as an explanation; if crack were coming to Australia, it would have been here by now.

The other frequently cited contingency used to explain the difference in the Australian pattern of cocaine use has to do with geographical distance. Australia is a long way from Latin America, which eliminates light aircraft and small ships as vehicles for importation. More significantly, smugglers often embed their wares in a broad flow of other traffic that already exists, but there is no regular traffic of goods or people between Latin America and Australia. Distance should not be entirely discounted as a factor, and were the geography different, more cocaine might have come into this country. Nonetheless, the differences between the American and Canadian experience with cocaine and crack (see Chapter 8) and the fair similarity of Canada with Australia suggest that geographical distance is a muted factor. Moreover, other drugs are shipped long distances to Australia (especially Southeast Asian heroin), albeit under circumstances slightly more propitious for traffickers. This, too, suggests that smuggling into Australia is not overly difficult.

Thus, neither time nor space is compelling as an explanation of the difference between the two countries, and perhaps this should not be surprising. As Harvey (1989) and Giddens (1990) have argued, one of the key features of modernity is its capacity to make time-space differences dwindle, so it would be unusual if so modern a phenomenon as drug use for leisure-based excitement[1] could be explained by such nonmodern features. Thus, a wider, more social-structural explanation is needed.

SOCIAL-STRUCTURAL EXPLANATIONS OF THE DIFFERENCES IN COCAINE AND CRACK USE LEVELS, U.S. VS. AUSTRALIA

Despite the similarities between the U.S. and Australia, there are subtle but important differences that are significant to my argument. The first has to do with the *modern metropolitan style of life,* which I have suggested is the underpinning for consumerist drug use (see the appendix to this chapter). One might think that Australia, a country located far from the U.S. and Europe and more a receiver than a generator of cultural ideas, must be less cosmopolitan than the U.S. If we compare Sydney and Melbourne with New York and San Francisco (or with London, Paris, and Berlin), this appears to be so. No doubt the latter cities are centers of power and influence within which we see the cutting edge of modern, metropolitan lifestyles. But this reasoning confuses cosmopolitan with metropolitan. Although U.S. cities are on the hypermodern edge of capitalist consumer culture, a substantial proportion of the total American population lives in small towns, suburbs, and provincial cities. Australia, by contrast, has a much larger proportion of its population living in big cities (the Sydney and Melbourne conurbations constitute about half the population). Thus, Australia is on average more metropolitan than the U.S.

Second, American cities are organized such that the suburbs in which many middle Americans live are socially dissimilar to Australia in important ways. In a large city like Sydney, many people live in suburbs that appear superficially similar to those that surround America's great cities. But American suburbs lie within county administrations that collect substantial taxes and state funds and use these to run their own schools, health services, police forces, and so forth. The strong tendencies toward residential and lifestyle *segregation* within modern U.S. cities are thus powerfully enhanced, as is the tendency for middle-class whites to "flee the city." Those escapees leave behind decaying inner-city areas that lack the resources to escape the clutch of poverty. These inner-city areas need more welfare services and yet have less ability to fund them because of the impoverished tax base. At the same time, the resource-rich suburban communities provide much better services, and this disparity accelerates the flight of those who can afford to flee. This sets up a vicious circle of further residential segregation. Indeed, it produces almost tribal loyalties in which the sense of "us versus them" is heightened, the divisions of class replicating and exaggerating those of race and ethnicity.[2]

Some of these tendencies exist in Australia, but they are much more muted. Although one can identify wealthy and attractive suburbs with high property values and better schools, the underlying structure of provision centers much more upon the state government. In Sydney, for example, schools, health care, and policing are all the function of the New South Wales state government—not of the city of Sydney or of some county board. Local government is not insignificant, but the old saw that Australian local government is about "rates, roads, and rubbish" remains relevant. So the affluent, white, middle- and upper-class people who live in Sydney's suburbs remain part of the overall political and taxation system within which the poor live. As a result, I suggest, the division that allows middle Americans in the suburbs to separate themselves off into enclaves of "traditional values" is much weaker in Australia.

The U.S., as a result, is a society that contains a much higher level of internal cultural contradiction than Australia. "Middle Australia," insofar as it exists, is a good deal more urbanized, secularized, and cosmopolitan than "middle America," and all Australians are tied into a single system of taxation, service provision, and electoral representation. The gaps between middle Australia and the metropolitan sophisticates (on one side) and the poor (on the other) are moderate, whereas the larger gaps in the U.S. generate a great deal of tension over issues of the morality of lifestyle (of which the drug issue is only one—see Hunter, 1991).

This analysis suggests three things about cocaine use. First, we ought to find consumerist-style use in both countries. Second, we should find more political controversy over drugs in the U.S. than in Australia because the former is more divided. Third, and relatedly, we should find greater (and more controversial) efforts to control cocaine use in the U.S., both for reasons of social control and for symbolic political reasons. In fact, we find all three of these characteristics.

Several other differences between the two countries bear upon the question of crack in particular. The U.S. has a *racial legacy* that connects back to antebellum slavery. The underclass in the U.S. is made up substantially of people of color in a way that is not true in Australia. Although Australia is by no means a model of racial tolerance, its racial conflict is significantly different in character. The aboriginal population of Australia, a victim of white colonialism rather than slavery, is tiny (around 1%), and much of it remains rural *cum* tribal. Moreover, so far as one may refer to an underclass in Australia, it is by no means defined so strongly by race or by residence.

This does not mean that Aborigines are not disadvantaged or do not have drug problems—far from it. Alcohol use in aboriginal groups is high, and alcohol is implicated in a wide variety of serious social problems, from very poor health and low life expectancy, through high arrest rates for minor crimes, including drunk and disorderly offenses, to their massive overrepresentation in Australian jails. Alcohol abuse is also a factor in the disturbingly high incidence of black on black violence, like that found in inner-city areas of the U.S., that has been documented in recent studies.[3]

Nonetheless, despite these manifest disadvantages, there are no large, black, urban ghettos where illicit drug trafficking flourishes as it does in the U.S. That reflects both the small numbers of aboriginal people and the fact that they are dispersed across the country, most in nonurban areas, rather than segregated in ghettos as in the U.S. The problems of black Americans, however—where disproportionately high use of alcohol and tobacco, poorer health, and crime and black on black violence also figure—are overlaid with problems having to do with illicit substance use. And this is connected to the second important difference, for it is not simply that the racial distribution of the underclass varies between the two countries. Were that the only significant difference, our underclass would display the same problems found in the U.S., but without a strongly racial character. The central point, simply put, is that *Australia does not have an underclass in the same way that the U.S. does.*

Of course, this simple statement needs qualification. Wealth is not evenly distributed in Australia, and through the 1980s, inequality has increased. The shape of that inequality is similar to the U.S.—a very few people own an immense amount of wealth and everyone else owns a little. But Australia, although not a welfare state dream, clearly has more of *a support net for the poor.* Unemployment and welfare benefits, although arguably meager, are still more generous and of longer duration than their equivalents in the USA. Nowhere in Australian cities, for example, can we find an area equivalent to Mott Haven, the South Bronx area graphically described in a *New York Times* special report (Gonzalez and Dugger, 1991). In this area, which is 69% Hispanic and 29% black, 38% of the nearly fifty thousand people are on public assistance, and the median family income is $7600, well below the official poverty line. About two-thirds of families are headed by a single mother; yet pregnant women receive poor if any prenatal care. The area is rife with drug dealing and criminal violence, and the picture painted of this troubled area is bleak: "At night, the rhythm of life is jolted by the crackle of gunfire and the crash of bottles flung off roofs. 20 year-old Joey Maysonet surveyed a horizon of ghosts. He pointed to one corner and recalled how in this year alone, three of his friends had died there."

Although the processes involved are immensely complex, the overall economic effect of the differences between American and Australian welfare systems, on top of the unique way poverty and race interact in the

U.S., is clear. In Australia, there is no racial ghetto where youth, deprived of economic opportunity, can make money and gain dignity selling crack (see Chapter 3). This is perhaps the most important single element in the equation I am examining. The close identification of crack with black and Latino residents of inner cities is all too real. Yet that connection arises not from any inherent criminality of black and Latino Americans, but from these broader structural considerations.

A final set of differences between the U.S. and Australia concerns *drug regulation*. These differences are difficult to define in conventional scientific ways. The general pattern of laws is similar in the two countries, and the same substances are legal and illegal in both. Both countries have internal variations at the state level, especially in regard to cannabis. Some state laws are close to decriminalization (*e.g.,* South Australia); others retain severe penalties. In both countries, trafficking is viewed as much more serious than use. Both countries have signed the same international drug control treaties, and both energetically seek to seize domestic drug products (particularly cannabis) and interdict illicit imports. Yet despite these similarities, the Australian drug control system is palpably *less zealous and punitive* than its American counterpart.

One example of this difference may be found in federal government action. In the mid-1980s, fueled by a variety of concerns, including the contemporary hysteria in the U.S., the Australian government launched a federal-state drug summit. After much huffing and puffing, the outcome was a multimillion-dollar budget for the National Campaign Against Drug Abuse (NCADA). Despite a clear focus on illegal drugs, NCADA ended up stressing legal drugs (alcohol and tobacco) as major determinants of ill health and other social costs in Australia. In this regard, NCADA's efforts fall into the long tradition of Australian drug policy: *concentrating more on health than on law enforcement* (NCADA is based in the Commonwealth Department of Community Services and Health). Moreover, when health concerns are raised in Australia, they are real concerns. In the U.S., by contrast, the apparent health and safety concerns that purport to be the rationale for random drug testing seem on closer examination to be a mere smoke screen for moral intervention (O'Malley and Mugford, 1991c).

NCADA has, overall, served to make the drug debate in Australia more, not less, rational and informed because the organization is neither staffed by prohibitionist ideologues nor under pressure from extreme political ideologues to suppress certain forms of drug use. As a result, the Australian public gained a complex understanding of the issues, and their expressed views are more knowledgeable and tolerant than those commonly expressed in the U.S. An illustration of this is provided by a recent opinion poll in Canberra, the national capital (Bammer, 1991). Respondents were asked about a proposed heroin maintenance experiment—a system in which registered addicts would receive drugs from a government outlet. Fully two-thirds of the respondents approved of such a trial. Furthermore, asked whether specific drugs were a "serious problem" in the community, 95% cited excessive drinking of alcohol, for heroin use 93%, cocaine 91%, amphetamines 82%, hallucinogens 80%, tobacco 79%, and marijuana 56%. That is, the highest priority was awarded to a legal drug (alcohol) and the lowest to an illegal drug (marijuana). Such a pattern bears tribute to a concerted campaign to understand the real health risks and social costs of *all* drugs.

In the U.S., drug policy discourse seems to have been driven far more by law and order concerns and to have hewn to a much more ideological line. In various research trips to the U.S., I could not help noticing that legal and illegal drugs are usually talked about as if they were fundamentally different phenomena, as if both did not entail health risks. Listening to political rhetoric, one would never guess that former Surgeon General Koop and former Drug Czar Bennett were talking about two sides of the same coin.

The two nations' different stances toward needle exchange programs makes a similar point. Such programs aim to minimize the spread of HIV and AIDS from the sharing of drug injection equipment. The evidence is clear that where clean equipment is made readily available, as in Sydney, intravenous drug users share needles less and as a result have much lower rates of HIV seropositivity. The level of HIV infection in Sydney's substantial injecting drug community remains low (as of 1995, around 2%) compared to U.S. cities like New York or Newark, New Jersey, which have infection rates as high as 50–60%. Although it would be an exaggeration to say that needle exchanges are not controversial in Australia, compared to the furor raised in the U.S. whenever they are proposed, Australia has been a model of calm. Rhetoric about needle exchanges "sending the wrong message" and "condoning drug use" has been the dominant political response in the U.S. In Australia, only a small minority of moral conservatives made such claims, and even these fell largely upon deaf ears.

Indeed, the U.S. government has responded to AIDS and to crack in a similarly unfortunate way. In both cases, the problems quickly spread through American cities; in the case of AIDS, a "second wave" was carried by drug users who were denied clean needles because that would "send the wrong message." In both cases, there was massive media attention and public debate. Yet that debate had an unreal character. Moral posturing about how people ought to live took pride of place over what actually worked to save lives because what seemed to work in other countries was ideologically unpalatable. By contrast, Australia has not had a crack epidemic and is also not experiencing a second wave AIDS epidemic driven by needle sharing. Here, too, variations in national political culture seem to account for the difference, with the Australian government prepared to respond to real problems with realistic policies rather than moralizing rhetoric. In short, Australian drug control policy has always been less morally absolutist and less enthusiastically punitive. In my view, this, too, helps account for our lack of a crack problem and our lower rate of drug-related problems more generally.

CONCLUSION

If we add up the foregoing strands of metropolitanism, racial stratification, welfare provision, and drug regulation, we can better understand why the U.S. is more ripe for drug problems than Australia. On one hand, to the extent that metropolitan U.S. society is at the hypermodern edge of consumer capitalism, there will be substantial middle- class drug use. That use is condemned as a moral outrage by those segments of "middle America" that cling to "traditional values," but this has had little, if any, effect on prevalence. On the other hand, the interaction of poverty, racism, and enfeebled public welfare provisions creates all the necessary conditions for both large-scale urban trafficking and a ready market for a powerful drug like crack, which offers moments of pleasure and escape. For the users and traffickers in America's inner cities, the propensity toward harsh, punitive drug control policies has only exacerbated the troubles that made both crack use and crack dealing attractive in the first place.

Meanwhile in Australia, where these key social-structural features are different, an otherwise similar country sees a very different picture of cocaine use. Here there is some consumerist use of powder cocaine among the metropolitan middle and working classes, but because of a greater racial tolerance and a stronger safety net for the poor, we have little basis for urban gang trafficking or escapist use. Finally, whatever drug problems we do have are more apt to be dealt with in terms of rational regulation and public health programs than with moral hysteria and repressive policies.

The use of a drug like crack can be seen as a function of supply, regulation, and demand. In the case of Australia, supply is restricted, partly by geographical contingency but more importantly by the absence of a class of people for whom illicit crack sales is perhaps the only available means of material success. With powder cocaine for snorting, the difference between the two nations is smaller. In both, there is a distribution network that involves many users in low-level distribution among themselves and friends, but in a context of privacy and friendship rather than fiercely competitive, for-profit street sales between strangers. Supply, then, is a part of the story.

On regulation, the less punitive system in Australia has restrained the excesses that attend full prohibitionism. Repressive regulations have a peculiar and destructive effect on the "settings" in which drug use occurs. The more a given form of drug use is criminalized and its users stigmatized, the more pressures there are toward the riskiest form of use. Dealers have an incentive to concentrate the product to maximize profit. Users have an incentive to use rapidly to reduce the visibility of use (just as speakeasies led more to drunkenness than "civilized drinking"). At the same time, the more moderate users and those with the highest attachment to conventional culture will be least likely to participate in use. Thus, user groups tend increasingly to consist of the disaffected, the unattached, and risk takers, those most likely to have sets and settings of excess. In short, the more repressively prohibitionist drug regulation is, the more negative and problematic the sets and settings of use will be.

This brings me back to the demand dimension. Both Australia and America are locked increasingly into the consumerism of modern life, and some drug use—especially activities like snorting cocaine—is best understood in this way. Where the two nations differ is in the areas conventionally focused on by drug theorists—the negative consequences of drug use. Without racial ghettos, Australia has far fewer despair-inducing conditions and consequently fewer people with the impetus to "escape" them by using (and/or selling) crack. Because cocaine use in Australia is more a middle-class activity, and because we lack the equivalent of American ghettos, we have a similar albeit smaller demand for drugs like cocaine and almost no demand for a drug like crack.

The differences between the two societies in supply, regulation, demand, and the resultant drug problems are all related to political-economic differences. Thus, by implication, reducing the harms of drug use (not the fantastical and unachievable "drug-free society") depends in part on internal economic and social reform. For example, social policies that truly improve the life circumstances and life chances of the growing ranks of poor people will, as many of the other contributors to this book show, almost certainly strengthen their bonds to conventional life and reduce their drug abuse. Clearly, such social policies would actually contribute to reducing drug-related harms, unlike high-tech panaceas like "bug wars" against coca crops or aircraft carriers in the Caribbean or increasing the already appalling level of imprisonment of young black men (Duster, 1987; Lusane, 1991).

Lamentably, as Australia has fallen under the spell of laissez-faire economic rationalism through the 1980s, some of the bulwarks that have saved us from American-style excesses have been eroded. Australian spending on public welfare, for example, is under threat. Nonetheless, differences in this arena remain marked. The Reagan-Bush years in the U.S. were characterized by a clear redistribution of wealth upward and a refusal to undertake public spending to create employment and to maintain the inner city, the effects of which exacerbated the long-run tendencies toward local fiscal crisis and white middle-class flight to the suburbs. This in turn further weakened the urban tax base and public support programs, the latter being already low by international standards. Many voters in the richest nation on earth convinced themselves that they could not afford to support what they saw as the parasitic poor. The poor, they seemed to say, echoing Reagan, should display a little more energy and initiative and earn money for themselves rather than "sponge" from the welfare system. What many Australians find ironic is that those same American voters seem willing to spend boundless sums to incarcerate those inner-city poor who display just such energy and initiative working in the only growth industry in their neighborhoods.

In Australia, we have not created the fertile soil in which such things as "crack epidemics" take root. We take better care of our citizens on a collective basis, preferring to deal as best we can with their problems rather than relying upon a combination of punitive measures and moralizing rhetoric as a response to the problems of the poor and needy. As a result, we have neither widespread, violent, illicit drug markets in our cities nor substantial numbers of heavy crack users who both suffer and seem to "cause" serious social problems.

APPENDIX: A NOTE ON THEORIZING THE PROBLEM OF COCAINE AND CRACK USE

It might be thought that there is no need of a special explanation for drug use in modern societies, for Weil (1972) and Siegel (1989) have shown that drug use has always been ubiquitous within human cultures and is even found among other species. But a general feature cannot explain a specific one, although it may be a necessary condition for it. Knowing that humans take drugs, for example, tells us nothing of the form that drug use takes in a particular culture, nor who takes which drugs and why. Nor does this general pattern establish the specific pattern of consequences that flows from drug use. This is a vital question, for with cocaine (as with other illicit and licit drugs), use is patterned in nonrandom ways. Indeed, one might sketch an ideal-type distinction between two extremes of cocaine use. One involves buying cocaine through friendship channels and snorting it in party settings as a sensual pleasure and celebration of success. The other involves buying crack on the street and smoking it for escape from the problems of a poor and threatening life. In both cases, pleasure and status are involved, but the former is more frequent among the middle class, and the latter is found largely among the poor.

Of course, reality is more complex than this, but the contrast is heuristically useful because such a pattern cannot be explained by reference to any general features of human drug taking. Rather, it requires explanation in terms of particular features of the social contexts in which drug use occurs. Part of the difficulty, however, with analyzing drug-related problems at a social-structural level is that a good theoretical framework has not yet been developed; much theorizing about drug use is locked into simplistic models that focus upon pathology and problems. I have dealt with some of these topics in part elsewhere[4] and will not reiterate the details of the argument here. In summary, however, the following seven points can be noted:

1. Most conventional approaches to drugs locate them inside discourses of health, law/deviance, or policy. In contrast, I think it vital to locate them principally (although by no means entirely) in a discourse about the commodity consumption and exciting leisure practices inherent in modernity.

2. Most conventional approaches to drugs emphasize psychomedical concerns. They concentrate upon such things as poor impulse control, deficits in the immediate environment, or the backgrounds and personalities of users. They assume that normal, educated, and informed people don't use drugs and that those who do must suffer from deficit or pathology. In contrast, I think it vital to see that the majority of users of all drugs, licit and illicit, employ them actively and in organized fashion. Like other lawbreakers (Katz, 1988; Presdee, 1991), they are "agents" (not merely creatures that react) who create and sustain meaning, in this case, by the use of drugs. Most are knowledgeable about drugs and successfully control the dangers, but the sense of risk is not irrelevant (see Lyng, 1990).

3. Most conventional approaches to drugs focus on the minority of users who show up in treatment or prison and thus conclude that drug use causes problems. In contrast, my own research on noncaptive populations confirms the picture documented by other writers in this volume (including Cohen, Cheung and Erickson, and Reinarman et al.), which is that most drug users manage their use without serious problems. Zinberg (1984), in his seminal work on drug control, referred to "setting," that is, the network of social ties in which the user is embedded and that constitutes the situation or context of use, as a major influence on use. Setting can operate in either direction (see Mugford, 1991c:37–42), so that users are constrained to use or not to use, depending on the nature of that setting. In the case of cocaine used for leisure purposes in conventional life contexts, setting limits use and prevents problems (see, *e.g.,* Waldorf et al., 1991).

4. Most conventional approaches to drugs assume that demand for drugs, especially illicit ones, arises from some pathological "deficit" and/or that demand is a reflex of supply. With the former, demand is seen as some kind of mistake—as if intelligent people would not freely do these things. With the latter, many writers assume that once one has explained the supply of a drug, demand needs no further explanation because people are powerless to resist it. In contrast, O'Malley and I have argued (Mugford and O'Malley 1990, 1991; O'Malley and Mugford, 1991a, 1991b) that the sources of demand must be theorized as part of modern society.

5. Most conventional approaches to drugs assume that illicit drug use undermines the fabric of modern life and is "un-American" (or "un-British," "un-Australian"). In contrast, I argue that drug use *epitomizes* one of the two (contradictory) aspects[5] of modern culture—the pursuit of self through

consumption and the "hedonist ethic" (see Bell, 1976; Bellah et al., 1985; Campbell, 1987; Featherstone, 1983, 1987; Reinarman, 1995).

6. Most conventional approaches to drugs document the problems of use in extensive fashion and see them, and deficit-driven demand, as the normal condition of drug use. I argue, in contrast, that although drug-related problems and deficit-driven demand clearly exist, these are found among a minority rather than the majority of illicit drug users. Consequently, we still need an explanation of drug use patterns for the majority of users, and this, I suggest, must focus on modern culture. (This does not mean that I ignore deficit explanations. As I will show, distinguishing between demand based upon the pursuit of excitement in leisure and demand that is largely deficit driven is at the core of my argument.)

7. The six points just outlined all concern modern culture, which embraces a particular and historically specific set of values about time, pleasure, and entertainment within which a variety of activities, including drug use, are given specific cultural meanings (see Chapter 16).

Of these seven points, the crucial issue that I must develop briefly here concerns the *normality* of demand for drugs within modern societies. Modern societies are structured by the development of capitalism; a money economy; capitalist relations of production, consumption, and exchange; and the development of the metropolis. Baudelaire long ago suggested that these developments brought with them a style of life characterized by "the transitory, the momentary and the contingent" (Frisby, 1986:14; see also Berman, 1983). Within this culture, time becomes commodified and "desacralized." The commodification of time, says Giddens (1981:131), holds "the key to the deepest transformations of day-to-day social life that are brought about by the emergence of capitalism. These relate both to the central phenomenon of the organization of production . . .and also the intimate textures of how daily social life is experienced." Desacralization of time leads to the development of the "stupefying number of forms of entertainment invented by modern civilizations. . . . [T]he situation is precisely the opposite of that found in traditional societies where 'entertainments' do not exist" (Provonost, 1986:10).

In contrast to the premodern, modern life becomes divided between two worlds: on one hand, production—a world of duty, effort, wage labor (for most people), and time that is not one's own—and on the other hand, consumption—a world of leisure, pleasure, free time. This division is particularly sharp in the metropolis, where the conditions of modernity are most advanced. Indeed, leisure time categories such as "the weekend" and especially "Saturday night" are crucial cultural signifiers in the metropolitan experience (Chambers, 1986). The demand for entertainment that is intrinsic to the modern sphere of consumption is, I submit, central for understanding modern use of drugs. While drugs continue to be used for quasi-religious and spiritual purposes and for self-medication (*e.g.*, Watson and Beck, 1991), widespread drug use as a leisure pursuit in its own right is part and parcel of modern life. Moreover, as Reinarman and Levine also argue in Chapter 16, this demand is—in a sociological sense—both normal and integral to the modern, industrial economy and society.

Modern cities are differentiated into several areas with varied moral statuses that are political in character. Debates about the "vices" found in certain areas are surrogates for debates about class and power. Stallybrass and White (1986), for example, show that new discourses that challenged insobriety (devaluing alcohol use and "carnival" time) and promoted sobriety and propriety (valuing polite debate and coffee drinking) were explicitly developed in the coffee houses of the eighteenth century by people who consciously distanced themselves from the older, established drinking traditions of both aristocracy and peasantry.

Both consumerism and moral politics, then, are intertwined with modern ideas of pleasure. The use of drugs for "recreational" purposes is one element of commodity-based entertainment and exemplifies the "fleeting, transitory and contingent" character of modern life. Because modernity is strongest in cities, the association of the city, entertainment, and drug use is predictable. Furthermore, it should be no surprise that certain drugs (*e.g.*, cocaine) have taken on cultural meanings strongly associated with the "sensual" side of modern urban life or that this should stand as a moral affront to those holding "traditional values." In short, the use of cocaine and other drugs is a practice that is both embedded in modern culture and at the same time a symbolic terrain for political and moral struggle. Both elements are relevant to understanding the politics of cocaine and crack use.

For any drug we wish to study, therefore, we have a dual task: first, to analyze the market position that various forms of it come to occupy and, second, to understand the moral-political struggles surrounding it. With regard to the first, what Zinberg (1984) calls "set"—the expectations that users bring to the use of a drug that influence how they use it and interpret its effects—can be understood as being constructed by the market position of a given drug or form of a drug. For example, the fact that cocaine and crack are chemically equivalent does not lead to equivalence in set—users think of them differently, use them differently, and derive different highs. More important, if we compare crack smoking in a "street" setting with cocaine freebasing in affluent homes—actions that are objectively identical—we do not find equivalent sets. The question then becomes whether we can connect the various sets that surround cocaine to the two ideal types of use outlined earlier.

Let us start with the more negative form of use. Illicit drug use is often seen as retreatism, and retreatist use is highly visible in treatment-based research. Impoverished underclass crack users may be seeking pleasure and celebrating (however momentarily) success just as more affluent freebasers do. But the ghetto crack users who have attracted so much attention are difficult to understand apart from the dire circumstances in which they live; their crack use tends to have an element of escape.

The second ideal-typical form of use—snorting to celebrate success or for leisure and pleasure in private party situations, using cocaine purchased through friendship networks rather than street-corner dealers—cannot be understood in quite the same way. This second type, much more typical among middle-class people, is better conceptualized as conformity to the norms of consumer culture—albeit by an illegal route. What could fit better into an exciting, youthful, metropolitan, leisure scene than cocaine? It is a powerful stimulant sold in a high-status commodity form, it makes users "feel like a million bucks" (as long as they don't overdo it), and it allows them to transcend workaday cares in a moment, transporting them into a world of excitement (see Gusfield, 1987, on drugs and context shifting). My research on recreational cocaine users in Australia (Mugford and Cohen, 1989) found exactly this type of use and user, as did Cohen (1989) in the Netherlands, Erickson et al. (1987) in Canada, and Waldorf et al. (1991) in the U.S.

These latter studies describe both a psychological set that sees cocaine as a pleasurable party drug and a social setting of largely conventional lives within which cocaine is used. For the majority of users who hold that set and take cocaine within that setting, the drug creates few problems for them or for society at large. Crack users may be seeking status-filled pleasures, too, but the psychological set they bring to their use tends to have a deficit dimension created by poverty and despair; and their crack use typically takes place in deeply troubled settings that help create problems for users and for others. My argument is summarized schematically in Table 9-2.

TABLE 9-2   Cocaine/Crack Contexts and Effects

Drug	Set	Setting	Wider Social Context	Problems
Powder cocaine	Great feelings of power/ success and pleasure	Leisure Friendship network Use moderated	Employed, educated users "Comfortable" suburbs	Relatively few, but some escalation to high levels
Crack	Escape, pleasure	Dead time "Street" Use not moderated	Unemployed, poor Inner city	Many, both direct to user and indirect to society

The use of cocaine in "epidemic" proportions, therefore, needs to be investigated very carefully, with attention paid to disentangling those elements that drive a consumerist, pleasure-based form of cocaine use from those that also have an escapist or deficit dimension. If we find surges of one or another type of use in one country but not in another, otherwise similar country, we must ask what social-structural conditions obtain in one but not the other that would account for this.

NOTES

1. I expand on this aspect of drug use in later sections.

2. I am aware that the detailed patterns of the U.S. are more complex than this simplified account implies. But I seek here to paint only in broad brush strokes. Australia also shows local complexity, but the difference at the broadest level is what matters for this comparative argument.

3. For shocking figures on the disproportionate arrest and incarceration rates and poor health of the aboriginal population, see the *Royal Commission into Aboriginal Deaths in Custody,* vol 1, 1990; *Medical Journal of Australia,* February 1991; and *Aboriginal and Islander Health Worker,* May/June 1991.

4. See Dance and Mugford, 1991; Mugford, 1991a, 1991b, 1991c, 1991d; Mugford and Cohen, 1989; Mugford and O'Malley 1990, 1991; O'Malley and Mugford, 1991a, 1991b.

5. The other is the well-known Protestant work ethic.

REFERENCES

Bammer, Gabrielle. 1991. *Feasibility Research into the Controlled Availability of Opioids.* Canberra: National Center for Epidemiology and Population Health, Australian National University.

Bell, Daniel. 1976. *The Cultural Contradictions of Capitalism.* New York: Harper Torchbooks.

Bellah, Robert, Richard Madsen, William Sullivan, Ann Swidler, and Stephen Tipton. 1985. *Habits of the Heart: Individualism and Commitment in American Life.* New York: Harper and Row.

Berman, Marshall. 1983. *All That Is Solid Melts into Air: The Experience of Modernity.* London: Verso.

Campbell, Colin. 1987. *The Romantic Ethic and the Spirit of Modern Consumerism.* Oxford: Basil Blackwell.

Chambers, Ian. 1986. *Popular Culture—The Metropolitan Experience.* London: Methuen.

Cleeland Report. 1989. *Drugs, Crime and Society: Report by the Parliamentary Joint Committee on the National Crime Authority.* Chaired by Peter Cleeland, MP. Canberra: Australian Government Publishing Service.

Cohen, Peter. 1989. *Cocaine Use in Amsterdam in Non-Deviant Subcultures.* Amsterdam, Netherlands: University of Amsterdam.

Collins, David J., and Helen M. Lapsley. Monograph #15. Canberra: Australian Government 1991. *Estimating the Economic Costs of Drug Abuse in Australia.* National Campaign Against Drug Abuse Publishing Service.

d'Abbs, Peter. 1989. "Indicators of Illegal Drug Use: Northern Territory," paper for the second National Drug Indicators Conference, Canberra, March.

Dance, Phyll, and Stephen Mugford. 1992. "The St. Oswald's Day Celebrations: 'Carnival' Versus 'Sobriety' in an Australian Drug Enthusiast Group," *Journal of Drug Issues* 22:591–606.

Duster, Troy S. 1987. "Crime, Youth Unemployment, and the Black Underclass," *Crime and Delinquency* 33: 300–315.

Erickson, Patricia, Edward Adlaf, Glenn Murray, and Reginald Smart. 1987. *The Steel Drug: Cocaine in Perspective.* Lexington, MA.: Lexington Books, D.C. Heath.

Featherstone, M. 1983. "The Body in Consumer Culture," *Theory, Culture and Society* 1: 18–33.

————. 1987. "Lifestyle and Consumer Culture," *Theory, Culture and Society* 4: 57–70.

Frisby, David. 1986. *Fragments of Modernity*. Cambridge, England: Polity Press.

Giddens, Anthony. 1981. *A Contemporary Critique of Historical Materialism*. Cambridge, England: Polity Press.

————. 1985. *The Nation-State and Violence*. Cambridge, England: Polity Press.

————. 1990. *The Condition of Modernity*. Cambridge, England: Polity Press.

Gonzalez, David, and Celia W. Dugger. 1991. "A Neighborhood Struggle with Despair," *New York Times*, Nov. 5: A1, A16.

Gusfield, J. R. 1987. "Passage to Play: Rituals of Drink in American Society," pp. 73–80 in M. Douglas, ed., *Constructive Drinking: Perspectives on Drink from Anthropology*. Cambridge, England: Cambridge University Press.

Harvey, David. 1989. *The Condition of Postmodernity*. Oxford, England: Blackwell.

Hunter, James Davison. 1991. *Culture Wars: The Struggle To Define America*. New York: Basic Books.

Katz, Jack. 1988. *Seductions of Crime: Moral and Sensual Attractions of Doing Evil*. New York: Basic Books.

Lee, Felicia R. 1991. "For Material Things and Protection, More Girls Are Taking the Road to Violence," *New York Times*, Nov. 25: A1, A16.

Lusane, Clarence. 1991. *Pipe Dream Blues: Racism and the War on Drugs*. Boston: South End Press.

Lyng, S. 1990. "Edgework: A Social Psychological Analysis of Voluntary Risk Taking," *American Journal of Sociology* 95: 887–921.

Mugford, Stephen K. 1981. "The Structure and History of the International Trade in Drugs—Some Implications for Social Policy," pp. 100–104 in *Man, Drugs and Society*. Canberra: Australian Foundation for Alcohol and Drug Dependence.

————. 1982. "Some Political and Economic Features of the Drug Trade: Historical Perspectives and Policy Implications," pp. 12–18 in Grant Wardlaw, ed., *Drug Trade and Drug Use*. Canberra: Australian Foundation for Alcohol and Drug Dependence for the Australian National University.

————. 1988. "Pathology, Pleasure, Profit and the State: Towards an Integrated Theory of Drug Use," paper presented to the Australia and New Zealand Society of Criminology, Sydney.

————. 1991a. "Alternative Methods, Alternative Realities," pp. 333–355 in Grant Wardlaw, ed., *Proceedings of the Second National Drug Indicators Conference*. Canberra: Australian Institute of Criminology.

————. 1991b. "Drug Policy and Harm Reduction: Towards a Unified Policy for Legal and Illegal Drugs," pp. 22–35 in J. Mathews et al., eds., *An Unwinnable War: The Politics of Drug Decriminalization*. Sydney: Pluto Press.

————. 1991c. "Drug Legalization and the 'Goldilocks' Problem: Thinking About the Costs and Control of Drugs," pp. 33–50 in Melvyn B. Krauss and Edward P. Lazear, eds., *Searching for Alternatives: Drug-Control Policy in the United States*. Stanford, CA: Hoover Institution Press.

————. 1991d. "Least Bad Solutions to the 'Drugs Problem,'" *Drug and Alcohol Review* 10: 401–415.

Mugford, Stephen K., and Phillip J. Cohen. 1989. *Drug Use, Social Relations and*

Commodity Consumption: A Study of Cocaine Users in Sydney, Canberra and Melbourne.
A report to the Research into Drug Abuse Advisory Committee, NCADA.

Mugford, Stephen K., and Pat O'Malley. 1990. "Policies Unfit for Heroin?," *International Journal on Drug Policy* 2: 16–22.

———. 1991. "Heroin Policy and the Limits of Left Realism," *Crime, Law and Social Change: An International Journal* 15: 19–36.

O'Malley, Pat, and Stephen K. Mugford. 1991a. "The Demand for Intoxicating Commodities: Implications for the 'War on Drugs,'" *Social Justice: A Journal of Crime, Conflict and World Order* 18:49–75.

———. 1991b. "Crime, Excitement and Modernity," paper presented to the annual meeting of the American Society of Criminology, San Francisco.

———. 1991c. "Moral Technology: The Political Agenda of Random Drug Testing," *Social Justice: A Journal of Crime, Conflict and World Order* 18:122–146.

Presdee, Mike. 1991. "Doing Right, Doing Wrong, Doing Crime: Young People and the Construction of Crime," paper presented to the annual meeting of the American Society of Criminology, San Francisco.

Provonost, G. 1986. "Introduction: Time in Historical Perspective," *International Social Science Journal* 107: 5–18.

Reinarman, Craig. 1995. "The 12-Step Movement and Advanced Capitalist Culture: Notes on the Politics of Self-Control in Postmodernity," pp. 90–109 in M. Darnovsky, B. Epstein, and R. Flacks, eds., *Cultural Politics and Social Movements.* Philadelphia: Temple University Press.

Siegel, R. K. 1989. *Intoxication: Life in Pursuit of Artificial Paradise.* New York: Simon & Schuster.

Stallybrass, P., and A. White. 1986. *The Poetics and Politics of Transgression.* London: Methuen.

Waldorf, Dan, Craig Reinarman, and Sheigla Murphy. 1991. *Cocaine Changes: The Experience of Using and Quitting.* Philadelphia: Temple University Press.

Wardlaw, Grant, ed. 1991. *Proceedings of the Second National Drug Indicators Conference.* Canberra: Australian Institute of Criminology.

Watson, Lynne, and Jerome Beck. 1991. "New Age Seekers: MDMA Use as an Adjunct to Spiritual Pursuit," *Journal of Psychoactive Drugs* 23: 261–270.

Weil, Andrew. 1972. *The Natural Mind: An Investigation of Drugs and the Higher Consciousness.* Boston: Houghton Mifflin.

Zinberg, Norman. 1984. *Drug, Set and Setting: The Basis for Controlled Intoxicant Use.* New Haven, CT: Yale University Press.

TEN

Crack in the Netherlands

Effective Social Policy is Effective Drug Policy

Peter D. A. Cohen

In this chapter, I describe what is known about the relatively small amount of crack use found in the Netherlands. In keeping with the spirit of this book, I believe that one cannot understand Dutch drug use and drug policy without understanding their historical and sociopolitical context. First, therefore, I offer a brief description of how the Dutch labor movements responded to our first "drug problem"—alcohol. This history is important both because it informed subsequent Dutch drug policy and because these labor movements shaped the reform legislation on income distribution and social services that has, in turn, exercised a powerful influence on the consequences of drug use in the Netherlands. Second, I summarize recent reactions to heroin use in the Netherlands, which also tell us something useful about how subsequent forms of use of drugs such as cocaine and crack are being dealt with in Dutch society. Third, I summarize Dutch social policies on drug use. Finally, I describe what we know about crack use in the Netherlands with an eye for what it can tell us about crack in the very different context of the U.S.

ALCOHOL AND THE WORKING CLASS
DURING DUTCH INDUSTRIALIZATION

In the nineteenth century, a strong anti-alcohol ideology was one of the elements in Dutch working-class movements for emancipation. Although working-class organizations were politically divided about the best strategies for contending with the industrialist elite, a remarkable unity existed in their views about alcohol.[1] As in America, alcohol was depicted as destroying families. But more importantly, in the Netherlands, alcohol was also seen as distracting people from what *really* mattered: organizing politically to win representation in parliament or even to overthrow the traditional structure of power altogether. Although it is difficult to determine retrospectively what drinking patterns and problems really existed, the objective size of alcohol-related health or behavior dysfunctions does not really matter for my purposes here. What does matter is the strength of the idea that combating alcohol was part of the struggle to raise the social and material status of the poor.[2]

I want to stress two aspects of this idea. First, alcohol was seen as a problem for the *working class*. The best known image of this is the man in a working-class pub being dragged out by his small working-class daughter, who is saying, "Daddy, please stop and come home." There was no equivalent concern for the *middle- and upper-class* drinkers, who were not perceived as problematic or in need of political emancipation. Second, there was a very strong alcohol abstinence or mitigation *movement* (often led by middle- and upper-class intellectuals) whose members wore a "blue button" on their lapels as a symbol of abstinence. The influence of this old movement of the "blue buttons" can still be recognized in legislation regulating the production and distribution of alcohol. (Most European nations have such alcohol regulations, with Nordic nations the most strict, although none are prohibitionist.) Concern over alcohol was a part of all formal working-class movements as well as the more diffuse ideology about improving the material and political status of "the laboring classes." Thus, anti-alcohol agitation was part of the same political phenomenon that led to the first reform legislation on child labor, housing conditions, working hours, and safety at work.

In short, in the Netherlands of the nineteenth century, drinking was seen as a problem for the working-class segment of the population, and antidrinking attitudes were part of a general struggle for political emancipation of that segment. In the last century and a half, all the industrialized democracies of Western Europe have experienced alcohol as problematic, and in general, all have interpreted drinking problems in terms of their effects on the *general* social development of the poor.

However, alcohol has now lost its former function as rallying point for political emancipation. Objectively, one might say that today, just as one hundred fifty years ago, the prevalence of alcohol-related health problems is high. The best estimate from prevalence studies of drinking suggest that slightly more than 3% of Dutch citizens drink enough to impair their health or social functioning.[3] But compared to one hundred fifty years ago, one of the striking differences is that alcohol-related problems are no longer seen as belonging to a certain class of the population. Nor are current concerns about alcohol connected to broader ideologies about the need to change the sociopolitical structure of society. Today, as in the U.S., alcohol concerns are connected to much narrower, individualistic ideologies about personal health.

But an important difference remains as a residue of this history. Working-class political activity over the last hundred and fifty years has left a legacy of welfare and social security systems in present-day northern Europe (and to some degree in southern Europe). In contrast to the U.S., the Netherlands and most other industrialized democracies of Europe have relatively well developed social legislation that strengthens the socioeconomic position of those who have the weakest position in capitalist systems of production. State-financed housing programs, health care systems, old age and disability insurance, licensing and workplace safety rules, and such are all secured by law. Of course, the quality of the results of such legislation varies between countries, as does their cost. But as a rule, these vast systems of public provision have markedly improved the standard of living of the poor and the working class and reduced inequality—without impairing Europe's ability to remain one of the richest economic entities of the modern world. And, most germane to my purpose here, these public programs have helped immensely in minimizing the negative consequences of alcohol, drug, and other problems.

HEROIN

In the Netherlands, the drug of most concern is and has long been heroin.[4] Even in Amsterdam, the largest urban metropolis in the nation (seven hundred thousand inhabitants), only about 1% of the household population over twelve years old has tried heroin even once in their lives (Sandwijk et al., 1991). Researchers estimate that the number of resident heroin addicts in this city (a group not normally caught by household surveys) is between three thousand (Korf and Hoogenhout, 1990) and forty-seven hundred, or between .5% and 1% of the age cohort over twelve years.[5] Despite this low prevalence, however, public concern about the use of heroin has been high since the early 1970s because the use of heroin is associated with poverty and the lowest social strata of the population.

The same cannot be said for marijuana. Marijuana use in the Netherlands has never been linked exclusively to underclasses. Rather, it is associated with the middle and upper classes. The result has been that, aside from societal conflict over the student movement and counterculture of the 1960s, marijuana use has attracted very little attention from the public or the government. To some degree, then, this parallels the absence of concern about alcohol use among the middle and upper classes a century ago.

So, in the Netherlands, heroin has replaced alcohol as the drug of most concern, in part because its use is most often linked to the lower strata, as was the case with alcohol a century ago. But the degree of concern over heroin is very different from the alcohol concerns of the period of industrialization. First, unlike alcohol, only a very small proportion of Dutch society has had any involvement with heroin. Second, concern about heroin comes and goes in relatively brief "attacks" (or "drug scares"). The apex of concern over heroin was 1980, when a group of mainly black heroin users[6] collectively occupied a large building in the center of Amsterdam in a protest against unsatisfactory social conditions. This incident made heroin use and its apparent causal connection to low social positions very visible, just as the public drunkenness of the laboring classes did in the eighteenth and nineteenth centuries. But, epidemiologically, heroin use was very rare in 1980, as it is now, despite the consistent quality (about 35% purity) and Europe's lowest heroin prices (Council of Europe, 1993).

In Dutch culture, heroin use serves as a harsh reminder of the existence of thousands of underprivileged people, even though everyone in the Netherlands knows that the objective size of the group of underprivileged persons is relatively small. This does not mean the problem is unimportant. In a society that has a vast complex of legal and social service institutions to deal with medical care, schooling, housing, and economic support for anyone in need, visible signs of apparent inefficiencies in this system— even for relatively small groups—raises questions about the system itself. This means that politicians fear these visible signs as almost nothing else, which is why they reacted to it so quickly.[7]

Throughout the modern history of the Netherlands, the heavy use of alcohol and more recently heroin by underclass groups has been a fact of important political significance. But *unlike in the U.S., in the Netherlands, such drug use has always been perceived as evidence of the need for social and political change.* Underclass drug use, and certainly what is called "addiction," are generally seen by Dutch society as intolerable—*not* merely because drugs make some of its members dysfunctional for society, but because the problems of some of its members suggest that their *society* is to some extent dysfunctional.

SOCIAL POLICIES TOWARD DRUG USE

It may be interesting to American readers that in the Netherlands the existing social welfare infrastructure has quickly adapted itself to the new phenomenon of regular heroin use and the nonmainstream lifestyles around it. In most locations in the Netherlands, the old, established institutions for dealing with alcohol problems were simply extended to cover drug problems. In the 1970s, Dutch policy makers, mainly in the cities, discovered that the abstinence ideology of these institutions was inappropriate and inadequate for dealing with heroin use. So this ideology lost its dominance, methadone maintenance programs were initiated, and the whole range of social welfare programs available for all Dutch citizens was mobilized. Thus, health care for "addicts," economic support, help with finding somewhere to live, and, if needed, even child care were made available to them.

Of course, these efforts did not completely integrate all such "addicts" into mainstream lifestyles and thereby render them invisible. In Amsterdam, it was exactly the visibility of a small group of about two hundred mostly black heroin users—and particularly the construction of a connection between visible addict behavior in the streets and the problems of certain neighborhoods—that led to suppressive actions toward "street addicts" in the 1980s. Americans are no strangers to this problem and response, but Dutch officials took such suppressive actions very reluctantly each time and only under heavy pressure from the population of these very restricted city areas. But aside from this subgroup, Dutch social policies have made the social and physical situation of most of the addicts in Amsterdam relatively good (see Korf and Hoogenhout, 1998); mortality is relatively low (see Sluis et al., 1990) and most lead relatively normal, rather inconspicuous lives that are generally not troubling to other citizens.

In short, the Dutch government's first response to the new heroin problem was to use the whole gamut of health and welfare programs to stabilize the lives of heavy users and integrate them into the community. This rendered their "deviance" largely invisible and relatively unproblematic for others. Officials used suppressive policies only for the small segment of heroin users who had not become integrated and invisible.

In the history of modern heroin use in the Netherlands, the political system has never had to cope with drug use as visible proof of the deep impoverishment of a large segment of the population. Of course, there is some impoverishment, but for most of the Dutch poor, the welfare system works adequately. Similarly, the welfare system works quite well for so-called heroin addicts, whose problems are seen as not merely drug related, but as the complex product of an impoverished environment and their reactions to it.

All that remain visible on city streets are small, marginal groups whose pastime is the use of all kinds of drugs, not least alcohol. Most of this street behavior occurs in very small geographical areas, which makes visible social marginalization a relatively limited phenomenon. Outside major cities, Dutch politics is almost untouched by illegal drug use (for example, a recent study by the scientific office of one of the political parties registered the complaint that lack of interest made serious discussion about progress in drug policy impossible.) Statistics about criminal activities, again mostly in the cities, do play some role in national politics, but both police and politicians speak of drug-related crime only as a small part of the general crime problem in the country. And, as in virtually all the social democracies of Western Europe, the general crime rate is a fraction of that found in the U.S. (see Currie, 1985).

CRACK, FREEBASE, AND COCAINE IN THE DUTCH CONTEXT

As in the U.S., cocaine use in the Netherlands emerged in the early 1970s. It is found mainly in Amsterdam, although even there on a very small scale. In the rest of the nation, the use of cocaine is either still rarer or completely absent.[8] The use of freebase (now "crack") cocaine began in 1983, when it was discovered by a group of experienced Surinamese heroin users in Amsterdam. These people ingested their heroin mainly by smoking it; intravenous use had never been fashionable among their circles. Thus, smoking cocaine came naturally to and spread easily among them. They simply smoked cocaine the same way as they smoked heroin (*i.e.*, "chasing the dragon"), and many continue to use cocaine by this method. They freebased in a casual yet cumbersome way with complicated glass pipes to cool and filter the smoke in water or alcohol.[9]

Medical personnel from the Amsterdam Health Authority reported some behavioral anomalies by early freebasers, and some regular freebasers complained of lung irritations. However, unlike the U.S., there was no evidence of citizen complaints or significant drug-related problems with freebasers or crack users. This form of cocaine use has gradually faded away except for a very small minority of the daily heroin users in the city who also smoke cocaine and small groups of freebasers outside the "junkie" scene.

No reliable quantitative information exists about the size of the group that freebased in 1983–1984 or about the proportion of this group that continues to freebase or smoke crack. However, in my 1987 study of 160 individuals from nondeviant subcultures in Amsterdam who used cocaine regularly, 18% reported having at least tried smoking crack or freebase. But this way of consuming cocaine was not popular in the mainly white, middle-class group of respondents in this study, among which past-month prevalence of this method of use was almost nonexistent (see Cohen, 1989, 1990).

In 1989 and 1990, I tried to find regular crack users by tapping the networks of regular cocaine users we had interviewed successfully in 1987. In spite of serious efforts to locate even a small sample, I was able to interview only four, three men and one woman. I also asked many other drug users in Amsterdam to contact regular crack or freebase users for me, a "snowball" sampling technique that had worked well in many earlier studies. This, too, failed to turn up any significant number of crack or freebase users. I was told that a few heavy crack users do exist, but even the promise of a $50 interview fee did not induce them to contact me. From the stories and estimates I gathered from my few respondents and other informants, one would not be far off in estimating that perhaps one or two hundred regular crack users or freebasers exist in all of Amsterdam.

None of the freebasers I interviewed belonged to the group of daily heroin users who lace their opiate consumption with some form of amphetamine or cocaine. Maximum consumption among these four was seven grams of crack a day. One of the four was almost abstinent and held a regular job. Two of the others had irregular jobs to maintain themselves. Only one was a cocaine dealer, a career ruptured by freebasing. This person (with his partner) smoked all of his supply meant for small-scale trade.

Like the American crack users described in earlier chapters, all four of my Dutch respondents reported bingeing, smoking all the crack or freebase available until it was gone. Interestingly, however, the frequency of these binges varied between daily and monthly. Only the cocaine dealer and partner planned to stop altogether; the others expressed no intention of becoming abstinent. They remarked that they found this high sufficiently pleasurable that they had to exercise deliberate control over their use. But both were confident that they would be able to continue to exercise that control. Their reports showed clearly that their ability to control their use of crack depended on the amount and seriousness of other social activities in their daily lives—work, holidays, home maintenance, partner relations, and so forth. Unfortunately, beyond the clues offered by these few respondents, there is simply not enough solid information on the variety of crack and freebase use patterns in Amsterdam to paint an adequate picture. But this fact is telling: crack use is apparently not widespread, and that which exists is not all that problematic for Dutch society.

To this Dutch observer, the speed with which crack use spread in America's inner cities cannot be understood apart from the fact that crack *sales* created real employment and entrepreneurial opportunities for an underclass population that has very few of them. By contrast, no form of commercial crack or freebase operation has been spotted in the Netherlands at this writing. It appears that those who favor the use of crack or freebase make it themselves from the locally available cocaine hydrochloride. I suspect that this absence of crack sales has to do with the fact that the Netherlands has not allowed a large underclass without legitimate economic options to develop, and so there are fewer citizens drawn to either crack sales or crack use.

We know more about cocaine hydrochloride use in Amsterdam from community prevalence studies and from other research done in specific groups that are difficult to trace by means of household surveys. The average price of such cocaine in Amsterdam is about $80 per gram at the gram-dealer level (average purity 60%) and about $30 per gram at the one-hundred-gram-dealer level. In general, there is a low prevalence of cocaine use in the Amsterdam population; only about 5% have tried cocaine one or more times in their lives, and less than one-tenth that number (.5%) have used it in the past month (Sandwijk et al., 1988; Sandwijk et al., 1991). Although about 80% of the local heroin "addicts" use cocaine with some regularity, cocaine has never been seen as a drug of the socially marginal. Because the use of crack or freebase cocaine has remained largely invisible, the only images of crack and freebase available in the Netherlands come from the U.S.

Local politicians in Amsterdam and in the Netherlands as a whole have never had to deal with the problem of cocaine use as a symbol of intolerable poverty. If such a problem had occurred, the Dutch government would have reacted first with the development of special branches or programs within its welfare and health systems, just as it has to all other new drug problems. One reason why crack use has not become visible is that the problems thought to flow from it (*e.g.*, poverty and crime) are managed adequately by public support, social service, and treatment programs.

In numerous research visits to the U.S., I have been struck repeatedly by how different the situation is there. Although until the early 1980s cocaine was not associated in public discourse with the poor, the introduction of crack among inner-city populations seems to have rendered it the symbolic "drug of the poor." And, in contrast to the Netherlands, American cities have large underclasses.[10] This means that almost all cities of any great size will have very visible populations whose social situation is comparable to that found in the Third World. This is one of the most important differences between the U.S. and Europe in general, where neither the mass scale of such poverty nor its depth are reached—not even in the poorest areas in Spain, southern Italy, or decaying British industrial towns.

To this observer, the forms of crack use found in ghettos seem to create very special problems for American governments for two reasons. First, U.S. elected officials, local or federal, do not have at their disposal the extensive network of legislative and institutional means to deal effectively with poverty and urban problems that European social democracies have. This means, for instance, that inner-city decay has not been countered with state- or city-initiated building programs that actually change the living situations of the poor. Even simple services like garbage collection in poorer neighborhoods in New York City stop when the government is strapped for resources. The result has been the incredible—to Dutch sensibilities—social and physical deterioration of America's inner cities, where masses of poor have to struggle simply to survive.

Second, the majority of Americans apparently do not support the initiation of social-democratic mechanisms to counteract such extreme forms of poverty. Remarkably, from the Dutch point of view, the dominant opinion in the U.S. seems to hold that the individuals who suffer such conditions are the cause of them. If they do not want to live in underclass conditions, they have to work to escape, the thinking goes. If they do not escape, this is somehow taken to mean that they do not "really" want to, as if the poor had control over the structure of economic opportunity. Thus, the poor are held responsible for their own poverty and all the consequences that flow from it. This, too, seems strange to Dutch sensibilities.

The combination of these two aspects of American politics means that American politicians have neither the tools to fight the presence of growing masses of underclass poor nor the political support for creating such tools. This problem could still be overlooked, however, if these poor would stay invisible in their decayed parts of the city and quietly sit there until they die. But many of America's poor have not cooperated in this invisibility; they "invade" parts of the city that "belong" to the richer segments of the American society, like subway stations and streets. They leave their ghettos—to work or look for work, to beg, to simply sit, to sleep in the streets, sometimes to sell drugs. They do not, in short, maintain a level of invisibility that mainstream American society, or even European societies, consider acceptable.

For the Dutch, and for most other Europeans, this would be a political problem of the first order. We tend to be shocked to find that, in American political culture, it is apparently possible to see mass poverty and underclass drug use and to neither recognize the links between them nor expand social programs to deal with them effectively.

NOTES

1. Hard liquor was considered the true "enemy" among alcoholic beverages.

2. According to Peter van Druenen (1989), when this movement began, alcohol production and consumption were lower than ever before.

3. Several prevalence studies of the Netherlands consistently show that about 7% of the adult population consumes twenty or more "standard units" of twelve centiliters of alcohol per week, or about three such units per day. To arrive at my estimate of 3% problem drinkers, I arbitrarily halved the 7% prevalence figure on the assumption that about half these regular drinkers could damage their health in some way. In Amsterdam, we found about 1% prevalence of alcohol consumption of ten or more standard units per day (Sandwijk et al., 1991).

4. This is true in most other Western nations, with the possible exception of Sweden, where intravenous use of amphetamines is considered the most prevalent and therefore most dangerous form of illicit drug use.

5. Many of these regular heroin users move in from areas in the Netherlands outside Amsterdam and its surroundings (Korf and Hoogenhout, 1990).

6. Of these, a majority had recently emigrated from Surinam to the Netherlands.

7. Another cause of this relative speed, of course, is the existence of the institutional system for dealing with distribution problems of health care, housing, and economic subsistence. This is different from, say, Italy, where concern about heroin use is at least as high as in the Netherlands, but where the absence of an efficient social care system has until now prevented politically efficient responses to this overt "sign" of the existence of underclasses.

8. For a nearly complete overview of existing data, see Korf, 1989.

9. I have observed them doing this hundreds of times in the so-called "heroin boat," a floating outfit in the center of Amsterdam donated to heroin addicts by the local community.

10. Some sense of the magnitude of poverty in the U.S. can be gleaned from the fact that, in 1985, 14% of the total population fell below the official government poverty line. But official poverty among African-Americans and Latino-Americans was over twice this rate (31.3% and 29%, respectively). When one excludes transfer payments, roughly one in four Americans is poor; again the figures are sharply higher for minorities and presumably have grown still worse with the ensuing recession and rising unemployment rates (Katz, 1989:241–243; see also Axinn and Stern, 1988; U.S. Bureau of the Census, 1991; Wilson, 1987).

REFERENCES

Axinn, June, and Mark J. Stern. 1988. *Dependency and Poverty.* Lexington, MA: Lexington Books.

Cohen, Peter D. A. 1989. *Cocaine Use in Amsterdam in Non-Deviant Subcultures.* Amsterdam, Netherlands: University of Amsterdam.

———. *Drugs as a Social Construct.* 1990. University of Amsterdam.

Council of Europe. 1993. *Draft Multi-City Report.* Strasbourg, France: Council of Europe.

Currie, Elliott. 1985. *Confronting Crime: An American Challenge.* New York: Pantheon.

Druenen, P. van. 1989. *Honderd Jaar Volksbond Rotterdam 1889–1989 [Hundred Years People's Union Rotterdam].* Rotterdam: Volksbond.

Katz, Michael B. 1989. *The Undeserving Poor.* New York: Pantheon.

Korf, Dirk. 1989. "Dutch Trends in Coke," paper prepared for the Council of Europe, Pompidou Group, University of Amsterdam.

Korf, Dirk, and Hoogenhout, H. 1990. *Zoden aan de dijk: Heroinegebruikers en hun ervaringen met en waardering van de Amsterdamse hulpverlening [Heroin Users: Their Experience with and Evaluation of the Amsterdam Drug Treatment System].* Amsterdam, Netherlands: University of Amsterdam.

Sandwijk, P., P. Cohen, and S. Musterd. 1991. *Licit and Illicit Drugs in Amsterdam* (report of the 1990 household survey in Amsterdam, 12 years and older). Amsterdam, Netherlands: University of Amsterdam.

Sandwijk, P., I. Westerterp, and S. Musterd. 1988. *Het gebruik van legale en ilegale drugs in Amsterdam* (report of the 1987 household survey in Amsterdam, 12 years and older, entitled *Licit and Illicit drugs in Amsterdam*). Amsterdam, Netherlands: University of Amsterdam.

Sluis, T., F. Cobelens, and P. Schrader. 1990. "Acute dood na druggebruik in Amsterdam" [Overdose Deaths in Amsterdam]. Amsterdam Municipal Health Service.

U.S. Bureau of the Census. 1991. *Poverty in the United States.* Washington, DC: Government Printing Office.

Wilson, William J. 1987. *The Truly Disadvantaged: The Inner City, the Underclass, and Public Policy.* Chicago: University of Chicago Press.

PART THREE

The Price of Repression

•　　•　　•　　•　　•　　•　　•

Lester Grinspoon has written that "our society cannot be both drug-free and free"* When we first read this, we agreed with him. However, when we learned that injection drug use is common in our maximum-security prisons—with their locked cells, strip searches, guards, and gun towers—we had to conclude that Dr. Grinspoon had understated the point. Apparently American society could not be drug-free even if it were completely unfree. Nonetheless, in the name of protecting us against the latest demon drug, politicians, police, judges, corporations, and schools have chipped away at well-established rights and liberties. For example, our government now routinely uses secret surveillance, informers, entrapment, and unwarranted searches and seizures to arrest and imprison citizens for ingesting substances. Most large corporations now test the urine of job applicants as well as employees in order to detect signs of illicit drug use among a handful. Many workers lose their livelihoods as a result even when their use took place after work hours and had no effect on their work. Some public schools employ drug-sniffing dogs to search student lockers. And the weight of all these repressive responses to crack has fallen most heavily on those groups in our society with the least power to resist it: the poor, women, and ethnic minorities.

Most of the earlier chapters in this book have discussed in passing some of the costs and consequences of the government's response to crack. In this section, those costs and consequences are laid out more explicitly. In Chapter 11, Ira Glasser and Loren Siegel document the assault on constitutional rights that has taken place since the start of the crack scare. Siegel shows in Chapter 12 how this assault has grown to Orwellian proportions for women who are pregnant and poor. In Chapter 13, Troy Duster examines the question of why the drug war has impinged so disproportionately on African-Americans. He provides the broad historical background necessary for understanding how the latest drug war led the most massive single wave of imprisonment in U.S. history and why this wave swept mostly minorities into prison cells. His analysis shows how the shifting structure of economic opportunities interacts with racism to push young black men into the underground economy—and into the sights of the drug war's artillery.

It has often been said that truth is the first casualty of war. This is also true of drug wars. One of the unfortunate consequences of twentieth-century drug scares has been the almost religious belief that "drugs" are a great evil. This belief has precluded open debate about the full costs and

*Lester Grinspoon, *Marihuana Reconsidered* (Oakland, CA: Quick American Archives, 1994), p. xv.

consequences of American-style drug prohibition. In Chapter 14, Ethan A. Nadelmann pulls together a great deal of data on these costs and consequences. He details a wide range of negative consequences that flow from harsh drug laws and examines the evidence on the intended benefits invoked to justify them. Finally, he compares this evidence with the likely costs, consequences, and benefits of the most radical drug policy alternative: controlled legalization.

ELEVEN

"When Constitutional Rights Seem Too Extravagant to Endure"

The Crack Scare's Impact on Civil Rights and Liberties

Ira Glasser and Loren Siegel

> *History teaches that grave threats to liberty often come in times of urgency, when constitutional rights seem too extravagant to endure. The World War II camp cases, and the Red Scare and McCarthy-era internal subversion cases, are only the most extreme reminders that when we allow fundamental freedoms to be sacrificed in the name of real or perceived exigency, we invariably come to regret it.*
>
> SUPREME COURT JUSTICE THURGOOD MARSHALL
> (*SKINNER V. RAILWAY LABOR EXECUTIVES' ASSOCIATION,*
> 109 S.CR. 1402 [1989])

In January 1991, the Sentencing Project, a small, Washington-based organization that promotes sentencing reform, released the results of a new study: the United States now has the highest known rate of incarceration in the world.[1] The study compared its findings with those of an oft-cited earlier report by the National Council on Crime and Delinquency. In 1979, the U.S. incarceration rate was third in the industrialized world, trailing behind South Africa and the Soviet Union;[2] in the intervening twelve years, the United States had passed them. By 1993, we had 426 prisoners per 100,000 people, compared to South Africa's 333. Even more disturbing was the Sentencing Project's second finding: black males in the United States are incarcerated at a rate more than four times that of black males in South Africa (we have 3109 black prisoners per 100,000 people, compared to South Africa's 729 per 100,000).[3]

How did this come to pass? The United States is a constitutional democracy with strong civil libertarian traditions. Our criminal justice system, with its constitutional protections for suspects, defendants, and offenders, is unique in the world. The Miranda warnings, the exclusionary rule, the presumption of innocence, the right to counsel, and our highly developed concepts of due process and equal protection of the law seem difficult to square with our astronomical incarceration rate. During the 1980s, people such as U.S. Attorney General Edwin Meese regularly complained that constitutional rights were a major impediment to law enforcement. Yet despite all these constitutional rights, it was precisely during this period that incarceration rates soared in the U.S.

As earlier chapters have mentioned, the dramatic increase in prisoners, especially of blacks and Latinos, was largely a result of the crack scare and the War on Drugs. The many young men and women jailed for drug possession or petty dealing are properly understood as domestic, civilian "prisoners of war." They are perhaps the most obvious (but by no means the only) civil rights and civil liberties victims of the Reagan, Bush, and Clinton administrations' drug policies.

The use of images of war, attack, and subversion in justifying repression has been a recurring pattern in American history. In 1798, for example, fear of war with France led to the Alien and Sedition Acts, which allowed the Adams administration to convict and imprison its Republican opponents. Around the time of World War I, and again in the 1950s, "red scares" brought intense assaults on First Amendment rights to freedom of speech, press, and association. The supposed threats of international communism and political subversion were used to justify police infiltration of political groups, ideological jailings, loyalty oaths, mass deportations, and congressional inquisitions. Many careers and lives were ruined. Similarly, during World War II, a potent combination of racism and war hysteria led to the internment of 110,000 Japanese-American citizens and confiscation of their property by the U.S government. Although no interred Japanese-American was ever charged or even suspected of treason or espionage, this crude deprivation of liberty and property actually withstood constitutional challenge: "Pressing public necessity," said the Supreme Court in upholding the constitutionality of the mass detention, "may sometimes justify the existence of such restrictions."[4] Many years later these fearful overreactions were seen for what they were. At the time, only the victims and a handful of supporters understood what was happening.

As Reinarman and Levine showed in the beginning of this book, drug scares have also been a recurring theme in American history. Inordinate fear of drugs has preoccupied ordinary citizens as well as many judicial minds. In his essay, "Images of Death and Destruction in Drug Law Cases," law professor Steven Wisotsky surveys court decisions from the Harrison Narcotics Act of 1914 on. He identifies two primary images that repeatedly surface in drug cases. The first is that of the addict enslaved by his drug. Phrases like "misery, destruction and death," "one of the walking dead," and "mind-, soul-, and body-destroying drugs" are common in drug cases. The second reappearing theme is that of drug trafficking as an "insidious crime" that inflicts "unimaginable sorrow" on society.[5] The following passage from a 1969 Supreme Court decision is illustrative:

> Commercial traffic in deadly mind-soul-and body-destroying drugs is beyond a doubt one of the greatest evils of our time. It cripples intellects, dwarfs bodies, paralyzes the progress of a substantial segment of our society, and frequently makes hopeless and sometimes violent and murderous criminals of persons of all ages who become its victims. Such consequences call for the most vigorous laws to suppress the traffic as well as the most powerful efforts to put these vigorous laws into effect.[6]

These twin themes of enslaved addicts and of evil traffickers peddling deadly and destructive substances have been used repeatedly to justify government repression and constitutionally questionable practices. In the battle against "the scourge of drugs," just as in the struggle against fears of foreign domination and political subversion, the ends frequently have been used to justify the means.

President Reagan tapped into America's long-standing fear of drugs when he declared a War on Drugs in 1982.[7] But it took the emergence of crack in the spring of 1986 to drive politicians, the media, and thus public opinion to the new heights of antidrug hysteria. The tragic, cocaine-related deaths of two young athletes, Len Bias and Don Rogers, and a flood of lurid press accounts of ghetto crack use, ushered in a period of intense public concern about illegal drugs that lasted into the 1990s.[8] And once again, although most drug use was among whites, the public's fears were primarily focused upon racial minorities. The crack scare helped create a political environment in which it was possible to adopt repressive laws and practices.

In 1986, in an election-year fury, Congress pushed through the Anti–Drug Abuse Act. The act ratcheted up the already long sentences for a host of mostly nonviolent federal drug offenses and contributed further to the U.S.'s dramatically rising incarceration rate. At the same time, state legislatures enacted dozens of Draconian laws, including long mandatory minimum sentences for many minor, nonviolent drug offenses. Even the most extreme proposals received mainstream acceptance. The Delaware legislature seriously debated the resurrection of the public whipping post for drug offenders. In North Carolina, the governor's "Drug Cabinet" proposed to reestablish the chain gang. Los Angeles police chief Daryl Gates seriously advocated shooting occasional drug users. And during a radio talk show, Drug Czar William Bennett stated he did not have a moral problem with "beheading" drug dealers. As in earlier periods of national stress, the Supreme Court was swayed by popular opinion and approved a range of intrusive governmental practices. Warrantless searches of citizens' garbage;[9] aerial searches of greenhouses, backyards, and surrounding fields;[10] drug courier profiles used as a substitute for objective evidence;[11] police roadblocks;[12] and suspicionless urine testing of government employees,[13] to name a few, all survived constitutional challenge. In some cases, two or three justices filed eloquent dissents. For example, Justice Thurgood Marshall's remarks that we quoted at the beginning of this chapter were part of his dissent in the Supreme Court's first drug-testing decision.

WAR: A DANGEROUS METAPHOR

The war metaphor has been very appealing to the architects of repressive drug policies. There is nothing like a war to galvanize public opinion and create singularity of national purpose. Typically, war promoters portray their enemies as extremely threatening and less than human and call for the use of extreme measures to vanquish them. Therefore, wars are almost inevitably accompanied by the loss of civil liberties.

Like the leaders of other wars, the drug warriors sought to mold public opinion. They said that victory cannot be realized if we stay within constitutional boundaries. That message was subtly evident in the Bush administration's 1989 war manifesto, the *National Drug Control Strategy* (NDCS). In it, Drug Czar William Bennett asserted, "We should be tough on drugs—much tougher than we are now" and "we should be extremely reluctant to restrict [drug enforcement officers] *within formal and arbitrary lines.*"[14] Then-director of the FBI, William Sessions, was more direct. In a speech at Southwest Texas State University in early 1989, Sessions named drugs as "one of the most awesome threats" to America's social order. He said that drugs force the nation "to strike a new balance between order and individual liberties."[15]

By September of 1989, much of the public had been persuaded. In his televised address to the nation to drum up support for the drug war, President Bush warned that "Drugs are sapping our strength as a nation." An opinion poll conducted shortly after Bush's address found 62% of the sample "willing to give up some freedoms we have in this country" to reduce drug use.[16] Eighty-two percent favored using the military to control illegal drugs *within* the United States, and 52% said they would agree to let police search homes of suspected drug dealers without a warrant, even if the houses "of people like you" were sometimes searched by mistake. Perhaps worst of all, 83% favored reporting drug *users* to the police, even if the suspects happened to be members of their own family.

Drug policy makers took the public's apparent tolerance for repression as an opportunity to escalate the war further. President Bush sent a new "battle plan" to Congress that would have expanded the list of drug crimes that could be punished by death. That act also had a section eerily reminiscent of the Palmer Raids during the Red Scare of the 1920s and would have given the Immigration and Naturalization Service sweeping new powers summarily to deport *legal* aliens convicted of drug offenses.[17] Two prominent conservative Republicans, Phil Gramm and Newt Gingrich, quickly followed with their National Drug and Crime Emergency Act. It declared "the existence of a National Drug and Crime Emergency" and called for the establishment of concentration camps, euphemistically called "temporary detention quarters," for drug law offenders at underutilized military installations.[18] The act also would have required those convicted of drug possession to pay for the cost of their own criminal trials.[19] The House Armed Services Committee included in its 1990 defense authorization bill its own solution to prison overcrowding: ship drug offenders off to "extremely remote Pacific Islands" where they would be subjected to forced labor and total isolation from friends and family.[20]

These proposals garnered press coverage and probably won some votes for the politicians who sponsored them. However, if enacted, they would not have had the slightest impact on the country's crime rate or its drug problem. Researchers have consistently found that neither the death penalty nor harsh sentencing has any substantial deterrent effect on crime.[21] Furthermore, wider use of the death penalty, the establishment of drug gulags, and the summary deportation of legal aliens are antithetical to traditional American values of fairness, due process, and proportionality. Nevertheless, the men and women who protested the policies of the War on Drugs, and who upheld the traditional American values of civil liberties, due process, and justice, were repeatedly accused of being "traitors" and "surrendering to the enemy." Daryl Gates, chief of police of Los Angeles and ardent drug war supporter, once said, "I suppose calling pushers of drug legalization treasonous would be too extreme. But I continue to wonder why they choose to weaken our war effort just when we, as a nation, are beginning to take the offensive."[22] During his two-year tenure as drug czar, William Bennett frequently tried to discredit advocates of alternative drug policies while refusing to debate them on the merits. He called their ideas traitorous, "intellectually and morally scandalous," "thin gruel," "disingenuous," and "perverse."[23] Even critics who advocated a shifting of national priorities away from law enforcement and toward prevention and treatment were accused of being weak and faint of heart. Such tactics insulated drug warriors from the burden of responding to criticism. Dialogue and debate were discouraged, and even scientific research that called the prevailing ideology into question was sometimes suppressed.[24]

WHO IS THE ENEMY IN THE WAR ON DRUGS?

The rhetoric of the War on Drugs painted the enemy with broad strokes. Presidents Reagan and Bush, Drug Czar Bennett, and others repeatedly depicted the drug war as a life-and-death struggle between good and evil, between moral abstainers and immoral users. Bennett's *National Drug*

Control Strategy portrayed the enemy as a vast criminal conspiracy made up of the approximately twenty-eight million Americans who use illicit drugs and their suppliers: "In the teeth of a crisis—especially one which has for so long appeared to spiral wildly out of control, we naturally look for villains. We need not look far; there are plenty of them. Anyone who sells— and (to a great if poorly understood extent) anyone who uses them—is involved in an international criminal enterprise that is killing thousands of Americans each year." [25] In the year Bennett said this, [26] four hundred thousand Americans died from smoking tobacco, [27] but only seven thousand Americans died from using all illegal drugs combined. Czar Bennett's anger was not directed at the drug addict, who, he said, was a "bottomed-out mess" who "makes the worst possible advertisement for new drug use" and is therefore "not very contagious." Most of his scorn was reserved for "the non-addicted casual or regular user" of currently illegal drugs whose life remained productive and intact. This unrepentant resistance to authority infuriated Bennett. He also believed that the casual or occasional users' intact lifestyle made their drug use "*highly* contagious." [28] According to the National Institute on Drug Abuse surveys, approximately 80% of America's cocaine users are white. [29] Bennett himself described the "typical cocaine user" as a middle-class, white suburbanite. [30] But although such predominately white occasional users were often the chief target of Bennett's rhetorical wrath, the full weight of the government's war machine was *not* aimed primarily at them. In terms of the day-to-day enforcement of our drug laws, black and Latino crack users and low-level dealers, and inner-city residents in general, have borne the brunt of the punitive war effort, even though they constitute the minority of users. This bias, which has finally been noticed by the press and civil rights leaders [31] and even by some in law enforcement, [32] has led to the appalling statistics released by the Sentencing Project. Once again, while the typical cocaine user is a white, middle-class suburbanite, the typical drug law offender in prison is an unemployed, twenty-eight-year-old, black male with an eleventh-grade education. [33] Professor Norval Morris of the University of Chicago Law School has accurately summed up the situation: "The whole law-and-order movement is—in *operation*—anti-black and anti-underclass. Not in plan, not in design, not in intent, but *in operation.*" [34]

"OPERATION PRESSURE POINT" AND ITS PROGENY: ANTI–BLACK AND ANTI–CIVIL LIBERTIES

In 1984, even before the crack epidemic was under way, the New York Police Department launched a major program on the Lower East Side of Manhattan to deal with street-level drug dealing. [35] Dubbed "Operation Pressure Point," the program was a massive attempt to rid the area of the drug trade: "Large numbers of rookie uniformed police on foot dispersed crowds, made searches and arrests, and questioned those perceived to be buyers or sellers. Housing Authority and Transit Authority police intensified patrols in the housing projects and subways. Plainclothes officers from the Narcotics Division carried out surveillance and 'buy and bust' operations."[36] Although the long-term effectiveness of Operation Pressure Point is questionable,[37] it did yield an impressive body count. By its two thousandth day in 1989, it had resulted in 46,903 arrests, 36,102 of them for drug offenses.[38] The high arrest rate received much praise, including honorable mention from Czar Bennett.[39]

Clones of Operation Pressure Point soon sprang up around the country: the Tactical Narcotics Team (TNT) program in New York City, Operation Invincible in Memphis, Operation Clean Sweep in Chicago, Operation Hammer in Los Angeles, the Red Dog Squad in Atlanta. All of these programs targeted poor, overwhelmingly minority, urban neighborhoods where drug dealing tended to be open and easy to detect. This kind of enforcement was certainly easier than raiding brokerage houses on Wall Street. Just as the police tend to arrest street prostitutes (mostly minorities) rather than expensive call girls (mostly white), drug arrests focused upon visible street traffic. The goal of these efforts was to make as many arrests as possible. And in that respect, virtually all of them succeeded. Jail and prison rates soared. In New York City, for example, TNT yielded a 35% increase in felony drug arrests between 1988 and 1989.[40] Nationwide, arrests for drug *possession* alone reported by state and local police rose from 400,000 in 1981 to 762,718 in 1988. Comparable figures for drug sale and manufacture rose from 150,000 in 1981 to 287,858 in 1988.[41] Predictably, minorities and especially African-Americans were disproportionately represented in these figures.[42]

These TNT-style street sweeps are not noted for their attention to the Bill of Rights. Much as their name suggests, sweeps invariably sweep up the innocent as well as the guilty. In dismissing the charges against one victim of a TNT sweep, a judge described a typical operation: "The back-up team . . . swept through the block and lined up, against the wall, any male who happened to be in the vicinity and since the defendant was in the vicinity he too was ordered out of his van."[43] The sweeps resemble indiscriminate military operations far more than they do careful police work, which is perhaps not surprising, given their role as part of a domestic war effort.

"NO PERSON SHALL KNOWINGLY LOITER . . ."

To the repressive arsenal of the War on Drugs, cities and towns across the country added loitering laws that punish people simply for congregating in so-called high drug activity areas. In March 1989, Kalamazoo, Michigan, enacted a law that stated "No person shall knowingly loiter about, frequent or live in any building, house, vacant lot, street, curb, lawn, ally, yard, apartment, store, automobile, boat, boathouse, airplane or other place ... where controlled substances or drug paraphernalia are sold, dispensed, furnished, given away or stored."[44] Convicted loiterers could receive a $500 fine and/or ninety days in jail. Alexandria, Virginia's loitering law allows up to two years' imprisonment for two people who loiter for several minutes and exchange "small objects."[45] Washington, D.C., enacted the Illegal Drug Zone Emergency Act of 1989, which allows the police to post "antiloitering notices" along one thousand feet of public street in a "recognized drug trafficking area." Residents and visitors are permitted to walk through the posted area or stand alone on the sidewalk. But if two or more people gather, the police can order them to disperse or arrest them for disorderly conduct.[46] Loitering laws are used as a substitute for real evidence. Where the police see actual drugs being sold, they can make arrests based on laws prohibiting such sales. Loitering laws are used when there is no evidence of illegal drug sales. "Hanging out" even in one's own neighborhood therefore becomes a crime. Such laws are not enforced in white, middle-class neighborhoods; they are strictly a ghetto phenomenon.[47]

ILLEGAL SEARCHES AND SEIZURES

The Fourth Amendment to the Constitution, which protects the people against unreasonable searches and seizures, has come under special attack during the past decade. In enforcing drug laws in inner-city communities, the police frequently ignore the core protections of the Fourth Amendment. For example, in Boston in early 1989, two highly questionable police practices came to light. First, during the course of a criminal trial, a detective with the Boston Police Drug Control Unit admitted he had falsified an affidavit upon which a search warrant was based. The *Boston Globe* then conducted an examination of three hundred fifty search warrants obtained during the previous year by members of the elite sixty-man unit.[48] The *Globe* found a pattern in which some detectives depended on single informants for dozens of cases. According to the warrants, one informant alone managed to infiltrate forty separate drug operations in one year. Moreover, the unit cited only twelve confidential informants for more than two hundred of the warrants. Chief counsel to the state public defender's office was incredulous. "It would be very unusual for anyone to get around to so many different drug-dealing operations in one year," he said. "Drug dealers try to limit the people they deal with because they don't know who might be an informant."[49] The police were submitting boilerplate affidavits in order to avoid inconvenient Fourth Amendment requirements. As a result, dozens of unlawful raids were carried out, mostly in minority communities.

In May of 1989, the Boston police announced a new plan to deal with drug dealers and gang members in three minority neighborhoods: Roxbury, Mattapan, and parts of Dorchester (the nonwhite parts). According to the deputy police superintendent in charge of those areas, "known drug dealers or gang members who in any way cause fear in the community" would be summarily searched on sight.[50] In dismissing the charges against a victim of the policy, Cortland A. Mathers, a black superior court judge, described it as "in effect, a proclamation of martial law in Roxbury for a narrow class of people—young blacks suspected of membership in a gang or perceived by the police to be in the company of someone thought to be a member."[51] Shortly thereafter, the Civil Liberties Union of Massachusetts filed a class action suit on behalf of all black and Hispanic people between the ages of fifteen and thirty living in areas where the "search on sight" policy was in effect. The complaint filed by the CLUM described what befell Rolando Carr, a thirty-year-old black resident of Dorchester, on the evening of October 10 as he was walking with two friends to a neighborhood store:

> As the three men attempted to pass along Shandon Road, defendant Pressley [a Boston police officer] ordered them to halt and place their hands against a wall. He pointed his gun in their direction. With his revolver trained on him, defendant Pressley shouted at Rolando Carr, words to the effect, "You . . . I said freeze . . . Up against the goddamn wall with your hands up and spread your legs." As Carr moved toward the wall, Pressley fired a shot, hitting Carr in the lower back area. Pressley then told plaintiff Carr, "Get Up," to which Carr responded, "I can't. You shot me." As Carr lay wounded on the ground near the wall on Shandon Road, Pressley began to search him. He removed a house key from his pocket. The search produced no weapon and no evidence of criminal activity.[52]

In the fall of 1988, the Chicago Housing Authority instituted a new policy designed to rid the city's public housing projects of drug dealers. Dubbed "Operation Clean Sweep," the policy authorized warrantless, random searches of tenants' apartments by Chicago police officers and housing authority agents. In December of that year, the Illinois Civil Liberties Union filed a class action lawsuit on behalf of the one hundred fifty thousand public housing tenants subject to the policy. The complaint describes the events of December 7, 1988—events that occurred while plaintiff "Jane Doe 2" was absent from her apartment:

> Chicago Police Department officers and Chicago Housing Authority officials came into the apartment and began searching all areas of the apartment.

They looked through and under the cushions of the couch, and looked into the freezer in Plaintiff Jane Doe 2's kitchen. During the course of the search, the police picked the lock on her bedroom door and entered and searched her bedroom. When Plaintiff Jane Doe 2 returned to her apartment she was stopped by the police. She was subjected to a personal search, which included· a search through her bags, in which she carried various Christmas gifts that she had just purchased.[53]

In airports, train stations, bus depots, and on state highways, people of color are being stopped and searched on the basis of subjective, racially biased "drug courier profiles." Narcotics police have been using profiles since the early 1970s, but their use has increased significantly since a 1989 Supreme Court decision declined to strike them down as unconstitutional.[54] Those thought to fit the profile can be stopped and subjected to a brief interrogation and frisk.[55] If anything about the person's demeanor raises suspicion, a full-scale search can then be initiated. As with the anti-loitering laws, profiles are used by the police when real evidence is not available; people get arrested not for what they've done, but because of how they look. It is inevitable, of course, that when police are allowed to decide who "looks like" a criminal, then prejudice will come into play.

In New Jersey, the public defender's office began noticing in 1987 that a disproportionate number of minority drivers from out of state were seeking representation after being stopped and arrested by state troopers on the New Jersey Turnpike. In 1988, the public defender's office hired a Rutgers University statistician to conduct a survey of traffic on a certain section of the turnpike. His findings were striking: of the 1634 vehicles observed by survey teams, 77, or 4.7%, were occupied by black people and had out-of-state plates. Yet of 271 arrests for contraband in 1988, 226 or 80% involved black motorists driving out-of state vehicles. In a lawsuit brought by the public defender's office and the New Jersey ACLU, the statistician, Dr. Joseph I. Naus, said the difference between the typical traffic pattern and the rate of arrests of blacks from other states "is dramatically above thresholds used to establish prima facie evidence of racial discrimination."[56]

In April 1990, a New York City criminal court judge suppressed the evidence against Annette Evans, who had been stopped and searched in the Port Authority Bus Terminal by a detective from the Port Authority's Drug Interdiction Unit. In her ruling, Judge Carol Berkman wrote, "I arraign approximately one-third of the felony cases in New York County and have no recollection of any defendant in a PAPD [Port Authority Police Department] drug interdiction case who was not either Black or Hispanic. Judges Soloff and Roberts, the two other arraigning Judges for New York County, also have no such recollection."[57] Although the PAPD denied relying upon a "drug courier profile" in its interdiction program, Judge Berkman found that the program focused disproportionately on blacks and Hispanics and concluded, "Minorities did not fight their way up from the back of the bus just to be routinely stopped and interrogated on their way through the terminal."[58]

There have been many incidents of well-known African-Americans being subjected to these humiliating stops. Several years ago Lamar Burton, the actor of *Roots* fame, was stopped while driving from Los Angeles to San Francisco. One common profile characteristic is a well-dressed black person driving an expensive car.[59] Linda Jones, a black reporter for the *Detroit News*, has been stopped and interrogated repeatedly at various airports around the country. She usually wears her hair in close-cropped braids wrapped in a colorful Caribbean scarf. Following one of the stops, the Drug Enforcement Administration agents told her they were "looking for people who looked foreign and appeared nervous."[60] The Fourth Amendment exists to protect citizens from the tyranny of searches and seizures based on the constable's bias or whim. The police practices that have flourished during the War on Drugs and that have been justified as a price we must pay to vanquish crack are antithetical to the spirit and the letter of the Fourth Amendment.

UNEQUAL JUSTICE

The Fourteenth Amendment's promise of "equal protection before the law" is being broken at the final stage of the criminal justice process: sentencing. In 1990, the *Indianapolis Star* reviewed two hundred Marion County cocaine-dealing cases and came to a disquieting conclusion: minorities were more likely to go to prison than their white counterparts, and they received sentences averaging nearly three years longer.[61] For example, a twenty-three-year old white restaurant cook with no arrest record was charged with dealing after he sold 9.6 grams of cocaine to an undercover officer. His privately retained attorney worked out a deal with the prosecutor in order to avoid the minimum twenty-year penalty mandated by Indiana law. The white defendant was allowed to plead guilty to a lesser charge and was sentenced to six weekends in a community corrections program, five hundred hours of public service work, and three years' probation. Two months later, an unemployed eighteen-year-old black man was charged with dealing after selling *less than 3 grams* to an undercover cop. His public defender also worked out a deal: he pleaded guilty as charged and was sentenced to six years in prison. Overall, the study found that first-time minority drug offenders received sentences twice as long as whites despite having an average of less than half as much cocaine.

A February 1990 study of young men aged twenty to twenty-nine under criminal justice custody in New York State produced similar findings.[62] The

Correctional Association of New York discovered that the sanctions for black and Latino men were far more severe than for young white men charged with similar crimes. Overall, 48% of minority male offenders were in prison or jail, compared to 18% of young white offenders. A high percentage of white offenders (48%) were on misdemeanor probation, compared to 26% of minority offenders. The report found that, on any given day, nearly one in four young black men is under the control of the criminal justice system in New York. These figures were nearly the same as those reported by the nationwide survey conducted by the Sentencing Project in February 1990.[63] The disparities documented by these studies are mainly attributable to two factors: the incontestable racial biases of sentencing judges throughout the country and the much weaker bargaining positions of most minority defendants, who must rely upon the overburdened services of public defenders for their defense. But in some states, the bias has been institutionalized in the laws themselves.

In 1988, for example, Minnesota enacted a law that increased the penalty for possession of "cocaine base" (crack) but not for powder cocaine. Although possession of three grams of powder cocaine carried a penalty of five years in prison and/or a fine of $10,000, under the new law, possession of three grams of crack cocaine carried a penalty of twenty years in prison and/or a $250,000 fine. In 1990, five black defendants charged under the crack law challenged its constitutionality.[64] Judge Pamela Alexander agreed. The judge was persuaded by the statistics presented by the defendants: 92.3% of all persons convicted of possession of crack in 1988 were black; 85.1% of all persons convicted of possession of powder cocaine in that year were white. The same pattern continued into 1989. In an opinion refreshing for its dispassionate tone, Judge Alexander rejected the state's claim that crack was so different from cocaine that it warranted harsher penalties: "Cocaine is cocaine. Eighty proof whiskey contains the same active ingredient as a can of beer, which is alcohol. There is no justifiable reason to uphold a statute which results in such unequal treatment of similarly situated individuals. The constitution is designed to prevent this type of injustice." The judge ruled that the statute violated the Equal Protection Clause of the Fourteenth Amendment as well as a comparable provision of the Minnesota Constitution. But the defendants may not fare as well on appeal. Although disparate sentencing practices based on race have always existed in the United States, the War on Drugs has made those disparities significantly greater.

THE WAR ON CRACK BECOMES A WAR ON CIVIL LIBERTIES

In the 1980s, drug warriors frequently claimed that crack is so dangerous that using it would cause violent behavior in otherwise law-abiding people and so powerful that even a single exposure might lead an otherwise stable person to addiction. This image was spread by sensational stories in national news weeklies, lurid front-page stories in major newspapers, and tabloid television reporting. As a result, many people came to believe that homicide and other violent crime were on the rise because ghetto residents were crazed by the chemical effects of crack. However, this was certainly not the case. One important government-sponsored study found that 85% of cocaine- and crack-related homicides in New York City during a three-month period in 1988 were the result of the illegal status of the drug business—not the result of the drug's pharmacological properties. The homicides were committed in the course of business disputes that, because the business is illegal, could not be handled by police or other formal agents of control (see Chapter 6). The pro–drug war hysteria, however, proved too strong for a single study to overcome; and the results were not well reported in the mass media, which were busily promoting the drug war.

As in previous drug scares, fears about crack merged easily with racial fears. It is true that a small minority of young African-Americans was drawn to crack sales during the mid-1980s (see Chapter 3). It is also true that, in the context of a collapsing public education system, a 50% unemployment rate for black teenagers, and Reagan's aggressive defunding of social programs that might have made a difference, drug dealing became the nation's principal new job program for ghetto youth in the 1980s. All this contributed to the climate in which it became possible to arrest and imprison disproportionately large numbers of young black men. At the same time that homicide was the leading cause of death among young black males,[65] imprisonment became epidemic among the survivors: by 1990, there were more young black men in prison than in college.[66]

The crack scare was also used to whip up support for repressive laws and policies with sometimes deadly results. Bans were enforced against the distribution of clean needles for intravenous drug users. It was said that allowing the distribution of needles would encourage illegal drug use and "send the wrong message." In this way, the increased transmission of AIDS became a direct consequence of repressive drug policies. In the Netherlands, for example, where clean needles are distributed by the government, only 9% of intravenous drug users carry the AIDS virus. In Liverpool, England, where there are several syringe exchange programs, the proportion of intravenous drug users with the AIDS virus is less than 1%. In the United States, it is 26%, and in New York City, it is over 60%. And most of these victims are not white. During the crack scare, the so-called "crack baby" became a common media image. However, as is now clear, nearly all the crack baby phenomenon was a result of severe poverty— which was increasing during the Reagan and Bush years. Infants with physical and medical problems were being born to the same demographic group and for the same reasons as always: no prenatal care, bad nutrition, spousal abuse and neglect, and the heavy use of many substances, including alcohol and cigarettes. However, identifying such infants as "poverty babies" would have asked the United States to focus on social policies of support and service to the poor; and such programs had become taboo during the Reagan-Bush years. Calling these infants "crack babies" fostered the illusion that there was a singular, pharmacological cause for low-weight infants with physiological, medical, or behavioral problems. And it allowed courts to respond to this problem by punishing mothers. More than two hundred women nationwide were charged with various crimes for taking illegal drugs during their pregnancies. Most of these victims were black (see Chapter 12).

In this chapter, we have pointed out some of the racist consequences of contemporary drug policies, and we have argued that the crack scare made those consequences worse. Civil liberties have been widely violated as a result of the War on Drugs, but disproportionately against blacks. More often than whites, African-Americans have been the victims of street sweeps, illegal searches, drug courier profiles, and antiloitering laws. Arrests for violations of drug laws soared from fewer than 200,000 a year in 1968, prior to the first drug war declared by Richard Nixon, to 1.2 million annually. Disproportionate numbers of blacks have been arrested and imprisoned. AIDS, attributable to contaminated needles, and homicide, including a rising number of bystander shootings as drug dealers settled their commercial disputes with automatic weapons, added to the carnage among minorities. It is no exaggeration to say that Americans are witnessing the decimation of young black men. That drug policies have made that worse should have been a major political scandal.

While African-Americans and other minorities have borne the brunt of the War on Drugs, they have not been the only victims. The incremental erosion of basic rights and liberties, justified by the drug crisis, affects all Americans. In particular, the evisceration of the core protections of the Fourth Amendment will have serious and long-term consequences for the privacy rights of everyone. The Fourth Amendment's prohibition against unreasonable searches and seizures by the government was not adopted in order to protect criminals. Rather, it was a hard-won political right that Americans fought a revolution to secure. During the colonial period, the American colonists came to hate the general searches conducted by British customs agents and authorized by the king. General searches did not require a specific warrant or probable cause to believe a crime had been committed. Agents of the crown could enter the home of any colonist at will and search for and seize any contraband, including pamphlets critical of British rule. After the revolution, the American people insisted on constitutional protection against such searches and seizures, and the Fourth Amendment was the result.

Today the core protections of the Fourth Amendment have been dangerously diluted because of the brew of racism and drug war hysteria. This has resulted in policies that negatively affect a great many Americans. A prime example is drug testing in the workplace, a practice unheard of prior to 1986 but now commonplace in both the public sector and private industry. Each year millions of presumably innocent workers must prove their chemical purity in order to get or keep a job. The legal doctrine that has evolved permitting suspicionless urine testing of both job applicants and employees represents a major departure from Fourth Amendment precedent. No longer is the government, in its capacity as employer, required to have individualized suspicion that a particular employee is hiding contraband before it may conduct a search. Now it must merely demonstrate a "special need" to conduct wholesale urine testing in order to pass constitutional muster. Similarly, the Supreme Court recently approved a Michigan program of setting up roadblocks and stopping *all* cars to check for intoxication rather than allowing the police to pull over only those drivers driving in an erratic manner.

Toward the end of his long and illustrious Supreme Court tenure, Justice Thurgood Marshall became a rather lonely defender of Fourth Amendment principles. It is fitting to conclude with the closing words of his dissent in *Skinner v. Railway Labor Executives' Association,* in which the Court's majority legalized suspicionless drug testing:

> I believe the Framers [of the Bill of Rights] would be appalled by the vision of mass governmental intrusions upon the integrity of the human body that the majority allows to become reality. The immediate victims of the majority's constitutional timorousness will be those railroad workers whose bodily fluids the Government may now forcibly collect and analyze. But ultimately, today's decision will reduce the privacy all citizens may enjoy, for . . . principles of law, once bent, do not snap back easily.

NOTES

1. Marc Mauer, "Americans Behind Bars: A Comparison of International Rates of Incarceration," Sentencing Project, Washington, D.C., 1991.

2. Eugene Doleschal and Anne Newton, "International Rates of Imprisonment," National Council on Crime and Delinquency, Information Center, 1979.

3. The study looked at the number of incarcerated adults in each country, both those awaiting trail and sentenced offenders, and divided this figure by the country's population to obtain an overall rate of incarceration. For the United States, combined figures for prison and jail populations were used.

4. *Korematsu v. United States,* 323 U.S. 214 (1944).

5. Steven Wisotsky, "Images of Death and Destruction in Drug Law Cases," *The Great Issues of Drug Policy,* Drug Policy Foundation (Washington, DC, 1990).

6. *Turner v. United States,* 396 U.S. 398, 426 (1969), cited in ibid., p. 52.

7. Ronald Reagan's War on Drugs was officially declared on October 14, 1982, during a speech to the U.S. Department of Justice. He pledged an "unshakable" commitment "to do what is necessary to end the drug menace." Leslie Maitland, "President Gives Plan To Combat Drug Networks," *New York Times,* October 15, 1982, p. A1.

8. In July of 1986, just after the deaths of Bias and Rogers, the three major television networks offered no less than seventy-four evening news segments on drugs, half of which dealt with crack (see Chapter 2).

9. *California v. Greenwood,* 107 S.Ct. 1625 (1987).

10. *Oliver v. United States,* 466 U.S. 170 (1984); *California v. Ciraolo,* 476 U.S. 207 (1986).

11. *United States v. Sokolow,* 109 S.Ct. 490 (1989).

12. *Michigan State Police v. Sitz,* 110 S.Ct. 2481 (1990).

13. *National Treasury Employees Union v. Von Raab,* 109 S.Ct. 1384 (1989); *Railway Labor Executives' Association v. Skinner,* 109 S.Ct. 1402 (1989).

14. White House, *National Drug Control Strategy* (NDCS), September 1989, pp. 7–8, emphasis added.

15. Henry Krausse, "FBI Director Says Drugs, Terrorism To Force New Balance of Law, Liberty," *Austin American Statesman,* February 11, 1989, p. C37. In a similar vein, Admiral William Crowe, then-chairman of the Joint Chiefs of Staff, stated that it would be necessary "to infringe some human rights" in pursuit of the War on Drugs. "My general feeling about drugs," he said, "is that this country is, at this point, not willing to do what it has to do to solve the drug problem. If this is truly a national crisis, and I've heard it referred to as war, you're probably going to have to infringe some human rights." Elizabeth Kurylo, "U.S. Military Chief: Stopping Drugs Impossible Without Some Limitations on Human Rights," *Atlanta Constitution,* April 5, 1989, p 5.

16. Richard Morin, "Many in Poll Say Bush Plan Is Not Stringent Enough," *Washington Post,* September 8, 1989, p. A1.

17. See Michael Isikoff, "U.S. Seeks Wider Anti-Drug Powers—Aliens Could Face Summary Expulsion," *Washington Post,* May 16, 1990, p. A1.

18. The World War II era internment camps for Japanese-Americans were similarly euphemistically called "relocation centers."

19. Gramm-Gingrich National Drug and Crime Emergency Act.

20. Michael Isikoff, "Penal Colonies for Drug Criminals?" *Washington Post,* September 19, 1990, p. A13. House Armed Services Committee member Rep. Richard Ray (D-Ga.), who took credit for the idea, explained, "There's not much chance they're going to get anything but rehabilitated on two small islands like these [Wake Island and Midway Island]. You can't go anywhere. You won't be interrupted by families coming to visit every weekend."

21. There is no credible evidence that the death penalty deters crime. States that have the death penalty do not have lower crime rates or murder rates than

states that have abolished the death penalty. And states that have abolished capital punishment, or instituted it, show no significant changes in either crime or murder rates. Similarly, contrary to the claims of politicians, there is no clear evidence that harsh sentencing laws deter crime. See, for example, the 1983 National Institute of Justice study, "Mandatory Sentencing: The Experience of Two States," which concludes that it was virtually impossible to determine if mandatory sentencing brought about any benefits.

22. Daryl F. Gates, "Some Among Us Would Seek to Surrender," *Los Angeles Times*, March 15, 1990, p. B7. Gates's adherence to a military solution to the drug problem was obvious during his September 5, 1990, testimony before Congress when he opined that casual drug users "should be taken out and shot." Ronald J. Ostrow, "Casual Drugs Users Should Be Shot, Gates Says," *Los Angeles Times*, September 6, 1990, p.A1. Although members of Congress, the media, and the public expressed some shock over the intemperance of these remarks, Gates never retracted them.

23. William J. Bennett, "Drug Policy and the Intellectuals," speech delivered at the Kennedy School of Government, Harvard University, December 11, 1989.

24. For example, several researchers from the University of Toronto conducted a survey to find out whether studies showing *no* adverse effects of cocaine in pregnancy had a different likelihood of being accepted for presentation at large scientific meetings than studies showing adverse effects. They found that between 1980 and 1989, fifty-eight abstracts on fetal outcome after gestational exposure to cocaine were submitted. Of the nine abstracts showing no adverse effect, only one (11%) was accepted. Of the forty-nine positive abstracts submitted, twenty-eight (57%) were accepted. The researchers concluded, "This bias against the null hypothesis may lead to distorted estimation of the teratogenic risk of cocaine and thus cause women to terminate their pregnancy unjustifiably." G. Koren, H. H. Shear, K. Graham, T. Einarson, "Bias Against the Null Hypothesis: The Reproductive Hazards of Cocaine," *Lancet*, December 16, 1989, pp. 1440–1442. See also the more detailed discussion of these issues by Morgan and Zimmer in Chapter 7.

25. NDCS, p. 7.

26. Arnold S. Trebach and Kevin B. Zeese, *Drug Prohibition and the Conscience of Nations*, Washington, DC: Drug Policy Foundation, 1990, p. 28.

27. S. Okie, "Smoking-Related Deaths Up 11% to 434,000 Yearly, CDC Reports," *Washington Post*, February 2, 1991, p. 1.

28. NDCS, p. 11; emphasis in original. Two legal scholars have observed that Bennett's vilification of the casual, nonaddicted user is "the most novel element" in the national drug control strategy. They posit that such a user particularly galls an authoritarian like Bennett because it is the nonaddicted user "who is most conspicuously thumbing his nose at state authority." Franklin E. Zimring and Gordon Hawkins, "What Kind of Drug War?" *Working Paper No.16*, Earl Warren Legal Institute, University of California, Berkeley, 1990.

29. National Institute on Drug Abuse, *National Household Survey on Drug Abuse; Population Estimates 1988*, Washington, DC: U.S. Government Printing Office.

30. *National Drug Control Strategy*, White House, September 1989, p. 4.

31. See Lisa Belkin, "Airport Anti-Drug Nets Snare Many People Fitting 'Profiles'—Racial Questions Raised," *New York Times,* March 20, 1990, p. A1; Ron Harris, "Blacks Take Brunt of War on Drugs," *Los Angeles Times,* April 22, 1990, p. A1; E. J. Mitchell, "Has Drug War Become a War Against Blacks?" *Detroit News,* April 26, 1990, p. 1; Bill McAllister, "Study: 1 in 4 Young Black Men Is in Jail or Court-Supervised," *Washington Post,* February 27, 1990, p. A3.

32. Immediately after the March 1991 University of Virginia fraternity drug bust, the law enforcement officials responsible for the raid stated that the investigation was undertaken partially to offset the fact that mostly inner-city minorities were being targeted by the War on Drugs.

33. David W. Rasmussen and Bruce L. Benson, "Drug Offenders in Florida," *An Economic Analysis of Recidivism Among Drug Offenders in Florida,* Policy Studies Program, Florida State University, Tallahassee, FL, 1990.

34. Quoted in Ron Harris, "Blacks Feel Brunt of Drug War," ibid., p. 1.

35. Lynn Zimmer, "Operation Pressure Point: The Disruption of Street-Level Drug Trade on New York's Lower East Side," Occasional Papers from the Center for Research in Crime and Justice, New York University School of Law, 1987.

36. Michael Z. Letwin, "Report from the Front Line: The Bennett Plan, Street-Level Drug Enforcement in New York City and the Legalization Debate," *Hofstra Law Review* 18: 799 (1990).

37. Zimmer, "Operation Pressure Point," p. 15.

38. Letwin, "Report from the Front Line," p. 799.

39. NDCS, p. 22.

40. Felicia R. Lee, "Attack on Crack: More Arrests, Fewer Long Sentences," *New York Times,* May 31, 1989, p. B1.

41. U.S. Department of Justice, Office of Justice Programs, Bureau of Justice Statistics, *Sourcebook of Criminal Justice Statistics—1989,* U.S. Government Printing Office.

42. Substance Abuse and Mental Health Services Administration, *National Household Survey on Drug Abuse: Population Estimates 1994,* Washington, DC: U.S. Department of Health and Human Services, SAMHSA, Office of Applied Studies, 1995. Sam Meddis, "Drug Arrest Rate Is Higher for Blacks," *USA Today,* December 20, 1989, p. A1.

43. *People v. Franklin,* N.Y.L.J., May 26, 1989, p. 23, cited in Letwin, "Report from the Front Line," p. 823, n. 154.

44. Craig A. Thomas, "ACLU Plan Challenge to Drug-Loitering Law," *Kalamazoo Gazette,* May 20, 1989, p. 1.

45. Jack Kelley, "Drug Tactics Raise Rights Fear," *USA Today,* May 17, 1990, p. 4A.

46. Linda Wheeler, "Anti-Loitering Law's Debut Impresses Neighbors in SE," *Washington Post,* June 1, 1989, p. D1.

47. In Seattle, Washington, the enforcement of a drug loitering law had another counterproductive effect: it drove drug users away from the areas of the city where clean needles were being distributed by the public health authorities in an AIDS prevention effort, so much so that health care officials found it difficult to find addicts who needed clean needles.

48. Sean Murphy, "Informant Pattern Is Called into Question," *Boston Sunday Globe,* March 26, 1989, p. 1.

49. Ibid., p. 9.

50. Richard Ray, "Police Begin To Crack Down on Known Drug Dealers, Gangs," *Boston Globe,* May 20, 1989, p. 22.

51. *Commonwealth v. Lamar Phillips and Melvin Woody,* No. 080275080276, Suffolk Superior Court, September 19, 1989.

52. This case was settled when the City of Boston agreed to pay an undisclosed sum of money to the named plaintiffs. Although the police department never formally rescinded the policy, it has ceased to implement it since the settlement of the CLUM lawsuit.

53. *Rose Summeries, Jane Does 1–3 and John Doe v. The Chicago Housing Authority,* complaint filed on December 18, 1988, in the U.S. Federal Court, Northern District of Illinois, Index No. 88 C 10566. The case was settled in 1989 after the Chicago Housing Authority entered into a consent decree specifying that apartments would be subjected to an "emergency inspection" only if there were "reasonable cause to believe that there is an immediate threat to the safety and/or welfare of tenants. . . ."

54. *United States v. Sokolow,* 490 U.S. 1 (1989). The Court avoided ruling on the constitutionality of the drug courier profile by finding that the totality of Sokolow's characteristics (paid for plane ticket in cash, used alias, wore black jump suit and copious amounts of gold jewelry) gave the police probable cause to stop and search him even in the absence of the profile.

55. In *Terry v. Ohio,* 392 U.S. 1 (1968), the Supreme Court held that the police could stop and frisk a person if the person's conduct gave rise to "an apprehension of danger." When written, the decision represented a narrow exception to the requirements of the Fourth Amendment. But over the years, it has been interpreted more and more broadly by the Court.

56. J. F. Sullivan, "New Jersey Police Are Accused of Minority Arrest Campaigns," *New York Times,* February 19, 1990, p. B1.

57. *People v. Evans,* 147 Misc.2d 811 at 813 (Sup.Ct., NY Co. 1990).

58. *People v. Evans* at 819.

59. For example, the Florida Highway Patrol relied on a drug courier profile that cautioned troopers to be suspicious of rented cars, "scrupulous obedience to traffic laws," and drivers wearing "lots of gold" or who do not "fit the vehicle" (*i.e.,* a black driving a Porsche), until the profile was ruled unconstitutional under state law by a state court judge. In Steven Wisotsky, *Breaking the Impasse in the War on Drugs,* Westport, CT: Greenwood Press, 1986, p. 127.

60. Lisa Belkin, "Airport Anti-Drug Nets Snare Many People Fitting 'Profiles,' " *New York Times,* March 20, 1990, p. A1.

61. George McLaren, "Minorities Do More Time for Cocaine Dealing," *Indianapolis Star,* April 30, 1990, p. 1.

62. *Imprisoned Generation,* a report by the Correctional Association of New York and the New York State Coalition for Criminal Justice, September 1990.

63. *Young Black Men and the Criminal Justice System: A Growing National Problem,* the Sentencing Project, February 1990.

64. *Minnesota v. Gerard Jerome Russell, Dmitry Deshone Armstead, Michael Odell Johnson, Steve Antonio Morrison and James NMN Alderson,* Hennepin County District Court, December 27, 1990.

65. According to a 1991 study by the Health and Human Services National Center for Health Statistics, more black adolescent boys die from gunshots than from all natural causes combined, and a black male teenager is eleven times more likely to be murdered with a gun than his white counterpart. Paul Taylor, "Guns and Youth: HHS's Grim Statistics," *Washington Post,* March 14, 1991, p. A1.

66. Marc Mauer, *Young Black Men and the Criminal Justice System: A Growing National Problem,* Sentencing Project, February 1990.

TWELVE

The Pregnancy Police
Fight the War on Drugs

Loren Siegel

The criminalization of poor women for ingesting drugs during pregnancy will surely be remembered as one of the most misguided of the repressive, constitutionally questionable tactics employed by the state during the War on Drugs. During the late 1980s, as the specter of "crack babies" haunted American political rhetoric, more than two hundred criminal prosecutions were initiated against women in almost twenty states. Overzealous prosecutors came up with a variety of pseudolegal theories upon which to base their cases. In North Carolina, Sandra Inzar was charged with assault with a deadly weapon (crack cocaine) with intent to kill her fetus, for which the maximum penalty is twenty years in prison.[1] In Virginia, Britta Smith was charged with felony child neglect after her newborn tested positive for a cocaine metabolite.[2] In New York, Melissa Morabito was charged with endangering the welfare of her unborn child.[3] Happily, the indictments against these women and most of the others were eventually dismissed by judges unwilling to stretch beyond all recognition the plain meaning of the penal laws.

One of the women, however, did not escape trial and conviction. On July 13, 1989, Jennifer Johnson of Altamonte Springs, Florida, became the first woman to be convicted under a drug trafficking statute for delivering drugs to her infant through the umbilical cord just moments after birth.[4] When she was arrested, Jennifer Johnson had been using cocaine for about three years. She had sought treatment for her addiction during her pregnancy, but no program would accept her. On January 23, 1989, Johnson gave birth to a baby girl. Her labor and delivery were normal, and, in the words of the attending obstetrician, the baby "looked and acted as we would expect a baby to look and act." Wanting the best for her baby, Johnson herself told the obstetrician that she had used cocaine during her pregnancy. This fact was confirmed by urine drug screens administered to both mother and infant. The hospital notified a state child protection investigator of the birth of a "cocaine baby." The investigator in turn notified the county sheriff, who initiated a criminal investigation that led to Johnson's arrest.

The prosecutor had to overcome a major legal obstacle in order to prosecute Ms. Johnson. Because under Florida law a fetus is not a person, he could not charge her with delivering cocaine during the pregnancy itself. So he argued instead that the cocaine was "delivered" after the birth during the sixty to ninety seconds before the umbilical cord was clamped. Judge O. H. Eaton of the Seminole County Circuit Court found Johnson guilty as charged, holding that the term "delivery" under Florida law included "passage of cocaine or a derivative of it from the body of the mother into the body of her child through the umbilical cord after birth occurs." Judge Eaton went on to rule:

> The fact that the defendant was addicted to cocaine at the time of these offenses is not a defense. The choice to use or not use cocaine is just that—a choice. . . . Pregnant addicts have been on notice for years that taking cocaine may be harmful to their children. This verdict puts pregnant addicts on notice that they have a responsibility to seek treatment for their addiction prior to giving birth. Otherwise, the state may very well use criminal prosecution to force future compliance with the law or, in appropriate cases, to punish those who violate it.[5]

Jennifer Johnson, who had no prior criminal convictions, was sentenced to one year of house arrest and fourteen years of closely supervised probation. The terms of her probation included a prohibition against entering a bar or nightclub without the permission of her probation officer. If Johnson became pregnant again during those fourteen years, she would have to follow a pregnancy care program approved by the court. She was also to be subject to random urine tests and warrantless searches of her home during her year of house arrest.

Jennifer Johnson was the first woman to be convicted. But she has not been the only victim of the "pregnancy police." In South Carolina, eighteen women were charged with criminal neglect of their fetuses during 1989 under a protocol developed by the public hospitals, the police, the department of social services, and prosecutors. Within days of giving birth, these women (who tested positive for drugs) were arrested, handcuffed, and taken to jail until they could make bail. Their babies were taken into "protective custody" by the state.

In Washington, D.C., Brenda Vaughn, a first-time offender, was convicted of check forgery and was sentenced to an unusually long prison term when the judge learned she was pregnant and had tested positive for cocaine. "I'm going to keep her locked up until the baby is born because she's tested positive for cocaine when she came before me," declared Judge Peter Wolf. "She's apparently an addictive personality and I'll be darned if I'm going to have a baby born that way."[6] Although the prosecutor had recommended probation, Judge Wolf sentenced her to remain in jail, with virtually no prenatal care, until her due date.

Less dramatic than the criminal prosecutions, but far more prevalent, are civil proceedings against new mothers who use drugs. Hundreds of women have lost custody of their newborns based upon a single positive drug test at birth.[7] In a particularly egregious case, a family court judge in New York removed an infant from her mother's custody because the mother had tested positive for marijuana. The woman admitted using marijuana during labor to ease the pain on the advice of a friend who was a nurse. This woman did regain custody of her baby, but only after several months of agonizing legal wrangling.[8]

Typically, these proceedings are triggered by the hospital's report of a positive drug screen to the local or state agency charged with providing services to neglected or abused children. Several states have enacted laws that redefine "neglect" to include prenatal exposure to controlled substances. In 1988, for example, Oklahoma enacted a statute defining "a deprived child" as "one born in condition of dependence on a controlled, dangerous substance." The same law requires the hospital to report "chemically dependent children" to social services, which in turn must give any evidence of drug abuse to the district attorney. Failure to report constitutes a crime.[9]

Although illicit drug use crosses all income levels and races, black women and poor women have been disproportionately targeted for prosecution. In a 1989 study conducted in one Florida county, 380 pregnant women in public clinics and 335 in private care were drug tested. The rate of positive test results was 15.4% among white women and 14.1% among black women. Yet black women were nearly ten times more likely to be reported for substance abuse than their white counterparts.[10]

This racial and class bias in prosecutions can be attributed to two factors. First, public clinics and hospitals, which primarily serve low-income, often minority women, comply with reporting regulations to a far greater extent than do private hospitals and doctors serving the middle and upper classes.[11] Second, doctors are influenced, either consciously or unconsciously, by a drug user profile based on racial stereotypes and are therefore much more likely to test the urine of poor black women than of middle-class white women in spite of empirical evidence showing comparable patterns of drug use. In South Carolina, one element of the profile used by public hospitals to identify probable drug users is no prenatal or late prenatal care (after twenty-four weeks). This is highly discriminatory because Medicaid, medical insurance for poor people, does not cover pre-natal care before nineteen weeks of pregnancy.

Judge Eaton's admonition to Jennifer Johnson that "pregnant addicts have a responsibility to seek treatment" indicates his indifference to the situation of poor women in need of medical care and his ignorance of the facts of the case. Ms. Johnson *had* sought drug treatment, and she testified at her trial that, on several occasions during her pregnancy, she had called for an ambulance out of concern for the baby: "I thought that . . . if I tell them I use drugs they would send me to a drug [treatment] place." But her pleas for help in getting treatment were ignored. As for her prenatal care, as Johnson put it, "It wasn't much, but it was enough that I had been checked by the doctor and I know I didn't have any diseases. . . ."

In spite of the universal recommendation that prenatal care is funda-mental to healthy pregnancies and healthy babies, such care does not exist for millions of American women. In fact, access to prenatal care and deliv-ery services has diminished in recent years for poor women. For example, a 1987 California study discovered that, for the 30% of women in Califor-nia who are poor and uninsured, there is no maternity care system. In Los Angeles, patients who use public clinics must wait as long as nineteen weeks after requesting an appointment for prenatal care before getting one. In San Diego, clinics turned away 1245 pregnant women during a three-month period in 1987 because of limited resources.[12] The lack of prenatal care has been particularly disastrous for drug-using women, who are already at special risk. Quality prenatal care is probably more essential to a good outcome for these women than drug treatment. As one expert has put it, "In the end, it is safer for the baby to be born to a drug-abusing, anemic or diabetic mother who visits the doctor throughout her preg-nancy than to be born to a normal woman who does not."[13]

Drug treatment for poor, pregnant women is even scarcer than is prena-tal care, although surveys indicate that the incidence of maternal substance abuse has tripled since 1981.[14] It is extraordinarily difficult even for highly motivated pregnant women to find drug treatment programs that will ac-cept them. Northwestern University Hospital is the only Chicago-area hos-pital that admits pregnant women for residential drug treatment, and it has only two beds reserved for them. In New York City, of seventy-eight drug treatment programs surveyed in 1989, 54% refused to treat pregnant women, 67% refused to treat pregnant women on Medicaid, and 87% had no services available for pregnant women on Medicaid who used crack. Moreover, less than half of the handful of programs that did accept preg-nant women provided or arranged for prenatal care.[15] This situation has not changed.

The prosecutors of pregnant women have had a misguided theory of deterrence. Their own justifications reveal their belief that their actions will deter not only the defendants, but pregnant women in general, from using drugs. As District Attorney Michael Ramsey of Butte County, California, put it, "We intend to send a strong message not only to mothers, but to the community at large that Butte County will not allow drug abuse to affect its babies." [16] Those directly involved in the care of substance-abusing pregnant women differ with D.A. Ramsey and other prosecutors over the effects of the "message." They have found that such punitive actions do not deter addicts from using drugs during pregnancy, but they do deter women from sharing important information with their doctors and indeed from using the health care system at all. In 1989, a Florida newspaper reported that "after uniformed officers wearing guns entered Bayfront Medical Center to investigate new mothers suspected of cocaine abuse, doctors reported that they could no longer depend on the mothers to tell them the truth about their drug use because the word had gotten around that the police will have to be notified." [17] The head nurse at Greenville Memorial Hospital in North Carolina, which was the site of similar police actions, was blunt in her appraisal: "I think these prosecutions are dangerous. The mothers won't seek medical help. If they don't seek medical help, we're going to have a lot of dead babies." [18]

A broad spectrum of professional and medical organizations has also expressed opposition to and grave concerns about prosecuting pregnant women for fetal abuse. The American Academy of Pediatrics was one of thirty-eight organizations that filed *amicus curiae* briefs with the Florida Supreme Court in *Florida v. Johnson*. In its brief, the academy argued:

> The public must be assured of non-punitive access to comprehensive care which will meet the needs of the substance-abusing pregnant woman and her infant. Believing that premature measures taken toward pregnant women, such as criminal prosecution and incarceration, have no proven benefits for infant health, the Academy is concerned that such involuntary measures may discourage mothers and their infants from receiving the very medical care and social support systems that are crucial to their treatment.

In addition to being the antithesis of a public health approach to a medical problem, the practice of prosecuting women for using drugs during pregnancy raises a host of very significant legal and ethical problems. With the lodging of criminal charges, the defendant's newborn is immediately removed from her custody and placed in foster care. Older children may suffer the same fate. For example, when Kimberly Hardy of Muskegon, Michigan, was charged ten days after giving birth, her baby and her two older children, who were five years old and fifteen months old, were all seized and sent into foster care. There were neither allegations nor evidence of child abuse or neglect against Hardy. Her children were taken away from her solely on the results of the drug test administered by the hospital and on the assumption that Hardy was an unfit parent because she used drugs. The presumption that foster care is necessarily preferable to leaving an infant with a mother who uses drugs is probably wrong. A study in Los Angeles followed thirteen such children; they were placed in a total of thirty-five foster homes before reaching the age of three.[19]

The pregnancy prosecutions have usually been triggered by a hospital's report of a positive drug test to a state agency. This practice violates both the woman's right to nondisclosure of private information and the physician's ethical obligation to protect doctor-patient confidentiality. Only a confidential and trusting relationship enables a physician to learn from the patient all the facts necessary to make a diagnosis. Knowing this, many practitioners are simply not reporting positive drug test results. But under the laws of some states, the failure to report constitutes a crime. Thus, physicians now face the dilemma of either violating the privacy rights of their patients and their own ethical obligations or running afoul of the law.

Although prominent medical, legal, civil rights, and civil liberties groups have condemned the prosecutions, prosecutors who have initiated these cases have found a measure of public support. In a poll conducted at the height of the crack scare, 46% of the respondents thought that "prenatal abuse" should be a criminal offense.[20] This support is rooted in the convergence of two powerful social movements: the antiabortion movement and the antidrug movement. The American antiabortion movement has been a potent political force in the country for more than a decade. Under the leadership of Christian fundamentalist groups and the Catholic Church, it has engaged in all forms of political action: litigation, lobbying, public education, and civil disobedience. Although its goal of recriminalizing abortion is rejected by the majority of American voters, it does enjoy the support of an active and vociferous minority.

The notion of "fetal rights" sits at the center of the philosophy of the antiabortion movement. Antiabortion activists describe themselves as civil rights advocates on behalf of "the unborn." Their campaign for the recognition of fetal rights as a valid legal concept has been an uphill one because firmly embedded in the nation's common law is the "born alive" rule: a fetus must be born alive in order to secure legal personhood.[21] The law has traditionally viewed mother and fetus as an indivisible unit whose legal interests are the same. The antiabortion movement has been trying for years to drive a legal wedge between mother and fetus.

One of the antiabortion movement's tactics for establishing fetal rights is to support legal actions that raise the issue, even in the nonabortion context. The criminal prosecution of drug-using pregnant women has provided such an opportunity. Ann Louise Lohr of Americans United for Life Legal Defense Fund, in commenting upon the prosecution of Kimberly

Hardy, a Michigan woman who was charged with delivering cocaine to her baby via the umbilical cord, said, "You do not have an absolute right to do with your body what you want. The state can require you to have vaccines. There are seat-belt laws, motorcycle helmet laws. Here's a class of people that aren't getting any protection, and it's the unborn." [22] Clearly, if you can criminally prosecute pregnant women for harming their fetuses by ingesting cocaine, then you can prosecute them for killing their fetuses by aborting.

America's recent antidrug movement grew contemporaneously with the antiabortion movement, and it too developed out of a backlash against the perceived hedonism of the 1960s. The antidrug movement of the late 1970s was a loose coalition of drug abuse professionals, parents' groups, individual "moral entrepreneurs," and government officials. It had strong conservative religious affiliations and orientations, and its guiding principles were total intolerance of all illegal drug use and strong support for criminal sanctions. The early antidrug movement's efforts at arousing the American public were not terribly successful. In fact, as late as 1986, only 2% of the population regarded drugs as the nation's most important problem. But by 1989, a staggering 64% of Americans named drugs as America's most critical problem, the highest percentage ever received by a single issue in any public opinion poll. William Bennett, appointed by President Bush to head the Office of National Drug Control Policy, embodied the blame-the-user ideology that seemed to grip the country. As drug czar, he waged a punishing moral crusade against all illicit drug use and all illicit drug users and rejected the "easy temptation" to blame drug use on deeper social problems like poverty, racism, and unemployment.

At the peak of the drug scare, the "crack baby"—a political and media creation—became one of the War on Drugs' most potent symbols. According to news accounts in major newspapers throughout the country, pregnant women who used crack gave birth to "crack babies" who were irritable, inconsolable, developmentally delayed, and incapable of love. They suffered from "Alzheimer's-like symptoms" and would be learning disabled as youngsters. Worst of all, it was claimed that three hundred seventy-five thousand crack babies were born each year. Given this political environment, the criminal prosecutions of Jennifer Johnson and other poor black women are not so surprising.

The U.S. Supreme Court's 1973 decision in *Roe v. Wade,* recognizing a woman's constitutional right to abort a pregnancy, gave women the right to privacy and personal autonomy previously reserved to men. The pregnancy prosecutions, by creating an adversarial relationship between the woman and her fetus, returned to the state the power to control her behavior during pregnancy. [23] The concept of fetal rights deprives women of child-bearing age of rights retained by all other citizens, and it completely ignores the powerful effect of men on fetal development. We know now that alcohol and drug use have an effect on the quality of a man's sperm.[24] Further, and probably more important, in the U.S., one woman in twelve is beaten during pregnancy. But violent husbands have not been charged with fetal abuse.[25] Advocates of fetal rights argue that only the pregnant woman has a special "duty of care" to her unborn fetus. The views of one such advocate demonstrate where we are heading if we go down this road:

> A reasonable pregnant woman's prenatal duties would include regular pre-natal checkups, a balanced diet with vitamin, iron and calcium supplementa-tion, weight control, and judicious use of medications, tobacco and caffeine. Alcohol and narcotic use in pregnancy should be avoided entirely. Negligent exposure to noxious chemicals and drugs, refusal to accept genetic counsel-ling and prenatal diagnosis, refusal to obtain prenatal therapy, or failure to provide a modified diet, could give rise to a cause of action.[26]

Under Judge Eaton's ruling in the Jennifer Johnson case, women in Florida who smoke or drink alcohol during pregnancy could be prosecuted because in that state delivery of alcohol and cigarettes to a minor is a crimi-nal offense. A woman in Wyoming was charged with criminal child abuse for endangering her fetus by drinking while pregnant, although the charges were subsequently dismissed.[27] Several women have even been prosecuted for allegedly passing drugs to their babies through their breast milk.[28] These events conjure up images from Margaret Atwood's prophetic novel, *The Handmaid's Tale*, in which the story's protagonist protests, "We are two-legged wombs, that's all; sacred vessels, ambulatory chalices."

Fortunately, the prosecutions have not gone unchallenged. The Ameri-can Civil Liberties Union and public defenders across the country have vigorously defended these women at trial and on appeal. The ACLU's ulti-mately successful appeal of Jennifer Johnson's conviction was supported by thirty-eight medical, public health, women's, and civil rights organizations, including the American Medical Association, the American Public Health Association, the National Council of Negro Women, the Drug Policy Foun-dation, and the Women's Legal Defense Fund. Around the country, indict-ments are being dismissed, and in some cases, grand juries are refusing to indict in the first place. Since the Florida Supreme Court's reversal of John-son's conviction, the pace of new prosecutions has slowed down markedly nationwide.

In another encouraging development, thanks to the outspokenness of some drug researchers and health care providers, the media have begun to deconstruct the "crack baby" myth. Journalists have begun to question whether the syndrome even exists. One syndicated columnist has observed, "Just when the name has stuck, it turns out that the 'crack baby' may be a creature of the imagination as much as medicine, a syndrome seen in the media more often than in medicine. Some three years after the epidemic of stories about these children began, some six years after hospitals began to see newborns in deep trouble, researchers are casting doubt on the popular demon of the war on drugs. Like the national panic about child-snatching—putting missing children on milk cartons—that raged until it was tempered by reality, the story of crack babies is in for some revision."[29] "Some revision" is an understatement. It is becoming increasingly clear, as follow-up research is done on cocaine-exposed children, that the "crack baby" story was based almost entirely on exaggeration and hyperbole.

Dr. Ira Chasnoff, whose 1985 study of cocaine-exposed infants, which appeared in the *New England Journal of Medicine,* originally piqued the interest of the media, now believes his dire predictions about these babies' prognoses were wrong: "It is wrong to paint a stereotypical picture of the so-called 'crack babies' as a lost generation. They have the ability to learn." Chasnoff followed many of these infants and found, three years later, that most of them appear quite normal with no detectable behavioral or learning disabilities.[30] Several other recent studies have reached the same conclusion.[31]

The widely reported and frightening claim that three hundred seventy-five thousand "crack babies" are born every year is also misleading and distorted. The figure was based on a Chasnoff survey of positive drug test results in hospitals serving inner-city residents. Chasnoff discovered that 11% of the babies he surveyed were exposed to illicit drugs of all sorts, including marijuana. Reporters then extrapolated from this that 11% of all babies born each year nationwide were exposed to cocaine. Not true. Experts now estimate that perhaps 2% of newborns have been exposed to cocaine at least once before birth and that this exposure rarely has any effect on health outcomes.[32]

It is becoming increasingly clear that "crack babies" are, in reality, poverty babies. Homelessness, despair, lack of medical care, poor nutrition, abusive childhoods, abusive relationships—these are the "complex of poverty-related factors that threatens the future of babies born to crack-using mothers."[33] Mothers who use crack were convenient scapegoats for conservative administrations to blame in order to divert the public's attention away from the declining social and economic conditions affecting increasing numbers of Americans. Educational opportunity, access to quality health care, universal drug treatment upon request, adequate housing and jobs—not arrest, prosecution, and punishment—are better answers to the problem of crack use during pregnancy. All of American society will be healthier for it.

NOTES

1. *North Carolina v. Inzar*, Sup.Ct. Robeson Co., April 9, 1991.

2. *Virginia v. Smith*, Cir. Ct. Franklin Co., September 23, 1991.

3. *New York v. Morabito*, City Ct. Ontario Co., January 28, 1992.

4. On July 23, 1992, the Supreme Court of Florida reversed Johnson's conviction on the grounds that the passage of a cocaine metabolite through the umbilical cord to a newborn did not constitute "delivery" within the meaning of the Florida statute prohibiting delivery of a controlled substance to a minor. The court also criticized the prosecution of Johnson on public policy grounds: ". . . prosecuting women for using drugs and 'delivering' them to their newborns appears to be the least effective response to this crisis. Rather than face the possibility of prosecution, pregnant women who are substance abusers may simply avoid prenatal or medical care for fear of being detected. Yet the newborns of these women are, as a group, the most fragile and sick, and most in need of hospital neonatal care. A decision to deliver these babies 'at home' will have tragic and serious consequences."

5. *Florida v. Johnson*, Cir. Ct., Seminole Co., July 13, 1989.

6. Victoria Churchville, "D.C. Judge Jails Woman as Protection for Fetus," *Washington Post*, July 23, 1988, p. A1.

7. K. Moss, "Legal Issues: Drug Testing of Post-Partum Women and Newborns as the Basis for Civil and Criminal Proceedings," *Clearinghouse Review* 23: 1406 (March 1990).

8. *Nassau County Department of Social Services v. Leavy*, Family Court, Nassau Co., 1989.

9. Okla. Stat. Ann. Title 10, Section 1101 (1988).

10. Ira J. Chasnoff, "The Prevalence of Illicit Drug or Alcohol Use During Pregnancy and Discrepancies in Mandatory Reporting in Pinellas County, Florida," *New England Journal of Medicine* 322: 1201 (April 26, 1990).

11. Phil Willon, "Cocaine Mothers May Be Victims of Bias, Coler Says," *Tampa Tribune*, September 19, 1989.

12. Southern California Child Health Network, "Back to Basics: Improving the Health of California's Next Generation," 1987. Lack of access to health care has always been the reality for America's poor, but the situation became much graver during the 1980s. Although America's infant mortality rate had been on the decline for decades, it took a sudden jump in 1985 when infant mortality increased nationwide by 3% among black infants. This was the first increase since 1964 (Children's Defense Fund, "The Health of America's Children: Maternal and Child Health Data Book," Washington, DC, 1988). Substantial reductions in federal funding for health care during the Reagan years are probably the cause of this reversal.

13. "Taxpayers Pay for Lack of Prenatal Treatment," *St. Petersburg Times*, 1986.

14. Wendy Chavkin, testimony presented to House Select Committee on Children, Youth and Families, 100th Congress, 1st Session (April 27, 1989).

15. Ibid.

16. T. V. Dell, "DA To Prosecute Moms of Addicted Newborns," *Chico Enterprise-Record*, October 28, 1988, p. 1A.

17. "Angry Doctors Cut Drug Tests After Police Interview Moms," *St. Petersburg Times,* May 13, 1989.

18. Garlock, "4 Accused of Drug Use During Pregnancy," *Charlotte Observer,* August 17, 1989.

19. K. Moss, "Recent Developments in the Law: Substance Abuse During Pregnancy," *Harvard Women's Law Journal* 13 (1989).

20. "This Is What You Thought: 46% Say Prenatal Abuse Should Be a Criminal Offense," *Glamour Magazine,* May 1988.

21. Holly McNulty, "Pregnancy Police: The Health Policy and Legal Implications for Punishing Pregnant Women for Harm to Their Fetuses," *N.Y.U. Review of Law and Social Change* 16: 277 (1987).

22. Kennan, "The Birth of a Felony," *Detroit News,* December 21, 1989.

23. See D. Johnsen, "The Creation of Fetal Rights: Conflicts with Women's Constitutional Rights to Liberty, Privacy and Equal Protection," *Yale Law Journal* 95: 599 (1986).

24. Cohen, "Paternal Contributions to Birth Defects," *Nursing Clinics of North America* 21: 1 (1986).

25. K. Pollitt, "'Fetal Rights': A New Assault on Feminism," *The Nation,* March 26, 1990, p. 409.

26. Shaw, "Conditional Prospective Rights of the Fetus," *Journal of Legal Medicine* 5: 63 (1984).

27. *Wyoming v. Pfannensteil,* County Court of Laramie, 1990.

28. In *State v. Hall,* No. 89 CR 2331 18th Jud. Dist. Ct., Sedgwick Co., Kansas Criminal Department, 1990, a woman was prosecuted for endangering her child by breast-feeding while using cocaine. The court eventually dismissed that charge on the grounds that the state's child endangerment statute was not intended to apply to breast-feeding. In October 1992, a California woman was sentenced to six years in prison for child endangerment. The county coroner had attributed the death of her twenty-four-day-old infant to traces of methamphetamine in the woman's breast milk. The woman pleaded guilty to child endangerment rather than go to trial on a second degree murder charge. "Mother Gets 6 Years for Drugs in Breast Milk," *New York Times,* October 28, 1992, p. A11.

29. E. Goodman, "Beyond the 'Crack Baby' Horror Lies the Pain of Troubled Kids," *Miami Herald,* January 16, 1992.

30. Fackelmann, "The Crack Baby Myth," *Washington City Paper,* December 13, 1991.

31. For a useful review, see G. Koren, K. Graham, H. Shear, and T. Einarson, "Bias Against the Null Hypothesis: The Reproductive Hazards of Cocaine," *Lancet* 16:1440–1442 (December 1989).

32. Joanne Jacobs, "The Whole Truth About 'Crack Babies,'" *San Jose Mercury News,* July 28, 1991.

33. Editorial, "Truth Is a Casualty," *San Jose Mercury News,* July 28, 1991, p. 6C.

THIRTEEN

Pattern, Purpose, and Race in the Drug War
The Crisis of Credibility in Criminal Justice

Troy Duster

From 1760 through the 1820s, the prisons and criminal justice systems in Western societies faced a growing crisis of credibility: punishment for crimes was wildly arbitrary and capricious. Some thieves were hanged for stealing cloth worth very little, and murderers often served only a few months in prison. In England alone, the statutes provided the death penalty for 160 different offenses, but there was neither pattern nor coherence to when the death penalty would be used (Cantor, 1932:251; see also Hay, 1975; Thompson, 1975). For the same crime, one person could get twenty years imprisonment while another served a few weeks and yet another was hanged. Victor Hugo immortalized the period with his enduring tale of the cruel long-term sentencing of Jean Valjean for stealing a loaf of bread. Philosophers Kant and Hegel and the premier theorist of the criminal law in the first part of the nineteenth century, Paul Johann Anselm von Feuerbach, each argued that it was imperative to find a way to "make the punishment better fit the crime" (Elliott, 1931; Ellis and Ellis, 1989; Ezorsky, 1972; Heath, 1963).

One after another, social analysts, essayists, historians, and moral philosophers observed, lamented, analyzed, and commented upon how the chaotically uneven punishments were undermining the legitimacy of the state's use of its power (Knox, 1967).[1] Indeed, one important nineteenth-century school of thought held that the primary purpose of the criminal law was to limit the abuses of authorities toward the accused (Radzinowicz, 1966:22). This position was best articulated by the Italian social theorist Franceso Carrara.[2] The emergence of legal rights for the accused, protection from the arbitrary and abusive behavior of the courts, was one of the signal accomplishments of the movement to limit the powers of the state, an extraordinary achievement of the Enlightenment. The first major reform of the penal codes, inspired by the concern to rationalize punishment, occurred between 1840 and 1855. Codification rapidly swept through most Western societies (Rusche and Kirchheimer, 1967). A dramatic and fundamental transformation of the criminal codes of Prussia (1851), Austria (1852), and Sweden and Denmark (1867) modeled the set of parallel changes that swept through Holland, Italy, and ultimately the whole European continent and the U.S.

A century and a half later there is another growing crisis of credibility in the criminal justice system, but this time with America as the focal point. As members of a nation going through the experience, we are perhaps too close to the phenomenon to see it fully in sociohistorical perspective, but the centerpiece of this development is the War on Drugs occasioned by crack cocaine. This war has played a dominant role in radically shifting incarceration figures and rates and legislatively mandated sentencing. For example, in September 1989, a federal judge in San Francisco openly wept because new federal laws required that he sentence a man to ten years in prison without possibility of parole. This was a first-time offense of a man gainfully employed for twenty-four years as a longshoreman, a man whose reputation for those two decades had been as a good and honest worker. His crime was driving a friend across town to make a drug drop-off. The driver himself was not a dealer, nor was he involved in any drug transaction. The trip netted him only $5, but because the jury found that he did know the purpose of the journey, he was sentenced to ten years in prison without possibility of parole. The prosecuting attorney expressed no remorse. Instead, he said that this would send a message to all those who don't think the drug war is serious business. In another case, a man in Los Angeles, was sentenced to life imprisonment in 1990 merely for possessing *six grams* of cocaine—this in the last decade of the twentieth century.

This chapter examines how the War on Drugs has contributed to injustice—especially racial injustice—in the U.S. criminal justice system. Several chapters have noted that the punitive effects of the drug war have fallen disproportionately on poor people, especially minorities. The first part of this chapter describes in detail the growth and darkening of U.S. prisons.

Why the War on Drugs had this effect, why it resulted in the arrest and imprisonment of disproportionate numbers of blacks, is a complicated issue. I discuss two major factors. The first is some long-term changes in the economy, especially the decline in manufacturing jobs and the increase in service jobs. For a variety of reasons, service sector employers are significantly less disposed than manufacturers to hire blacks. Faced with fewer regular jobs, some inner-city black youth find work in the underground economy—notably in street-level drug sales. The second major factor is the drug war's almost exclusive focus on street-level sellers rather than, for example, on white bankers laundering huge sums of drug money. This selective aim also contributed to the rising incarceration rates of blacks.

THE GROWTH AND DARKENING OF U.S. PRISONS

In 1954, black and white youth unemployment in America were equal, with blacks actually having a slightly higher rate of employment in the age group sixteen to nineteen. By 1984, the black unemployment rate had nearly quadrupled, while the white rate had increased only marginally (see Table 13-1). Just as unemployment rates among African-American youth were skyrocketing during these three decades, so were their incarceration rates. If we turn the clock back just about fifty years, whites constituted approximately 77% of all prisoners in America, while blacks were only 22% (Hacker, 1992:197). This provides the context in which we might best review Table 13-2 and the astonishing pattern in the recent historical evolution of imprisonment rates by race. Notice that in the last half century, the incarceration rate of African-Americans in relation to whites has gone up dramatically. In 1933, blacks were incarcerated at a rate almost three times that of whites (see Table 13-2). In 1950, the ratio had increased to approximately four times; in 1960, it was almost five times; in 1970, it was six times; and in 1989, it was seven times that of whites.

During the last two decades, we have seen the greatest shift in the racial composition of the inmates of our prisons in all of U.S. history. According to our most recent figures (Hacker, 1992:197), 45% of those in our state and federal prisons are African-American. Of the more than 275,000 awaiting trial, more than 40% are black. And if those figures are not sufficient to alert us to the special importance of the relationship between race,

TABLE 13-1   Employment and Unemployment Rates Among Black and White Male Youths 1954–1981

Age	Blacks and Other Nonwhites					Whites				
	1954	1964	1969	1977	1981	1954	1964	1969	1977	1981
	Percentage of the Population Employed									
16–17	40.4	27.6	28.4	18.9	17.9	40.6	36.5	42.7	44.3	41.2
18–19	66.5	51.8	51.1	36.9	34.5	61.3	57.7	61.8	65.2	61.4
20–24	75.9	78.1	77.3	61.2	58.0	77.9	79.3	78.8	80.5	76.9
	Percentage of the Labor Force Unemployed									
16–17	13.4	25.9	24.7	38.4	40.1	14.0	16.1	12.5	17.6	19.9
18–19	14.7	23.1	19.0	35.4	36.0	13.0	13.4	7.9	13.0	16.4
20–24	16.9	12.6	8.4	21.4	24.4	9.8	7.4	4.6	9.3	11.6

SOURCE: Employment and Training Report of the President, 1982.

TABLE 13-2   Incarceration Rates by Race

Year	Population[1]			Incarceration[2]			Rate (%)[3]		
	Total	White	Black	Total	White	Black	Total	White	Black
1933	125,579	112,815	12,764	137,997	102,118	31,739	0.11	0.09	0.25
1950	151,684	135,814	15,870	178,065	115,742	60,542	0.12	0.09	0.38
1960	180,671	160,023	19,006	226,065	138,070	83,747	0.13	0.09	0.44
1970	204,879	179,491	22,787	198,831	115,322	81,520	0.10	0.06	0.36
1989	248,240	208,961	30,660	712,563	343,550	334,952	0.29	0.16	1.09

[1]Total population of the United States by ethnicity (in thousands). Source: Series A 23–28: Annual Estimates of the Population, by Sex and Race: 1900 to 1970. In *Historical Statistics of the United States, 1976:* Department of Commerce, Bureau of the Census, 1976, pp. 9–28. No. 19: Resident Population—Selected Characteristics: 1790–1989. *Statistical Abstract of the United States 1991,* 111th ed., Bureau of the Census, 1991, p. 17.

[2]Total number of prison population by ethnicity. Note: Data for incarceration reflects the estimated number of prisoners surveyed on a particular date. Source: Table 3-31, Characteristics of Persons in State and Federal Prisons. *Historical Corrections Statistics in the United States,* Bureau of Prison Statistics, 1986, p. 65.

[3]Incarceration/population.

the economy, and criminal justice, African-Americans account for 61% of all robbery suspects (Hacker, 1992: 181).

Table 13-3 captures one part of the problem graphically. These data demonstrate that while (1) there are more than ten times as many white males in higher education (4,485,000) than incarcerated (330,258), (2) there are more black males in prison or jail (341,662) than attending colleges and universities on a full-time basis (270,301).

Since 1980, America built more prisons and incarcerated more people than at any other time in our history. In the brief period from 1981 to 1991, we went from a prison population of 330,000 inmates in state and federal prisons to 804,000—substantially more than a doubling in a single decade—the greatest rise in a prison population in modern history.[3] (This does not include jail populations, persons in drug-related facilities, or juveniles.) Federal drug offense convictions went up 213% in this same period, signaling the importance of the drug war in this development. There is now a near complete consensus among criminologists that drug control strategies account for most of the increase of the U.S. prison population of the last decade. As late as 1980, only 25% of the federal prison population was incarcerated for drug charges. By January 1992, this figure had more than doubled to 58% (Clark Foundation, 1992).

It is difficult to exaggerate the extent to which this expanding net of the criminal justice system has selectively enveloped the lives of so many young African-American males. During 1989, 35% of all black males between the ages of sixteen and thirty-five were arrested (Freeman, 1991). Tillman's

TABLE 13-3   Incarceration Versus Matriculation in the U.S.,
1986–1988

Situation	Black Males	White Males
Incarcerated[1]		
In prison	240,117[2]	186,879[3]
In jail	101,545[3]	143,379
Total	341,662	330,258
In college or university[4]		
Four-year, full-time	185,407	Not available
Two-year, full-time	84,894	
Four-year, part-time	66,272	
Two-year, part-time	99,255	
Total (full- and part-time)	435,828[2]	4,485,000

[1] Source: "Profile of State Prison Inmates for 1986," U.S. Department of Justice, Bureau of Justice Statistics, January 1988; "Prisoners in 1987," U.S. Department of Justice, Bureau of Justice Statistics, April 1988; "Jail Inmates in 1986," U.S. Department of Justice, Bureau of Justice Statistics, October 1987.
[2] In 1987 figures
[3] In 1986 figures
[4] Full-time total: 270,301, part-time total: 165,527. Source: "Survey Report," Center for Education Statistics, April 1988, U.S. Department of Education.

(1986) arrest data for the state of California reveal that among white youth ages eighteen to twenty-eight, chances of an arrest are three in ten—but for black youth of the same age, chances of an arrest are seven in ten. Nationwide, in the age group sixteen to nineteen, 15% of black males face arrest in any given year (Gibbs, 1984). These patterns are mainly caused by three factors: increased participation of black male youth in street sales in the new underground drug economy, the selective enforcement of drug laws for street dealers, and the harsher mandatory sentencing guidelines aimed at crack cocaine versus powder cocaine (Meierhoefer, 1992).

According to the government's own best statistics, blacks constitute only 15–20% of the nation's drug users (Flanagan and Maguire, 1990; NIDA, 1990), but in most urban areas, they constitute half to two-thirds of those arrested for drug offenses. Indeed, in New York City, a recent study concluded that, in 1989, African-Americans and Latinos constituted 92% of all those arrested for drug offenses (Clark Foundation, 1992). In Florida, annual admissions to the state prison system nearly tripled from 1983 and 1989, from 14,301 to nearly 40,000 (Austin and McVey, 1989:4). This was a direct consequence of the War on Drugs because well over two-thirds of these felonies were drug related.

The nation gasped at the national statistics reported by the Sentencing

Project in 1990, citing the figure that nearly one-fourth of all black males twenty to twenty-nine years of age were in prison or jail or on probation or parole on any given day in the summer of 1989. This figure has been re-cited so often that it may have inured us; there was less astonishment when a study of Baltimore revealed that 56% of that city's young black males were under some form of criminal justice sanction on any given day in 1991 (Miller, 1992). Indeed, of the nearly thirteen thousand individuals arrested on drug charges in Baltimore during 1991, more than eleven thousand were African-Americans.

The explanation for this extraordinary racial imbalance between pat-terns of drug consumption and patterns of drug arrests—between who uses and who gets arrested—is not difficult. It is the selective aim of the artillery in the drug war. For example, interviews with public defenders in both the San Francisco Bay Area and Atlanta reveal that over half of their caseload is young, overwhelmingly black males who are arrested through "buy and bust transactions" by the police. Most of these transactions are of quantities of crack or cocaine valued at less than $75. In contrast, drug sales in the fraternity houses or "in the suites" routinely escape the net of the criminal justice system. Police police the streets, so it is street sales that are most vulnerable to the way in which the criminal justice apparatus is currently constituted and employed.

Racial bias in the administration of drug laws has become so obvious that some judges have begun to throw out cases. A white Manhattan judge, for example, allowed crucial evidence to be suppressed in a drug arrest case at the Port Authority Bus Terminal on the grounds that the drug en-forcement efforts were aimed exclusively at minorities.[4] It is a well-known and accepted police practice to intercept citizens who fit a "profile" of a likely offender. As Chapter 11 shows, that profile has increasingly taken on an exclusively racial dimension. When a superior court judge was informed that 80% of all illegal drug transactions involve whites, he replied in as-tonishment that he thought it was the opposite. Now even the police are beginning to raise questions about the legitimacy of their own activities in the drug war.

The drug war has also affected the races quite differently with regard to rates of imprisonment. One of the most striking figures showing this is the shift in the racial composition of prisoners in the state of Virginia. In 1983, approximately 63% of the new prison commitments for drug offenses in that state were white; the rest, 37%, were minority. Just six years later, at the peak of the crack scare, the situation had reversed; only 34% of the new drug commitments were white while 65% were minority.

It is not just the higher rates of arrest and incarceration, but the way in which the full net of the criminal justice system all the way through manda-tory sentencing falls selectively on blacks. For example, powder cocaine is most likely to be sold and consumed by whites, and blacks are more likely to sell and consume crack (Flanagan and Maguire, 1990; NIDA, 1990). Federal law is not race neutral on these two very much related chemical substances: possession with intent to distribute five grams of cocaine brings a variable sentence of ten to thirty-seven *months;* but possession with intent to distribute an identical amount of crack brings a mandatory minimum sentence of five *years.*[5] A study by the Federal Judicial Center in Washington, D.C., reveals that the mandatory minimum sentencing in drug cases has had a dramatically greater impact on blacks than on whites (Meierhoefer, 1992). In 1986, before the mandatory minimum sentences for crack offenses became effective, the average sentence was 6% higher for blacks than for whites. Just four years later, in 1990, the average sentence was 93% higher for blacks. Although these figures are most shocking for crack, the shift toward longer sentences for blacks also includes other drugs. In the same time period, from 1986 to 1990, the average sentence for blacks vis-à-vis whites (for offenses related to powder cocaine, marijuana, and the opiates) went from 11% greater to 49% greater (Meierhoefer, 1992:20). Table 13-4 shows the steady increase in numbers of offenders sentenced for various drugs from 1984 through 1990 and reveals the direct bearing upon race and ethnicity.

This differential impact of sentencing is explained by a closer look at systematic practices developed out of the sentencing guidelines. The term "guidelines" is actually a misnomer, in that they have statutory status, and judges are generally restricted to remaining within a set formula when setting the length of a sentence. An important part of the formula is "cooperation with the prosecution."

Here is an actual case before a federal judge in the Northern District of California, Ninth Circuit, an area in which drug arrests are particularly high. The judge in question reports that this is a typical situation in which the pattern of sentencing is strongly biased to provide longer terms to those lower down in the hierarchy of drug dealing. Higher level dealers have more bargaining chips; namely, they can inform on many others in the organization because they simply know more:

> The accused, a low-level "runner" for a drug operation, knew only a very few people in the operation. Therefore, he had nothing to "bargain" in terms of giving information to prosecutors. He was sentenced to a minimum of 20 years in prison. In the same courtroom, same judge, same drug operation, a drug dealer very high up in the organizational structure could and did name over a dozen people around and below him. For his "cooperation with the prosecution" he received a reduced sentence of only two years in prison.

There is a direct connection between the new statistics relating race, crime, incarceration rates, and long term sentencing and the routine

TABLE 13-4 Number of Offenders by Drug Type and Race, 1984–1990

	1984	1985	1986	1987	1988	1989	1990
Drug							
Marijuana	785	734	714	905	1,004	1,115	542
Cocaine	1,273 (54%)	1,496 (56%)	2,421 (67%)	2,779 (67%)	3,377 (69%)	4,153 (68%)	2,402 (70%)
Opiates	307	416	480	475	489	875	510
Race*							
White	1,394	1,544	2,075	2,309	2,269	2,665	1,431
Black	185 (8%)	257 (10%)	386 (11%)	511 (12%)	861 (18%)	1,308 (22%)	943 (28%)
Hispanic	741	788	1,094	1,284	1,673	2,062	1,029

*443 "other" offenders not included.

SOURCE: Meierhoefer, 1992:28–29.

NOTE: Figures represent only Federal offenders in the Federal Probation Sentencing and Supervision Information System (FPSSIS) who were convicted for drug quantities which would or do trigger the mandatory minimum sentences under the 1987 drug laws.

experiences of a new group of youth seeking entry-level employment in the service sector. In a recent study, the National Bureau of Economic Research found that men who had been jailed had markedly less chance of gainful employment because of their incarceration; 50% had held a job before incarceration, but only 19% afterwards. The researchers, Bound and Freeman (1992), calculated that the soaring rate of imprisonment (noted previously) accounted for nearly three-quarters of the sharp drop in employment of young black dropouts in the 1980s.

"WHO NEEDS THE NEGRO/BLACK/AFRICAN-AMERICAN?": THE DECLINE OF MANUFACTURING AND THE RISE OF THE SERVICE SECTOR

More than two decades ago, Sidney Wilhelm (1970) published a book with the provocative title, *Who Needs the Negro?* In this work, Wilhelm argues that America is effectively done with blacks, that the free slave labor that they had provided during the colonial period and the cheap labor during the early and middle periods of industrialization are no longer needed. Here is a prescient passage that now has the ring of clairvoyance:

> Following the Negro exodus out of the South to the industrial technology of the North, unemployment took on a different meaning—a complete break with the land and the absence of sympathetic white bosses on the basis of intimate acquaintance. And now, in terms of automation, joblessness loses the peculiar quality of being a mere transitory moment that will fade upon the resumption of economic prosperity. The new technology informs the Negro of permanent, workless years even as the economy establishes new productive records and profits. The Negro's fate is no longer tied into an economy in high gear; displacement rather than unemployment spells the difference. *Both poverty and joblessness exist, not outside the economic system as aberrations that come and go when recessions and depressions come and go but, instead, as fundamental aspects of an ongoing economic order* custom designed to maximize investment returns from the new technology. (Wilhelm, 1970:214–215; emphasis added)

At the time, because the U.S. was still enjoying a flourishing economy, few paid much attention to the ominous element in Wilhelm's argument. Indeed, because he concluded that genocide was the logical trajectory of the African-American's situation, critics treated Wilhelm's conclusions as more provocative than serious, more rhetorical than substantive. As we near the end of the century, the nation has witnessed a dramatic shift from being an industrial power to being heavily dominated by service sector employment. Soaring rates of long-term and seemingly intractable unemployment and poverty envelop more and more of the black community. In fiscal 1991, America spent more money on building and operating prisons ($26.2 billion) than on the central component of its welfare system, Aid to Families with Dependent Children ($22.9 billion).[6] Wilhelm's dark and gloomy prediction now seems far more evocative of the drug war than merely provocative and heuristic.

The shift from an industrial to a service economy has taken a far greater toll on black youth unemployment than on white youth unemployment. In fact, while the latter has increased only slightly in the past four decades, black youth unemployment has nearly quadrupled (see Table 13-1). Why has there been such a dramatic differential impact of deindustrialization on selected segments of the population?

The recent history of Detroit auto production is instructive for understanding trends in workforce makeup that impact different parts of the labor market. In the 1940s, there were eight production workers to every skilled worker at General Motors. By the middle of the 1980s, that figure had been halved, to four to one (Jacobs, 1987). This looks like a bland statistic that is hardly race specific, but it was in the production jobs that blacks had historically their greatest proportion of workers (Jacobs, 1987:6). At the same time, machine shops that supply screws to the auto industry are also a vital source of production jobs, but they are now concentrated in places like Jackson, Michigan, which has a population of less than 20% black. Moreover, because of the U.S.-Canada Auto Pact, American auto magnates from Detroit have shifted major production facilities to neighboring Ontario Province, in the city of Windsor. Indeed, Windsor has become something of an industrial suburb of Detroit, and in recent years, the number of Canadian auto workers has grown to an all-time high of 120,000. This admittedly tells only a part of the story, because new jobs are developing in the area of "high technology." But it is most emphatically in the high-tech arena where minorities are doing poorly (Markusen, et al., 1986:177–178). A survey of the fifty largest "high-tech" companies in the state of Michigan revealed that not a single firm had manufacturing operations within the city limits of Detroit, where African-Americans are concentrated.

The shift from manufacturing to service and high-tech industries helps explain the sharply increasing rates of black youth unemployment. Only in the last three decades has the United States witnessed the development of an aggregation of people, mainly black but increasingly Latino, who live in the central cities, suffer unprecedented levels of unemployment, participate at unparalleled levels in both alternative and underground economies, and have extraordinarily high rates of contact with the criminal justice system. Our cultural memory is so short that there is a tendency to regard this very recent development as endemic and a long-standing feature of American society.

The move from an agricultural to a manufacturing society required far less schooling of workers than does the move from manufacturing to service. People could and did move from the farms to the cities, to where the jobs were. They needed little in the way of formal education. Some could and did drop out of school in order to obtain employment. But a closer look at the issue of school dropouts as a historical phenomenon shows that it is not dropping out, but the larger context in which students drop out, that makes it a problem. In 1910, the dropout rate for whites was higher than it currently is for blacks. But in 1910, teenagers were dropping out of school and dropping into factory jobs in a booming and expanding secondary sector of the economy. Even into the 1940s, blacks could move from more rural areas to Gary, Pittsburgh, and Chicago to take factory jobs.

Currently, both the conventional wisdom and much scholarly analysis emphasize the importance of schooling as it relates to new service sector jobs (e.g., Moss and Tilly, 1991; Wilson, 1987). In 1940, only 70% of white youth in America aged sixteen to seventeen were attending secondary schools; and only 55% of black youth were attending secondary schools (Farley, 1984:18). By the early 1970s, that gap was nearly closed, with whites attending at about 90% and blacks at 87%. Today there is virtually no difference, with both groups enrolled in excess of 90%.[7] This increase in high school enrollment for both blacks and whites is a major change from 1960, when secondary school enrollment was 70% for whites and only 40% for blacks. Yet although African-Americans are experiencing more schooling, they are experiencing more unemployment than in the 1950s. If schooling is supposed to connect with jobs and preparation for careers, why this peculiar development?

Employment for white and black youth in the manufacturing sector has been relatively equal in the last four decades (see Table 13-1). It has not, however, been equal in the service sector, and increasingly that is where the jobs are. In a fascinating study, a group of researchers sent matched pairs of white and black high school graduates from the class of 1983 in Newark, New Jersey, out in the world to seek employment (Culp and Dunson, 1986). These job applicants were not "faking" an interest in employment. They had been screened as actually seeking work and were "matched" for academic achievement. Blacks and whites had about equal success in obtaining employment in the manufacturing sector. However, in the service sector, differences in the experiences of these matched pairs were dramatic: whites were four times more likely than blacks to be fully employed in this sector (Culp and Dunson, 1986:241). The most important finding for my argument here is that retail service establishments were far more likely to discriminate against black youth than manufacturing establishments. Yet this service sector is precisely where the economy has grown and will grow (see Tables 13-5–13-8).

In a 1990 update, elaboration, and adjustment of the methodology used by Culp and Dunson in the 1983 study, Struyk et al. (1991) conducted a total of 576 hiring audits in the two metropolitan areas of Chicago and Washington, D.C. In this study, two young men, one black, the other white, were carefully matched on all characteristics, including education, job qualifications, and experience. Jobs were from classified ads in major metropolitan newspapers. Discrimination is presumably lower for advertised jobs than for those passed by word of mouth. All auditors participating in the study were actually college students described as "articulate and poised" and dressed conventionally. These were all entry-level jobs. The applicants were also coached to be as similar as possible regarding demeanor.

The researchers found that when differential treatment occurs, it is three times more likely to favor the white applicant. "Reverse discrimination," where a black is favored, is far less common than white preference. What might be happening here? Why should whites and blacks have such similar fates in the manufacturing sector of the economy, while blacks have so much less success in the service sector? Education is supposed to be the key to success in the new service economy, with skin color and race receding in importance over time. Why is there this apparently anomalous finding that runs so far counter to the conventional wisdom? There are two related reasons. The first is active racial discrimination on the part of the employer, something we have just glimpsed in the previous studies of matched pairs seeking employment. The second is more subtle and has to do with the "lack of fit" between the clashing cultures and expectations of employers in the service sector and young African-Americans.

This cultural clash is due in part to increases in cultural and educational segregation. As firms leave the American city, the revenue base of the city deteriorates severely, leaving public education in a shambles. For example, between 1960 and 1980, the tax base of the city of Detroit declined by $650 million (Jacobs, 1987:12). Whites have begun to abandon the public schools of the central cities. Across the nation, as early as 1980 one white child in five (aged four through fifteen) was attending a private school (Farley and Allen, 1987:203). That figure has increased in the last decade and is now approaching one in four. For our major urban centers, a better estimate would be one in three. Meanwhile for blacks, nearly 90% attend public schools. As the tax base has declined, there has been a simultaneous increasing concentration of blacks in the inner cities. This segregation of our urban life has some obvious consequences, but it also has some that are less obvious.

TABLE 13-5 Employment Change, Various Industry Groups, from 1979 to 1989 (numbers in thousands)

Industry	1979	1989	Change N	Change %
Total nonagricultural	89,823.0	108,581.0	18,758.0	20.9
Total private	73,876.0	90,854.0	16,978.0	23.0
Goods producing	26,461.0	25,634.0	−827.0	−3.1
Mining	958.0	722.0	−236.0	−24.6
Metal mining	101.0	61.8	−39.2	−38.8
Bituminous coal and lignite mining	255.6	139.3	−116.3	−45.5
Oil and gas extraction	474.2	403.5	−70.7	−14.9
Nonmetallic minerals, except fuels	123.8	115.4	−8.4	−6.8
Construction	4,463.0	5,300.0	837.0	18.8
General building contractors	1,272.0	1,390.6	118.6	9.3
Heavy construction contractors	930.5	801.6	−128.9	13.9
Special trade contractors	2,260.1	3,107.4	847.3	37.5
Manufacturing	21,040.0	19,612.0	−1,428.0	−6.8
Durable goods	12,760.0	11,536.0	−1,224.0	−9.6
Lumber and wood products	766.9	769.5	2.6	0.3
Furniture and fixtures	497.8	531.0	33.2	6.7
Stone, clay, and glass products	708.7	602.9	−105.8	−14.9
Primary metal industries	1,253.9	782.5	−471.4	−37.6
Fabricated metal products	1,717.7	1,445.3	−272.4	−15.9
Machinery, except electrical	2,484.8	2,145.5	−339.3	−13.7
Electrical and electronic equipment	2,116.9	2,037.7	−79.2	−3.7
Transportation equipment	2,077.2	2,053.6	−23.6	−1.1
Instruments and related products	691.2	777.3	86.1	12.5
Miscellaneous manufacturing	444.8	391.2	−53.6	−12.1
Nondurable goods	8,280.0	8,076.0	−204.0	−2.5
Food and kindred products	1,732.5	1,665.2	−67.3	−3.9
Tobacco manufactures	70.0	52.9	−17.1	−24.4
Textile mill products	885.1	726.1	−159.0	−18.0

Apparel and other textile products	1,304.3	1,091.5	−212.8	−16.3
Paper and allied products	706.8	697.2	−9.6	−1.4
Printing and publishing	1,235.1	1,606.9	371.8	30.1
Chemicals and allied products	1,109.3	1,092.9	−16.4	−1.5
Petroleum and coal products	209.8	162.5	−47.3	−22.5
Rubber and miscellaneous plastics products	781.6	839.7	58.1	7.4
Leather and leather products	245.7	140.7	−105.0	−42.7
Service producing	63,363.0	82,947.0	19,584.0	30.9
Transportation and public utilities	5,136.0	5,705.0	569.0	11.1
Railroad transportation	556.3	294.8	−261.5	−47.0
Local and interurban passenger transit	262.6	331.3	68.7	26.2
Trucking and warehousing	1,339.4	1,659.9	320.5	23.9
Water transportation	215.9	176.0	−39.9	−18.5
Transportation by air	438.2	691.8	253.6	57.9
Pipelines, except natural gas	20.1	18.8	−1.3	−6.5
Transportation services	188.7	341.6	152.9	81.0
Communication	1,309.0	1,254.0	−55.0	−4.2
Electric, gas, and sanitary services	805.7	936.3	130.6	16.2
Wholesale trade	5,204.0	6,234.0	1,030.0	19.8
Durable goods distribution	3,081.0	3,696.0	615.0	20.0
Nondurable goods distribution	2,123.0	2,539.0	416.0	19.6
Retail trade	14,989.0	19,575.0	4,586.0	30.6
Building materials and garden supplies	629.2	769.8	140.6	22.3
General merchandise stores	2,287.4	2,483.4	196.0	8.6
Food stores	2,296.8	3,269.5	972.7	42.4
Automotive dealers and service stations	1,812.3	2,157.1	344.8	19.0
Apparel and accessory stores	949.4	1,191.9	242.5	25.5
Furniture and home furnishings stores	614.9	811.2	196.3	31.9
Eating and drinking places	4,513.1	6,369.9	1,856.8	41.1
Miscellaneous retail	1,885.7	2,521.7	636.0	33.7
Finance, insurance, and real estate	4,975.0	6,814.0	1,839.0	37.0
Banking	1,498.5	1,774.3	275.8	18.4
Credit agencies other than banks	554.0	907.5	353.5	63.8

(continued on next page)

TABLE 13-5 *(continued)* (numbers in thousands)

Industry	1979	1989	Change N	Change %
Security, commodity brokers, and services	204.2	435.2	231.0	113.1
Holding and other investment offices	111.2	212.0	100.8	90.6
Insurance carriers	1,199.8	1,468.0	268.2	22.4
Insurance agents, brokers, and service	430.1	659.8	229.7	53.4
Real estate	954.5	1348.0	393.5	41.2
Combined real estate, insurance, etc.	22.8	9.0	−13.8	−60.5
Services	17,112.0	26,892.0	9,780.0	57.2
Hotels and other lodging places	1,059.8	1,603.4	543.6	51.3
Personal services	904.0	1196.1	292.1	32.3
Business services	2,905.9	5,788.7	2,882.8	99.2
Auto repair, services, and garages	575.1	898.7	323.6	56.3
Miscellaneous repair services	281.8	359.9	78.1	27.7
Motion pictures	227.6	265.2	37.6	16.5
Amusement and recreation services	712.0	975.6	263.6	37.0
Health services	4,992.8	7,635.3	2,642.5	52.9
Legal services	459.9	896.3	436.4	94.9
Educational services	1,089.7	1,628.8	539.1	49.5
Social services	1,081.3	1,736.9	655.6	60.6
Museums, botanical and zoological gardens[1]	32.2	52.5	20.3	63.0
Membership organizations	1,516.2	1,761.6	245.4	16.2
Miscellaneous services	940.7	1,459.3	518.6	55.1
Government	15,947.0	17,727.0	1,780.0	11.2
Federal Government	2,773.0	2,988.0	215.0	7.8
State government	3,541.0	4,134.0	593.0	16.7
Local government	9,633.0	10,606.0	973.0	10.1

NOTE: Figures shown for 1979 and 1989 are annual averages from the CES program. Although published monthly estimates begin in 1982, the previously unpublished annual average for 1979 was computed and used for these comparisons.
SOURCE: Plunkert, 1990:8.

TABLE 13-6   The Twenty Fastest Growing Industries from 1979 to 1989
(numbers in thousands)

		Employees		Change	
Rank	Industry	1979	1989	N	%
1	Computer and data-processing services	270.8	763.4	492.6	181.9
2	Outpatient care facilities[1]	113.0	317.3	204.3	180.8
3	Personnel supply services	526.5	1,351.2	824.7	156.6
4	Mortgage bankers and brokers[1]	62.3	148.8	86.5	138.8
5	Correspondence and vocational schools[1]	44.9	105.1	60.2	134.1
6	Business credit institutions[1]	30.2	67.1	36.9	122.2
7	Individual and family services[1]	161.0	353.1	192.1	119.3
8	Mailing, reproduction, stenographic	113.3	245.1	131.8	116.3
9	Residential care[1]	201.1	426.4	225.3	112.0
10	Sanitary services	47.0	96.8	49.8	106.0
11	Guided missiles, space vehicles, parts	101.5	207.8	106.3	104.7
12	Air transportation services[1]	47.3	96.8	49.5	104.7
13	Security brokers and dealers	164.7	336.5	171.8	104.3
14	Legal services	459.9	896.3	436.4	94.9
15	Holding and other investment offices	111.2	212.0	100.8	90.6
16	Miscellaneous publishing	46.1	82.8	36.7	79.6
17	Miscellaneous business services[1]	1,277.5	2,256.5	979.0	76.6
18	Advertising	145.9	256.4	110.5	75.7
19	Accounting, auditing, and bookkeeping	299.0	520.4	221.4	74.0
20	Local and suburban transportation	75.8	130.3	54.5	71.9

[1]Although published monthly estimates begin in 1982, the previously published annual average for 1979 was computed and used for these comparisons.
NOTE: Figures shown for 1979 and 1989 are annual averages from the CES program. Industries are compared at the three-digit standard industrial classification (SIC) level, unless the CES program publishes monthly estimates only at the two-digit level.
SOURCE: Plunkert, 1990:10.

In America, the segregation of blacks has had a distinct outcome in a surprising place: language. William Labov, a linguist at the University of Pennsylvania, has been studying speech patterns of racial and ethnic groups for decades. Labov taped the ordinary speech patterns of English white and black children at play in Battersea Park in London. When he replayed the tapes, neither he nor his English colleagues could tell whether the voices belonged to black or white children. In sharp contrast, Labov claims that in America he can detect from his tape recordings in Philadelphia whether a child is white or black approximately four times in five. This linguistic difference is becoming more and more pronounced.[8] Over two decades ago, Labov (1972) published a major empirical study establishing the formalistic underpinnings for the technical argument that black English was a coherently different linguistic system from standard

TABLE 13-7   The Twenty Most Rapidly Declining Industries
from 1979 to 1989 (numbers in thousands)

		Employees		Change	
Rank	Industry	1979	1989	N	%
1	Iron ores	24.8	9.3	−15.5	−62.5
2	Combined real estate, insurance, etc.	22.8	9.0	−13.8	−60.5
3	Watches, clocks, and watchcases	27.7	11.3	−16.4	−59.2
4	Copper ores	33.3	14.1	−19.2	−57.7
5	Blast furnaces and basic steel products	570.5	274.3	−296.2	−51.9
6	Rubber and plastics footwear	22.7	11.0	−11.7	−51.5
7	Handbags and personal leather goods	32.8	16.1	−16.7	−50.9
8	Railroad equipment	74.3	39.0	−35.3	−47.5
9	Railroad transportation	556.3	294.8	−261.5	−47.0
10	Footwear, except rubber	148.9	79.6	−69.3	−46.5
11	Bituminous coal and lignite mining	255.6	139.3	−116.3	−45.5
12	Musical instruments	24.0	13.1	−10.9	−45.4
13	Operative builders	83.3	45.7	−37.6	−45.1
14	Taxicabs	59.6	35.1	−24.5	−41.1
15	Cement, hydraulic	32.7	19.4	−13.3	−40.7
16	Iron and steel foundries	240.7	143.6	−97.1	−40.3
17	Farm and garden machinery	182.3	109.8	−72.5	−39.8
18	Construction and related machinery	382.8	237.0	−145.8	−38.1
19	Primary nonferrous metals	72.5	45.4	−27.1	−37.4
20	Weaving mills, cotton	150.9	95.9	−55.0	−36.4

SOURCE: Plunkert, 1990:11.

English. Until Labov, the notion that black English was indeed "a second language" that could be treated as such for the purposes of education and learning was hotly contested. Although Labov's findings on language use and social segregation are fascinating in and of themselves, a particular aspect of this work may bear upon the differential success rates of matched pairs of white and black youth in the secondary and service sectors.

Growing differences in language and style tend to make black youth less desirable to service sector employers. Employers in the industrial sector are more likely to be concerned with a worker's productivity than with how that worker relates to the outside world. That is the nature of employment in the manufacturing sector. Conversely, employers in the service sector are more likely to be concerned with a worker's way of relating to the customers, clients, and the general public.

For analytic parsimony, economic and social analysts of employment patterns usually emphasize one or the other side of the relationship between employer/employee and the job market. However, in an increas-

TABLE 13-8   The Thirty Industries Adding the Most Jobs
from 1979 to 1989 (numbers in thousands)

		Employees		Change	
Rank	Industry	1979	1989	N	%
1	Eating and drinking places	4,513.1	6,369.9	1,856.8	41.1
2	Miscellaneous business services[1]	1,277.5	2,256.5	979.0	76.6
3	Grocery stores	2,001.9	2,889.1	887.2	44.3
4	Hospitals	2,608.4	3,490.7	882.3	33.8
5	Personnel supply services	526.5	1,351.2	824.7	156.6
6	Hotels, motels, and tourist courts	1,019.9	1,548.9	529.0	51.9
7	Computer and data-processing services	270.8	763.4	492.6	181.9
8	Offices of physicians	716.8	1,206.8	490.0	68.4
9	Legal services	459.9	896.3	436.4	94.9
10	Nursing and personal care facilities	950.8	1,384.2	433.4	45.6
11	Miscellaneous shopping goods stores	568.5	905.4	336.9	59.3
12	Services to buildings	487.0	807.6	320.6	65.8
13	Machinery, equipment, and supplies	1,260.8	1,574.0	313.2	24.8
14	Trucking and trucking terminals	1,248.8	1,537.7	288.9	23.1
15	Colleges and universities	716.9	990.9	274.0	38.2
16	Amusement and recreation services	712.0	975.6	263.6	37.0
17	Engineering and architectural services	515.0	756.1	241.1	46.8
18	Insurance agents, brokers, and service	430.1	659.8	229.7	53.4
19	Residential care[1]	201.1	426.4	225.3	112.0
20	Accounting, auditing, and bookkeeping	299.0	520.4	221.4	74.0
21	Outpatient care facilities[1]	113.0	317.3	204.3	180.8
22	Air transportation	390.9	595.0	204.1	52.2
23	Commercial and stock savings banks	1,369.3	1,572.8	203.5	14.9
24	Individual and family services[1]	161.0	353.1	192.1	119.3
25	Real estate agents and managers	360.2	550.6	190.4	52.9
26	Groceries and related products	648.1	837.9	189.8	29.3
27	Offices of dentists	322.0	511.6	189.6	58.9
28	Department stores	1,878.1	2,056.2	178.1	9.5
29	Security brokers and dealers	164.7	336.5	171.8	104.3
30	Savings and loan associations	236.0	402.8	166.8	70.7

[1]Although published monthly estimates begin in 1982, the previously unpublished annual average for 1979 was computed and used for these comparisons.

NOTE: Figures shown for 1979 and 1989 are annual averages from the CES program. Industries are compared at the three-digit standard industrial classification (SIC) level, unless the CES program publishes monthly estimates only at the two-digit level.

SOURCE: Plunkert, 1990:13.

ingly competitive economy with a low rate of growth, employment in the service sector involves a more complex set of conditions that notably constrain economic opportunities, entry-level employment, and career trajectories for all workers. The problems this creates for all employees are exacerbated for young workers, and even more particularly for young workers with styles of speech and presentation that employers often see as threatening or less attractive. Service sector employers are particularly sensitive to behaviors, attitudes, and social and physical attributes of employees that make up a certain "presentation of self" because they assume that prospective customers will find these behaviors and attributes undesirable and take their business elsewhere.

In this setting, more mature female workers replace younger male workers, immigrant workers replace native-born workers from racial and ethnic minorities (Segura, 1984, 1989), and suburban workers replace the workers from the more ethnic urban cores. The new demographic reality of two-worker households has meant that more women are engaged in the part-time or full-time workforce (Bianchi and Spain, 1986; Tienda et al., 1987). This combines with the flight of retail trade, supermarkets, and discount stores to the suburban periphery. This migration of jobs away from "certain parts of town" is now so commonly observed and understood that it has become part of our taken-for-granted assumptions:

> For example, nearly all new export and regional-serving jobs moved north of Atlanta during the 1980s; the vast majority of low-income, Black neighborhoods are on the south side of town. In Dallas, nearly all new jobs have been created in the north and northwest quadrants of the metropolitan area; the Black and Hispanic populations are concentrated to the east and south. In the Philadelphia metropolitan area, from 1970 to 1990 the number of export and regional-serving jobs that located in the high-income Main Line to the north-west of the city, as well as in the white middle-income areas of lower Bucks County to the northeast and New Jersey to the east, increased by more than 50 percent. The number of these types of jobs in the increasingly Black and Hispanic city dropped by 15 percent over the same time period. (Leinberger, 1992)

In short, the misfit between the location of urban young minority workers and suburban service jobs complements the employer preference for female and white workers to serve the predominantly white and female suburban retail trade and services clientele.[9]

Anthropologist Phillipe Bourgois provides a good ethnographic description of the lack of cultural fit between inner-city minority youth and service sector jobs. Bourgois lived for five years as a street ethnographer in Spanish Harlem, "(living) in an irregularly heated, rat-filled tenement opposite one of the largest conglomerations of segregated and impoverished public housing projects in the world [where he became] close friends with the addicts, thieves, dealers and con artists . . ." (1991:3–4). It is worth briefly reiterating here some of the core findings from Chapter 3 and from his other recent work.

He found that many of the crack dealers had actually been employed earlier in marginal factory-related jobs, but the factories had closed down or left Spanish Harlem. This left the workers looking for other kinds of employment. Several found low-paying entry-level jobs in the service sector. The factory jobs had an ancillary culture that contained an "oppositional culture" of defiance and resistance, and even the most rudimentary factory work produced some collective sense of opposition/defiance. However, jobs in the service sector require more direct contact with the culture of the supervisors and thus more of a subordination of the behavioral and linguistic styles of these youth. The black and Latino workers in the service sector voice a combination of class-race anger at the subordination of their values, in part because their resentments are not mediated through a union or any other form of collective resistance. The workers in these service jobs routinely complained of being *disrespected. The nature and quality of the disrespect was different in kind and more poignantly experienced.* It penetrated their armor, pierced through to their self-worth and self-conception (see Williams, 1989, 1992). Too often, it left them with a level of strong emotional antagonism toward "straight society" quite different from what industrial workers report as their feelings after being "laid off" or experiencing "unemployment." Bourgois writes:

> Mingo and Willie's street triumph prevents them from genuflecting in the service economy. The fundamental issue here is the qualitative change in the nature of social interaction in service sector employment. When you are sweating in the mail room or behind the xerox machine you cannot maintain your cultural autonomy. First of all, there's no union; secondly, you've got very few fellow workers protecting you. In fact, you're surrounded by supervisors and bosses from an alien and obviously dominant culture. If they are not scared of street culture, they ridicule it. You look like a bumbling fool to them, incapable of enunciating all the syllables in the complicated strung out words they mouth at you. You have a hard time deciphering the sloppy abbreviations on the notes they jot out for you each morning. Besides, none of the logic behind the filing of triplicate copies or post-dated invoices makes any sense to you. And worse, you don't even know how to look them in the eye without making them nervous or even how to walk down the hallway without bopping your shoulders like you do on your way to cop around the corner.
>
> From the prospective crack dealer's perspective, it appears as if your supervisors want you to imitate them, hook, line, and sinker. They want you to smile their tight-lipped way every time they tell you what to do. In the service sector, the cultural clash between white yuppie power and inner-city "scrambling jive" is much more than style. It is experienced as terror to the

drop-outs who suddenly realize that they are idiotic buffoons in the eyes of the folks with all the power over them. As Julio explained to me once, the humiliation only gets worse when you stick it out and "when they get to know you." On the street, it is referred to as being "dissed," from the word "disrespected." (Bourgois, 1991:10)

The difficulty these young people face while working in the service sector was captured well by one of Bourgois's street dealer informants who was once numbered among the gainfully employed in the straight economy: "So you, you know, you try to do good, but then people treat you like shit. Man, you be cool at first and then all of sudden when they get to know you they try to 'diss' you. When I first got to my jobs, I was busting my ass and everything but after awhile, it's like, you get to hate your supervisor" (Bourgois, 1991:10). This points to a peculiar conjunction of class and race alienation from employment opportunities in entry-level jobs in the service sector. When such alienation is combined with the discriminatory preferences on the employers' side of the equation, it becomes easier to understand why some young black men end up in the underground economy—and in the cross hairs of the drug war artillery.

THE DRUG WAR BACKFIRES:
CATAPULTS CRACK COCAINE OVER MARIJUANA

By any pharmacological or physiological measure, marijuana is a more benign drug than crack cocaine. In the late 1970s, marijuana was much cheaper and far more available than cocaine in the U.S. (Adler, 1985; Gorriti, 1989). In 1980, the average cost of an ounce of marijuana in the five major U.S. cities was approximately $80. Ten years later the cost had more than tripled and on average was close to $250 per ounce. In sharp contrast, by 1989, cocaine had become so cheap and so widely available that it cost only a fraction of what it had in 1980 (Gorriti, 1989:49). At the same time, cocaine purity increased markedly. *There is strong empirical evidence to suggest that this inversion of the fates of marijuana and cocaine occurred not despite a tripling in the federal budget for the War on Drugs, but because of it.* The War on Drugs in effect took a relatively benign drug off the streets and put in its place a harsher drug that would have much more violence associated with its sale and distribution (see Chapter 6). Here are some reasons why this occurred.

Marijuana is relatively easy to grow. During the 1960s and 1970s, small "cottage industries" run by amateurs and by consumer growers were common. In its various antidrug crusades, the federal government indiscriminately grouped all illicit drugs together as equals and effectively brought marijuana under the same moral banner as heroin. In the course of its high-profile drug wars, the U.S. government drove most of the amateurs out of marijuana production. In their place came the professionals, who could use big money to circumnavigate surveillance.

Small "operators, from adventurous youth to amateur groups who used to account for a large percentage of the illegal border crossings were increasingly driven out of business. In their stead more professional groups flourished: people who could rise to the new sophistication demanded by the law enforcement challenge and who could afford the technology and equipment capable of avoiding detection" (Adler, 1985:33; see also Murphy et al., 1990).[10]

When the U.S. government engineered the spraying of chemicals over marijuana fields in Mexico and Northern California, the professionals responded by building special high-technology greenhouses far from the scrutiny of authorities or by finding more remote fields. However, those costs were considerable, were passed on to the consumer, and ultimately drove the price of marijuana sky high. If the issue was only marijuana availability, this particular development may have received the applause of those who wanted to get drugs off the street. However, the soaring cost and decreased availability did not occur in a vacuum; it was accompanied by a development that would actually put far more drugs on the street, a cheaper, more plentiful drug that would bring with it increased violence in street-level transactions: crack cocaine.

Cocaine is much easier to transport than marijuana and easier to conceal from the authorities. It is far less bulky, has far less odor, and is smuggleable in imaginative and inventive ways that have proved to be the bane of the Drug Enforcement Administration. All over the U.S., warehouses with tons of powder cocaine are uncovered every few months, but the price keeps dropping because the supply is plentiful. When the DEA and the FBI beefed up border patrol operations in the mid and late 1970s, they made surface transport and smuggling of drugs very dangerous. Airplanes had always been used for drug smuggling, but when the drug war really got serious, it inadvertently made air smuggling the preferred and less risky strategy. It was one of the unanticipated and less than fully appreciated features of the drug war that, by forcing the smugglers into the air, drug enforcement agents would create a situation that would make detection and interception far more difficult and would ultimately help flood the U.S. market with powder cocaine. Smugglers "would send two or three airplanes to fly across together—one full, the others empty—and then have them split off into different directions to confuse and lose the 'Feds.' Another tack was to fly two planes piggyback, one right above the other, so they came across the same on the radar blip. Then the empty one would fly to the airport while the loaded one went to the arranged meeting place" (Adler, 1985:37).

These shifts unexpectedly flooded the warehouses with tons of cocaine, sending its street price plummeting to a half, then to a third of what it had been in less than a decade. To add to this strange twist of fate, in the mid-1980s, there was a discovery that would hasten the violence associated with cocaine distribution. It was a new and cheap and simple technology that would convert the now plentiful and relatively cheap powder cocaine into crack, which could then be sold for as little as $5 a rock. This technology was so simple that with a microwave oven, baking soda, and minimal skill, one could make crack cocaine in very short shrift. This meant that, with very little capital, anyone, including a sixteen-year-old high school drop-out, could convert this money into a drug bonanza. Unlike the old heroin trade, which required factories in Marseilles, France, and transport be-tween Turkey and Syria through Lebanon; unlike the old heroin trade, which required seven tiers of hierarchy in a bureaucratic organization that started with the import "connection" and fanned into several intermediaries in a line of authority and control before it finally hit the streets, the potential profits from the new drug, crack, were readily available to many inner-city youth with a little money and a willingness to enter this risky business.

While these youth became the targets in the drug war and filled the prisons, bigger targets were ignored. In a remarkable piece of investigative journalism, Jefferson Morley (1989) reported how the U.S. government under Reagan and Bush knowingly abandoned its most significant lead against the truly powerful in the drug war. Indeed, Bush directly presided over the dismantling of a team of investigators hot on the trail of an enor-mous drug money laundering scandal, not in Latin America, but right here in the U.S.

Every bank turns over its cash deposits to the local Federal Reserve branch office. In most areas of the country, deposits and payouts are roughly balanced. However, from 1970 to 1976, as cocaine use began to spread, cash surpluses in Florida banks tripled, from a currency surplus of $576 million to $1.5 billion. This activity was sufficiently unusual to trigger public scrutiny. After media publicity about federal inaction in 1979, the government finally swung into action. Only then did the government launch Operation Greenback, which consisted of an interagency task force of the Departments of Treasury and Justice and the Federal Reserve. Mor-ley reported that, in 1982, a branch office of the suburban Capital Bank of Miami had accepted $242 million in cash in less than eighteen months. Indeed, on the basis of a preliminary examination, twenty-four Miami banks were due to receive "close scrutiny" from the task force.

However, this was the period in which the Reagan administration was on a search and destroy mission for "crippling regulations" on financial institutions. (This strategy was also directly to usher in the savings and loan scandals that would put the nation in a $277 billion debt.) Moreover,

Reagan had put a freeze on government hiring, so the Federal Reserve and Operation Greenback could not hire the competent examiners needed to follow up on this most promising of leads. In March 1982, George Bush, then vice president, was appointed head of the Reagan administration's antidrug task force. Within one year of his appointment, Operation Greenback was downgraded from an interagency task force to a single office inside the U.S. attorney's office in Miami. Even so, this operation was sufficient to force several of the big money launderers to diversify and move operations to California. In 1988, Southern California banks reported an unprecedented excess of $3 billion in cash. There were sufficient grounds to suspect that this was directly attributable to the laundering of drug money.

In the spring of 1989, the Federal Reserve Bank in Washington released statistics on the currency surpluses in Miami and Los Angeles at $8 billion. We got no summoning to arms for an all-out attack on the criminal bankers from then–Drug Czar Bennett. Instead, he courageously aimed his drug war artillery at the most legally vulnerable by obtaining eviction notices for sixty low-income, mostly black residents of public housing projects in southeast Washington.

This chapter opened with the case of a black longshoreman who was sentenced to ten years in prison without possibility of parole. In April 1990, Michael Milken, who made billions from fraudulent manipulations of "junk bonds"—one of the major factors in the savings and loan crisis—pled guilty to six felonies but was fined for less than half of his illicit earnings, a mere $600 million. At the time, the judge sentenced Milken to a ten-year prison sentence for his crimes. However, just two years later, the same judge reduced the sentence by seven years. Milken spent only a small fraction of a decade in prison, and he will get to spend many of his remaining millions. There was no mandatory ten-year sentence without possibility of parole.

One does not need a conspiracy theory to account for such disparities. Indeed, conspiracy theories are usually fundamentally flawed in that they attribute too much agency to particularly powerful cabals or individuals. Rather, what happened during this period is better explained by the coming together of forces that required no "genocidal intent" in the minds of any key actors. Nonetheless, when we look at who gets jobs and who doesn't, and at who ends up in the mainstream service economy and who in the underground crack economy, the nonconspiratorial conjuncture of forces sketched here leads to the same result. As Bourgois, Murphy and Rosenbaum, and Goldstein et al. have suggested in earlier chapters, whether the issue is the consequences of crack use or of crack selling, those affected are overwhelmingly young, impoverished blacks and Latinos.

I began this chapter by noting the crisis of credibility of the criminal justice system that occurred in Europe at the end of the eighteenth century. Hegel, Kant, Carrara, Beccaria, and Feuerbach confronted the problem of injustice caused by arbitrariness, whim, and caprice. To bring about justice, they sought to make the criminal law and its administration more orderly, coherent, and rational. We in America at the end of the twentieth century face perhaps an even greater challenge.

A hundred years from now some historian will observe that the injustices of our criminal justice system were not arbitrary and capricious. Rather, she will note that there was a striking pattern in who was attacked, and who was not attacked, when the criminal justice system waged war on crack. The question is: will the historian write that this clear pattern of injustice led to major reforms—or to a collapse of legitimacy?

NOTES

The first segment of this chapter is based upon testimony delivered to the United States House of Representatives Subcommittee on Legislation and National Security, Committee on Government Operations, July 2, 1990. I would like to thank Jennifer Reck for her assistance in retrieving and analyzing archival background materials.

1. The list includes French social theorists, essayists, and philosophers Montesquieu, Rousseau, and Voltaire; Jeremy Bentham in England; and perhaps most significant of all for the actual developments in a movement that was to reshape the criminal justice system, the Italian Cesare Bonesana, Marchese di Beccaria (1738–1794).

2. Because Carrara wrote before the unification of Italy, it is more appropriate to refer to him as Carrara of Pisa.

3. Bureau of Justice Statistics, U.S. Department of Justice, Office of Justice Programs, January 1992, Vol 1., No. 3, NCJ-133097, Washington, DC.

4. Reported in R. Sullivan, "Judge Finds Bias in Bus Terminal Search," *New York Times,* April 25, 1990, p. A16.

5. Section 21 U.S.C. 841(a).

6. The figures on prison costs were compiled from the Department of Justice statistics for 1991 and complemented by a report of the Edna McConnell Clark Foundation. The figures on the costs of AFDC are from the Department of Health and Human Services, reported in the *New York Times,* July 19, 1992.

7. However, there is still a gap between the races with respect to who is completing high school. In 1980, about 85% of the whites but only 70% of the blacks finished high school.

8. Cited in Jim Quinn, "Linguistic Segregation," *The Nation,* Nov. 9, 1985, pp. 479–482.

9. A good summary of the empirical literature on this topic appears in Moss and Tilly (1991). There is also recent comparative work on geographical location and employment opportunities for young black males in New York and Los Angeles (Jargowsky and Bane, 1990).

10. For a detailed and more recent analysis of how intensified law enforcement has driven the relatively harmless small-time marijuana dealers out in favor of larger, more organized, profit-oriented, and violent dealers, see Dorn et al., 1992.

REFERENCES

Adler, Patricia, *Wheeling and Dealing: An Ethnography of an Upper-Level Drug Dealing and Smuggling Community* (New York: Columbia University Press, 1985).

Austin, James S., and Aaron David McVey, "The Impact of the War on Drugs," *Focus* (Prison Population Forecast 39) (San Francisco, CA: The National Council of Crime and Delinquency, December 1989:1–7).

Bachman, Jerald G., and John M. Wallace, Jr., "The 'Drug Problem' Among Adolescents: Getting Beyond the Stereotypes," *Ethnicity and Disease* 1:315–319 (1991).

Bachman, Jerald G., John M. Wallace, Jr., Patrick M. O'Malley, Lloyd D. Johnston, Candace L. Kurth, and Harold W. Neighbors, "Race/Ethnic Differences in Smoking, Drinking, and Illicit Drug Use Among American High School Seniors, 1976–89," *American Journal of Public Health* 81:372–377 (1991).

Bianchi, Suzanne M., and Daphne Spain, *American Women in Transition* (New York: Russell Sage Foundation, 1986).

Bluestone, Barry, and Bennett Harrison, *The Deindustrialization of America* (New York: Basic Books, 1982).

Bound, John, and Richard B. Freeman, "What Went Wrong? The Erosion of Relative Earnings and Employment Among Young Black Men in the 1990s," *Quarterly Journal of Economics*, February 1992: 201–232.

Bourgois, Philippe, "In Search of Respect: The New Service Economy and the Crack Alternative in Spanish Harlem," Working Paper No. 21. New York: Russell Sage Foundation, 1991.

Cantor, Nathaniel F., *Crime, Criminals and Criminal Justice* (New York: Henry Holt, 1932).

Clark, Edna McConnell Foundation, *Americans Behind Bars* (New York: May, 1992).

Culp, Jerome, and Bruce H. Dunson, "Brothers of a Different Color: A Preliminary Look at Employer Treatment of White and Black Youth," pp. 233–260 in R. B. Freeman and Harry J. Holzer, eds., *The Black Youth Unemployment Crisis* (Chicago: University of Chicago Press, 1986).

Dorn, Nicholas, Karim Murji, and Nigel South, *Traffickers: Drug Markets and Law Enforcement* (London: Routledge, 1992).

Elliott, Mabel A., *Conflicting Penal Theories in Statutory Criminal Law* (Chicago: University of Chicago Press, 1931).

Ellis, Ralph D., and Carol S. Ellis, *Theories of Criminal Justice: A Critical Reappraisal* (Wolfeboro, New Hampshire: Longwood Academic, 1989).

Ezorsky, Gertrude, ed., *Philosophical Perspectives on Punishment* (Albany: State University of New York Press, 1972).

Farley, Reynolds, *Blacks and Whites: Narrowing the Gap* (Cambridge, MA: Harvard University Press, 1984).

Farley, Reynolds, and Walter R. Allen, *The Color Line and the Quality of Life in America* (New York: Russell Sage Foundation, 1987).

Flanagan, Timothy J., and Kathleen Maguire, eds., *Sourcebook of Criminal Justice Statistics 1989* (Washington, DC: U.S. Department of Justice, Bureau of Justice Statistics, 1990).

Freeman, Richard B., "Crime and the Employment of Disadvantaged Youth," National Bureau of Economic Research, NBER Working Paper No. 3875, 1991.

Gibbs, Jewelle Taylor, "Black Adolescents and Youth," *American Journal of Orthopsychiatry* 54:6–19 (1984).

Goldstein, Paul, and Henry Brownstein, "Report on National Institute of Justice study," *New Perspectives Quarterly* 6:24 (1989).

Gorriti, Gustavo, "Southern Exposure: The View from Peru," *New Perspectives Quarterly* 6:49–51 (Summer 1989).

Hacker, Andrew, *Two Nations: Black and White, Separate, Hostile, Unequal* (New York: Scribner's, 1992).

Hay, Douglas, "Property, Authority and the Criminal Law," pp. 17–64 in D. Hay, P. Linebaugh, J. Rule, E.P. Thompson, and C. Winslow, eds., *Albion's Fatal Tree: Crime and Society in Eighteenth-Century England* (New York: Pantheon, 1975).

Heath, James, *Eighteenth Century Penal Theory* (Glasgow: Oxford University Press, 1963).

Jacobs, James, "Black Workers and the New Technology: The Need for a New Urban Training Policy," Industrial Technology Institute, Ann Arbor, MI, September 1987.

Jargowsky, Paul A., and Mary Jo Bane, "Neighborhood Poverty: Basic Questions," in Michael T. McGeary and Lawrence E. Lynn, eds., *Concentrated Urban Poverty in America* (Washington, DC: National Academy of Sciences Press, 1990).

Knox, T. M., ed. and trans., *Hegel's Philosophy of Right* (Oxford: Clarendon Press, 1967).

Labov, William, *Language in the Inner City: Studies in the Black English Vernacular* (Philadelphia: University of Pennsylvania Press, 1972).

Leinberger, Christopher, "Business Flees to the Urban Fringe," *The Nation*, July 6, 1992: 10–14.

Lusane, Clarence, *Pipe Dream Blues: Racism and the War on Drugs* (Boston: South End Press, 1991).

Markusen, Ann, Peter Hall, and Amy K. Glasmeier, *High Tech America* (Boston: Allen & Unwin, 1986).

Meierhoefer, Barbara S., "The General Effect of Mandatory Minimum Prison Terms: A Longitudinal Study of Federal Sentences Imposed," Federal Judicial Center, Washington, DC, 1992.

Miller, Jerome G., "Hobbling a Generation: Young African American Males in the Criminal Justice System of America's Cities," National Center on Institutions and Alternatives, Alexandria, Virginia, 1992.

Moberly, Walter, *The Ethics of Punishment* (Hamden, CO: Archon Books, 1968).

Morley, Jefferson, "Contradictions of Cocaine Capitalism: The Great American High," *The Nation*, October 2, 1989, pp. 341–347.

Moss, Philip, and Chris Tilly, "Why Black Men Are Doing Worse in the Labor Market: A Review of Supply-Side and Demand-Side Explanations," Social Science Research Council, New York, 1991.

Murphy, Sheigla, Dan Waldorf, and Craig Reinarman, "Drifting into Dealing: Becoming a Cocaine Seller," *Qualitative Sociology* 13:321–343 (1990).

NIDA (National Institute on Drug Abuse), National Household Survey on Drug Abuse, DHHS Publication No. (ADM) 91–1789, 1990.

Plunkert, Lois M., "The 1980's: A Decade of Job Growth and Industry Shifts," *Monthly Labor Review*, September 1990: 3–16.

Quinn, Jim, "Linguistic Segregation," *The Nation*, November 9, 1985: 479–482.

Radzinowicz, Leon, *Ideology and Crime* (New York: Columbia University Press, 1966).

Reuter, Peter, Robert MacCoun, and Patrick Murphy, *Money from Crime: A Study of the Economics of Drug Dealing in Washington, D.C.* (Santa Monica, CA: Rand Corporation, 1990).

Rusche, Georg, and Otto Kirchheimer, *Punishment and Social Structure* (New York: Columbia University Press, 1967).

Scott, Peter Dale, and Jonathan Marshall, *Cocaine Politics: Drugs, Armies, and the CIA in Central America* (Berkeley: University of California Press, 1991).

Segura, Denise, "Labor Market Stratification: The Chicana Experience," *Berkeley Journal of Sociology* 29:57–91 (1984).

———, "Chicana and Mexican Immigrant Women at Work: The Impact of Class, Race and Gender on Occupational Mobility," *Gender and Society* 3:37–52 (1989).

Struyk, R.J., M.A. Turner, and M. Fix, "Opportunities Denied, Opportunities Diminished: Discrimination in Hiring," research paper, The Urban Institute, Washington, DC, 1991.

Thompson, E.P., *Whigs and Hunters: The Origins of the Black Act* (New York: Pantheon, 1975).

Tienda, Marta, Shelley A. Smith, and Vilma Ortiz, "Industrial Restructuring, Gender Segregation, and Sex Differences in Earnings," *American Sociological Review* 52:195–210 (1987).

Tillman, Robert, "The Prevalence and Incidence of Arrest Among Adult Males in California," Bureau of Criminal Statistics Special Report Series (Sacramento: State of California, Department of Justice, December 1986).

Wallace, John M. Jr., and Jerald G. Bachman, "Explaining Racial/Ethnic Differences in Adolescent Drug Use: The Impact of Background and Lifestyle," *Social Problems* 38:333–354 (1991).

Wilhelm, Sidney M., *Who Needs the Negro?* (Cambridge, MA: Schenkman, 1970).

Williams, Terry M., *The Cocaine Kids* (New York: Addison-Wesley, 1989).

———, *Crack House* (New York: Addison-Wesley, 1992).

Willis, Paul, *Learning to Labour: How Working-Class Kids Get Working-Class Jobs* (New York: Columbia University Press, 1981).

Wilson, Kenneth, and Allen Martin, "Ethnic Enclaves: A Comparison of the Cuban and Black Economies in Miami," *American Journal of Sociology* 78:135–160 (1973).

Wilson, William J., *The Truly Disadvantaged: The Inner City, the Underclass, and Public Policy* (Chicago: University of Chicago Press, 1987).

Woo, Deborah, "The People v. Fumiko Kimura: But Which People?" *International Journal of the Sociology of Law* 17:403–428 (1989).

FOURTEEN

Drug Prohibition in the U.S.

Costs, Consequences, and Alternatives

Ethan A. Nadelmann

Current policies toward crack have failed to eliminate its abuse and have exacerbated its consequences, as previous chapters have suggested. More and more Americans have realized this in recent years. After decades of drug prohibition's failures, growing numbers of political leaders, law enforcement officials, drug abuse experts, and ordinary citizens have been insisting that a radical alternative to current policies be considered: the controlled legalization of drugs. Just as "Repeal Prohibition" became a catch phrase that swept together the diverse objections to alcohol prohibition in the 1930s, so "Legalize Drugs" has become a catch phrase that has galvanized opposition to drug prohibition.

"Drug legalization" means many things to many people. I use the term "legalization" to refer to the removal of criminal sanctions against drug users, producers, and sellers and the institution of various forms of regulation. Many of the arguments against drug prohibition and in favor of legalization also hold for decriminalization, which still retains prohibition against production and large sales while eliminating criminal sanctions against use and petty sales. Chapters 15–17 discuss the possibilities for reducing the punitiveness of U.S. drug policy within the framework of prohibition. This chapter focuses on the problems with drug prohibition largely in contrast to forms of controlled, regulated legalization.

The policy analyst views legalization as a model for critically examining the costs and benefits of drug prohibition policies. Libertarians, both civil and economic, view it as a policy alternative that eliminates criminal sanctions on the use and sale of drugs that are costly in terms of both individual liberty and economic freedom. Others see it simply as a means to "take the crime out of the drug business," which in the case of crack is a major issue. In its broadest sense, however, legalization incorporates the many arguments and growing sentiments for de-emphasizing our traditional reliance on criminal law enforcement to deal with drug abuse. Legalization models instead emphasize education, prevention, treatment, noncriminal restrictions on availability and use of psychoactive drugs, and positive inducements to abstain.

There is no one legalization option. At one extreme, some libertarians advocate the removal of all criminal sanctions, restrictive regulations, and taxes on the production and sale of psychoactive substances—with the exception of restrictions on sales to children. More modest proposals would limit legalization to one of the safest (relatively speaking) of all illicit substances: marijuana. Others prefer a "medical model" similar to today's methadone maintenance programs. More ambitious are those options that combine legal availability of some or all currently illicit drugs with vigorous efforts to restrict consumption by means other than criminal sanctions. Many advocates of this type of legalization simultaneously advocate much greater efforts to limit tobacco consumption and the abuse of alcohol as well as a transfer of government resources from law enforcement to prevention and treatment. Indeed, the best model for this version of legalization is precisely the tobacco control model advocated by those who want to do everything possible to discourage tobacco use short of criminalizing it.

Clearly, no single drug legalization model, nor any drug prohibition or decriminalization model, is capable of "solving" our problems with crack or most other currently illicit drugs. Nor is there any question that legalization would entail some risks. Legalization would almost certainly increase the availability of drugs, decrease their price, and remove the deterrent power of the criminal sanction—all of which may well invite some increase in drug use and abuse. Such risks must be taken seriously, especially with a powerful drug like crack. But there are at least three reasons to *consider* taking these risks. First, drug control strategies that rely primarily on criminal law enforcement are significantly and inherently limited in their capacity to curtail drug abuse. Second, prohibitionist approaches to drug control are not just of limited value but also highly costly and counterproductive; indeed, as earlier chapters have shown, most of the violence and crime that many people attribute to crack itself in fact stem from drug prohibition policies. Third, the risks of legalization may well be less than most people assume—particularly if intelligent alternative measures are implemented.

THE LIMITS OF DRUG PROHIBITION POLICIES

Few law enforcement officials any longer contend that their efforts can do much more than they already are doing to reduce drug abuse in the U.S.

This is true of international drug enforcement efforts, interdiction, and both high-level and street-level domestic drug enforcement efforts. Indeed, the massively increased law enforcement efforts against crack since 1986 can be seen as an experiment that fared rather poorly.

U.S. international drug control efforts seek to limit the export of illicit drugs to the U.S. by a combination of crop eradication and crop substitution plans, financial inducements to growers to abstain from illicit production, and punitive measures against producers and traffickers. These efforts have met with scant success in the past and show no indications of succeeding in the future. Eradication faces serious obstacles. For example, marijuana and opium can be grown in a wide variety of locales, and even the coca plant from which cocaine and crack are made "can be grown in virtually any subtropical region of the world which gets between 40 and 240 inches of rain per year, where it never freezes, and where the land is not so swampy as to be waterlogged. In South America this comes to 2,500,000 square miles," of which less than 700 square miles are now being used to cultivate coca.[1]

Producers in many countries have reacted to crop eradication programs by engaging in "guerrilla farming" methods, cultivating their crops in relatively inaccessible hinterlands and camouflaging them with legitimate crops. Some illicit drug producing regions, particularly in the Andes area where coca growing is concentrated, are controlled not by the central government but by drug trafficking gangs, thereby rendering eradication efforts still more difficult and hazardous. Even where eradication efforts prove relatively successful in one country, the "push down–pop up" phenomenon ensures that production will emerge in other countries. This has occurred with both the international marijuana and heroin markets during the past two decades and is certain to recur with coca if eradication efforts in Bolivia, Peru, and Columbia prove more successful in the future than they have in the past. Because the foreign export prices of illicit drugs are such a tiny fraction of the retail price in the U.S.—about 4% with cocaine, 1% with marijuana, and less than 1% with heroin[2]—international drug control efforts are not even successful in raising the cost of illicit drugs to U.S. consumers.

International drug control efforts also confront substantial, and in some cases well-organized, political opposition in foreign countries.[3] Given the huge profits made possible by criminalization, major drug traffickers retain the power to bribe and intimidate government officials into ignoring or even cooperating with their enterprises.[4] The parallels between the crack economy of U.S. inner cities described by Bourgois in Chapter 3 and in many Latin American and Asian countries are clear: illicit drug traffic is an important source of income and employment, bringing in billions of dollars in hard currency each year and providing the only source of adequate wages for hundreds of thousands. The illicit drug business has been described—not entirely in jest—as the best means ever devised by the U.S. for exporting the capitalist ethic to potentially revolutionary Third World peasants.

By contrast, U.S.-sponsored eradication efforts risk depriving those same peasants of their livelihoods and thereby stimulating support for insurgencies ranging from Peru's Sundero Luminoso (Shining Path)[5] to the variety of ethnic organizations active in drug-producing countries such as Colombia and Burma. Moreover, many of those involved in producing illicit drugs overseas feel no moral obligation to prevent what they see as decadent *gringos* from snorting cocaine, smoking crack, or injecting heroin. Rather, their moral obligation is to earn the best living possible for their families. Under the conditions in which they live, there is little the U.S. can do to change this perception.

Interdiction efforts offer no greater chances of success in stemming the flow of cocaine and heroin to the United States.[6] Indeed, during the 1980s, the wholesale price of a kilo of cocaine dropped by 80% while the retail purity of a gram of cocaine quintupled from 12% to about 60%; the trend with heroin was similar through the 1990s.[7] Easily transported in a variety of aircraft and sea vessels, carried across the Mexican border by legal and illegal border crossers, hidden in everything from furniture to flowers to private body parts and cadavers, cocaine and heroin shipments are extraordinarily difficult to detect.[8] Despite powerful congressional support for increasing the military's role in drug interdiction, and Clinton's recent appointment of General Barry McCaffrey as drug czar, most military leaders insist that they can do little to make a difference. The Coast Guard and U.S. Customs have expanded their efforts dramatically in this area since the mid-1980s, but they too concede that they will never seize more than a small percentage of total shipments. With cocaine, crack, and heroin worth far more than their weight in gold, the economic incentives to take the risk of transporting these drugs to the U.S. are so great that we can safely assume there will never be a shortage of those willing to take the chance. To assume otherwise is to fly in the face of everything we know about markets, profit motives, and human nature.

The one partial success that interdiction efforts can claim concerns marijuana. Because marijuana is far bulkier per dollar of value than either cocaine or heroin, it is harder to conceal and easier to detect. Stepped-up interdiction efforts throughout the 1980s appeared to reduce the flow of marijuana to the U.S. and to increase its price to American consumers.[9] Yet, paradoxically, this success had two unintended consequences: the U.S. emerged as one of the world's leading producers of marijuana—indeed, U.S. producers are now believed to produce among the most potent strains in the world[10]—and many international traffickers redirected their efforts

from marijuana to cocaine. The principal consequence of U.S. drug interdiction efforts, many contend, was a glut of increasingly potent cocaine,
which is easily transformed into crack, and a shortage of comparatively
benign marijuana (see Chapter 13).[11]

Domestic drug enforcement efforts have proven increasingly successful
in apprehending and imprisoning at least some of the rapidly growing
number of illicit drug merchants. The principal benefit of law enforcement efforts directed at major drug trafficking organizations is probably
the rapidly rising value of drug trafficker assets forfeited to the government. There is, however, little indication that such efforts have any significant impact on the price or availability of illicit drugs. Intensive and expensive street-level drug enforcement efforts mounted by many urban police
departments resulted in the arrests of thousands of low-level drug dealers
and users and helped improve the quality of life in some targeted neighborhoods.[12] In most large urban centers, however, these efforts had little
impact on either the overall availability of illicit drugs or the quality of life
in poor neighborhoods.

The logical conclusion of the foregoing analysis is not that drug enforcement efforts do not work at all; rather, it is that even substantial increases
in drug enforcement efforts have little effect on the price, availability, and
consumption of illicit drugs. Law enforcement officials acknowledge that
they alone cannot solve the drug problem but contend that their role is
nonetheless essential to the overall effort to reduce illicit drug use and
abuse. What they are less ready to acknowledge, however, is that the criminalization of drug markets has proven highly costly and often counterproductive in much the same way that national prohibition of alcohol did sixty
years ago.

THE COSTS AND CONSEQUENCES
OF DRUG PROHIBITION POLICIES

Fears of crack drove government officials to expend at least $10 billion in
1987 and more than double that by 1995. Federal expenditures on drug
enforcement rose from less than $1 billion per year in 1980 to approxi-
mately $8.2 billion in 1995.[13] State and local law enforcement agencies
spent an estimated $5 billion on police enforcement of drug laws at the
start of the crack scare in 1986, amounting to about one-fifth of their total
investigative resources.[14] By 1995, this figure had risen dramatically, and
expenditures for incarcerating the four hundred thousand drug law violators in local jails and state and federal prisons were approaching $10 bil-
lion.[15] In 1995, over 60% of the ninety-five thousand inmates in federal
prisons, and more than one-fifth of inmates in state prisons and local jails,

were there for drug law violations, at a cost of \$20,000 to \$40,000 per inmate per year.[16]

State prison systems witnessed similarly dramatic increases in their inmate populations during the 1980s due in no small measure to increasing crack arrests.[17] Approximately two hundred twenty thousand drug law violators were in state prison in 1995, compared to nineteen thousand in 1980.[18] In New York prisons, the proportion of inmates who were drug law violators more than tripled, from 9.4% in 1982 to 34.1% in 1995; they also represented 44% of the new commitments in 1995. In New Jersey's prisons, the percentage of drug law violators quintupled, from 6.1% in 1981 to 31% in 1995; during the same period, the number of drug law violators among new commitments increased even more dramatically, from 6% to about 50%.[19] Many other states, including Massachusetts, Texas, Oklahoma, and Nebraska, also witnessed enormous increases in drug law violators in their prisons, many for crack offenses. In California, the state with the largest prison population, there was a thirty-four-fold increase in drug law violators from 1980 to 1996. And, as Chapter 13 suggests, these skyrocketing rates of incarceration for drug offenses are disproportionately made up of racial minorities. For example, as in many other states, the percentage of nonwhites committed to Virginia's prison system for drug law violations rose from 38.2% in 1983 to 65% in 1989.[20] Nationwide, 67% of drug offenders committed to state prisons in 1992 were African-American. One-third of the massive increase in prison and jail populations between 1980 and 1996 was due to the increased number of drug law violators.[21]

Drug possession and trafficking offenses accounted for approximately 135,000 (23%) of the 583,000 individuals convicted of felonies in state courts as the war against crack got into full swing in 1986.[22] In 1992, this figure had increased to 280,232 (31%) of the 893,630 convictions. Seventy percent of the same convicted drug offenders were sentenced to an average of forty-three months in prison.[23] In the federal courts, the 11,356 drug cases filed in 1994 accounted for 25.4% of all criminal cases filed that year, more than triple the 3127 filed in 1980. The 2542 drug trials in 1994 accounted for 49.9% of all trials, and the 5104 appeals in drug cases represented 47.8% of all criminal appeals.[24] The four statutes providing for mandatory minimum sentences for drug offenses also had a major impact. During the year ending September 1992, for example, more than 3000 drug law violators who had no histories of violent crime for at least the previous fifteen years received mandatory minimum sentences of five years or more.[25] The direct costs of building and maintaining enough prisons to house this growing population are rising at an astronomical rate. The opportunity costs, in terms of alternative social expenditures foregone and other types of criminals not imprisoned, are perhaps even more severe. And these figures do not even include the many inmates sentenced for "drug-related" crimes.

Arrests for drug law violations rose from an average of about 750,000 per year during the mid-1980s to almost 1.4 million per year by the end of the decade.[26] Approximately three-quarters of these were not for manufacturing or dealing drugs, but solely for *possession* of an illicit drug, typically marijuana.[27] These arrests represent about 3% of the 35–40 million Americans estimated to have illegally consumed a drug during the past year.[28] Yet, even in the mid-1980s, these arrests had already clogged many urban criminal justice systems. In New York City, for example, drug law violations in 1987, the second year of the crack scare, accounted for more than 40% of all felony indictments—up from 25% in 1985[29]; in Washington, D.C., the figure was 52% in 1986—up from 13% in 1981.[30] In the seventy-five largest counties, over 30% of felony defendants during 1992 had been arrested for drug law violations.[31] This preoccupation with crack and other illicit drugs has distracted criminal justice officials from violent and property crimes. In many cities, urban law enforcement has become virtually synonymous with drug enforcement.

Ironically, the greatest beneficiaries of this massive increase in drug law enforcement are drug traffickers. Criminalization of drugs effectively imposes a de facto value-added tax that is collected by the traffickers in the form of higher prices. More than half of all organized crime revenues are believed to derive from the illicit drug business; estimates of the dollar value range between $10 billion and $50 billion per year.[32] If the marijuana, cocaine, and heroin markets were legal, state and federal governments would collect billions of dollars annually in tax revenues. Instead, they expend billions on what amounts to a subsidy to organized crime.

The drug-crime connection continues to resist coherent analysis both because cause and effect are so difficult to distinguish and because the role of drug prohibition in causing "drug-related crime" is so often ignored. There are five possible connections between drugs and crime, at least three of which would be weakened if prohibitionist drug laws were changed. First, the production, sale, purchase, and possession of marijuana, crack, heroin, and other banned substances are in and of themselves crimes that occur billions of times each year in the U.S. In the absence of drug prohibition laws, these activities would largely cease to be crimes. Selling drugs to children would, of course, remain a crime, and other evasions of drug control regulations in a legal market would continue to be prosecuted. But a major part of the criminal justice costs noted previously would be avoided.

Second, many illicit drug users commit crimes such as robbery, burglary, drug dealing, prostitution, and numbers running at least in part to earn enough money to purchase crack, heroin, or other illicit drugs[33]—drugs that cost far more than alcohol and tobacco not because they cost much more to produce but because they are illegal. Legalization would inevitably reduce the cost of the drugs that are now illicit and thus significantly reduce the number of crimes committed to buy drugs. Current methadone maintenance programs represent a limited form of drug legalization that attempts to address this drug-crime connection by providing an alternative opiate at little or no cost to addicts who might otherwise steal to support their illicit heroin habits. Such programs have proven effective in reducing the criminal behavior and improving the lives of tens of thousands of illicit drug addicts.[34] Methadone needs to be made far more accessible, both by expanding the number of programs and by making the drug more readily available—as is the case in Europe, Australia, and Asia—through general physicians, pharmacists, and mobile distribution sites.[35]

At the same time, the "British system" of prescribing not just oral methadone but also injectable and smokeable heroin, methadone, and cocaine to injection drug addicts persists on a small scale despite continuing pressures against prescribing injectables.[36] And in 1994, Switzerland began a heroin prescription program that now has six hundred fifty patients and has had considerable success. The Netherlands plans to begin a similar program in 1997. This idea, too, merits consideration in the U.S.—particularly if one accepts the assumption that the primary objective of drug policy should be to minimize the harms that drug abusers do to others.[37]

The third drug-crime connection is more coincidental than causal in nature. Contrary to myth, most illicit drug users do not engage in crime aside from their drug use, and many criminals do not use or abuse illicit drugs or alcohol. Nonetheless, most studies of criminal careers show much higher levels of substance use among criminals than among noncriminals. For example, a 1986 survey of state prison inmates found that 43% were using illegal drugs on a daily or near daily basis in the month before they committed their crimes. However, this study also found that roughly half the inmates who had used an illicit drug had not done so until *after* their first arrest.[38] Although drug abuse does lead some people into crime, criminal subcultures lead others into drug abuse. It is less accurate to point the causal arrow one way than it is to say that *both* drug abuse and crime are part of the deviant milieux of many marginalized groups. Many of the same factors that lead individuals into lives of crime probably also push them in the direction of substance abuse.[39] Legalization would at least diminish this drug-crime connection by removing from the criminal subculture most of the lucrative opportunities that now derive from the illegality of the drug market. But the world of crime will probably continue to attract drug abusers whether or not drugs are legalized. As Chapters 8–10 suggest, the general failure of U.S. social policy to deal with inequality and marginalization ensures that the conditions underlying both crime and drug abuse will persist.

The fourth drug-crime link is the commission of violent and other crimes by people under the influence of illicit drugs. This connection seems to infect the popular imagination the most. Many people believe that some drugs "cause" some people to commit crimes by reducing normal inhibitions, unleashing aggressive and other asocial tendencies, and lessening senses of responsibility. Crack gained such a reputation in the 1980s, just as PCP (phencyclidine) did in the 1970s, heroin did in the 1960s, marijuana did in the 1930s, and cocaine did at the turn of the century.[40] Crack's reputation for directly causing violent behavior seems to be no more deserved than were those of marijuana, heroin, and cocaine. As Chapters 4 and 6 show, crack use in itself does not automatically cause crime and violence.[41]

No illicit drug is as strongly associated with violent behavior as is alcohol, and this should make us skeptical of all assertions that any drug directly causes any criminal or violent behavior. According to Justice Department statistics, 47% of all jail inmates convicted of violent crimes in 1989 reported having used alcohol just prior to committing their offense.[42] A 1986 survey of state prison inmates similarly found that most of those convicted of arson, murder, involuntary manslaughter, and rape were far more likely to have been under the influence of alcohol, or both alcohol and illicit drugs, than under the influence of illicit drugs alone.[43] Yet we all know that the vast majority of the 140 million Americans who drink do not turn criminal under the influence of alcohol. Because only relatively few users under certain conditions become violent or criminal when they have used alcohol or other drugs, it is very difficult to assess the possible impacts of drug legalization on this drug-crime connection.

The fifth drug-crime connection is the violent, intimidating, and corrupting behavior of drug traffickers. In many Latin American countries, notably Colombia, this connection virtually defines the "drug problem." But even within the U.S., trafficker violence rapidly became a major concern of criminal justice officials and the public at large. The connection is not difficult to explain. Illegal markets tend to breed violence, both because there are huge profits at stake thanks to prohibition and because participants in such markets cannot resort to legal institutions to resolve their disputes.[44]

During alcohol Prohibition, violent struggles between bootlegging gangs and hijackings of booze-laden trucks and sea vessels were notoriously frequent. Today's equivalents are the pirates of the Caribbean looking to rip off drug-laden vessels en route to U.S. shores, the machine gun battles and executions of the more sordid drug gangs, and the generally high levels of violence that attend many illicit drug relationships. More often than not the victims are other drug dealers, but witnesses, bystanders, and law enforcement officials have too frequently been victimized as well. Most law enforcement authorities agree that the dramatic increases in urban murder rates during the 1980s were largely caused by the rise in drug dealer killings, mostly of one another.[45] As shown in Chapter 6, far more drug-related homicides stem from the illicit market system than from the effects of the drugs themselves. The same point may be made about corruption: the powerful allure of illicit drug dollars is responsible for rising levels of corruption, not just in Latin America and the Caribbean, but also in federal, state, and local criminal justice systems throughout the U.S.[46] Drug legalization strategies would certainly deal a severe blow to both the violence and corruption that are inherent in illicit drug markets.

Perhaps the most unfortunate victims of the drug prohibition policies have been the poor and law-abiding residents of urban ghettos. Prohibitionist policies have proven largely futile in deterring large numbers of ghetto dwellers from becoming drug abusers, but they do account for much of what ghetto residents identify as the drug problem. In many neighborhoods, the aggressive, gun-toting drug dealers seem to upset law-abiding residents more than the addicts per se.[47] Other residents, however, perceive the drug dealers as heroes and successful role models. In impoverished neighborhoods from Medellin and Rio de Janeiro to many of America's leading cities, dealers often stand out as symbols of success to children who see no other options. At the same time, the increasingly harsh criminal penalties imposed on adult drug dealers have led to the widespread recruiting of juveniles.[48] Where once only children who used drugs for a long time started dealing them, today many young people start to use illegal drugs only after they have worked for older dealers. And the juvenile justice system offers no realistic options for dealing with this growing problem.

Among the most difficult costs to evaluate are those that relate to the widespread defiance of drug prohibition laws. Whether or not they cause themselves or their neighbors any problems, tens of millions of Americans who use illicit drugs are obliged to enter into relationships with illegal dealers, labeled criminals, and subjected to the risks of criminal sanction. More diffuse costs include the cynicism that such legislation generates toward law in general and the sense of hostility and suspicion that many otherwise law-abiding individuals feel toward police. Costs such as these led many conservatives to oppose alcohol Prohibition and seek its repeal. As John D. Rockefeller put it in 1932:

> When the 18th Amendment was passed I earnestly hoped—with a host of advocates of temperance—that it would be generally supported by public

opinion and thus the day be hastened when the value to society of men with minds and bodies free from the undermining effects of alcohol would be generally realized. That this had not been the result, but rather that drinking has generally increased; that the speakeasy has replaced the saloon, not only unit for unit, but probably two-fold if not three-fold; that a vast array of law-breakers has been recruited and financed on a colossal scale; that many of our best citizens, piqued at what they regarded as an infringement of their private rights, have openly and unabashedly disregarded the 18th Amendment; that as an inevitable result respect for all law has been greatly lessened; that crime has increased to an unprecedented degree—I have slowly and reluctantly come to believe.[49]

Among the most dangerous consequences of current drug laws are the harms that stem from the unregulated nature of illicit drug production and sale.[50] Consumers of heroin and the various synthetic substitutes sold on the street, for example, face fatal overdoses and poisonings from impure or unexpectedly potent supplies. Emergency room physicians suspect that many of the toxicological syndromes associated with cocaine abuse may be the result of adulterants, which are found in most street samples of cocaine.[51] In short, one of the costs of criminalization is the absence of anything resembling a Food and Drug Administration to ensure quality control and provide users with accurate information on the drugs they consume. Moreover, the quality of a drug addict's life often depends greatly upon his or her access to reliable supplies. Drug enforcement operations that temporarily disrupt supply networks are thus a double-edged sword: they may encourage some addicts to seek treatment, but they oblige many others to seek out new and hence less reliable suppliers, with the result that more, not fewer, drug-related emergencies and deaths occur.

Arguably the greatest costs of prohibitionist policies are the many lives that have been and will be lost to AIDS. By 1993, 33.5% of all AIDS cases in the U.S., and the vast majority of HIV-infected heterosexuals, children, and infants, had contracted the dreaded disease directly or indirectly from illegal injection drug use (IDU).[52] Three-quarters of all new HIV infections in the U.S. in 1994 contracted the virus via IDU. Today in New York City, 53% of all reported AIDS cases involve IDU, and approximately half the city's injection drug users are infected with HIV.[53] Still, needle exchange programs serve only about 15% of the IDU population.[54] With public health approaches to this problem constrained by criminal law, some drug dealers have begun to provide clean syringes to their customers.[55]

In Switzerland, increases in the number of HIV-infected users led clinicians to establish heroin prescription programs throughout the country. Data on these patients show stabilizing or decreasing use of heroin, fewer illegal activities, less use of illegally obtained drugs, fewer psychiatric episodes, improved quality of life, and renewed contact with family and friends.[56] England continues to allow provision of oral and injectable methadone and injectable heroin on a limited level, and the Netherlands plans to begin a program following the Swiss lead. England, Scotland, Canada, Switzerland, Australia, the Netherlands, Thailand, and other countries actively attempt to limit the spread of HIV by and among injection drug users by removing restrictions on syringes and instituting free syringe exchange programs.[57] Yet many municipal governments in the U.S. still resist following suit, and the federal government maintains a ban on federal funding.

Despite mounting evidence to the contrary,[58] many U.S. officials argue that such policies would "send the wrong message" and "encourage" or "condone" the use of illegal drugs.[59] Only in late 1988 did needle exchange programs begin emerging in U.S. cities, almost always at the courageous initiative of nongovernmental organizations. By 1990, programs were under way in Tacoma, Washington; Boulder, Colorado; Portland, Oregon; New Haven, Connecticut; San Francisco; and Honolulu.[60] By 1996, needle or syringe exchange programs were operating in at least sixty American cities and had gained the support of the U.S. Centers for Disease Control, National Research Council, National Commission on AIDS, General Accounting Office, National Academy of Sciences, American Medical Association, and American Public Health Association. But resistance remains. Due in part to the ban on federal funding, only about 10% of injection drug users nationwide and only about 15% in New York City, home of nearly half of America's injection drug users, are served by existing syringe exchanges.[61] In New York City, a pilot program was canceled by then-Mayor David Dinkins shortly after he assumed office in 1990 despite evidence that it had proven successful in reducing the needle sharing that spreads HIV and helped bring addicts into treatment. By 1992, the AIDS epidemic and pressure from community groups led to a reinstatement of the program. But for the thousands of IV drug users, their spouses, sexual partners, and children who have died or will soon die from AIDS, this was too little too late. Their lives, too, must be counted as costs of drug prohibition. Meanwhile, as tens of billions of dollars are being spent to arrest, prosecute, and imprison illegal drug users, tens of thousands of addicts are turned away from treatment programs that remain notoriously underfunded.

Among the other costs of current drug policies are the restrictions on using illicit drugs for legitimate medical purposes.[62] Marijuana has proven useful in alleviating pain in some victims of multiple sclerosis, enhancing the appetites of AIDS patients dying prematurely from wasting syndrome, reducing the nausea that accompanies chemotherapy, and treating people who would otherwise go blind from glaucoma.[63] In September 1988, the administrative law judge of the DEA accordingly recommended that marijuana be made legally available for such purposes,[64] but his decision was overturned for political reasons. Heroin has proven highly effective in helping many terminally ill cancer patients deal with severe pain; some researchers have found it more effective than morphine and other opiates in treating pain in many patients.[65] It is legally prescribed for such purposes in Britain and Canada.[66] Some doctors in the U.S. continue to use cocaine to treat pain in some patients despite recently imposed bans.[67] Drugs such as LSD, peyote, and MDMA (Ecstasy) have shown promise in aiding psychotherapy and in reducing tension, depression, pain, and fear of death in the terminally ill;[68] they also have demonstrated some potential, as yet unconfirmed, to aid in the treatment of alcoholism.[69] Current drug laws, however, greatly hamper even the investigation of these and other potential medical uses of illegal drugs. It is virtually impossible for any of these illegal drugs to be legally provided to those who would benefit from them, and it contributes strongly to the widely acknowledged undertreatment of pain by the medical profession in the U.S.[70]

Among the strongest arguments in favor of decriminalization are moral ones. On the one hand, the standard refrain regarding the immorality of drug use crumbles in the face of most Americans' tolerance for alcohol and tobacco use, which are responsible for many times more social and health costs than all illicit drugs combined. Only the Mormons and a few other like-minded sects, who regard as immoral any intake of substances to alter one's state of consciousness or otherwise cause pleasure, are consistent in this respect. They eschew not just the illicit drugs, but also alcohol, tobacco, caffeinated coffee and tea, and even chocolate. Most Americans are hardly so consistent with respect to the propriety of their pleasures. Their "moral" condemnation of some substances and not others amounts to little more than a prejudice rooted in the demonization that has accompanied all drug wars.

On the other hand, drug enforcement risks its own immoralities. Because most drug law violations do not create victims who call the police, drug enforcement agents must rely heavily on undercover operations, electronic surveillance, and informants. In 1994, 76% of the 1154 court-authorized orders for wiretaps in the U.S. involved drug trafficking investigations.[71] Police see these techniques as indispensable, but for the public, they are among the least desirable tools available. The same is true of drug testing. It may be useful for determining liability in accidents, but it also threatens our Fourth Amendment protections against invasive searches and seizures, the Fifth Amendment right not to testify against oneself, and the presumption of innocence and right of privacy to which Americans are morally entitled. There are good reasons for requiring that such measures be used sparingly (see Chapter 11).

Equally disturbing are the increasingly vocal calls for people to inform not just on drug dealers but on neighbors, friends, and even family members who use illicit drugs. Intolerance of illicit drug use and users is heralded not merely as an indispensable ingredient in the war against drugs, but as a mark of good citizenship. Certainly every society requires citizens to assist in the enforcement of criminal laws. But societies, particularly democratic and pluralistic ones, also rely strongly on an ethic of tolerance toward those who are different but do no harm to others. Overzealous enforcement of the drug laws risks undermining that ethic and propagating in its place an Orwellian society of informants. Indeed, enforcement of drug laws makes a mockery of an essential principle of a free society: that those who do no harm to others should not be harmed by others, particularly not by the state. Most of the twenty million Americans who consume illegal drugs each year do no harm to anyone else; indeed, most do relatively little harm even to themselves. Directing criminal and other sanctions at them, and rationalizing the justice of such sanctions, may well represent the greatest societal cost of our current drug prohibition system.

ALTERNATIVES TO DRUG PROHIBITION POLICIES

Repealing the drug prohibition laws clearly promises substantial advantages. Between reduced government expenditures on enforcing drug laws and new tax revenue from legal drug production and sales, public treasuries would enjoy a net benefit of at least $10 billion per year and possibly much more. Billions in new revenues would thus be available—and ideally targeted—for funding much-needed drug treatment programs as well as the types of social and educational programs that often prove most effective in preventing children from using drugs in the first place. The quality of urban life would rise significantly. Homicide rates would decline, as would robbery and burglary rates. Organized criminal groups would be dealt a devastating setback. The police, prosecutors, and courts would focus their resources on combating violent and property crimes. And the health and quality of life of many drug users and even drug abusers would improve significantly. Internationally, U.S. foreign policy makers would get on with more important and realistic tasks, and foreign governments would reclaim the authority that they have lost to drug traffickers.

All these benefits of legalization would be for naught, however, if millions more people were to become drug abusers. Our experience with alcohol and tobacco provides ample warnings. But the impact of legalization upon the nature and level of consumption of currently illicit drugs is impossible to predict with any accuracy. On the one hand, legalization implies greater availability, lower prices, and the elimination of the deterrent power of the criminal sanction—all of which would suggest higher levels of use. Indeed, some fear that the extent of drug abuse and its costs would rise to those of alcohol and tobacco.[72] On the other hand, there are many reasons to doubt that a well-designed and intelligently implemented policy of controlled drug legalization would yield such costly consequences.

The logic of legalization depends in part upon two assumptions: that most illegal drugs are not as dangerous as is commonly believed and that those types of drugs and methods of consumption that are most risky are unlikely to prove appealing to many people precisely because they are so obviously dangerous. Consider marijuana. Among the roughly sixty million Americans who have smoked marijuana, not one has died from a marijuana overdose[73]—a striking contrast with alcohol, which is involved in approximately ten thousand overdose deaths annually, half in combination with other licit or illicit drugs.[74] Although there are good health reasons for people not to smoke marijuana daily and for children, pregnant women, and some others not to smoke at all, there is little evidence that occasional marijuana consumption is harmful. Certainly, it is not healthy to inhale marijuana smoke into one's lungs; the National Institute on Drug Abuse (NIDA) has declared that "marijuana smoke contains more cancer-causing agents than is found in tobacco smoke."[75] However, the number of "joints" smoked by all but a very small percentage of marijuana users is a tiny fraction of the twenty cigarettes a day smoked by the average cigarette smoker. Indeed, NIDA's own data show that even among the minority that uses with some regularity, the average is closer to one or two "joints" per week than one or two per day.[76] Nor is marijuana strongly identified as a dependence-causing substance.[77] The available evidence suggests that daily marijuana use is a phase through which only a small minority of users pass, after which even their use becomes moderate or occasional.

The dangers associated with cocaine, heroin, the hallucinogens, and other illicit substances are greater than those posed by marijuana, but not nearly so great as we have been led to believe. Consider cocaine. In 1986, NIDA reported that over 20 million Americans had tried cocaine, that 12.2 million had consumed it at least once during 1985, and that nearly 5.8 million had used it within the past month. Among eighteen to twenty-five-year-olds, 8.2 million had tried cocaine; 5.3 million had used it within the past year; 2.5 million had used it within the past month; and 250,000 had used it on the average weekly. One could extrapolate from these figures that a quarter of a million young Americans are potential problem users. But one could also conclude that only 3% of those eighteen to twenty-five-year-olds who had ever tried the drug fell into that category.[78] Nor is there any reason to believe that even this small percentage of problem users *remains* problem users; most seem to learn their lessons and cut back or quit.

All of this is not to say that cocaine is not a risky drug, especially when it is smoked in the form of crack or freebase, injected, or consumed with other powerful substances. Indeed, the accounts of crack users and free-basers in Chapter 4 offer compelling testimony that the more concen-trated forms and direct modes of ingesting cocaine can lead to compulsive bingeing and other serious problems. Clearly, tens of thousands of Ameri-cans have suffered from their abuse of cocaine, and a tiny fraction has died. But there is also clear evidence that the vast majority of cocaine users does not get into significant trouble.[79] So much media attention has fo-cused on the relatively small percentage of cocaine users who become ad-dicted that popular perceptions have become badly distorted. In one sur-vey of high school seniors' drug use, for example, researchers asked those who had used cocaine recently whether they had ever tried to stop using cocaine and found that they couldn't. Only 3.8% of that small group said yes, in contrast to the 18% of cigarette smokers who answered similarly.[80]

Even the exaggerated antidrug advertisements of the Partnership for a Drug-Free America claim that only "about ten percent who try [cocaine] get addicted."[81] Although all forms of cocaine use have declined among the middle and upper classes, crack addiction remains a very serious prob-lem among the most impoverished and vulnerable segments of the popula-tion. Yet most cocaine users remain intranasal users, and the evidence on patterns of cocaine use suggests that only a small percentage of people who snort cocaine end up having a problem with it. Even in inner cities, where crack is widely available, most people either never try it or never get into trouble with it. In this respect, most people are radically different from the rats and monkeys that, when caged in isolation and deprived of all other activities, repeatedly chose cocaine over food and starved.[82] Human beings are not caged in isolation and usually do have other activities in their lives.

With respect to the hallucinogens such as LSD and psilocybin mush-rooms, the potential for addiction is virtually nil. The dangers arise primar-ily from using them improperly or irresponsibly.[83] Although some of those who have used one or another of the hallucinogens have experienced a "bad trip," far more have reported positive experiences, and very few have suffered any long-term harm.[84] Moreover, the likelihood of negative expe-riences is largely a function of criminalization, which actively inhibits the spread of user knowledge about proper doses and safe settings.[85] As for the great assortment of stimulants, depressants, and tranquilizers produced illegally or diverted from licit channels, each can be used safely or abused, depending more on the characteristics of the user and his or her circum-stances and use patterns than on its chemical properties.

Prior to the explosion in crack use during the mid and late 1980s, no drugs were regarded with as much horror as opiates, especially heroin. As with most drugs, opiates can be eaten, snorted, smoked, or injected. But unfortunately, the criminalization of the less concentrated eatable and smokeable opiates in the early twentieth century helped push users toward heroin injection. Now, growing fear of AIDS appears to be causing a shift among younger opiate addicts toward intranasal ingestion and smoking ("chasing the dragon").[86] There is no question that heroin is potentially highly addictive, almost as addictive as nicotine. Although there are many down-and-out street addicts, heroin itself causes relatively little physical harm to the human body. When it is consumed on an occasional or even regular basis under sanitary conditions, its worst side effect other than addiction is constipation.[87] That is one reason why many doctors in early twentieth-century America saw opiate addiction as preferable to alcoholism and prescribed the former as treatment for the latter where abstinence did not seem realistic.[88]

Thinking about the illicit drugs as we do about alcohol and tobacco can provide important insights. Like tobacco, some illicit substances are highly addictive but can be consumed on a regular basis for decades without any demonstrable harm. Like alcohol, many illicit substances can be, and are, used by most consumers in moderation, with little or no harmful effects. But like alcohol, they also lend themselves to abuse by a minority of users who become addicted or otherwise harm themselves or others. And like both the legal substances, the effects of each of the illegal drugs vary greatly from one person to another. To be sure, the pharmacology of the substance is important, as is its purity and the manner in which it is consumed. But as other contributors to this volume have stressed, much more depends on the user's expectations regarding the drug, his or her social milieu, and the broader cultural environment—what Zinberg called the "set and setting" of drug use.[89] It is these factors that might change dramatically, albeit in indeterminate ways, were illicit drugs decriminalized.

Thus predicting whether legalization would lead to much greater levels of drug abuse is impossible. The lessons that can be drawn from other societies are mixed. China's experience with the British opium pushers of the nineteenth century, when millions reportedly became addicted to the drug, offers one worst-case scenario.[90] The devastation of many Native American tribes by alcohol presents another. But the decriminalization of marijuana by eleven states in the United States during the mid-1970s did not lead even to increased marijuana consumption, much less problems.[91] In the Netherlands, which went even further in decriminalizing cannabis in the 1970s, consumption initially *declined*. Although lifetime use of cannabis has gradually increased in the city of Amsterdam in recent years—from 22.8% in 1987 to 28.5% in 1994—even this higher level remains well below the lifetime use figures for the U.S. The Dutch policy has succeeded, as the government intended, "in making drug use boring."[92] In the U.S., alcohol consumption was not out of control before Prohibition, nor did it increase sharply after repeal. Finally, late nineteenth-century America was a society with almost no drug laws or even drug regulations, but levels of drug use were about what they are today.[93] Drug abuse was regarded as a problem, but the legal system was not regarded as the solution.[94]

There are strong reasons to believe that none of the currently illicit substances would become as popular as alcohol or tobacco even if they were legalized. Alcohol has long been the principal intoxicant in most societies, including many in which other substances have been legally available. Presumably, its diverse properties account for its popularity—it quenches thirst, enhances food, pleases the palate, promotes sociability, and so on. The widespread use of tobacco stems not just from its powerful addictive qualities but from the fact that its psychoactive effects are sufficiently subtle that smoking does not interfere with most other human activities. None of the illicit substances now popular in the U.S. shares either of these qualities to the same extent, nor would they automatically acquire them if they were legalized. Moreover, none of the illicit substances can compete with alcohol's special place in American culture and history, which it retained even during Prohibition.

Much of the damage caused by illegal drugs today stems from their being consumed in particularly potent and dangerous ways, and there is good reason to doubt that many more Americans would smoke crack or inject heroin into their veins even if given the chance to do so legally. Just as heroin use both rose and fell in the 1960s for reasons apparently having little to do with law enforcement, so the number of people smoking crack seemed to peak by the end of the 1980s.[95] Indeed, preliminary evidence suggests that initiation into crack use among inner-city youth began to decline at precisely the time—late 1989—when crack was cheapest and most abundant. Drugs are never so addictive, nor are users ever so stupid, that curiosity cannot be contained by commonsense caution or that lessons cannot be learned. Just as the vast majority of drinkers do not guzzle hundred proof vodka, so too would the vast majority of drug users avoid the riskiest drugs under decriminalization.

Perhaps the most reassuring reason for believing that repeal of the drug prohibition laws would not lead to tremendous increases in drug abuse is the fact that we have learned something from our past experiences with alcohol and tobacco abuse. We now know, for instance, that consumption taxes are an effective method for limiting consumption rates and related costs—especially among young people.[96] Substantial evidence also suggests that restrictions and bans on advertising, as well as educational negative advertising, can make a difference.[97] The same is true of other government measures, including restrictions on time and place of sale,[98] bans on vending machines, prohibitions of consumption in public places, packaging requirements, mandated adjustments in insurance policies, crackdowns on driving while under the influence,[99] and laws holding bartenders and hosts responsible for the drinking of customers and guests. There is even evidence that education about the dangers of cigarettes has deterred many children from beginning to smoke.[100] At the same time, we also have come to recognize the great harms that can result when drug control policies are undermined by powerful corporate lobbies such as those that now block efforts to lessen the harms caused by abuse of alcohol and tobacco.

The irony in the previous list of helpful regulatory mechanisms is that criminalization *precludes* their use. Thus, legalization might well allow greater opportunities to control drug use and abuse than do current criminalization policies. Under prohibition, the type, price, purity, and potency of drugs, as well as the participants in the business, are determined largely by drug dealers, the peculiar dynamics of unregulated competition in illicit markets, and the perverse interplay of drug enforcement strategies and drug trafficking tactics.

The results have not been encouraging. During the 1980s, the average retail purity of cocaine increased fivefold, wholesale prices dropped by 50–80%, the number of children involved in dealing rose dramatically, and crack became readily and cheaply available in hundreds of American cities.[101] By contrast, marijuana became more scarce and expensive, in part because it is far more vulnerable to drug enforcement efforts than cocaine or heroin. Thus, criminalization has encouraged both dealers and users to move away from a safer drug to more potent and dangerous ones. By contrast, spurred by regulations, education, and health concerns, licit drug users chose to switch from hard liquor to beer and wine, from high tar and nicotine to lower tar and nicotine cigarettes as well as smokeless tobaccos and nicotine gums, and even from caffeinated to decaffeinated coffees, teas, and sodas. It is entirely possible that these diverging trends are less a reflection of the nature of the drugs than of their legal status.

A noncriminal drug control policy thus offers several significant advantages over the current criminal justice approach. It shifts control of production, distribution, and, to a lesser extent, consumption out of the hands of criminals and into the hands of government and/or government licensees. It affords consumers the opportunity, and allows dissemination of the information necessary, to make far more informed decisions about the drugs they buy than is currently the case. It dramatically lessens the likelihood that drug consumers will be harmed by impure, unexpectedly potent, or mislabeled drugs. It corrects the hypocritical and dangerous message that, because alcohol and tobacco are legal, they are somehow safe. It reduces by billions of dollars annually government expenditures on drug enforcement and simultaneously raises additional billions in tax revenues. And it allows policy to shape consumption patterns toward relatively safer psychoactive substances and modes of consumption.

Toward the end of the 1920s, when the movement to repeal alcohol prohibition rapidly gained momentum, numerous scholars, journalists, and private and government commissions undertook thorough evaluations of Prohibition and potential alternatives. Prominent among these were the Wickersham Commission appointed by President Hoover and the study of alcohol regulation abroad directed by the leading police scholar in the United States, Raymond Fosdick, and commissioned by John D. Rockefeller.[102] These efforts examined the successes and failures of Prohibition and evaluated the many alternatives for controlling the distribution and use of beer, wine, and liquor. They played a major role in stimulating the public reevaluation of Prohibition and in envisioning alternatives. Precisely the same sorts of efforts are required today.

The controlled drug legalization option is not an all-or-nothing alternative to current policies. Indeed, political realities ensure that any shift toward legalization will evolve gradually, with ample opportunity to halt, reevaluate, and redirect drug policies that begin to prove too costly or counterproductive. The federal government need not play the leading role in devising alternatives; it need only clear the way to allow state and local governments the legal power to experiment with their own alternative policies. The first steps are relatively risk-free: legalization of marijuana and of low-potency coca products such as the coca teas, tonics, and wines popular a century ago; easier availability of illegal and strictly controlled drugs for treatment of pain and other medical purposes; and a broader and more available array of drug treatment programs, including those in which opiates and cocaine are prescribed to addicts in a variety of forms.

Remedying the drug-related ills of impoverished inner-city neighborhoods will require more effective social policies that can change opportunity structures and the quality of life. The risks of controlled drug legalization—increased availability, lower prices, and removal of the deterrent power of the criminal sanction—are relatively less in the inner cities than in most other parts of the U.S. because drug availability is already so high, prices so low, and the criminal sanction so ineffective in deterring illicit use that legalization can hardly worsen the situation. However, legalization could yield its greatest benefits precisely in the most impoverished areas, where it would take the profit out of drug dealing, sever much of the drug-crime connection, seize the market away from criminals, deglorify involvement in the illicit drug business, help redirect entrepreneurial élan from illegitimate to legitimate business, help stem the transmission of AIDS by intravenous drug users, and significantly improve the safety, health, and well-being of those who do use and abuse drugs. Simply stated, making even relatively risky drugs legally available may well be the most effective way to reduce harmful consequences of drug use and current drug policies in our most troubled urban areas.

There is no question that legalization entails real risks—risks that may lead to an increase in the number of people who use drugs and thus to a smaller increase in the number who abuse them. But that risk is by no means a certainty. The risks of current drug control policies *are* certain, and despite their enormous costs and consequences, they have yielded precious little progress to date. We know that repealing the drug prohibition laws would eliminate or greatly reduce many of the ills that people commonly identify as part of the "drug problem." Yet that option is repeatedly and vociferously dismissed without any attempt to evaluate it openly and objectively. The past twenty years have demonstrated that a drug policy shaped by rhetoric and fear mongering can lead only to our current disaster. Unless we are willing to evaluate honestly *all* policy options, including various legalization and decriminalization strategies, we will have no chance to devise better solutions for our drug problems.

NOTES

The author wishes to acknowledge the valuable research assistance of Phillip O. Coffin, research associate of the Lindesmith Center, in revising and updating this chapter.

1. Statement by Senator Daniel Patrick Moynihan, citing a U.S. Department of Agriculture report, in the *Congressional Record*, May 27, 1988, p. S7049.

2. Drug Enforcement Administration, U.S. Department of Justice, *Intelligence Trends*, vol. 14, no. 3, 1987.

3. See, for example, Kevin Healy, "Coca, the State, and the Peasantry in Bolivia, 1982–1988," *Journal of Interamerican Studies and World Affairs*, 30:105–126 (1988).

4. E. A. Nadelmann, "The DEA in Latin America: Dealing with Institutionalized Corruption," *Journal of Interamerican Studies and World Affairs*, 29:1–39 (1987/1988).

5. Cynthia McClintock, "The War on Drugs: The Peruvian Case," *Journal of Interamerican Studies and World Affairs*, 30:127–142 (1988); Roger Cohen, "Cocaine Rebellion: Peru's Guerrillas Draw Support of Peasants in Coca-Rich Regions," *Wall Street Journal,* January 17, 1989, p. 1.

6. Peter Reuter, "Can the Borders Be Sealed?" *The Public Interest*, 92:51–66 (1988).

7. See the annual reports of the National Narcotics Intelligence Consumers Committee, edited by the U.S. Drug Enforcement Administration. According to a report issued by the Unified Intelligence Division of the DEA's New York office in 1989, "heroin purities in Harlem and the Bronx—historically in the 3–5% range—now range in the 40% level. Lower East Side purities, traditionally in the 10–30 percent range, are currently running from 28–45%." See "Trends in Traffic—Her-

oin," *International Drug Report*, December 1989, p. 15. By 1994, purity levels had reached 60% in New York City, Philadelphia, and Newark, New Jersey, and 40% nationwide (U.S. Department of Justice, Drug Enforcement Administration, *DMP City Summary Data, 1994*).

8. Christopher Wren, "Big Cocaine Cache Is Found Stashed in Airliner Cockpit," *New York Times*, March 23, 1996, p. A6; Stewart Tendler, "Customs Trap Led to 350m Pounds of Cocaine," *The Times* (London), September 15, 1995, p. 3; Joseph P. Fried, "Cocaine Found Smuggled Inside a Dog," *New York Times*, December 6, 1994, p. B1.

9. See the annual reports of the National Narcotics Intelligence Consumers Committee, edited by the U.S. Drug Enforcement Administration.

10. Ibid.

11. The negative impact of the shifts in the availability and price of marijuana and cocaine on Caribbean communities in New York is analyzed in Ansley Hamid, "The Political Economy of Crack-Related Violence," *Contemporary Drug Problems*, 17:31–78 (1990).

12. See M. R. Chaiken, ed., *Street-Level Drug Enforcement: Examining the Issues* (Washington, DC: National Institute of Justice, September 1988).

13. National Drug Enforcement Policy Board, *National and International Drug Law Enforcement Strategy* (Washington, DC: U.S. Department of Justice, 1987); Office of National Drug Control Policy, *National Drug Control Strategy—Budget Summary* (Washington, DC: Executive Office of the President, January 1990), pp. 2–12; Bureau of Justice Statistics (hereinafter BJS), *Sourcebook of Criminal Justice Statistics, 1994*.

14. Specially prepared document by the BJS, February 7, 1996. See also the report prepared for the U.S. Customs Service by Wharton Econometrics, *Anti-Drug Law Enforcement Efforts and Their Impact* (1987), pp. 2, 38–46; and BJS, *Sourcebook of Criminal Justice Statistics, 1994*.

15. BJS, press release, December 3, 1995.

16. BJS, "Jurisdictional Population of Federal Prisons, 1994." See also BJS, *Sourcebook of Criminal Justice Statistics, 1994*. See also U.S. General Accounting Office, *Prison Crowding: Issues Facing the Nation's Prison Systems* (November 1989), and *Federal Prisons: Trends in Offender Characteristics* (October 1989). On prison costs, see Criminal Justice Institute, *The Corrections Yearbook* (New York: Criminal Justice Institute, 1995).

17. Drug offenders were about 22% of state inmates according to the BJS, "Correctional Populations of the U.S., 1992" (Washington, DC: U.S. Department of Justice, 1992), p. 53. The state-specific figures were obtained from either the annual reports of the state corrections systems or from correspondence received by the author from officials in those systems.

18. BJS, press release, December 3, 1996; BJS, *Correctional Populations in the U.S., 1992*, p. 53.

19. New Jersey Department of Corrections.

20. See James Austin and Aaron D. McVey, "The 1989 NCCD Prison Population Forecast: The Impact of the War on Drugs," *NCCD Focus*, December 1989, p. 6. (San Francisco: National Council on Crime and Delinquency).

21. These data were taken from BJS, *Sourcebook for Criminal Justice Statistics, 1980–1994;* BJS, press release, December 3, 1995; and New York, New Jersey, California, and other state correctional agencies.

22. U.S. Department of Justice, BJS bulletin, "Felony Sentences in State Courts, 1986" (February 1989).

23. BJS, "Felony Sentences in State Courts, 1992."

24. BJS, *Sourcebook of Criminal Justice Statistics, 1994,* pp. 435, 462, 501.

25. Executive Summary, "An Analysis of Non-Violent Drug Offenders with Minimal Criminal Histories" (Washington, DC: U.S. Department of Justice, 1994); Wendy Kaminer, "Federal Offense: The Politics of Crime Control," *Atlantic Monthly,* 273:102 (1994).

26. FBI, *Uniform Crime Reports, 1995,* p. 216.

27. BJS, *Sourcebook of Criminal Justice Statistics, 1987,* pp. 400–401.

28. Substance Abuse and Mental Health Services Administration, *Data from the 1995 National Household Survey on Drug Abuse* (Washington, DC: SAMHSA, Office of Applied Studies, 1996).

29. See Selwyn Raab, "Special Courts To Hasten Disposal of Drug Cases," *New York Times,* June 7, 1987, p. 38.

30. Greater Washington Research Center, *Drug Use and Drug Programs in the Washington Metropolitan Area: An Assessment* (Washington, DC: Greater Washington Research Center, 1988), pp. 16–17.

31. BJS, "Felony Defendants in Large Urban Counties" (Washington, DC: U.S. Department of Justice, 1992), p. 2.

32. Wharton Econometric Forecasting Associates, "The Income of Organized Crime," in President's Commission on Organized Crime, *The Impact: Organized Crime Today* (Washington, DC: U.S. Government Printing Office, 1986), p. 460.

33. Bruce D. Johnson et al., *Taking Care of Business: The Economics of Crime by Heroin Abusers* (Lexington, MA: Lexington Books, 1985); Bruce D. Johnson et al., "Drug Abuse in the Inner City: Impact on Hard-Drug Users and the Community," pp. 9–68 in *Drugs and Crime* 13, Michael Tonry and James Q. Wilson, eds. (Chicago: University of Chicago Press, 1990); BJS, *A National Report: Drugs, Crime, and the Justice System* (Washington, DC: U.S. Department of Justice, 1992) p. 7.

34. Bruce D. Johnson, Douglas Lipton, and Eric Wish, *Facts About the Criminality of Heroin and Cocaine Abusers and Some New Alternatives to Incarceration* (New York: Narcotic and Drug Research, 1986), p. 30.

35. J. Ward, R. Mattuck, and W. Hall, *Key Issues in Methadone Maintenance Treatment* (New South Wales University Press, 1992), pp. 29–32; Marc Reisinger, vice president, European Methadone Association, personal communication, February 5, 1996; Marc Reisinger, "Methadone Treatment and AIDS in Western Europe," paper presented at the National Conference on Methadone, Geneva, June 23, 1995; M. Reisinger, "Methadone as Normal Medicine," paper presented at the European Methadone Association Forum, American Methadone Treatment Association Conference, Phoenix, AZ, October 31, 1995; M. Reisinger, ed., *AIDS and Drug Addiction in the European Community* (Brussels, Belgium: European Monitoring Centre for Drugs and Drug Addiction, Commission of European Communities, 1993); Council of Europe, Cooperation Group To Combat Drug Abuse and Illicit Trafficking in Drugs (Pompidou Group), *Multi-City Study: Drug Misuse Trends in*

Thirteen European Cities (Strasbourg, France Council of Europe Press, 1995); Ernst C. Buning, Giel van Brussel, and Gerrit van Santen, "The 'Methadone by Bus' Project in Amsterdam," *British Journal of Addiction*, 85:1247–1250 (1990).

36. Information about prescription of cocaine in the form of nasal sprays, injections, and reefers (cocaine powder dissolved in colifurm and injected into cigarettes) is contained in correspondence to the author from Carole Woodley, coordinator, Drug Dependency Clinic, Warrington, England, February 16, 1990.

37. A leading controlled trial in which ninety-six confirmed heroin addicts requesting a heroin maintenance prescription were randomly allocated to treatment with injectable heroin or oral methadone found that "refusal to prescribe heroin is . . . associated with a considerably higher abstinence rate, but at the expense of an increased arrest rate and a higher level of illicit drug involvement and criminal activity among those who did not become abstinent." Richard L. Hartnoll et al., "Evaluation of Heroin Maintenance in Controlled Trial," *Archives of General Psychiatry*, 37:877 (1980). The more recent heroin prescription program in Switzerland has found that, after six months to a year, patients have a higher rate of employment, less use of most illicit and licit drugs, less illegal income, fewer relapses into old psychiatric episodes, more contact with family and old friends, and greater life satisfaction. In addition, the retention rate has been an astounding 73% after one year. Correspondence with Ueli Locher, drug coordinator, Zurich Social Welfare Department, April 1996.

38. See U.S. Department of Justice, BJS special report, "Drug Use and Crime" (July 1988).

39. See John K. Watters, Craig Reinarman, and Jeffrey Fagan, "Causality, Context, and Contingency: Relationships Between Drug Abuse and Delinquency," *Contemporary Drug Problems*, 12:351–373 (1985).

40. John P. Morgan and Dorreen Kagan, "The Dusting of America: The Image of Phencyclidine (PCP) in the Popular Media," *Journal of Psychedelic Drugs*, 12:195–204 (1980); Jerome L. Himmelstein, *The Strange Career of Marihuana* (New York: Greenwood Press, 1983); Edward M. Brecher, *Licit and Illicit Drugs* (Boston: Little, Brown, 1972); Steven Duke and Albert Gross, *America's Longest War* (New York: Putnam, 1993); David Musto, *The American Disease: Origins of Narcotic Control* (New York: Oxford University Press, 1987).

41. See also the discussion in Paul J. Goldstein, Patricia A. Bellucci, Barry J. Spunt, and Thomas Miller, "Frequency of Cocaine Use and Violence: A Comparison Between Men and Women," pp. 113–138 in *The Epidemiology of Cocaine Use and Abuse*, NIDA Research Monograph #110 (Washington, DC: National Institute of Drug Abuse, 1991).

42. BJS, *Sourcebook of Criminal Justice Statistics, 1991*, p. 629.

43. BJS, *Sourcebook of Criminal Justice Statistics, 1987*, p. 497.

44. In addition to Chapter 6 in this volume, see Paul J. Goldstein, "Drugs and Violent Crime," pp. 16–48 in *Pathways to Criminal Violence*, N. A. Weiner and M. E. Wolfgang, eds. (Newbury Park, CA: Sage, 1989).

45. See "A Tide of Drug Killing," *Newsweek,* January 16, 1989, p. 44.

46. See Philip Shenon, "Enemy Within: Drug Money Is Corrupting the Enforcers," *New York Times*, April 11, 1988, p. A1; Philip Shenon, "Coast Guard Says It Suspects 10 of Drug Dealing," *New York Times*, May 23, 1990, p. 26; Jim Consoli

and Michael Moore, "Seized Funds Pay for Frills: $500,000 for Conventions," *The Record,* December 31, 1995, p. A1; Ronald Smothers, "Atlanta Holds Six Policemen in Crackdown," *New York Times,* September 7, 1995, p. A17; N. R. Kleinfield, "Chinatown Officers Said To Be Partners on Both Sides of the Law," *New York Times,* June 19, 1995, p. A1.

47. Wade Nobles, Lawford Goddard, William Cavil, and Pamela George, *The Culture of Drugs in the Black Community* (Oakland, CA: Institute for the Advanced Study of Black Family Life and Culture, 1987).

48. Thomas Mieczowski, "Geeking Up and Throwing Down: Heroin Street Life in Detroit," *Criminology,* 24:645–666 (1986).

49. *New York Times,* June 7, 1932, pp. 1, 12, as cited in David Kyvig, *Repealing National Prohibition* (Chicago: University of Chicago Press, 1979), p. 152.

50. Charles L. Renfroe and T. A. Messinger, "Street Drug Analysis: An Eleven-Year Perspective on Illicit Drug Alteration," *Seminars in Adolescent Medicine,* 1:247–257 (1985).

51. Michael Shannon, "Clinical Toxicity of Cocaine Adulterants," *Annals of Emergency Medicine,* 17:1243–1247 (1988); Shawn Furlong, "Common Cocaine Adulterants," U.S. Department of Justice, Drug Enforcement Administration, personal communication, April 5, 1996.

52. Centers for Disease Control, *HIV/AIDS Surveillance Report: Second Quarter Edition,* "U.S. AIDS Cases Reported Through June, 1993," July 1993, vol. 5, no. 2.

53. The "three-fourths of all new HIV infections" figure is taken from the latest epidemiological data from the Centers for Disease Control as reported in Gina Kolata, "New Picture of Who Will Get AIDS Dominated by Addicts," *New York Times,* February 28, 1995, p. B6. New York figures are from New York City Department of Health, Office of AIDS Surveillance, "AIDS Surveillance Update," January 1993 and January 1995.

54. Syringe exchange program cumulative enrollment on December 31, 1995. New York State Department of Health, AIDS Institute, Harm Reduction Unit; New York City Department of Health, Office of AIDS Surveillance, "AIDS Surveillance Update," January 1993.

55. Samuel R. Friedman et al., "AIDS and Self-Organization Among Intravenous Drug Users," *International Journal of the Addictions,* 22:201–219 (1987).

56. Ueli Locher, drug coordinator, Zurich Social Welfare Department, "Switzerland's Heroin Prescription Program: Update," seminar at the Lindesmith Center, New York, January 4, 1996.

57. Robert J. Battjes and Roy W. Pickens, eds., *Needle Sharing Among Intravenous Drug Abusers: National and International Perspectives,* NIDA Research Monograph #80 (Washington, DC: National Institute on Drug Abuse, 1988).

58. Don C. Des Jarlais and Samuel R. Friedman, "HIV and Intravenous Drug Use," *AIDS* 2:S65–69 (suppl. 1) (1988); Denise Paone, Don Des Jarlais, Rebecca Gangloff, Judith Milliken, and Samuel R. Friedman, "Syringe Exchange: HIV Prevention, Key Findings, and Future Directions," *International Journal of the Addictions,* 30:1647–1683 (1995).

59. Michael Marriott, "Needle Exchange Angers Many Minorities," *New York Times,* November 7, 1988, p. B1; Michael Marriott, "Needle Plan Fails To Attract Drug Addicts, So It's Revised," *New York Times,* January 30, 1989, p. A1.

60. *International Working Group on AIDS and IV Drug Use Newsletter,* 3:3–4 (December 1988).

61. Dr. Denise Paone, Beth Israel Medical Center, September 1995, personal communication.

62. See, for example, Patrick Fitzgerald, "Members of Congress as Medical Experts: Heroin and the Compassionate Pain Relief Act," *Saint Louis University Public Law Review,* 6:371–394 (1987).

63. Lester Grinspoon and James Bakalar, *Marijuana, the Forbidden Medicine* (New Haven, CT: Yale University Press, 1993); Lester Grinspoon and James Bakalar, "Marihuana as Medicine: A Plea for Reconsideration," *Journal of the American Medical Association,* 273:23 (1995); American Public Health Association Resolution, "Access to Therapeutic Marijuana/Cannabis" (1995); Federation of American Scientists, "Medical Use of Whole Cannabis" (Washington, DC, 1995); Robert C. Randall, ed., *Marijuana, Medicine, and the Law* (Washington, DC: Galen Press, 1988); Tod H. Mikuriya, *Marijuana: Medical Papers, 1839–1972* (Oakland, CA: Medi-Comp Press, 1973).

64. "In the Matter of Marijuana Rescheduling Petition, Docket No. 86–22," September 6, 1988, U.S. Department of Justice, Drug Enforcement Administration.

65. See A. S. Trebach, *The Heroin Solution* (New Haven, CT: Yale University Press, 1982), pp. 59–84.

66. Ibid. Re: Canada, see Lon Appleby, "The Big Fix," *Saturday Night,* November 1985, p. 13ff.

67. Felicia Lee, "Doctor Defends Cocaine Treatments," *New York Times,* February 10, 1989, p. B3; Felix Barre, "Cocaine as an Abortive Agent in Cluster Headache," *Headache,* 22:69–73 (1982); Lester Grinspoon and James Bakalar, *Cocaine: A Drug and Its Social Evolution* (New York: Basic Books, 1976), pp. 154–175.

68. See Grinspoon and Bakalar, *Marijuana, the Forbidden Medicine;* Lester Grinspoon and James Bakalar, *Psychedelic Drugs Reconsidered* (New York: Basic Books, 1979); R. Yensen, "LSD and Psychotherapy," *Journal of Psychoactive Drugs,* 17:267–277 (1985); A. Griece and R. Bloom, "Psychotherapy with Hallucinogenic Adjuncts," *International Journal of the Addictions,* 16:801–827 (1981); Lester Grinspoon and James Bakalar, "Can Drugs Be Used To Enhance the Psychotherapeutic Process?" *American Journal of Psychotherapeutics,* 40:393–404 (1986); R. Straasman, "Human Hallucinogenic Drug Research in the U.S.," *Journal of Psychoactive Drugs,* 23:29–38 (1991).

69. Lester Grinspoon and James Bakalar, pp. 205–207 in *Dealing with Drugs: Consequences of Government Control,* Ron Hamowy, ed. (Lexington, MA: Lexington Books, 1987).

70. Marilee Donovan, Paula Dillon, and Lora McGuire, "Incidence and Characteristics of Pain in a Sample of Medical-Surgical In-Patients," *Pain* 30: 69–78 (1987); Ronald Melzack, "The Tragedy of Needless Pain," *Scientific American,* 262:27–33 (1990); David E. Weissman, "Why Doctors Are Afraid To Prescribe Narcotics," *The Narc Officer,* 5:47–80 (1989); Daniel Goleman, "Physicians Said To Persist in Undertreating Pain and Ignoring the Evidence," *New York Times,* December 31, 1987, p. B5; David C. Lewis, "Medical and Health Perspectives on a Failing U.S. Drug Policy," *Daedalus,* 121:165–194 (1992).

71. BJS, *Sourcebook of Criminal Justice Statistics, 1995*, p. 448.

72. Morton Kondracke, "Don't Legalize Drugs," *New Republic*, June 27, 1988, pp. 16–19.

73. "In the Matter of Marijuana Rescheduling Petition, Docket No. 86–22," September 6, 1988, U.S. Department of Justice, Drug Enforcement Administration.

74. Dean R. Gerstein, "Alcohol Use and Consequences," pp. 109–112 in *Alcohol and Public Policy: Beyond the Shadow of Prohibition*, Mark H. Moore and Dean R. Gerstein, eds. (Washington, DC: National Academy Press, 1981).

75. National Institute on Drug Abuse, *Marijuana* (Washington, DC: U.S. Government Printing Office, 1983).

76. See Lynn Zimmer and John P. Morgan, *Exposing Marijuana Myths: An Objective Review of the Scientific Literature* (New York: Lindesmith Center, 1995).

77. Judith Droitcour Miller and Ira H. Cisin, *Highlights from the National Survey on Drug Abuse: 1982* (Washington, DC: U.S. Department of Health and Human Services, National Institute on Drug Abuse, 1983), pp. 1–10. Figures from the 1993 national survey were even lower: 47.4% of eighteen- to twenty-five-year-olds had tried marijuana, 42.3% had used it at least ten times, and 19.9% had smoked it in the last month. *National Household Survey on Drug Abuse: Main Findings, 1993* (Washington, DC: SAMHSA, Office of Applied Studies, 1994).

78. Ibid. It should be noted that NIDA surveys do not sample persons in military or student dormitories, prison inmates, or the homeless.

79. See, for example, Patricia G. Erickson and Bruce K. Alexander, "Cocaine and Addictive Liability," *Social Pharmacology*, 3:43–55 (1989); Sheigla B. Murphy, Craig Reinarman, and Dan Waldorf, "An 11-Year Follow-Up of a Network of Cocaine Users," *British Journal of Addiction*, 84:427–436 (1989); Dan Waldorf, Craig Reinarman, and Sheigla B. Murphy, *Cocaine Changes* (Philadelphia: Temple University Press, 1991); Peter D. A. Cohen, *Cocaine Use in Amsterdam in Non-Deviant Subcultures* (Amsterdam, Netherlands: University of Amsterdam, Institute for Social Geography, 1987).

80. Patrick M. O'Malley, Lloyd D. Johnston, and Jerald G. Bachman, "Cocaine Use Among American Adolescents and Young Adults," pp. 50–75 in *Cocaine Use in America: Epidemiological and Clinical Perspectives*, NIDA Research Monograph #61, Nicholas J. Kozel and Edgar H. Adams, eds. (Washington, DC: National Institute of Drug Abuse, 1985), p. 73.

81. Committee on the Value of Advertising, "What We've Learned About Advertising from the Media-Advertising Partnership for a Drug-Free America" (New York: American Association of Advertising Agencies, 1990), p. 12.

82. T. G. Aigner and R. L. Balster, "Choice Behavior in Rhesus Monkeys: Cocaine Versus Food," *Science*, 201:534–535 (1978); see also Chris-Ellen Johanson, "Assessment of the Dependence Potential of Cocaine in Animals," pp. 54–71 in *Cocaine: Pharmacology, Effects, and Treatment of Abuse*, NIDA Monograph #50, J. Grabowski, ed. (Washington, DC: National Institute on Drug Abuse, 1984).

83. Grinspoon and Bakalar, *Psychedelic Drugs Reconsidered*, pp. 157–191.

84. Ibid.

85. H. S. Becker, "History, Culture, and Subjective Experience: An Exploration

of the Social Bases of Drug-Induced Experiences," *Journal of Health and Social Behavior,* 8:163–176 (1967).

86. John F. French and James Safford, "AIDS and Intranasal Heroin," *Lancet* 1(8646):1082 (May 13, 1989); D. C. Des Jarlais, S. R. Friedman, C. Casriel, and A. Kott, "AIDS and Preventing Initiation into Intravenous Drug Use," *Psychology and Health,* 1:179–194 (1987).

87. See, for example, Jerome H. Jaffe, "Drug Addiction and Drug Abuse," pp. 284–324 in *The Pharmacological Basis of Therapeutics,* 5th ed., L. S. Goodman and A. Gilman, eds. (New York: Macmillan, 1975); John C. Ball and John Urbantis, "Absence of Major Medical Complications Among Chronic Opiate Addicts," *British Journal of Addiction* 65:182–224 (1970); Brecher, *Licit and Illicit Drugs;* John Kaplan, *The Hardest Drug: Heroin and Public Policy* (Chicago: University of Chicago Press, 1983), p. 127.

88. See Shepard Siegel, "Alcohol and Opiate Dependence: Re-Evaluation of the Victorian Perspective," *Research Advances in Alcohol and Drug Problems,* 9:279–314 (1986); John A. O'Donnell, *Narcotics Addicts in Kentucky,* U.S. P.H.S. Publication # 1881 (Chevy Chase, MD: National Institute of Mental Health, 1969), discussed in Brecher, *Licit and Illicit Drugs,* pp. 8–10.

89. Norman E. Zinberg, *Drug, Set and Setting: The Basis for Controlled Intoxicant Use* (New Haven, CT: Yale University Press, 1984).

90. It is worth noting, however, that both trade and use of opium were actually illegal in China and that addiction was less widespread than commonly thought. Opium use there was not the result of legalization but of insistent supply and demand coupled with ineffective prohibition. See Richard K. Newman, "Opium Smoking in Late Imperial China: A Reconsideration," *Modern Asian Studies,* 29:765–794 (1995), and "Prohibition: The Chinese Experience," *Druglink,* July/August 1990, pp. 12–13.

91. Eric Single, "The Impact of Marijuana Decriminalization," *Journal of Public Health Policy,* Winter 1989, pp. 456–466; Lloyd Johnston, Jerald Bachman, and Patrick O'Malley, "Marijuana Decriminalization: The Impact on Youth 1975–1980," Monitoring the Future Occasional Paper #13, Ann Arbor, University of Michigan, Institute for Social Research, 1981.

92. Quote is from the Dutch Ministry of Welfare, Health, and Cultural Affairs, "Policy on Drug Users," Rijswijk, the Netherlands, 1985. Figures on lifetime use are from P. Sandwijk, P. D. A. Cohen, S. Musterd, and M. P. S. Langemeijer, *Licit and Illicit Drug Use in Amsterdam II: Report of a Household Survey in 1994* (Amsterdam: University of Amsterdam, Institute for Social Geography, 1995), pp. 48–56.

93. David Courtwright, *Dark Paradise: Opiate Addiction in America Before 1940* (Cambridge, MA: Harvard University Press, 1982).

94. See Brecher, *Licit and Illicit Drugs,* pp. 1–41.

95. Joseph B. Treaster, "U.S. Cocaine Epidemic Shows Signs of Waning," *New York Times,* July 1, 1990, p. A14.

96. See Philip Cook, "The Effect of Liquor Taxes on Drinking, Cirrhosis, and Auto Accidents," pp. 255–285 in *Alcohol and Public Policy,* Mark Moore and Dean Gerstein, eds. (Washington, DC: National Academy Press, 1981); Douglas Coate and Michael Grossman, "Effects of Alcohol Beverage Prices and Legal Drinking

Ages on Youth Alcohol Use," *Journal of Law & Economics,* 31:145–171 (1988); also see Kenneth E. Warner, "Consumption Impacts of a Change in the Federal Cigarette Excise Tax," pp. 88–105 in *The Cigarette Excise Tax* (Cambridge, MA: Harvard University Institute for the Study of Smoking Behavior and Policy, 1985).

97. Joe B. Tye, Kenneth Warner, and Stanton Glantz, "Tobacco Advertising and Consumption: Evidence of a Causal Relationship," *Journal of Public Health Policy,* 8:492–508 (1987).

98. Orvar Olsson and Per-Olof H. Wikstrom, "Effects of the Experimental Saturday Closing of Liquor Retail Stores in Sweden," *Contemporary Drug Problems,* 11:325–353 (1982); Milton Terris, "Epidemiology of Cirrhosis of the Liver: National Mortality Data," *American Journal of Public Health,* 57:2085–2086 (1967). More generally, see Harry G. Levine and Craig Reinarman, "From Prohibition to Regulation: Lessons from Alcohol Policy for Drug Policy," *Milbank Quarterly,* 69:461–494 (1991).

99. Ray McAllister, "The Drunken Driving Crackdown: Is It Working?" *ABA Journal,* September 1, 1988, pp. 52–56.

100. J. Michael Polich, Phyllis L. Ellickson, Peter Reuter, and James P. Kahan, *Strategies for Controlling Adolescent Drug Use* (Santa Monica, CA: Rand Corporation., 1984), pp. 145–152.

101. See the annual reports of the National Narcotics Intelligence Consumers Committee edited by the U.S. Drug Enforcement Administration.

102. Raymond B. Fosdick and Albert L. Scott, *Toward Liquor Control* (New York: Harper & Brothers, 1933). Also see Levine and Reinarman, "From Prohibition to Regulation."

PART FOUR

From Punitive Prohibition
to Harm Reduction

. . . .

"The crisis consists precisely of the fact that the old is dying and the new cannot be born; in this interregnum a great variety of morbid symptoms appear." Italian political theorist Antonio Gramsci wrote this about the political situation in Europe following the First World War. But his description captures equally well the current dilemma in U.S. drug policy. Ethan Nadelmann showed in the previous chapter that, as a regime of social control, drug prohibition in the United States has never been very successful and that since 1980 it has become increasingly ineffective, expensive, and even counterproductive. Unfortunately, in the current political climate—in the current "interregnum"—most of the more humane and effective alternatives to current U.S. drug policy cannot yet be fully imagined much less instituted.

We suggest that the story of "crack in America"—from crack's appearance, sales, and heavy use in inner cities to the intense political responses to it—is best understood as a "morbid symptom" of two larger contemporary crises. Crack's sales and use are morbid symptoms of the crisis of unemployment, poverty, and racism in U.S. cities. From the beginning, crack was a drug of escape from poverty and despair for inner-city men and women—of psychopharmacological escape (through the high) and of economic escape (through the business). And the political responses to crack, especially of harsh policing and of large-scale imprisonment, have fallen most of all on those men and women.

The punitive responses to crack use, and their stunning ineffectiveness, have also been morbid symptoms of a different crisis—of U.S. drug prohibition itself. The political responses to crack are symptoms that have made more apparent the truly nonrational and authoritarian character of U.S. drug policy, its extraordinary costliness, and its failure to reduce drug problems. All of this has deepened the crisis of U.S. drug policy and created an increasingly legitimate, organized, and knowledgeable opposition. Most of this book has focused on crack in the context of poverty, racism, and social injustice. The concluding chapters look at the character and crisis of U.S. drug prohibition itself.

In Chapter 15, we briefly discuss the criminalization of drug use in the U.S. in a broad historical context. We use the term "punitive prohibition" to name the dominant U.S. policy toward illicit drugs since about 1920. Punitive prohibition is distinguishable from more humane and tolerant forms of drug prohibition by its heavy reliance on criminal law and imprisonment for use and personal possession of illicit drugs. For nearly eighty years, the centerpiece of U.S. drug policy has been punishment of drug users by criminal law for possessing small quantities of drugs for personal consumption or for small-scale dealing. This committed punitiveness toward drug users sets the U.S. apart from most other Western societies, each of which has some form of drug prohibition. These other advanced industrial societies have instituted a broader range of drug policy options than the U.S. And U.S. drug prohibition has become more punitive over the years—dramatically so in the 1980s. Further, in the short run, punitive prohibition retains powerful institutional and ideological support.

In Chapter 16, we suggest that, in the long run, punitive prohibition will face substantial problems in maintaining its legitimacy. Punitive prohibition will probably continue loosing support because of its own internal contradictions (mounting costs with declining benefits). It also will likely be increasingly regarded as problematic because of enormous changes in modern society and culture. We suggest that there is a contradiction between a society organized around changing feelings, moods, and experiences by consuming commodities for pleasure and punitive drug prohibition. The policy of severely punishing a few specific forms of (drug-based) consciousness alteration will, we suggest, increasingly appear out of sync with the mass-consumption culture of the twenty-first century.

In Chapter 17, we discuss the rise of a formal, "respectable" opposition to the War on Drugs and the development in other countries and many U.S. cities of alternative "harm reduction" policies at the end of the 1980s. For many years in the U.S., punitive prohibition was rarely even criticized. The debate among policy makers was only on *how long* drug users of this or that type should spend in prison. Since the mid-1980s, the excesses and failures of the War on Drugs have led a growing number of Americans to question current policy and to seek alternatives. Other Western societies have begun to follow the "harm reduction" path of cities such as Amsterdam, Liverpool, Frankfurt, Madrid, Hamburg, Sydney, San Francisco, New Haven, and Zurich. Harm reduction policies, public health strategies, and varieties of decriminalization of use appear to be in the future of many other Western societies.

As the concluding chapters suggest, we believe that, in the very long run, the U.S. is also facing the end of the epoch of punitive prohibition. What is not clear is whether in the next ten years or so the United States is capable of much change—whether, in America, punitive prohibition's impasse will yield more progress than reaction, more liberty than repression, and more generosity than cruelty.

FIFTEEN

Punitive Prohibition in America

Craig Reinarman and Harry G. Levine

PUNITIVE PROHIBITION AND REGULATORY PROHIBITION

On Christmas eve of 1995, the governor of New York State, George Pataki, announced that he was granting clemency to two people who, as the *New York Times* put it, had served "long prison terms under the state's harsh Rockefeller drug laws." One of the two was Judy Perez, thirty-one years old, who had served nine years of a fifteen years to life sentence for drug *possession*. According to the *New York Times:* "Ms. Perez was convicted of drug possession in 1986 after the police raided a Brooklyn apartment she was visiting and found heroin, cocaine and drug paraphernalia. Though the police did not find any drugs in her possession, Ms. Perez was convicted of possession charges on the grounds that she was present in a room where drugs were in plain view. It was her first felony conviction" (Dao, 1994:A1). The governor selected Ms. Perez for clemency *not* because her case was unusual or her sentence especially severe, but because she had been an "exemplary inmate." During her nine years in prison, Ms. Perez had finished high school, received her bachelor's degree, served as a translator for other prisoners, and developed a program to teach English to inmates.

We use the term "punitive prohibition" to name the system of drug law and policy that imprisoned Judy Perez and the hundreds of thousands of inmates like her, whether exemplary or not. Punitive prohibition came into existence in the United States in the 1920s and has been the dominant U.S. drug policy since that time. The essential character of punitive prohibition was summarized well by the U.S. government's Task Force on Narcotics and Drug Abuse three decades ago:

> Since early in the 20th century we have built our drug control policies around the twin judgments that drug abuse was an evil to be suppressed and that this could most effectively be done by the application of criminal enforcement and penal sanctions. Since then, one traditional response to

an increase in drug abuse has been to increase the penalties for drug offenses. . . . Typically this response has taken the form of mandatory minimum
terms of imprisonment [for possession, use, and small-scale distribution],
increasing in severity with repeated offenses, and provisions making the drug
offender ineligible for suspension of sentence, probation and parole. (President's Commission, 1967:11)

Punitive prohibition along the lines of U.S. policy is not the only form
of drug prohibition. Punitive prohibition can be distinguished from more
tolerant and humane forms of drug prohibition that do not rely so heavily
on arresting and imprisoning men and women for possessing and using
illicit drugs or for small-scale dealing. Our co-authors showed in Part III
that Canada, Australia, and the Netherlands all have forms of drug prohibition that allow for comparatively effective public health policies for reducing drug abuse and harm. Yet each of these societies arrests and impris-
ons a much smaller proportion of their drug users, and for shorter
sentences, than the U.S. does. Other nations, notably Germany, Switzerland, and Italy, also formally have systems of drug prohibition, but have
decriminalized personal possession of some drugs or are moving in that
direction.

Because U.S. drug prohibition is so extreme, we find it useful to distinguish punitive prohibition from less harsh forms of prohibition—from
what we term "regulatory prohibition." Punitive prohibition and regulatory prohibition are ideal types that can be pictured on a continuum.
American policies fall toward the extreme punitive and criminalizing end;
the policies of the Netherlands, for example, especially its marijuana policies, fall toward the noncriminalizing and regulatory end. In the Netherlands, cannabis use and petty sales are still formally prohibited. Nonetheless, several hundred "coffee shops"—a type of cafe that sells soft drinks,
sandwiches, and espresso coffee—are also permitted by the police to sell
small quantities of hashish and marijuana. The Netherlands also allows
on-premises consumption of cannabis at the coffee shops. Sales of small
amounts, typically less than one-eighth of an ounce, are not formally legal
and are not directly taxed, but according to national policy, the police may
not interfere with the activities of the coffee shops unless they violate some
other regulation. The coffee shops are typically clean and pleasant places.
Some do very little business in cannabis; for some shops (especially in the
tourist areas of Amsterdam), cannabis sales constitute the majority of their
business. Distribution of larger amounts of cannabis outside of the coffee
shops is formally criminalized, and there are occasional seizures.

To choose another example, all forms of alcohol prohibition in the U.S.
(throughout the nineteenth century and up to the present) are unambigu-
ously varieties of regulatory prohibition because they never criminalized
personal possession and use of alcohol. Even today, at the end of the twen-

tieth century, many towns and counties in the U.S. still retain forms of alcohol prohibition. But no matter what the form of alcohol prohibition, personal possession and use, even for minors, have not been criminalized. The idea of "regulatory prohibition" may seem peculiar to those used to U.S.-style punitive drug prohibition, but it has been much more prevalent than punitive prohibition.

THE TEMPERANCE MOVEMENT'S WAR ON ALCOHOL AS THE ORIGIN OF THE WAR ON DRUGS

As we noted in Chapter 1, the history of modern drug scares, antidrug crusades, and punitive drug prohibition begins with the anti-alcohol or temperance movement of nineteenth-century America. Alcohol was the first drug in modern Western society to be the object of a large-scale mobilization against it. The temperance movement was not a kooky, fringe cause but, like the present-day War on Drugs, a respectable, mainstream affair. The temperance movement was the largest enduring, middle-class, mass movement in nineteenth-century America.

In making their case against alcoholic drink, nineteenth-century temperance crusaders first articulated *all* the fundamental antidrug arguments later adopted by twentieth-century antidrug crusaders in defense of punitive prohibition. Temperance physicians and laypersons popularized the modern conception of addiction as "loss of control." Temperance physicians argued that alcohol was an inherently addicting drug in exactly the same way that people today think that heroin and crack are inherently addicting; they said that moderate users come to need more and more and eventually become "hooked." Alcohol was also the first drug to be regarded in popular ideology as a major cause of crime and violence. Temperance speakers and writers said that, because of its effects on the brain, alcohol caused men to lie, rob, steal, and beat their wives. And, they said, because it made men do these all these things, alcohol was responsible for most of the social problems in American society. As we noted in Chapter 1, alcohol was the first drug to be scapegoated in modern society for larger social and economic problems, including crime, violence, poverty, homelessness, and slums.[1]

For most of the nineteenth century, temperance organizations did not routinely apply their arguments about alcohol to marijuana, morphine, heroin, and other psychoactive drugs. In nineteenth-century America, many grocery stores sold opium-based medicines, and most drugstores sold medicinal remedies containing cocaine, opium, morphine, heroin, and sometimes cannabis. The original Coca-Cola—advertised as a "temperance beverage," a safe "soft drink" alternative to alcoholic "hard drinks"—contained cocaine. As we noted in Chapter 1, in the late nineteenth and early twentieth centuries, there were some local drug scares and antidrug campaigns attacking certain groups, usually racial minorities, for their alleged drug use. And antidrug rhetoric was certainly used to secure the passage and reinterpretation of the Harrison Narcotics Act of 1914. But unlike the anti-alcohol movement, where scapegoating rhetoric and ideology fully developed prior to and independent of the legal prohibition of drink, antidrug rhetoric and ideology developed most of all *after* national drug prohibition was in effect. In contrast to national alcohol prohibition, national drug prohibition was not the product of a mass antidrug movement. Instead, drug prohibition rode to power on the back of the campaign for alcohol prohibition in the context of the social upheaval and conservative political climate of World War I.[2]

THE EPOCH OF PUNITIVE DRUG PROHIBITION: 1920 TO . . .?

Punitive prohibition became the governing regime in U.S. drug control policy around 1920. By that year, national alcohol prohibition was in effect, and prominent prohibitionists and top alcohol prohibition enforcement agents had worked to establish the prohibition of cocaine and opiates. The alcohol prohibitionists claimed that, with alcohol increasingly unavailable, there was a real danger that drinkers would begin using other drugs. Therefore, they argued, rigorous drug prohibition was also necessary. Extending the spirit of prohibitionism and the power of the state, prohibitionists pushed the courts to reinterpret and strengthen the first federal law on narcotics, the Harrison Narcotics Act of 1914. In a series of decisions between 1916 and 1922, the Supreme Court ruled that the Harrison Act implicitly allowed for the criminalization of the nonmedical use of opiates and cocaine and of any attempt by physicians to maintain opiate addicts medically on their drugs. These decisions transformed the Harrison Narcotics Act into the basis for national drug prohibition—into what we have termed "punitive prohibition" (Musto, 1987:121–193). By about 1920, after the passage of alcohol prohibition, the Narcotics Division was established as a subset of the Federal Alcohol Prohibition Enforcement Unit. The Narcotics Division then undertook, among other tasks, the closing down of the remaining morphine maintenance clinics in the U.S. and the arrest of hundreds of physicians who maintained their addicted patients by prescription (Musto, 1987; Waldorf et al., 1974).

The same sorts of arguments and imagery that had been at the heart of the anti-alcohol crusade since the early nineteenth century were widely used in the 1920s campaign against drugs. Moral entrepreneurs such as Richmond Hobson, newspaper owners such as William Randolph Hearst, and eager politicians kept scary images of the "menace" of "narcotics" in the public eye (Epstein, 1977). One of the "great works" of 1920s antidrug literature, the 1926 book *Opium the Demon Flower,* shows the prominence and legitimacy such ideas achieved. The author, Sara Graham-Mulhall, was the first deputy commissioner in the Department of Narcotic Drug Control of New York State, and the book won the Pictorial Review Annual Distinguished Achievement Award from a jury of eminent citizens that included the writers William Allen White, Charlotte Perkins Gilman, and Ida Tarbell. Graham-Mulhall acknowledged the assistance and invaluable service of a list of distinguished government officials and prominent citizens, from Governor Alfred E. Smith to Rabbi Stephen S. Wise. In short, the ideas in general, and the book in particular, had been endorsed by many prominent and mainstream reformers, intellectuals, and politicians.

Opium the Demon Flower argued strongly for criminalizing drug use and for imprisoning users because of the destructive power of the substance. The book's opening pages explained that "*Opium the Demon Flower* is a biography, a personality sketch, of a demon that destroys men's souls, ruins homes, debauches governments, enslaves India and China for revenue, assiduously recruits in America and fears nothing but light and law enforcement. . . . It smuggles, seduces, bribes, deceives, threatens, fights, destroys and secretly plans and executes" (p. x). The author called cocaine "opium's first cousin" and viewed it as an equally dangerous and pernicious enemy. In the last chapter, Graham-Mulhall confidently looked forward to the ultimate effect of what we have been calling punitive prohibition: the elimination of the drugs: "In picturing briefly . . . a whole world without opium, I am not romancing. I am prophesying, and am confident that . . . this picture [can] come through within a generation. . . . My civilized world without drug addiction is a world without the opium poppy. . . . Opium peddlers will be as rare as well-poisoners . . . [and] drug addiction will be as obsolete as legalized human slavery" (pp. 288–289). This sort of rhetoric long had been a mainstay of temperance and prohibitionist writing. Most anti-alcohol writers, however, did not also endorse criminalizing use and imprisoning physicians, pharmacists, and users. From the beginning of drug prohibition, then, antidrug ideology and rhetoric were more punitive than anti-alcohol ideology. As Graham-Mulhall put it:

> Leadership in the nation-wide fight against addiction has thus been definitely taken by America's federal government. The problem henceforth is one of administration. . . . What is needed is more inspection; more inspectors; *more certain and more severe punishment; more imprisonment.* . . . Among the supplementary steps that need to be emphasized, probably none is of greater importance than giving the utmost publicity to the penalties inflicted and actually paid for violation of the drug laws. (pp. 240–241, emphasis added)

The program that drug prohibitionists called for was indeed put into effect. In 1930, Congress established the Federal Bureau of Narcotics

(FBN) as a kind of sister agency to the Federal Bureau of Investigation. President Herbert Hoover soon appointed Harry J. Anslinger, at the time the assistant commissioner of the (alcohol) Prohibition Bureau, as the commissioner of narcotics. Like Hobson and other drug prohibitionists, Anslinger encouraged and spread lurid, sensationalist stories about all sorts of psychoactive substances. In 1937, for example, he engineered marijuana prohibition via the passage of the Marijuana Tax Act. After many centuries of medicinal and (some) recreational use, under intense pressure from the Federal Bureau of Narcotics and against the advice of an expert witness from the American Medical Association, the U.S. Congress added cannabis to the list of prohibited substances (see Becker, 1963; Dickson, 1968; Grinspoon and Bakalar, 1993).

After Anslinger's retirement in 1962, the Federal Bureau of Narcotics (eventually renamed the Drug Enforcement Administration [DEA]) continued to carry on both increasingly extensive antidrug policing activities and the antidrug propaganda that justifies them. Like the FBI, the CIA, and other federal police agencies, and working closely with them, the DEA continued to grow in size and influence. Its offices and agents now spread throughout American cities and around the world. Since at least the 1920s, the U.S. government has led a worldwide police, military, and ideological battle for punitive prohibition (Bruun et al., 1975). It continues to do so today despite the increasing reluctance of many of its Western allies.

Since 1960, the appearance of new forms of drug use have led to more drug menace rhetoric, more funding for antidrug police, military, and propaganda activities, and more prisons. Over time, new drugs have been brought under national prohibition policies criminalizing drug possession and use and punishing users with prison. In the 1960s, LSD and a few other hallucinogens were added to federal drug prohibition. In the late 1960s and early 1970s, President Richard Nixon, New York Governor Nelson Rockefeller, and then-governor of California Ronald Reagan adopted "drugs" as a campaign issue, promising to use police, prisons, and the military to "crack down" and "get tough" on drug users. The phrase "War on Drugs" was apparently first used by Nixon (Epstein, 1977). When Ronald Reagan became president in 1981, he again declared drugs to be a major problem in American society and pledged to devote more police and military resources to the problem, a pledge he certainly kept. Alcohol prohibition was repealed after a dozen years, but drug prohibition has become ever more punitive and entrenched.

Punitive drug prohibition has been part of the rise of the powerful, centralized police and military state characteristic of much of the twentieth century. As we noted in Chapter 2, the crack crisis made this more visible. The Reagan and Bush administrations and willing Democrats in Congress passed increasingly harsh new drugs laws almost every year from

1986 to 1992. Punitive prohibition has come to be extremely repressive and costly—far more so than alcohol prohibition ever was. Punitive prohibition in the U.S. now employs the full apparatus of military surveillance and intervention brought home: high-tech airplanes, combat helicopters, state-of-the-art weapons, a massive network of paid informants, specially trained troops, undercover agents, computerized dossiers, hi-tech spy equipment capable of intercepting scrambled phone and fax messages, electronic tracking devices, urine testing in the workplace, and much more.

In addition to the Drug Enforcement Agency, there are antidrug units in city, county, and state police, in all branches of the military, in the FBI, the CIA, the Customs Service, and the Coast Guard. "War" is absolutely the correct metaphor for American drug policy. Moreover, punitive prohibition requires jails to hold all those users and dealers arrested for possessing drugs as well as prisons to hold all those convicted. The new laws passed during the crack scare provided for long mandatory sentences, and the prison population in the U.S. roughly doubled in this period largely because of the incarceration of users and petty dealers. Punitive drug prohibition also has required a rising crescendo of propaganda to justify the financial drain, the deaths of police and civilians, and repressive policies like imprisoning pregnant women and ten-year sentences for teenagers found to have sold tiny amounts of crack. It may sound harsh, but in administrative terms, punitive drug prohibition as it currently exists in the U.S. bears more resemblance to the enormous policing apparatus of fascist and communist states than to the humanitarian visions of social reform of nineteenth-century antidrink crusaders. Finally, in the U.S., these military, policing, and surveillance activities are coupled with an extremist ideology. This ideological and rhetorical extremism (the direct descendent of Graham-Mulhall and the first generation of punitive prohibitionists) is evident in calls for measures such as "zero tolerance" and in the U.S. government's campaign to create a "drug-free America."

THE PERSISTENCE OF PUNITIVE PROHIBITION

Two important studies of the rise of criminalized drug prohibition, by David Musto (1987) and by Troy Duster (1970), both emphasize the importance of the larger context of the first two decades of the twentieth century. As Musto points out, the patriotic furor around the First World War, the red scare, Palmer Raids, the suppression of political dissent, the revival of the Ku Klux Klan, the perceived threats posed by Bolshevism and the Russian Revolution, and more made it much easier to shut down maintenance clinics, incarcerate physicians, and criminalize opiate use. And as Duster points out, there was in the same period a shift in the opiate addict population from mainly white, middle-class, middle-aged women to mainly urban, poor, immigrant, and nonwhite addicts. Once addicts could be perceived as threatening "others," it became much easier to institute what we have termed "punitive prohibition."

Punitive drug prohibition was born at a remarkable time, but, as we have tried to show in this book, its attractiveness to so many Americans far transcends that time. Further, our colleague Lynn Zimmer has shown us that earlier antidrug legislation, including the Harrison Act, contained rudiments of what would become punitive prohibition. Punitive prohibition is truly a policy of the twentieth century as a whole, and it has thus far survived intact the huge increase in nonproblematic middle-class marijuana use in the 1960s and 1970s and then grown even larger and more punitive.

In the 1970s, many observers believed that the spread of marijuana use among the white middle class would bring decriminalization in its wake—that American drug policy would become less punitive and, in effect, would move toward the more regulatory end of the prohibition continuum. With millions of otherwise respectable people using marijuana and other illicit drugs, this reasoning went, it was only a matter of time before the idea of imprisoning people for their drug use would seem altogether barbaric. In fact, a dozen states did decriminalize marijuana use in the early 1970s. President Carter proposed experimental marijuana decriminalization, and during his administration, the National Academy of Sciences established a commission of drug experts and physicians to review the evidence on various approaches to marijuana policy and make recommendations for reform.

But, as we noted in Chapter 1, this process was reversed starting with the election of 1980. By 1985 and 1986, the Reagan administration's rejuvenated antidrug campaign found a new "good enemy"[3] in crack (see Bayer, 1993). Throughout the 1980s, both President Reagan and President Bush made the War on Drugs their most important domestic policy initiative. The media and politicians of both parties joined in and enthusiastically supported the drug war. Thus, instead of decriminalization or even new public health approaches, policy makers massively increased spending for military initiatives, drug policing, and imprisonment. When conservative Republicans gained control of Congress in 1995, punitive prohibition probably had more political support than ever before.

Many people have shared the hope that the harshness of American drug prohibition would prove to be temporary, in part a product of the context of its birth. In fact, the opposite is the case. Punitive drug prohibition has proven to be much more at home in the twentieth century than alcohol prohibition was. National, constitutional alcohol prohibition actually was something of a fluke, a product of its unusual times. Other than the U.S., only a few countries even experimented with alcohol prohibition. But various types of drug prohibition were endorsed and enacted by all Western European countries. As we have tried to show in this book, the scapegoating rhetoric that was important in making the early case for drug prohibition in the 1920s in the U.S. continued be useful in all the drug scares of subsequent decades. For the many reasons we have discussed, drugs have continued to be "the good enemy." As a result, there are a number of reasons for believing that, in the short run and the not-so-short run, punitive prohibition will persist as the dominant U.S. drug policy despite its costs, consequences, and contradictions.

Punitive prohibition has powerful constituents who have vested material and ideological interests in it. Punitive prohibition in general, and the crack scare and the War on Drugs in particular, have provided a fiscal bonanza for the drug control complex—the many interlocking police, military, and drug enforcement agencies at all levels of government. The crack scare and drug war have also helped fuel the growth of a large for-profit treatment industry. Hundreds of scientists have built their careers on government grants given with the aim of documenting the dangerous effects of drugs (although never those of drug policy itself). Few of the professional "experts" who have benefited from punitive prohibition have questioned it, and even those who have doubts rarely admit them publicly. This is unlikely to change.

As we showed in Chapter 2, the mass media have also been crucial in constructing a climate of public opinion favorable to punitive prohibition. The extensive coverage of crack and other drug problems has rarely strayed beyond dramatic horror stories and the routine pronouncements of politicians or experts with opinions safely within the prohibitionist paradigm. The media have ignored or downplayed the growing number of dissenting experts questioning current drug policy and offering alternatives. The slide toward sensationalism, "info-tainment," and "pack" journalism has further eroded the craft of journalism. Therefore, most reporters and editors are still unlikely to ask tough questions about a costly, ineffective national policy and the constructed conventional wisdom on which it rests.

For any public policy to persist for most of a century, however, it takes more than government antidrug propaganda, entrenched beneficiaries, and media magnification. Punitive prohibition has resonated with enough voters to ensure their support or at least ward off their opposition, and the reasons for this resonance are unlikely to disappear. Harsh drug laws have continuing appeal to U.S. voters in part because, thanks largely to punitive prohibition, drug use is often associated with crime, prostitution, overdose deaths, and a range of other problems. On a deeper cultural and social-psychological level, such harsh laws "make sense" to many Americans because they believe that "drugs" loosen the grip of self-control long viewed as central to economic success and social order in America. This helps make it easy for drugs to be portrayed and perceived as profoundly dangerous and threatening.[4]

The contributors to this book have argued in various ways that heavy crack use, the War on Drugs, and the harsh new drug laws were caused by far more than the appearance of a potent new mode of cocaine use. The crisis consisted of the use of this risky new "high" by the young black and Latino poor in a context that included increased racial and class inequalities and reduced opportunities for a decent life. As this book is being finished, political and economic trends strongly indicate that economic and social conditions in the U.S. are likely to worsen in ways that will fuel drug abuse and drug sales and therefore also fuel elite and popular support for punitive prohibition.

First, the global economic restructuring and intensifying market competition of recent years have resulted in corporate and government policies that have systematically redistributed wealth upward and reduced the living standards and economic opportunities of the bottom half of the population. Despite relatively robust economic growth in much of the 1980s and 1990s, rates of unemployment, poverty, and homelessness in the U.S. have remained high or increased while standards of living for most Americans have stagnated or declined (see, *e.g.*, Currie et al., 1994; Phillips, 1990). More than thirty million Americans now live below the poverty line, and almost that many live only slightly above it. Further, more working- and middle-class Americans have been made economically insecure by corporate mergers, disinvestment, "downsizing," and "streamlining," all of which translate into layoffs, wage and benefit cuts, and the use of temporary and part-time workers.

Second, although the U.S. has always had the most anemic system of public provision of any industrial democracy, even this system has been under concerted attack since 1980. The corporate sector has relentlessly pushed for lower taxes and less generous income support programs (see, *e.g.*, Piven and Cloward, 1982). At the same time, the political Right has made electoral gains by playing on racial fears and vilifying "welfare cheats" and "reverse discrimination" to mobilize the resentments of economically insecure voters. Both these strategies have cut social services and thus reduced the government's ability to cushion the blows of joblessness, poverty, and economic insecurity.

Third, as we suggested at the beginning of the book, poverty, unemployment, economic insecurity, and declining opportunities for building decent lives all increase the prevalence of the psychological sets and social settings that make hard-drug abuse and drug sales more likely, especially in impoverished, inner-city communities. In the U.S., as in other industrial societies, long-term, heavy, hard-drug use (both crack and heroin) occurs mainly among a small minority of people at the bottom strata of society, especially among the poorest and most deprived people. A larger percentage of our population is poor and has far fewer social, medical, and economic services than in any other modern industrial society. As a result, more of the poor in America have persistent and destructive hard-drug problems than do the urban poor of other industrial societies. When, as is happening now, external circumstances make the lives of the poor even more economically precarious and difficult, the drug use of some tends to become heavier and more oriented to intoxication and escape. And in such economic hard times, the drug business (with opportunities for sellers, lookouts, drivers, guards, couriers, and more) is more likely to become the only growing business in poor neighborhoods.

Faced with such worsening conditions, politicians and the media are likely to see increased repression, policing, and imprisonment as sensible policies. They will do so not because such measures work to reduce drug abuse, but because they are still politically popular. They create the appearance of "doing something" about drug problems while exerting greater control over a growing "dangerous class."

NOTES

1. Blocker, 1989; Clark, 1976; Gusfield, 1986; Levine, 1978, 1980, 1984, 1992; Rumbarger, 1989.

2. Alcohol prohibitionists in the nineteenth and early twentieth centuries did not believe in the kind of punitive state apparatus that was created in the 1920s to enforce drug prohibition. No one in the nineteenth century or the early twentieth century proposed (or believed) that national alcohol prohibition would have to be enforced by a huge police force or would require a massive expansion of the prison system. In the 1920s, during national alcohol prohibition, despite widespread violations, prohibitionists did not seek to criminalize use. Finally, national alcohol prohibition was repealed in the early 1930s, when many longtime prohibitionists recognized that the moral authority of the Constitution was not stopping people from drinking and that Prohibition was creating severe new problems, especially of crime and "lawlessness." Repeal of constitutional alcohol prohibition returned control of alcohol policy to the states and to state-run alcohol control systems with considerable local control (including, of course, various kinds of regulated, noncriminalized prohibitions) (Blocker 1976, 1989; Gusfield 1989; Levine 1984; Levine and Reinarman 1993).

3. We take the phrase "good enemy" from the great Finnish alcohol sociologist and historian, Kettil Bruun. In his last work, Bruun argued that Nordic countries, especially Sweden, tend to view drugs as a "good" or "suitable" enemy—a target and scapegoat for all kinds of problems that have their origins elsewhere. Bruun's argument has not yet been translated into English. However, *The Gentlemen's Club: The International Control of Drugs*, a major study of the creation of contemporary international narcotics policy, is available in English (1975).

4. Modernization, industrialization, and mass consumption culture have eroded the power of the older, inner-directed culture of self-restraint, no matter how hard cultural conservatives try to reimpose it. Yet the U.S. is still a deeply individualist society with a market economy that makes self-control important for survival and success. At the same time, modern mass consumption culture makes available a growing array of incentives for indulgence—more and more ways to *lose* self-control. These contradictory cultural demands tend to make people continuously anxious about regulating all sorts of behaviors (see Levine, 1992; Reinarman, 1994). One result is the explosion of new "twelve-step anonymous" groups for people who feel they have lost control over not merely alcohol and other drugs but food, sex, work, credit card use, gambling, love, shopping, and many other aspects of modern life that involve no intoxicants at all (Reinarman, 1995). Another result is that antidrug campaigns and scares that explain breakdowns of self-control as the result of drug use continue to find wide acceptance and legitimacy.

REFERENCES

Bayer, Ronald, "Introduction: The Great Drug Policy Debate," pp. 1–23 in Ronald Bayer and Gerald M. Oppenheimer, eds., *Confronting Drug Policy: Illicit Drugs in a Free Society* (New York: Cambridge University Press, 1993).

Becker, Howard S., *Outsiders: Studies in the Sociology of Deviance* (Glencoe, IL: Free Press, 1963).

Blocker, Jack S., Jr., *Retreat from Reform: The Prohibition Movement in the United States, 1890–1913* (Westport, CT: Greenwood, 1976).

———, *American Temperance Movements* (Boston: Twayne, 1989).

Bruun, Kettil, Lynn Pan, and Ingemar Rexed, *The Gentlemen's Club: International Control of Drugs and Alcohol* (Chicago: University of Chicago Press, 1975).

Clark, Norman H., *Deliver Us from Evil: An Interpretation of American Prohibition* (New York: Norton, 1976).

Courtwright, David T., *Dark Paradise: Opiate Addiction in America Before 1940* (Cambridge, MA: Harvard University Press, 1982).

Currie, Elliott, *Reckoning: Drugs, the Cities, and the American Future* (New York: Hill and Wang, 1993).

Currie, Elliott, Robert Dunn, and David Fogarty, "The Fading Dream: Economic Crisis and the New Inequality," pp. 103–127 in J. Skolnick and E. Currie, eds., *Crisis in American Institutions,* 9th ed. (New York: Harper Collins, 1994).

Dao, James, "Pataki Grants Clemency to Two Prisoners," *New York Times,* Dec. 24, 1994, p. A1.

Dickson, Donald T., "Bureaucracy and Morality," *Social Problems* 16:143–156 (1968).

Duster, Troy, *The Legislation of Morality* (New York: Free Press, 1970).

Epstein, Edward J., *Agency of Fear: Opiates and Political Power in America.* (New York: G. P. Putnam's Son's, 1977).

Graham-Mulhall, *Opium the Demon Flower* (New York: Montrose, 1926).

Gramsci, Antonio, *Selections from the Prison Notebooks,* Quintin Hoare and Geoffrey N. Smith, eds. (New York: International Publishers, 1971 [1920]).

Grinspoon, Lester, and James B. Bakalar, *Marijuana: The Forbidden Medicine* (New Haven, CT: Yale University Press, 1993).

Gusfield, Joseph R., *Symbolic Crusade: Status Politics and the American Temperance Movement*, rev. ed. (Urbana: University of Illinois Press, 1989).

Kobler, John, *Ardent Spirits: The Rise and Fall of Prohibition* (New York: G. P. Putnam's Sons, 1973).

Levine, Harry G., "The Discovery of Addiction: Changing Conceptions of Habitual Drunkenness in America," *Journal of Studies on Alcohol* 39:143–174 (1978).

———, "Temperance and Women in 19th Century America," pp. 525–567 in O. Kalant, ed., *Research Advances in Alcohol and Drug Problems* (New York: Plenum, 1980).

———, "The Alcohol Problem in America: From Temperance to Alcoholism," *British Journal of Addiction* 79:109–119 (1984).

———, "Temperance Cultures: Concern About Alcohol Problems in Nordic and English-Speaking Cultures," pp. 16–36 in G. Edwards et al., eds., *The Nature of Alcohol and Drug Related Problems* (London: Oxford University Press, 1992).

Levine, Harry G., and Craig Reinarman, "From Prohibition to Regulation: Lessons from Alcohol Policy for Drug Policy," pp. 160–193 in Ronald Bayer and Gerald M. Oppenheimer, eds., *Confronting Drug Policy: Illicit Drugs in a Free Society* (New York: Cambridge University Press, 1993).

Musto, David, *The American Disease: The Origins of Narcotic Control*, exp. ed. (New York: Oxford University Press, 1987).

Phillips, Kevin, *The Politics of Rich and Poor: Wealth and the American Electorate in the Reagan Aftermath* (New York: Harper Perennial, 1990).

Piven, Frances Fox, and Richard Cloward, *The New Class War: Reagan's Attack on the Welfare State and Its Consequences* (New York: Pantheon, 1982).

President's Commission on Law Enforcement and Administration of Justice. *Task Force Report: Narcotics and Drug Abuse* (Washington, DC: U.S. Government Printing Office, 1967).

Reinarman, Craig, "The Social Construction of Drug Scares," pp. 92–104 in Patricia Adler and Peter Adler, eds., *Constructions of Deviance* (Belmont, CA: Wadsworth, 1994).

———, "The Twelve-Step Movement and Advanced Capitalist Culture," pp. 90–109 in M. Darnowsky, B. Epstein, and R. Flacks, eds., *Cultural Politics and Social Movements* (Philadelphia: Temple University Press, 1995).

Rumbarger, John J., *Profits, Power, and Prohibition: Alcohol Reform and the Industrializing of America, 1800–1930* (Albany: State University of New York Press, 1989).

Waldorf, Dan, Martin Orlick, and Craig Reinarman, *Morphine Maintenance: The Shreveport Clinic, 1919–1923* (Washington, DC: Drug Abuse Council, 1974).

SIXTEEN

The Cultural Contradictions
of Punitive Prohibition

Craig Reinarman and Harry G. Levine

> *An ideology is reluctant to believe that it was ever born, since to do so is to acknowl-*
> *edge that it can die. . . . It would prefer to think of itself as without parentage,*
> *sprung parthenogenetically from its own seed. It is equally embarrassed by the*
> *presence of sibling ideologies, since these mark out its own finite frontiers and so*
> *delimit its sway. To view an ideology from the outside is to recognize its limits.*
> TERRY EAGLETON (1991:58)

Since 1920, Americans have never known anything but punitive drug prohibition, so it is difficult to think of it as a political and ideological system with limits. Many Americans still believe that the answer to the failures of punitive prohibition is more punitive prohibition. This is close to believing that when a medicine is found to fail and have nasty side effects, the patient should be made to take a double dose of it. Such a belief does not rest so much on a lack of policy imagination as on the sort of fundamentalist ideology that has given us the backward-looking utopian slogans of the latest drug war: "zero tolerance," "just say no," "drug-free America." When arresting half a million Americans each year did not stop illicit drug use, the fundamentalist response was to arrest a million.

We call this ideology fundamentalist because what Christian fundamentalism, Islamic fundamentalism, and all other forms of religious and moral absolutism share is a refusal to engage in the democratic discourse of modernity (Giddens, 1991). Fundamentalists reject the pluralism that is at the center of modern, urban society by denying the existence of beliefs and behaviors that depart from their imagined *ancien regime* of morality. Fundamentalists refuse to engage in reasoned dialogue with "the other"—those who neither think nor act as they do. Fundamentalists do not recognize that the modern world is riddled with competing claims, realities, and authorities. They see no shades of grey, only black and white; their values are literally sacred, beyond discussion. Those who advocate punitive prohibition in the face of its failures, costs, and consequences are selectively fundamentalist. They believe that most of the individual freedoms of American democracy and the pleasures of modern society can be preserved while those they judge immoral can be forcibly eliminated.

In this chapter, we argue that the selective fundamentalism of punitive prohibition's defenders cuts against the grain of modern society and will, therefore, be perceived as problematic by more and more people. This argument is rooted in an observation found in virtually all classical social theory and most modern historical writing: the spread of modern capitalism loosens the grip of tradition, especially ascetic traditions. In *The Protestant Ethic and the Spirit of Capitalism* (1985 [1920]), Max Weber argued that the affluence generated by capitalism has cultural consequences that undermine the asceticism that helped generate that affluence in the first place (see also Bell, 1976; Marcuse, 1964). For better or worse, the consumption of commodities for pleasure appears to be growing inexorably more central to the economy and culture of modern capitalist society, and therefore more legitimate. Modern capitalism depends upon the consumption of commodities for pleasure, and the appeal of such consumption is often that they affect our senses and alter our moods. In this chapter, we suggest, therefore, that the consumption of commodities for pleasure has become so intrinsic to modern capitalist society that punitive prohibition's selective use of criminal law and the state to enforce abstinence from one group of commodities is likely to be increasingly ineffective and increasingly perceived as illegitimate.

MASS CONSUMPTION CULTURE
AND CONSCIOUSNESS ALTERATION

The consumption of the relatively few drugs that are currently illicit has become a proverbial small fish in an enormous sea of commodities and commodified experiences that are advertised, sold, and consumed precisely because they alter feelings, mood, and consciousness. This is because the U.S. and other Western societies have become what many scholars call "mass consumption cultures." By the late nineteenth century, the industrial revolution had given rise to mass production and assembly-line manufacturing, thereby changing forever the ways modern societies produce the things citizens need to live. However, most people were not then accustomed to purchasing manufactured goods to satisfy their needs. Most people still either made a great deal of what they needed or made do with what they had. This created a problem for the captains of commerce and industry. If their huge investments in new mass-production technologies were to be profitable, the new products had to be sold on a huge scale— that is, mass production required mass consumption. Americans had to be converted into a nation of consumers.

In the early decades of the twentieth century, a number of influential business leaders began to solve this problem by luring Americans to break their old habits of saving and home producing and to start consuming instead. Captains of industry transformed themselves into what Stuart Ewen (1976) has called "captains of consciousness" in order to create demand for mass-produced consumer goods. They developed innovative marketing and advertising techniques, and they used the insights of the new discipline of psychology to establish techniques of convincing people to satisfy their needs and wants—and to assuage the anxieties and insecurities that advertising was often designed to create—through the consumption of commodities.

At first, mass consumption spread slowly, existing alongside traditional lifestyles that valued scrimping and saving, making things, mending things, or making do. The construction of the consumer was also slowed by the Great Depression and World War II. But in the postwar economic boom, and with the rampant suburbanization in the 1950s and 1960s, mass consumption began to spread across the nation, among working-class and affluent families alike. By the time television stations were beaming out the new consumer lifestyle and the cornucopia of available consumer goods into nearly every postwar suburban ranch house and split level in the nation, mass consumption had became as American as apple pie, and apple pie itself had became another mass-produced, mass consumption commodity.

The architects of mass consumption not only translated traditional needs for the "hardware" of social life—food and furniture—into the commodity form; they also increasingly created new needs for "software": beauty products, health and mental health services, movies, music, massage, amusement parks, video games, vacations, art, and spectator sports. Their ingenious use of advertising and other pioneering marketing techniques created a growing array of new "needs" and wants in a process that philosopher Richard Lichtman (1982) has called "the production of desire."[1]

From the present vantage point at the end of the twentieth century, it seems plain that American culture and character have been transformed almost as dramatically as the assembly line transformed the handicraft labor of blacksmiths. Shopping malls and shopping districts have become the most important arenas of public life in cities, towns, and suburbs. Shopping has become a leisure activity in itself. The modern economy has become dependent upon mass consumption: without it, aggregate demand declines, and so do industrial production, profits, growth, jobs, taxes, public services, and the quality of our lives. Economists speak of "underconsumption" as the essence of economic recession.

Daniel Bell (1976) has pointed out the contradiction between America's old work culture and its new mass consumption culture. The Protestant work ethic and delayed gratification still remain relatively strong in the work sphere. But, Bell argues, in leisure and private life, people are incessantly encouraged to enjoy, indulge, and consume—and they do. Mass consumption has become intrinsic to modernity, one of the defining features of advanced industrial societies (see also Marcuse, 1964). Most Americans whose incomes put them above the poverty line spend a great deal of their leisure time and disposable income consuming commodities for entertainment and pleasure. The word "pleasure" is important here, for whether one likes it or laments it, the pursuit of pleasure has become a rather normal "vocabulary of motive" (Mills, 1940). When asked why they buy all these commodities, Americans tend to answer that they derive pleasure from them. *Modern society, we are suggesting, is organized around the consumption of commodities to satisfy an ever expanding array of wants. Further, more and more of this consumption is done not merely to satisfy basic needs, but simply for pleasure—the same reasons drug users give for their drug use.*

From this vantage point, the consumption of consciousness-altering commodities is not so much alien to modern American culture as *intrinsic* to it.[2] Modern men and women inhabit a world where they routinely get "high" on music, feel moved by movies, hope to improve their chances for sexual ecstasy by consuming Calvin Klein cologne or Johnny Walker scotch, and endlessly "improve" their selves with commodities ranging from hair coloring to psychotherapy to cosmetic surgery. In such a world, the consumption of consciousness-altering commodities—drugs—is not a large leap down a dark, unknown road, but just another short step along a well-worn and familiar path.

PROZAC PRESENT, PHARMACOLOGICAL FUTURE

The future will likely bring ever more consumption of commodities, including those that alter consciousness. The technical capacities for changing the self with chemicals continue to multiply at an astonishing rate. The pharmaceutical industry is prospering in part by inventing ever more drugs that improve, control, or otherwise alter our moods and minds. Millions of Americans, for example, ingest Valium, Librium, and an expanding array of other common tranquilizers and antianxiety and antidepressant drugs.

Prozac is one such drug. We think it provides a window on the pharmacological future. Many psychiatrists have hailed this relatively new antidepressant as a mental health miracle, and it has been immensely popular and profitable. Since its invention in 1987, over fourteen million people have used it, most of them Americans. More than any other single drug, Prozac was responsible for a 50% increase in the 1980s in the number of patients who were prescribed consciousness-altering drugs by psychiatrists

(Rothman, 1994). It is taken by people who feel too "down" or too "up," for various forms of depression, obsessive-compulsive disorders, anxieties, attention deficit disorders, general malaise, and a growing array of other "conditions" that a decade ago were considered within the normal range of human mood and personality variation. Now doctors are prescribing Prozac to hundreds of thousands of young people for "teenage problems" that were seen until recently as only the normal problems of teenagers.

Psychiatrist Peter Kramer praises Prozac in his book *Listening to Prozac* (1993), which jumped onto the *New York Times* bestseller list and stayed there for months. The book's subtitle contains the telling phrase "the Remaking of the Self." The author cheerfully writes of "cosmetic psychopharmacology" in which people who are not by any standard definition mentally ill take Prozac because, like the millions of ordinary looking people who opt for cosmetic surgery, they found that they liked their "selves" on the drug better than their "selves" without it. Little wonder, for the effects of this new drug seem to fit American culture and character like a glove. Prozac, Kramer writes, tends to "give social confidence to the habitually timid, to make the sensitive brash, to lend the introvert the social skills of a salesman."

We think Prozac, Ritalin, the benzodiazapines (Valium, etc.), and other pharmaceuticals should be seen not only as exemplars of the new psychopharmacology, but also as part of a revolution in mood and consciousness alteration that is well under way. There is little historical or scientific reason to believe that drug prohibition will be able to manage all the rapidly proliferating mood-altering and performance-enhancing drugs. Indeed, this revolution is already overwhelming existing physician- and pharmacy-based regulation (Murray et al., 1984). As historian David Rothman (1994:38) put it: "Today we stand and listen to Prozac; tomorrow we will listen to a new hormone, and the day after tomorrow, to a new genetic manipulation. I can conceive of strict rules and procedures, but I have grave difficulty imagining them being implemented and respected. We would need a very different breed of patient and doctor, and we would have to be a very different kind of society." In short, the pharmaceutical technology for altering consciousness is racing ahead of the political technology for controlling it.

If this is true for drugs that are, in theory, controlled by prescription, it is certainly no less true for illicit drugs that are not controlled at all. Just as alcohol prohibition led to dangerous, concentrated forms of liquor from illicit distilling, so has prohibition of heroin, for example, led underground chemists to make synthetic heroin (fentanyl). In fact, dozens of "designer drugs" have sprung up underneath the nation's drugs laws. Congress and the Food and Drug Administration now take longer to make a new drug control law (even if we assume it will be effective) than chemists take to invent or discover a new drug. Indeed, one recent memoir by a well-known pharmaceutical chemist contains five hundred pages of chemical formulae for 179 new psychedelic drugs (Shulgin and Shulgin, 1991).

Even if effective controls on chemists were conceivable, how long will the one hundred or more little-known psychoactive plants in places like the Amazon rain forest remain out of reach when communication and transportation technologies are shrinking the globe (see, *e.g.*, Schultes and Hoffman, 1979; Siegel, 1989; Weil, 1972:98–111)? Nor does one need drugs from distant places to show the futility of prohibition's efforts to keep up with the drugs that exist or will be brought into existence. In March of 1994, the *Wall Street Journal* offered a front-page story on the "hallucinogenic venom" contained in a species of Colorado River toad found in the southwestern U.S. Although the article of course proclaims the dangers of this substance, it also describes a Boy Scout leader who had four such frogs as pets and details how extracting, drying, and then smoking the venom yields the hallucinogen Bufotenine (Richards, 1994).

Further, the line separating psychoactive recreational drugs from other substances is becoming increasingly blurred. There has been much news about anabolic steroids, for example, in connection with the Olympics or other athletic competitions. But there is also growing use of such steroids by body builders in high schools, colleges, and local fitness spas across the country. Steroid use entails well-known health risks, but tens of thousands of young athletes and body builders have found underground sources and continue to inject them anyway—and not just because steroids add muscle bulk quickly, but because at least some steroid injectors "get off" on the extra aggressiveness they feel in their bulked-up state. Just as anorexic cover girls and models have led many young women to internalize unnatural feminine beauty ideals, so have many young men internalized the Arnold Schwartzenegger body image as the essence of masculinity and sought a chemical shortcut to achieving it. In a culture that is achievement oriented, values aggressiveness, and advertises all manner of products purporting to help individuals look, feel, and do better, market demand for performance-enhancing substances is very likely to grow.

As for supply, Prozac and steroids are only recent cases in a longer pharmaceutical history that suggests that chemists will continue to find or invent new performance-enhancing substances. And because these substances fall in between our current chemical categories, they will cause yet more problems for prohibition. For example, so-called "smart drugs"—combinations of vitamins and more exotic ingredients that can alter consciousness—have been common for years in health food stores and in the semi-above-ground "rave scene," where MDMA or Ecstasy use is common (Beck and Rosenbaum, 1994). Recent *New York Times* reports have noted that, since 1990, millions of doses of a legal Chinese herb, ma huang or ephedra, have been sold over the counter as an organic, herbal cousin of illicit drugs like Ecstasy or methamphetamine. Dozens of brands of this substance, such as Herbal Ecstasy, Ultimate Xphoria, and Cloud 9, promise "a floaty, mind-expanding euphoria," "increased sexual sensations," "enhanced sensory processing," and "mood elevations." More such substances are on the way, and the key ingredient, ephedrine or pseudoephedrine, is already present in numerous nonprescription cold and allergy medicines. The herb itself is inexpensive, and the synthetic form of it is very easy to produce. Thus, the government will have a very difficult time even regulating such substances, much less prohibiting them. According to Dr. David Kessler, commissioner of the U.S. Food and Drug Administration, "You are always chasing harm after it has occurred. What companies do is reformulate, and we have to start all over again, and because there are many different products and many different combinations, you end up chasing forever" (Burros and Jay, 1996:B8; Lambert, 1996:A12).

College newspapers across the U.S. have reported that new "smart drugs" and other herb-based substances can enhance test taking and other dimensions of intellectual performance. Students have long known that over-the-counter caffeine products like No-Doze can help them stay awake to cram for exams, and they are likely to be faced with many new alternatives. Coffee, tea, and cold caffeinated beverages are already present in most workplaces precisely because they are performance enhancers. With the growth of super vitamins, smart drugs, and the many other performance-enhancing and consciousness-altering substances that are likely to come along, it is not clear where the border of acceptability will be drawn in the future, much less how it could ever be effectively patrolled by the state.

Finally, the efficacy and legitimacy of punitive prohibition look bleaker still if one gazes into the crystal ball of science fiction. Science fiction is fiction, of course, but it also has one foot in science and real trends, and it has sometimes been quite prescient. The science fiction novels of the 1950s contain some still unimaginable technological feats, but they also contain a great number of innovations that we now take for granted. When Orson Wells performed his famous "War of the Worlds" radio hoax, how many of his listeners imagined that Americans would walk on the moon in their lifetimes? We already have organ transplant surgery, whole encyclopedias condensed onto tiny CD Rom disks, genetically engineered strawberries and medicines, as well as space travel. How long will it take the Human Genome Project, avant-garde neuroscientists, hormone therapy researchers, and software designers to astound us with entirely new chemical and even electronic means of consciousness alteration? Comedian Lilly Tomlin once quipped, "I worry that the inventor of muzak is busy inventing something else." With respect to the future of consciousness alteration, we wonder what the inventor of Virtual Reality is busy inventing. When *The Six Million Dollar Man* first appeared on television, its cyborg hero seemed quite far-fetched. But as the twentieth century comes to a close, pacemakers, artificial hips, and all manner of plastic surgery have fallen into the realm of normalcy. Meanwhile, cutting-edge computer engineers, artificial intelligence experts, and other cyberspace technicians are already working on miniature computers that can be implanted in the body to enhance human capabilities and other means of escaping the body by electronically "downloading" knowledge, sights, sounds, and highs into consciousness (see, *e.g.*, Dery, 1996; Haraway, 1985). Can anyone who has lived through the breathtaking technological advances since World War II credibly claim that the early twentieth-century invention of punitive prohibition will effectively control all the consciousness-altering technology that is likely to be invented in the early twenty-first century?

CONCLUSION

The historical evidence shows unequivocally that, legal or illegal, drug use is not going away. Persons of all ages, genders, races, and classes have ingested chemicals to alter their consciousness in virtually every culture and epoch (see, *e.g.*, Rudgley, 1993; Schivelbusch, 1993; Weil, 1972). No regime of drug control, no matter how repressive, has ever been able to eliminate such practices. Surely as industrialization and modernization spread, so too will mass consumption culture and all that goes with it. This means that whether one is a fan or a foe, punitive prohibition is in trouble—and not just because it has so many noxious effects on human rights and civil liberties or because it is increasingly costly and ineffective. Punitive prohibition is constrained toward obsolescence because it more and more cuts against the structural grain of the society that invented it and contradicts how most citizens of that society actually live.[3] We think these broad structural and cultural forces help explain why drug prohibition has become less effective even as it has become more punitive and why current prohibitionists have had to go to such ideological and rhetorical lengths to legitimate it.

Punitive prohibition cannot hope to keep up with the technological developments in psychopharmacology, which are coming faster and in greater numbers than ever before. Nor is punitive prohibition likely to be a match for the remarkable ingenuity that human beings have historically demonstrated in their search for altered states of consciousness. If the future is likely to bring both a growing variety of demands for and supplies of consciousness-altering substances, then punitive prohibition is likely to become even less effective. The twin pillars of drug prohibition are supply reduction and demand reduction. A succession of administrations has expanded each of these strategies and reaped only diminishing returns. The reason has not been lack of effort, ingenuity, or money. Both supply reduction and demand reduction have fallen short, and are likely to fall shorter in the future, because they fly in the face of the basic economic and cultural organization of our society. Supply reduction strategies are all designed to increase the costs of drug dealing, but this inevitably increases the potential for profits in illicit drug markets. According to basic economic theory, such potential means that rational economic actors will move into this industry in the hopes of reaping such profits. Similarly, as we have suggested in this chapter, demand reduction cuts against the logic of mass consumption that is the lifeblood of our economy and a basic fundament of our modern culture.

At the start of the modern era, powerful feudal regimes tried mightily to hold off the rise of market-based capitalist society. They failed. Nor could the farmers and artisans of preindustrial capitalism hold off the rise of mass production/mass consumption capitalism. By the same long-term logic, we doubt that the punitive prohibitionist regime of the present will be able to hold off the hi-tech pharmacological future. And, if we may stretch this metaphor, it is worth remembering that the solution to the problems of capitalism is not the prohibition of markets, which is what communism tried to do. Rather, the solutions to the problems of capitalism (such as they are so far) have been enlightened regulations and public provisions that reduce the market's harms while harnessing its potentials.[4] We think a similar approach to drug problems will emerge in the long run.

Does all this mean that the end of the epoch of punitive prohibition is in sight? If prohibition could speak, it might well respond with Mark Twain's famous line: "Rumors of my death have been greatly exaggerated." The spread of mass consumption culture and the trajectory toward greater individual liberty in American democracy do not have the playing field of drug policy all to themselves. As we noted in the previous chapter, punitive prohibition has persisted for generations and is likely to have continuing political utility and public appeal, especially in a context of inequality, economic insecurity, and fear. In the short run, then, the contradictory forces pushing and pulling on American drug policy make its immediate future indeterminate. This may mean a continuation of the *selective prohibitionism* we already have, in which marginalized "others" who use drugs get incarcerated while the majority of working-and middle-class users rarely feel the sting of harsh drug laws or, when they do, end up in treatment. Indeed, most Americans have demonstrated their willingness to live quite comfortably with just such an arrangement.

But some of the key constituencies of punitive prohibition are beginning to express discomfort. The harsh drug laws of the crack era caught more than a few "respectable" middle-class drug users in its net—and rarely for selling or even using crack (the FBI's Uniform Crime Reports for 1995 showed that over four-fifths of drug arrests were of marijuana offenders). Many of their "respectable" families and friends who had found it possible to live with punitive prohibition for ghetto crack dealers are worried that the drug war has come to overkill. Prohibitionists often combat such worries and legitimate harsh drug laws by citing the suffering of the poor and people of color at the hands of drugs. But as the racist consequences of punitive prohibition become more and more clear, many people in African-American and Latino communities have begun to wonder whether the cure is worse than the disease. It is not clear how long they will continue to support punitive prohibition when it sends mostly their family members away to prison while drug problems remain behind in their communities. Whether all this means that punitive prohibition has gone beyond the limits of its legitimacy remains to be seen. What we can see clearly is that this legitimacy is being questioned as never before and that the search for alternatives has begun.

NOTES

1. In his classic book, *The Affluent Society,* economist John Kenneth Galbraith makes much the same point: "As a society becomes increasingly affluent, wants are increasingly created by the process by which they are satisfied. This may operate passively. Increases in consumption, the counterpart of increases in production, act by suggestion or emulation to create wants. Or producers may proceed actively to create wants through advertising and salesmanship. . . . The higher level of production has, merely, a higher level of want creation necessitating a higher level of want satisfaction" (1958:128).

2. In a similar vein, Paul Scriven (1992:xi) has noted that because the U.S. is a "medicine society," illicit drug use is "rooted in legal drug use. We are a society of members who routinely use drugs to maintain and enhance our lifestyle. In a sea of behavioral drug usage, a certain portion is contained and declared immoral and dangerous. Why should we be surprised that so many venture into the roped off area. . . . ?"

3. The father of American criminology, Edwin H. Sutherland, once said, "Where customary restraints are adequate, no laws are necessary; where customs are inadequate, laws are useless." His point seems especially relevant to prohibition.

4. The authors are grateful to Dr. Peter Cohen of the University of Amsterdam for this metaphor, which he first presented in a speech at a United Nations conference on social development, Geneva, Switzerland, July 1993.

REFERENCES

Beck, Jerome, and Marsha Rosenbaum, *The Pursuit of Ecstasy: The MDMA Experience* (Albany: State University of New York Press, 1994).

Bell, Daniel, *The Cultural Contradictions of Capitalism* (New York: Basic Books, 1976).

Burros, Marian, and Sarah Jay, "Concern Is Growing Over an Herb That Promises a Legal High," *New York Times,* Apr. 10, 1996, p. B1.

Dery, Mark, *Escape Velocity: Cyberculture at the End of the Century* (New York: Grove, 1996).

Eagleton, Terry, *Ideology* (London: Verso, 1991).

Ewen, Stuart, *Captains of Consciousness: Advertising and the Social Roots of Consumer Culture* (New York: McGraw-Hill, 1976).

Galbraith, John Kenneth, *The Affluent Society* (Boston: Houghton Mifflin, 1958).

Giddens, Anthony, *Modernity and Self-Identity* (Stanford, CA: Stanford University Press, 1991).

Haraway, Donna, "A Manifesto for Cyborgs," *Socialist Review* 80:65–107 (1985).

Kramer, Peter D., *Listening to Prozac: A Psychiatrist Explores Antidepressant Drugs and the Remaking of the Self* (New York: Viking, 1993).

Lambert, Bruce, "Fears Prompting Crackdown on Legal Herbal Stimulant," *New York Times,* April 23, 1996, p. A12.

Lichtman, Richard, *The Production of Desire* (New York: Free Press, 1982).

Marcuse, Herbert, *One-Dimensional Man: Studies in the Ideology of Advanced Industrial Society* (Boston: Beacon Press, 1964).

Mills, C. Wright, "Situated Actions and Vocabularies of Motive," *American Sociological Review* 5:904–913 (1940).

Murray, Thomas H., Willard Gaylin, and Ruth Macklin, *Feeling Good and Doing Better: Ethics and Nontherapeutic Drug Use* (Clifton, NJ: Humana Press, 1984).

Richards, Bill, "Toad-Smoking Gains on Toad-Licking Among Drug Users," *Wall Street Journal,* March 7, 1994, p. 1.

Rothman, David J., "Shiny Happy People: The Problem with 'Cosmetic Psychopharmacology,' " *The New Republic,* February 14, 1994, pp. 34–38.

Rudgley, Richard, *Essential Substances: A Cultural History of Intoxicants in Society* (New York: Kodansha, 1993).

Schivelbusch, Wolfgang, *Tastes of Paradise: A Social History of Spices, Stimulants, and Intoxicants* (New York: Vintage, 1993).

Schultes, Richard E., and A. Hoffman, *Plants of the Gods* (Maidenhead, England: McGraw Hill, 1979).

Scriven, Paul, *The Medicine Society* (East Lansing: Michigan State University Press, 1992).

Shulgin, Alexander, and Ann Shulgin, *PIHKAL: A Chemical Love Story* (Berkeley, CA: Transform Press, 1991).

Siegel, Ronald, *Intoxication* (New York: Dutton, 1989).

Weber, Max, *The Protestant Ethic and the Spirit of Capitalism* (London: Unwin, 1985[1920]).

Weil, Andrew, *The Natural Mind: An Investigation of Drugs and the Higher Consciousness* (Boston: Houghton Mifflin, 1972).

SEVENTEEN

Real Opposition, Real Alternatives
Reducing the Harms of Drug Use and Drug Policy

Craig Reinarman and Harry G. Levine

The failures and excesses stemming from the expansion of punitive prohibition in the crack scare have given rise to real, formidable opponents who have pointed out the true costs of punitive prohibition, articulated alternative policies, and made drug policy a contested terrain for the first time in decades. These opponents of drug wars have introduced previously heretical ideas ranging from moderate drug policy reforms, to harm reduction and needle exchange programs, all the way to decriminalization and full legalization. They have made drug prohibition itself a topic of debate and research and called attention to the fact that U.S. drug prohibition is more expensive and repressive than that in any other industrial democracy. These drug policy reformers have been successful enough to prompt the Drug Enforcement Administration to hire a panel of experts to prepare a pamphlet for DEA agents and other prohibitionists explaining how to argue against them. The DEA pamphlet is entitled "How To Hold Your Own in a Drug Legalization Debate" (DEA, 1994).

THE RISE OF "RESPECTABLE" OPPOSITION

At the peak of the drug war in 1989, Drug Czar William Bennett devoted a whole speech at Harvard to criticizing critics of the drug war. He attacked all those who did not share his belief that the way to solve our drug problems was to make drug policy *more* punitive. He claimed that those scientists and scholars who disagreed with him were taking an "intellectually as well as morally scandalous" position (Bennett, 1989). Bennett's speech did not result in long lines of intellectuals eager to enlist in his war. The "academic cynics" he ridiculed were not cynical; nor were they "the usual suspects" from academia, the libertarian Left, or the 1960s counterculture.

345

Punitive prohibition's critics cut across the political spectrum. They include the wealthy and powerful as well as the poor and powerless. They come from the political Right and the Left. There are elite professionals and grassroots activists. These opposition voices include such *unusual* suspects as former prosecutor and now mayor of Baltimore, Kurt Schmoke; conservative publisher William F. Buckley, Jr.; Nobel Prize–winning free-market economist Milton Friedman of Stanford University; former Reagan administration secretary of state, George Shultz; longtime TV news anchors Walter Cronkite and Hugh Downs; international financier and philanthropist George Soros; former U.S. surgeon general, Dr. Joycelyn Elders; Nobel Prize–winning novelist Gabriel Garcia Marquez; and members of Congress such as George Crockett and Barney Frank. They have been joined by numerous judges across the court system, those appointed by Republicans as well as Democrats, and by a much larger array of scientists and university professors in medicine, law, and the social and physical sciences. After alcohol prohibition had been in effect for a number of years, longtime prohibitionist John D. Rockefeller, Jr., saw its ill effects and funded a public policy think tank to design new, nonprohibitionist models of alcohol control. Similarly, in recent years, a number of prominent conservatives have come to see the harmful consequences of punitive prohibition and lent their support to drug law reform organizations such as the Drug Policy Foundation in Washington, D.C., and the Lindesmith Centers in New York City and San Francisco.

By the mid-1990s, so many knowledgeable and influential people, from all professions and all points on the political spectrum, had raised so many critical questions about punitive drug prohibition that they had become not only a recognizable but a "respectable" opposition. Between 1989 and 1995, trenchant critiques of punitive prohibition appeared in a broad range of highly regarded scholarly journals and popular periodicals, including *Science, Lancet, Harper's, New York Times, Wall Street Journal, American Heritage, Harvard Law Review, American Journal of Public Health, Atlantic Monthly, Daedalus, Los Angeles Times, Public Interest, Mother Jones, Washington Monthly, Milbank Quarterly, Scientific American, Stanford Magazine, British Medical Journal, The Nation, The Economist, Journal of the American Medical Association, Washington Post, Foreign Policy, The New Republic, National Review, New England Journal of Medicine,* and *Notre Dame Journal of Law, Ethics and Public Policy.* These writings dissected the flaws in and laid out workable, effective alternatives to punitive prohibition for a large and influential readership. At the level of ideas, floodgates have been opened that moral fundamentalists and other prohibitionists will probably not be able to close again.

In the professions closest to drug problems, for example, there appears to be majority support for some kind of alternative to punitive prohibition.

The American Bar Association, the American Public Health Association, and the American Medical Association are not known for taking radical stands on public policy issues. Yet each has passed an official resolution criticizing existing drug policies and advocating reforms.

Biomedical science has long been a key source of legitimacy for prohibition, but, even here, there are signs of change. When opiates first became widely used in the late nineteenth and early twentieth centuries, their risks were not well known, and many people became addicted through physicians' prescriptions. In the process of criminalizing drug use, prohibition agents arrested and imprisoned physicians who tried medically to maintain opiate-addicted patients, and over time, the medical profession was pressed into the service of punitive prohibition (Lindesmith, 1965; Musto, 1987). Gradually, what John Morgan has called "opiophobia" and a kind of pharmacological Calvinism spread through organized medicine (Klerman, 1972; Morgan and Pleet, 1983). Most physicians eventually came to fear psychoactive drugs as much as other Americans (see Zinberg, 1984:vii). In practice, physicians came to err on the side of more pain rather than more drugs, and in politics, they provided scientific legitimization for punitive prohibition.

In recent years, however, opiophobia and pharmacological Calvinism have come to make less sense as medical technology and practice render more forms of human suffering less necessary. Patients are less willing to endure extreme pain quietly and are demanding more sensitive treatment. At the same time, physicians have learned through systematic studies that the risks of physical dependence inadvertently caused by physician treatment ("iatrogenic addiction") are extremely low. Experiments in which patients were allowed to regulate their own doses of opiates and other allegedly addictive painkillers found no tendency toward abuse or addiction. Increasing numbers of hospitals now allow patients themselves to administer measured doses of intravenous opiate-based painkillers through a hand-held plunger. Many physicians are moving in the direction of doing whatever is necessary to reduce patient pain, sometimes even if that means recommending the use of an illicit drug (see, *e.g.,* Doblin and Kleiman, 1991; Leary, 1994).[1] At the level of policy discourse, a growing number of physicians have seen too much harm and too little health come from punitive prohibition to remain silent.

Many of the criminal justice professionals who confront drug offenders every day are also opposing current drug policies. In 1993, more than fifty senior federal judges started a boycott of drug cases because they felt the drug control system was not working and that long mandatory sentences were often unjust. Many other local judges have also refused to hand out mandatory minimum sentences for minor drug offenses or are refusing to take drug cases altogether (Treaster, 1993; see also Myers, 1989). Dozens of police chiefs across the country have quietly made illicit drug use a low priority. The police chief of New Haven, Connecticut, openly helped establish needle exchange programs and procedures to divert drug offenders to treatment and social service agencies. Former police chiefs such as Anthony Bouza, Joseph McNamara, Wes Pomeroy, and Frank Jordan (who later became the mayor of San Francisco) have publicly criticized punitive prohibition and called for decriminalization or public health approaches. A recent survey of some 365 police chiefs, police officers, district attorneys, and judges found that about 90% in all groups felt "the U.S. was losing the war on drugs," many of whom supported alternative approaches to drug policy (McNamara, 1995). Even Raymond Kendall, head of the leading international police force, Interpol, admitted in 1993 that the War on Drugs was "lost" and that "making drug use a crime is useless and even dangerous."[2]

The reasons why so many criminal justice officials have spoken out against punitive prohibition are not difficult to discern. First, overwhelming majorities are frustrated by the fact that drug offenders are clogging the criminal justice system at every level. A 1994 Department of Justice survey of twenty-five hundred police chiefs, sheriffs, jail administrators, prosecutors, public defenders, judges, and probation and parole directors found nearly nine in ten agreeing that the drug war had created workload problems for their agencies (McEwen, 1995). Second, too many good cops are called upon to put their lives on the line for minor busts when they know that the bulk of the violence associated with drugs is a function of our drug laws. Third, police officers know that there are many other laws they could be enforcing. The War on Drugs was sold to the public as a crime control measure, but in many ways, it has become a fetter on crime control. Officers who might be walking beats keeping streets safe are siphoned off into drug dragnets, after which they spend endless hours processing paperwork and appearing in court. Finally, police also know that many violent criminals have been let out of jail early to make room for nonviolent drug offenders.

In November 1994, U.S. Attorney General Janet Reno gave the keynote address to the forty-sixth annual meeting of the American Society of Criminology, the nation's leading professional association of social scientists who specialize in crime. She formally requested that they share their findings about feasible crime control options with policy makers. The society responded by forming a series of task forces comprised of over forty top criminologists. The Drug Policy Task Force examined the empirical evidence on drug policy across three recent "epidemics," including crack. The "cornerstone" of their report to the attorney general was expanded "treatment opportunities at all stages of the criminal justice system," not more and harsher laws:

The lessons from decades of legalistic policies suggest that deterrence strategies have not been successful in reducing drug use. Enforcement strategies have consumed resources, aggravated health risks associated with drugs, and increased the levels of violence surrounding drug markets. Drug policy has also increased profits for drug dealers and attracted other young people into selling, as the exaggerated symbols of conspicuous consumption by dealers act as a siren for younger people. Severe sentencing laws applied broadly and indiscriminately have undermined, rather than reinforced, the moral authority of the law. (American Society of Criminology, 1995:8).

Earlier we suggested that the media are likely to continue to support drug wars and prohibition, but there have been a number of notable exceptions and signs that more will join them. By the mid-1990s, dissenting voices and alternative visions had moved beyond the confines of scholarly journals and public affairs magazines to the more popular and mainstream media. MTV aired a documentary highlighting drug harm reduction programs and approaches. The CBS news show *Sixty Minutes* did a segment on the Liverpool harm reduction programs. Walter Cronkite, who had once narrated a Partnership for a Drug-Free America TV spot, produced for his own TV series an hour-long critique of the failures of the drug war and a positive review of alternative policies. An increasing number of nationally syndicated political columnists (Russell Baker and Anthony Lewis of the *New York Times,* for instance) have written critically of drug wars and punitive prohibition. Many political cartoonists have satirized punitive prohibition for yielding a prison building boom when funding for schools and job training had been cut.

In 1994, Max Frankel, editor in chief at the *New York Times* during the crack scare, wrote in his new column in the *Times*'s Sunday magazine that the drug war had cost a fortune and had not really worked. Retired as editor, Frankel explicitly criticized coverage of the drug war, including (implicitly) that of the *New York Times* under his stewardship. He argued that journalists should have covered the drug war *as a war,* in which case they would have discovered its true costs, "body counts," and other consequences. This type of more complete and truthful coverage, Frankel argued, would have engendered a much needed public debate about prevailing drug policy (Frankel, 1994:30). We believe that Frankel's strong statements are signs of the significant undercurrents of opposition to U.S. drug policies at major institutions of influence and power. If nothing else, the media's penchant for new story lines has led at least some journalists to begin reporting some of the failures, costs, and consequences of the drug war.

Until recently, most African-Americans have been correctly perceived as staunch supporters of the drug war and often of punitive prohibition. Since at least the 1940s, heroin and other hard drugs have been more visibly available in urban black neighborhoods than white neighborhoods; black communities have also had disproportionately more people with intractable life problems and vulnerable to hard drug abuse. Black churches have served for over a century as the main focus for community organizing and as a major source of community leadership and civil rights activists. But community-based black church leaders (like local white church leaders) tend to have very traditional views on lifestyle and moral questions such as alcohol and drugs. The black middle class and wealthy, including professionals, celebrities, and stars, whether churchgoing or not, have usually avoided questions of drug policy or have taken relatively conventional and conservative stands. Black politicians, whatever their personal views, have typically represented the more culturally conservative sectors of the black community. For many years, the single most visible and vocal drug warrior in the U.S. Congress was Representative Charles Rangel, a black congressman from Harlem and part of the Upper West Side of Manhattan.

But there have always been opponents of drug wars and prohibition among African-Americans. In 1986, the mayor of Baltimore, Kurt Schmoke, electrified a meeting of the U.S. Conference of Mayors with his keynote address urging them to consider alternatives to drug prohibition, including decriminalization. Schmoke, a graduate of Harvard University and Yale Law School, served five years as an assistant district attorney prosecuting drug cases. His experiences convinced him that drug prohibition was bad for Americans in general and African-Americans in particular. Drug prohibition, he reasoned, created much needed employment for poor young men, especially blacks and Latinos, but only in criminal enterprises; and the "gangster" lifestyle of young drug dealers distorted values and priorities in black neighborhoods. As a result, prohibition probably increased the spread of hard drugs in poor communities, and those young men in the drug business who were not killed frequently wound up in prison for a long time. Schmoke has not softened his views. He has continued to speak out for drug policy reform, he helped convince the governor to allow needle exchange in Maryland, he has introduced other harm reduction measures in Baltimore, and he has been continually reelected.

Over time, increasing numbers of black politicians and professionals have withdrawn their support for repressive drug policies or have openly endorsed alternatives. In 1990, the African-American mayor of New Haven, Connecticut , along with the police and the Yale School of Management, instituted a large-scale and innovative needle exchange program, modeled on those in Amsterdam, Rotterdam, and Liverpool (Johnson, 1990). At the press conference announcing the needle exchange program, the mayor explained that they would be closely studying the effects of the program by comparing New Haven to a "control group" that did not have needle exchange. The control group, he said, was New York City. A year later the first results of the New Haven program showed the spread of the AIDS virus had been reduced significantly compared to New York City (Navarro, 1991). Partly as a consequence, Congressman Rangel, who had vehemently and effectively opposed all needle exchange, eventually withdrew his objections to it.

In recent years, black politicians have outspokenly criticized the huge disparity in mandatory sentencing laws between those convicted of selling powder cocaine and those convicted of selling smokeable cocaine (crack). Most of the former are white, the latter, black; typically, crack sellers possess much less cocaine but receive mandatory sentences several times to ten times as long as the powder cocaine dealers. African-Americans in Congress, along with civil rights, civil liberties, and legal reform organizations, have been actively working together to reduce or eliminate this disparity. In 1996, the U.S. Sentencing Commission studied this issue and recommended ending these disparities. But the Clinton administration rejected the commission's recommendation, and Congress overwhelmingly voted to retain the disparate sentences. That vote then sparked several riots in prisons overcrowded with young black men serving long mandatory sentences for selling small amounts of crack.

These injustices, along with rising AIDS deaths due to needle sharing, are leading more and more African-Americans to abandon their traditional support for punitive prohibition. Black social workers in New York, Boston, Chicago, and other cities are increasingly recommending harm reduction approaches. In 1995, black elected officials in Oakland, California, engaged in civil disobedience to support needle exchange and stop the spread of AIDS in their city. Four members of the city council were willingly arrested and tried for distributing sterile syringes. They presented the defense of necessity and were quickly acquitted by a jury.[3] Growing numbers of black journalists, lawyers, doctors, educators, and ministers are talking about alternatives to prison for drug offenders and questioning the use of prisons and criminal law to deal with drug problems. In part, the black middle class has been taught by young African-American men and women who have become needle exchange and harm reduction activists in their own communities. Many of these activists are themselves former drug abusers; some are HIV positive or already have AIDS. They are insisting to their neighbors and families that the devastating effects of the drug war in their communities are more damaging and permanent than the effects of drug abuse. These activists have been passionate and articulate exponents of humane approaches to drug problems and advocates of more just social and economic policies. We believe that more and more

African-Americans will come to join them in building more just, humane, and effective alternatives.[4]

Drug policy reform sentiments also have been making substantial headway in other Western industrial democracies. The U.S. has pushed punitive prohibition on other nations since the first international treaties outlawing opium at the start of the twentieth century (Bruun et al., 1975; Musto, 1987). But the cumulative consequences of such laws have recently reduced U.S. powers of persuasion. In 1994, Germany and Columbia joined Spain, Italy, the Netherlands, and Poland in moving away from punitive prohibition. In 1996, a commission of the European Parliament voted to support decriminalization of cannabis. Canada and Australia have also taken steps to shift the axis of their drug policies away from criminal law toward public health. A growing number of local elected officials in Europe have embraced alternative drug policies, sometimes in defiance of their own federal laws. Their reasons are practical: public health–based drug policies offer more promising results at the local level.

In 1990, for example, the mayors and chief drug policy officials of several major European cities formed a transgovernmental alliance against rigid drug prohibition laws called the European Cities on Drug Policy (ECDP). As in the U.S., national legislators can sometimes score electoral points by supporting "tough" drug policies, but they rarely have to live with the consequences on city streets. At their meeting in Frankfurt, officials who actually have the responsibility for running cities signed a bold policy declaration (the Frankfurt Resolution) denouncing drug wars and stating that they would henceforth find their own ways of managing drug problems. These alternatives now include expanded, user-friendly methadone programs, supervised hygienic injection facilities, de facto decriminalization, needle exchange programs, and cooperative agreements linking the police with treatment, health, and social service agencies. Drug sales and drug-related crime and deaths have dropped dramatically.

These ideas quickly spread in Europe and in the U.S. Within three years, the number of European city governments that joined European Cities on Drug Policy more than doubled. Their 1993 meeting drew official representatives from fifty-eight cities in fourteen countries (ECDP, 1993; Nadelmann et al., 1994). The same year, the Drug Policy Foundation organized an American version of the Frankfurt meeting and had difficulty accommodating delegates from over forty cities and nearly twenty countries, including many more American mayors than they had anticipated. All these officials were interested in developing practical public health alternatives to punitive prohibition because they knew firsthand the costs and consequences of relying predominantly on repressive criminal law.

THE EMERGENCE OF HARM REDUCTION AT THE GRASS ROOTS

In recounting all these prominent opponents of punitive prohibition, we do not want to appear to be subscribing to the "great man" theory of history, according to which kings, generals, popes, and presidents seem to be the sole authors of human events. Long before most of the people cited previously went public with their criticisms, grassroots activists were directly defying drug laws, often at great risk, to do what they found necessary to meet the human and health needs of drug users. Their work helped open the space in public discourse for the critics and laid the foundation for the alternatives to punitive prohibition that are taking shape.

For example, beginning in the early 1980s, AIDS activists and addicts spread the word in the hard-to-reach social worlds of injection drug users that sharing needles and syringes can lead to AIDS.[5] They trained each other as volunteer "community health outreach workers" (CHOWs). They walked through the worst neighborhoods and flophouses of America's cities distributing information on AIDS risks and safe injecting procedures. They devised pocket-sized bottles of bleach for cleaning syringes and distributed them to injection drug users. They made referrals to drug treatment, health, and social service agencies. They passed out condoms and safe sex information so that needle sharers who might be infected with HIV would be less likely to spread the virus to their sexual partners and their children. When their shoe-leather ethnographic research found that this was not enough to halt the deadly epidemic, they organized, staffed, and scraped together funds for free needle exchange programs. They found ways to get supplies of technically illegal syringes. They formed associations like the North American Syringe Exchange Network and organized national and international conferences to share their epidemiological and practical knowledge. They got social scientists to help them collect the data necessary to evaluate the effectiveness of their efforts when the government refused to fund such research. And they did all this at their own expense, for no pay.

After years of working underground and risking arrest and jail, these activists had convinced many police chiefs and city officials that needle exchange works and should be allowed to operate. By the mid-1990s, numerous scientific studies supported their claims (see Centers for Disease Control, 1993; DesJarlais and Friedman, 1992), and over sixty major U.S. cities had needle exchange programs that reduce needle sharing, help addicts get the help they need, and remove tens of thousands of potentially HIV contaminated needles each week from streets and parks.

The punitive prohibition paradigm fostered and hindered needle exchange. By making syringes illegal, scarce, and expensive, punitive prohibition made needle sharing inevitable and needle exchange necessary.

However, members of Congress ignored the mounting evidence favoring needle exchange and consistently voted for a ban, sponsored by Senator Jesse Helms, against any federal drug funds for needle exchange. Their justification was that needle exchange might "encourage" injection drug use by giving it a government "stamp of approval." But there was never any evidence that this was the case, and subsequent studies from around the world have shown that needle exchanges reduce the spread of HIV/AIDS and have other beneficial public health effects, *without* increasing injection drug use (see, *e.g.*, Centers for Disease Control, 1993; DesJarlais and Friedman, 1992; Watters et al., 1994).[6]

Grassroots activists have been fighting the consequences of punitive prohibition in other ways. Julie Stewart is the sister of an otherwise lawabiding man whose life was nearly destroyed by a twenty-year mandatory sentence for growing some marijuana plants. She discovered that thousands of other families had members in similar situations, and she started a group called Families Against Mandatory Minimums (FAMM). Stewart and other FAMM activists have argued that the crack-era drug laws are unjust, counterproductive, racially discriminatory, and costly. They maintain, and the attorney general's own review of drug offender sentencing showed, that over one in five inmates in federal prisons were low-level, nonviolent drug offenders, two-thirds of whom were serving long mandatory minimum sentences (Massing, 1993; U.S. Department of Justice, 1994).[7] As FAMM publications point out, "for all other crimes—rape, murder, child molestation, burglary—a judge *must by law* consider at least 10 other factors about the individual case when sentencing," mitigating factors that expressly cannot be taken into account in drug cases (FAMM, 1992:1). The organization's membership has grown rapidly, and it now has a newsletter, full-time workers, and a national network of cooperating attorneys who challenge the legality of these sentences. FAMM members continue to present public testimony favoring the repeal of the harsh crack-era drug laws in Congress, statehouses, churches, community centers, and a variety of other venues.

On another front, medical marijuana "buying clubs" have sprung up underneath punitive prohibition. Thousands of people suffering from serious diseases have found marijuana the most effective medicine, sometimes even a lifesaving one, and very often their own physicians have quietly recommended it. Marijuana was a valued medicine in the physicians' pharmacopoeia until the early twentieth century. William Osler, the dean of medical textbook writers, recommended it for a number of conditions. Again in the early 1970s, several medical journal articles reported physicians' successful experiences with patients who used marijuana medicinally. Smoked cannabis became widely recognized as an effective antinausea drug for the side effects of chemotherapy[8] and as a means of stimulating the appetites and thus prolonging the lives of AIDS patients. Since then, marijuana has been found to help many patients with glaucoma, epilepsy, AIDS, multiple sclerosis, migraines, quadriplegia, paraplegia, and other painful conditions (Grinspoon and Bakalar, 1993).

The ban on the medical use of marijuana is probably one of the most politically vulnerable parts of punitive prohibition. The federal government has repeatedly refused to allow even the research needed to test the medical efficacy of marijuana even though the medical use of marijuana has considerable public support. In 1995, an independent polling firm surveyed a random representative sample of over a thousand American voters on their attitudes about medical marijuana. More than nine in ten were aware of marijuana's medical uses for glaucoma and nausea from chemotherapy. A surprising majority of 55% favored legalization of marijuana for medical purposes, even when the survey question specified that evidence of its efficacy was not yet "conclusive." When the question included the phrase "when proven effective," support rose to nearly nine in ten.[9] These survey data suggest why a number of state legislatures have passed laws allowing physicians to prescribe marijuana to patients who need it, despite the federal government's refusal to allow such prescriptions. The California Legislature passed medical marijuana bills in 1994 and 1995, each of which was vetoed by the Republican governor. But in 1996, voters in California and Arizona passed medical marijuana initiatives by substantial margins, neither subject to veto. A national medical marijuana bill (HR 2618) that would allow physician prescription has attracted sixteen cosponsors in Congress, including several Republicans.

On this issue, as with needle exchange, a few courageous individuals began by invoking the tradition of civil disobedience of Ghandi and Martin Luther King, Jr., to make an enormous difference in the lives of thousands of desperately ill Americans. Their defiance of punitive prohibition in the interest of humane medical treatment is a moral example that has inspired many others to take up this cause. Given the growth in public support for medical marijuana, continued suppression of it will probably only help raise public awareness of this additional cost of punitive prohibition: seriously ill and often dying patients suffer needless pain because they are denied a relatively safe and effective medicine for the sake of antidrug ideology.

THE PRINCIPLES OF HARM REDUCTION

The term "harm reduction" has been applied to needle exchange and a wide variety of other practices aimed at reducing the harms related to drug use—including the harms caused by harsh drug laws—without attempting to eliminate drug use per se. When this concept first arose in the 1980s, it was not yet a developed alternative model of how to deal with drug problems more humanely and effectively; rather, harm reduction was mostly a name put on an array of practices invented by street-level community health workers trying to deal with drug problems.

The basic principle of what became the harm reduction approach is very much in keeping with the tradition of American pragmatism. Spouses and siblings have long used informal cajoling and expressions of concern to get drinkers and drug users to use smaller amounts, less often, or more carefully so that they would suffer fewer harms. Similarly, no parents want their teenagers to drink alcohol, but most are smart enough to recognize that despite their warnings teenagers are likely to drink. So they act to reduce the risk of harm. Thus, generations of parents have been practicing their own forms of harm reduction when, for example, they have warned their teenagers not to mix wine and whiskey or offered them rides home, "no questions asked," should they find themselves in a car with an intoxicated driver.

The original theory of methadone treatment for heroin addicts was also based on a harm reduction logic, though the term itself had not yet been invented (Dole and Nyswander, 1965). Virtually all traditional treatments available to heroin addicts began by demanding the one thing most could not achieve: abstinence. So methadone maintenance was designed to be more user-friendly; it provided a longer-acting substitute opiate that could be taken orally, along with health, job training, and social services to help addicts stabilize their lives and leave the criminal world.[10] Their addiction would remain, but they and society as a whole would suffer radically fewer harms because of it. At its best, methadone maintenance still does this (but see Rosenbaum, 1995).

The first formal statements of the principles of a "harm reduction model" were developed by drug outreach and education workers in Liverpool, England, in the mid-1980s (*e.g.,* Dorn, 1988; Newcombe and Parry, 1988; O'Hare, 1988; Strang and Farrell, 1992). Their model rests on the assumption that drug users are not enemy deviants or pariahs, but reasonable citizens who use and sometimes misuse drugs, but who nonetheless have a stake in reducing risks and improving their health. Thus, harm reduction eliminates the inherent disapproval of drug use that has been the essence of temperance, prohibitionist, and drug war ideologies. The model's first premise is that abstinence cannot be the only goal of drug policy or of agencies providing services to drug users. The Liverpool drugs workers had seen too many long-term users at too close a range to believe that many would be drawn to services that insisted on abstinence first. Indeed, such a goal had effectively excluded a great many of the high-risk users they most wanted to reach and marginalized those users in deviant subcultures where drug abuse was likely. Therefore, in developing their new approach, the drugs workers defined abstinence as the last in a graduated series of harm reduction objectives. As the national Harm Reduction Coalition (HRC) in the U.S. later put it, "Any reduction in harm is a step in the right direction" (1995:1).

The second premise of the harm reduction model is that the best way to get drug users to alter their behavior and reduce the harms associated with their drug use is to provide services that the users value and trust (*e.g.,* providing sterile syringes, information about safer injecting and drug use practices, AIDS prevention materials, referrals to treatment, health, and social service agencies). This way, instead of being alienated from conventional society and its helping institutions, users can be attracted to them. Thus, the harm reduction model assumes that if contact can be made in a context of user-friendly social services rather than user-hostile social control, drug users can be empowered to take intermediate steps to reduce their risks. Harm reductionists both "affirm and seek to strengthen the capacity of people who use drugs to minimize the harms associated with their drug use" (HRC, 1995:1). Rather than isolating drug users, harm reduction concentrates on "integrating them or reintegrating them into the community" (Nadelmann et al., 1994). This integration, empowerment, and help allow and encourage drug users to take responsibility for their drug use and its consequences.

When the Liverpool drugs workers implemented this new harm reduction approach in the Merseyside region around Liverpool, there was a marked reduction in risk behaviors like needle sharing and a clear increase in the number of drug users who took advantage of treatment and other services (O'Hare et al., 1993). The model quickly spread across England and now informs drug policy in nearly all regions of the country. The same basic approach was used in the Netherlands at the time and has been adopted by many other European and American cities.

Harm reduction now is more a philosophy or perspective on dealing with drug problems than it is a precise set of activities. No list of harm reduction policies and practices could be complete because activists are constantly using the harm reduction perspective to invent new practices tailored to local conditions. A basic list includes expanded availability of high-quality, low-threshold methadone maintenance programs for all opiate addicts who seek them (including such user-friendly formats as methadone buses as used in Amsterdam); nonjudgmental treatment of all types on request; repeal of drug paraphernalia laws and other restrictions on the sale and possession of sterile injection equipment; expansion of needle exchange programs and the equipment they provide (*e.g.,* adding sterile "cookers" and "cottons") so that no injection drug user need ever risk AIDS by sharing equipment; hygienic injection rooms for addicts supervised by medical staff like those in Zurich and Frankfurt; accessible and accurate information on the purity of drugs to inform users of adulterants and prevent overdoses; integration of law enforcement activities with harm reduction, health, and social service programs; and reform or repeal of harsh laws that inhibit rational distinctions between drugs on the basis of relative risk to users.

If this sounds at all reasonable to American readers, it may be because it is similar to what the U.S. has done about drinking problems since the repeal of alcohol prohibition. For example, U.S. alcohol policy is based on the assumption that most drinkers care about their health and are capable of making reasonable decisions. Alcohol policy recognizes that most users are not abusers, distinguishes among different types of alcohol according to risk, monitors quality and purity, and requires that alcohol content be listed on each container. The U.S. provides for various forms of counseling, treatment, health care, and social services for those with alcohol-related problems through employee assistance programs, health insurance, and public agencies. Just as important, by keeping drinkers integrated into conventional society, alcohol policy subjects them to the full range of informal social controls that helps most of them keep their drinking within bounds. And none of this involves massive imprisonment of drinkers for possessing or consuming alcohol.[11]

As was true for alcohol prohibition, the largest potential constituency for harm reduction and other drug policy reforms are the users themselves. Drug users are overwhelmingly white, and most are middle class or solidly working class. Drug users (especially marijuana users, but also cocaine snorters; Ecstasy, LSD, and mushroom trippers; amphetamine users; and even some recreational heroin snorters) are in every profession and are among the ranks of the famous and high achievers in every field. Drug users have won Nobel Prizes, Pulitzer Prizes, Oscars, Emmys, Grammys, and World Series and Superbowl rings. Most drug users have remained silent, their opposition to punitive prohibition implicit in their flouting of its laws. Should they ever find their voice and the political space to speak, they would constitute a huge movement for reform. The National Household Surveys on Drug Abuse have shown that about seventy million Americans have at least tried illicit drugs in spite of punitive prohibition and that twenty million people have used illegal drugs in the last year. The dirty little secret of drug prohibition is that most recreational users find their drug experiences valuable for a wide variety of reasons, including physical pleasure, release from stress, mental health, spirituality, intellectual stimulation, self-medication, enhanced sociability, or just plain fun. And because their drug use arises from these purposes rather than some pathology, the vast majority do not become abusers or addicts. In pursuing experiences with drugs, moderate users have developed a wide variety of rules and rituals to regulate their drug use so as to prevent or reduce harmful effects. Zinberg and others have called these unlegislated, unwritten rules *informal social controls*. Because these informal controls are part of custom and culture, most drug users adhere to them voluntarily, even enthusiastically, just as most drinkers self-regulate their alcohol consumption according to informal drinking rules (Becker, 1967; Zinberg, 1984; Zinberg et al., 1977).

As we suggested in Chapter 4, a small minority of illicit drug users seeks extreme drug experiences. For all its harms over the course of the twentieth century, punitive prohibition has done almost nothing to reduce this phenomenon. To paraphrase the Bible, "Some crazies shall always be with us." Public discourse about drugs (and public health) would be much improved if Americans refused to be misled when extreme cases are presented as typical by politicians seeking votes or media looking for dramatic stories. The vast majority of illicit drug users, like the vast majority of drinkers, use their preferred intoxicants moderately to enhance their lives. As much as any of us, they informally regulate their drug use to minimize pain and maximize pleasure.

Punitive drug prohibition is rooted in the assumption that all illicit drugs are inherently dangerous and that, left to their own devices, most if not all illicit drug users are or will likely become abusers or addicts. Ironically, much of the behavior cited to support this assumption stems from the sets and settings of use that are shaped by prohibition itself. By making drug users deviants, our laws marginalize them in deviant subcultures. In a kind of self-fulfilling prophecy, their contact with criminal worlds is maximized while the potentially moderating influences of "normal" society are minimized. Harm reduction policies, by contrast, build upon informal social controls and approach users as people who are full citizens of society and who have a self-interest in getting and using information about the risks of the drugs they use.

Of course, as we noted at the start of this book, self-regulated drug use and informal social controls are more likely among those who have balanced lives, who can look forward to a decent life in the future, and who therefore have some stake in conventional life and society (Waldorf et al., 1991). Just as marginalizing drug use into deviant subcultures increases the likelihood of abuse, so does socioeconomic marginalization increase the likelihood of sets and settings that increase the likelihood of drug problems. All the contributors to this book have become convinced of the strong causal connection between social justice and public health. This connection holds whether the U.S. moves toward more drug wars or toward harm reduction policies. If social inequality continues to increase, whatever the drug policy, a larger portion of the population will be unable to build balanced lives or look forward to a decent life in the future. Under these conditions, some minority of these dispossessed citizens will almost certainly develop the distressed mind-sets and will find themselves in the distressed social settings that make escape via hard-drug abuse likely.

But if more Americans join those who have already recognized that drug problems are imbedded in and grow out of broader social problems, then the United States can start shedding the worst aspects of punitive prohibition and move in the direction of a more just, humane, and effective drug policy—toward harm reduction, regulatory prohibition, and decriminalization. Together with the sorts of broader social policies that would better meet basic human needs, these would constitute crucial steps in reorganizing American society so that more people have the sorts of lives and life chances, and the sorts of sets and settings, in which the risks of drug-related harm are markedly reduced.

CONCLUSION

We do not need to end this book with detailed, thoughtful proposals for reforming punitive prohibition because these already exist in abundance. Many insightful and accessible books on drug policy reform have been published over the past decades, including those by Nyswander (1956:139–170), Lindesmith (1965), Bakalar and Grinspoon (1984), Trebach and Zeese (1990, 1992), Zimring and Hawkins (1992), Bayer and Oppenheimer (1993), Currie (1993), Heather et al. (1993), Duke and Gross (1994), Sharp (1994), Baum, (1996), and Bertram et al. (1996). There have also been a dozen blue-ribbon national commissions in the U.S., England, and Canada in the twentieth century, *all* of which have suggested helpful and workable alternatives to punitive prohibition (see Trebach and Zeese, 1990:34–38 for an overview). Each of these commissions was comprised of prominent, respectable establishment figures such as judges, governors, members of Congress and Parliament, mayors, university presidents, police chiefs, and world famous scientists and staffed by highly trained scientific, medical, and legal experts. They each did their homework—careful research on all available evidence, often over several years. They all wrote reports that were circumspect, conservative, restrained, and measured. Each and every one of them recommended new drug policies that moved away from punitive prohibition (*e.g.*, decriminalization of marijuana and other drugs, elimination of harsh criminal penalties for possession and petty dealing, heroin maintenance clinics and physician prescription systems). Although some of their recommendations have been adopted in England, the Netherlands, Switzerland, Germany, and other European countries. U.S. policy makers have ignored or repudiated them.

The developing opposition to punitive prohibition is also creating new alternatives all the time. Ironically, the unworkability of prohibition has

spurred not only opposition from many camps, but also professional reform efforts, grassroots alternatives, and user-generated informal social
controls, all of which offer insights about how to reduce drug-related harm
more effectively and humanely than is possible under punitive prohibition. These activities have opened up new social spaces in the widening
cracks of punitive prohibition. In these spaces, a rich array of experiments
in democratic drug control is growing. Together, they are building toward
a future less strewn with drug-related damage—and drug *policy*-related
damage—than the punitive present.

NOTES

1. See Scriven (1992) on the notion that the U.S. has become a "medicine
society." Physicians have long noted that patients have come to expect, even ask
for, prescriptions as a routine outcome of office visits. More generally, one facet of
modernity may be consciousness of the induced (*i.e.*, noninevitable) character of
consciousness (Berger, 1981:209), including consciousness of suffering; thus, people expect to be able to buy something, swallow it, and relieve their suffering.

2. Kendall quoted in *Le Nouvel Observateur,* as cited in Fratello (1993). It should
be noted that the McNamara survey was of a nonrandom sample of criminal justice
system officials.

3. Craig Staats, "Council Members Risk Jail To Arrest Spread of HIV," *Oakland
Tribune,* January 18, 1995, p. A11.

4. All of what we have written about the disproportionate effects of the drug
war on African-Americans holds true for Latinos as well. Latino harm reduction
and needle exchange activists have also bravely brought alternative perspectives
on drug use and policy to their communities as well. And Latino professionals in
medicine, law, education, social work, and policing, and from all national groups,
are also increasingly rejecting punitive prohibition and looking for less harmful
alternatives.

5. The drug harm reduction movement was born in the early 1980s on the
streets of Amsterdam, Rotterdam, and Liverpool. Drug users and their friends began distributing sterile hypodermic needles to other injection drug users (IDUs)
in order to stop the spread of a potentially deadly form of hepatitis. They understood that IDUs were at great risk of contracting and spreading hepatitis when they
shared needles. Because the local public health authorities were unwilling or unable to distribute syringes for fear of appearing to support illicit drug users, the
users decided to do it themselves. They collected donations and began showing up
with boxes of sterile syringes at places frequented by injection drug users, for example, near the train stations in Amsterdam and Rotterdam. In order to reduce the
number of contaminated needles in circulation, the syringe distributors began collecting the used syringes in exchange for new ones. This became known as "needle
exchange." A few years later, when the AIDS epidemic hit, these small bands of
needle exchangers had already established what would prove to be the cheapest
and most effective program for preventing the spread of HIV and AIDS among
drug users.

6. In 1992, the U.S. Centers for Disease Control (CDC) commissioned a team of medical scientists to review all the scientific evidence on the effectiveness of needle exchange. The researchers reviewed thousands of reports, data sets, and scientific articles and interviewed hundreds of scientists around the world. Eighteen months later, their report concluded that the evidence that needle exchanges reduced the spread of AIDS was unequivocal and overwhelming, and it recommended that the government lift its ban. Apparently fearing yet more attacks from the Right for being "soft on drugs," the Clinton administration did not release this report, but rather ordered an "internal review" by a panel of independent scientists at the CDC. That review confirmed the findings of the initial report, but the Clinton administration refused to release this report, too, even denying numerous Freedom of Information Act requests from journalists. After suppressing these reports for over a year, the administration finally acceded to repeated requests for a copy by the House Subcommittee on Health and Environment, but only on the condition that it not be released publicly. Once copies of both studies were leaked to the press, a hale of criticism ensued. As Ethan Nadelmann argued in Chapter 14, the lives of thousands of injection drug users, their sexual partners and children, and others who might have been saved from AIDS by needle exchange must be counted as a cost of punitive prohibition. They have been, in effect, sentenced to death because officials put drug war politics and moral ideology ahead of evidence and epidemiology (Louis Freedberg, "Needle-Swap Report Being Kept Secret: U.S. Findings on AIDS Prevention," *San Francisco Chronicle*, December 6, 1994, p. A1; John Schwartz, "Reports Back Needle Exchange Programs: Administration Has Not Acted on Recommendations to Lift Funding Ban," *Washington Post*, February 16, 1995, p. A6; Richard O'Mara, "Scientists Urge Lifting of Ban on Needle Exchanges for Addicts," *Baltimore Sun*, March 11, 1995, p. 3).

7. The White House at first ordered this Justice Department review withheld. But after rumors began to circulate that the attorney general was being hushed up, the report was released.

8. For nausea, smoking a drug is often much more effective than pills because patients frequently cannot keep oral medication in their stomachs, and pills take much longer to work. Smoking cannabis gets the antinausea medicine (THC) almost immediately into the brain; it is easier for the patients to adjust dosage; there is no interaction with the stomach and nothing to throw up. Synthetic THC is available only in pill form and thus is much less effective than smoking for most cancer and AIDS patients. A survey of oncologists found that about half would prescribe marijuana if it were legal (Doblin and Kleiman, 1991), and some recommend it anyway. Many physicians also recommend cannabis to AIDS patients. Ironically, much stronger and more dangerous drugs can be prescribed.

9. Poll conducted by Belden and Russonello Research and Communications, Washington, DC, March 31 through April 5, 1995, for the American Civil Liberties Union.

10. Unfortunately, the dominant antidrug ideology underlying policy and funding decisions has pushed methadone maintenance away from Dole and Nyswander's original vision (*e.g.*, Dole, 1988; Dole and Nyswander, 1965; Nyswander, 1956:148–170; Payte, 1991) and toward a social control–oriented, "short-leash"

model characterized by rigid rules and inadequate doses. Unlike virtually all other chronic diseases, in which physicians count *functional improvement* as treatment success (Lewis, 1994), most modern methadone programs take abstinence from all other drugs and even detoxification from methadone itself as the treatment objective. Predictably, by all but abandoning the original harm reductionist goals, this approach has made methadone less appealing to addicts and less successful (see Rosenbaum, 1995; Rosenbaum et al., 1988).

11. We do not mean to suggest that U.S. alcohol policy is ideal or even very good. Elsewhere (Levine and Reinarman, 1991) we have discussed at length some lessons to be learned from alcohol prohibition and control for understanding drug prohibition and control. In that article, we point out that alcohol policy "was the outcome of self-conscious public policy and not the 'natural' result of market forces or national zeitgeist. The alcohol control system has worked sufficiently well that it usually goes unnoticed, even by students of prohibition or American history. For purposes of devising new drug policy options, however, it is important to remember that this particular system was the self-conscious creation of a political and economic elite with the power to institute what it regarded as good and necessary. The alcohol control system they devised is not especially democratic; it does not really address public health or social welfare concerns; it does not even attempt to address the range of alcohol-related health problems in our society; and it has produced enormous profits for a handful of large corporations that continue to fight public health measures" (p. 181). However, compared to America's current drug policy, alcohol policy is humane, gentle, and relatively effective.

REFERENCES

American Society of Criminology, "Task Force Reports from the ASC to Attorney General Janet Reno," reprinted in *The Criminologist* 20(6):1–17 (1995).

Bakalar, James, and Lester Grinspoon, *Drug Control in a Free Society* (New York: Cambridge University Press, 1984).

Baum, Dan, *Smoke and Mirrors: The War on Drugs and the Politics of Failure* (Boston: Little, Brown, 1996).

Bayer, Ronald, "Introduction: The Great Drug Policy Debate: What Means This Thing Called Decriminalization?," pp. 1–23 in R. Bayer and G. M. Oppenheimer, eds., *Confronting Drug Policy: Illicit Drugs in a Free Society* (Cambridge, England: Cambridge University Press, 1993).

Becker, Howard S., "History, Culture, and Subjective Experience: An Exploration of the Social Bases of Drug-Induced Experiences," *Journal of Health and Social Behavior* 8:162–176 (1967).

Bennett, William, "Drug Policy and the Intellectuals," speech at the Kennedy School of Government, Harvard University, December 11, 1989.

Berger, Bennett, *Survival of a Counterculture* (Berkeley: University of California Press, 1981).

Bertram, Eva, Morris Blachman, Kenneth Sharpe, and Peter Andreas, *Drug War Politics: The Price of Denial* (Berkeley: University of California Press, 1996).

Brecher, Edward, *Licit and Illicit Drugs* (Boston: Little, Brown, 1972).

Bruun, Kettil, Lynn Pan, and Ingemar Rexed, *The Gentlemen's Club: International Control of Drugs and Alcohol* (Chicago: University of Chicago Press, 1975).

Centers for Disease Control, *The Public Health Impact of Needle Exchange Programs in the U.S. and Abroad* (Rockville, MD: National AIDS Clearinghouse, 1993).

Courtwright, David T., *Dark Paradise: Opiate Addiction in America Before 1940* (Cambridge, MA: Harvard University Press, 1982).

Currie, Elliott, *Reckoning: Drugs, the Cities, and the American Future* (New York: Hill and Wang, 1993).

DesJarlais, Don, and Samuel Friedman, "AIDS and Legal Access to Sterile Injection Equipment," *Annals of the American Academy of Political and Social Science* 521:42–65 (1992).

Doblin, Rick, and Mark Kleiman, "Marijuana as Antiemetic Medicine: A Survey of Oncologists' Experiences and Attitudes," *Journal of Clinical Oncology* 9:1314–1319 (1991).

Dole, Vincent P., "Implications of Methadone Maintenance for Theories of Narcotic Addiction," *Journal of the American Medical Association* 260:3025–3029 (1988).

Dole, Vincent P., and Marie Nyswander, "A Medical Treatment for Diacetylmorphine (heroin) Addiction—A Clinical Trial with Methadone Hydrochloride," *Journal of the American Medical Association* 193:646–650 (1965).

Dorn, Nicholas, "Minimisation of Harm: A U-Curve Theory," *Druglink* 2:3–5 (1988).

Drug Enforcement Administration, *How To Hold Your Own in Drug Legalization Debate* (Washington, DC: U.S. Department of Justice, Drug Enforcement Administration, 1994).

Duke, Steven B., and Albert C. Gross, *America's Longest War: Rethinking Our Tragic Crusade Against Drugs* (New York: Putnam's, 1994).

European Cities on Drug Policy, *Report* (Frankfurt, Germany: ECDP Co-Ordination Bureau, 1993).

Families Against Mandatory Minimums, "What's Wrong with Mandatory Minimum Sentences" (Washington, DC: FAMM Foundation, 1992).

Frankel, Max, "O.K., Call It War," *New York Times Magazine*, December 18, 1994, p. 30.

Fratello, David H., "Parallel Universes," *The Drug Policy Letter* (Spring 1993), p. 9.

Grinspoon, Lester, and James B. Bakalar, *Marijuana: The Forbidden Medicine* (New Haven, CT: Yale University Press, 1993).

Harm Reduction Coalition, *Mission Statement* (pamphlet) (Oakland, CA: HRC, 1995).

Heather, Nick, Alex Wodak, Ethan Nadelmann, and Pat O'Hare, eds., *Psychoactive Drugs and Harm Reduction* (London: Whurr, 1993).

Johnson, Kirk, "New Haven Plans To Give Drug Addicts New Needles," *New York Times*, May 24, 1990, p. B1.

Klerman, Gerald L., "Psychotropic Hedonism vs. Pharmacological Calvinism," *Hastings Center Report* 2:1–3 (1972).

Leary, Warren E. "Cancer Patients in Needless Pain, U.S. Guidelines Say: Unfounded Fears of Addiction Discourage Narcotics Use, Medical Experts Report," *New York Times,* March 3, 1994, p. A1.

Levine, Harry G., and Craig Reinarman, "From Prohibition to Regulation: Lessons from Alcohol Policy for Drug Policy," *Milbank Quarterly* 69:461–494 (1991).

Lewis, David, "Methadone Maintenance: Still Fighting for Credibility After 30 Years of Effective Outcomes," *Digest of Addiction Theory and Application* 13:12 (1994).

Lindesmith, Alfred, *The Addict and the Law* (Bloomington: Indiana University Press, 1965).

Massing, Michael, "Delusions of the Drug Cops," *New York Review of Books,* July 15, 1993, pp. 30–32.

McEwen, Tom, *National Assessment Program: 1994 Survey Results* (Washington, DC: U.S. Department of Justice, Office of Justice Programs, National Institute of Justice, 1995).

McNamara, Joseph D., "Changing Police Attitudes Support Reform of National Drug Control Policies," paper presented at the 37th Annual International Congress on Alcohol and Drug Dependence, San Diego, August 20–25, 1995.

Morgan, John P., and David L. Pleet, "Opiophobia in the United States: The Under-Treatment of Severe Pain," pp. 313–318 in John P. Morgan and Doreen V. Kagan, eds., *Society and Medication* (Lexington, MA: Lexington Books, 1983).

Musto, David, *The American Disease: Origins of Narcotic Control* (New Haven, CT: Yale University Press, 1973[1987]).

—— "Opium, Cocaine, and Marijuana in American History," *Scientific American* 265:40–47 (1991).

Myers, Martha A., "Symbolic Policy and the Sentencing of Drug Offenders," *Law and Society Review* 23:295–315 (1989).

Nadelmann, Ethan, Peter Cohen, Ernest Drucker, Ueli Locher, Gerry Stimson, and Alex Wodak, "The Harm Reduction Approach to Drug Control: International Progress," The Lindesmith Center, New York, 1994.

Navarro, Mireya, "Yale Study Reports Clean Needle Project Helps Check AIDS," *New York Times,* August 1, 1991, p. A1.

Newcombe, Russell, and Allan Parry, "The Mersey Harm-Reduction Model," presented at the International Conference on Drug Policy Reform, Bethesda, MD, October 22, 1988.

Nyswander, Marie, *The Drug Addict as Patient* (New York: Grune and Stratton, 1956).

O'Hare, Pat, "Drug Education: A Basis for Reform," presented at the International Conference on Drug Policy Reform, Bethesda, MD, October 22, 1988.

O'Hare, Pat, Russell Newcombe, Alan Matthews, Ernst Buning, and Ernest Drucker, eds., *The Reduction of Drug-Related Harm* (London: Whurr, 1993).

Payte, J. Thomas, "A Brief History of Methadone in the Treatment of Opioid Dependence," *Journal of Psychoactive Drugs* 23:103–107 (1991).

Room, Robin G. W., "Cultural Changes in Drinking and Trends in Alcohol Problems Indicators: Recent U.S. Experience," pp. 149–162 in Walter B. Clark and Michael E. Hilton, eds., *Alcohol in America: Drinking Practices and Problems* (Albany: State University of New York Press, 1991).

Rosenbaum, Marsha, "The Demedicalization of Methadone Maintenance," *Journal of Psychoactive Drugs* 27:145–149 (1995).

Rosenbaum, Marsha, Jeanette Irwin, and Sheigla Murphy, "De Facto Destabilization as Policy: The Impact of Short-Term Methadone Maintenance," *Contemporary Drug Problems* 15:491–517 (1988).

Scriven, Paul, *The Medicine Society* (East Lansing: Michigan State University Press, 1992).

Sharp, Elaine B., *The Dilemma of Drug Policy in the United States* (New York: Harper Collins, 1994).

Strang, John, and M. Farrell, "Harm Minimisation for Drug Users: When Second Best May Be Best First," *British Medical Journal* 304:1127–1128 (1992).

Treaster, Joseph B., "2 U.S. Judges, Protesting Policies, Are Declining To Take Drug Cases," *New York Times*, April 17, 1993, p. A7.

Trebach, Arnold, and Kevin Zeese, *Drug Prohibition and the Conscience of Nations* (Washington, DC: Drug Policy Foundation, 1990).

———, *Strategies for Change: New Directions in Drug Policy* (Washington, DC: Drug Policy Foundation, 1992).

United States Department of Justice, *An Analysis of Non-Violent Drug Offenders with Minimal Criminal Histories* (Washington, DC: U.S. Department of Justice, 1994).

Waldorf, Dan, Craig Reinarman, and Sheigla Murphy, *Cocaine Changes* (Philadelphia: Temple University Press, 1991).

Watters, John K., Michelle J. Estilo, George L Clark, and Jennifer Lorvick, "Syringe and Needle Exchange as HIV/AIDS Prevention for Injection Drug Users," *Journal of the American Medical Association* 271:115–120 (1994).

Weil, Andrew, *The Natural Mind* (Boston: Houghton Mifflin, 1972).

Wilson, William, J., *The Truly Disadvantaged: The Inner City, the Underclass, and Public Policy* (Chicago: University of Chicago Press, 1987).

Zimring, Franklin E., and Gordon Hawkins, *The Search for Rational Drug Control* (Cambridge, England: Cambridge University Press, 1992).

Zinberg, Norman E., *Drug, Set, and Setting: The Basis for Controlled Intoxicant Use* (New Haven, CT: Yale University Press, 1984).

Zinberg, Norman E., W. M. Harding, and M. Winkeller, "A Study of Social Regulatory Mechanisms in Controlled Illicit Drug Users," *Journal of Drug Issues* 7:117–133 (1977).

We've Been Here Before

Excerpts from the 1967 Report
of the Task Force on Narcotics and Drug Abuse
of the President's Commission on Law Enforcement
and Administration of Justice

In January 1967, the President's Commission on Law Enforcement and Administration of Justice, created by President Johnson, issued its reports. The commission was comprised of nine task forces on various topics, including the Task Force on Narcotics and Drug Abuse. Each task force issued its own report that was published by the U.S. government and sold for $1. The Narcotics and Drug Abuse Task Force report contained a foreword by Commission Chair Nicholas Katzenbach, a chapter summarizing the findings of the task force, and six additional chapters that had been prepared as "background documentation" for the chapter on narcotics and drug abuse. The first excerpts that follow are from the task force's own chapter, and the second set is from the background chapter prepared by Richard Blum and Mary Lou Bunkhouse-Balbaky titled "Mind-Altering Drugs and Dangerous Behavior: Dangerous Drugs." We came upon the task force report as we were finishing this book and found some of the descriptions, findings, and conclusions eerily similar to the ones we were presenting thirty years later. The emphasis in the quotes is ours.

FROM THE TASK FORCE'S CHAPTER

Since early in the century we have built our drug control policies around the twin judgments that drug abuse was an evil to be suppressed and that this could most effectively be done by the application of criminal enforcement and penal sanctions. Since then, one traditional response to an increase in drug abuse has been to increase the penalties for drug offenses. The premise has been that the more certain and severe the punishment, the more it would serve as a deterrent. Typically, this response has taken the form of mandatory minimum terms of imprisonment, increasing in severity with repeated offenses, and provisions making the drug offender ineligible for suspension of sentence, probation and parole. . . .

[In 1951] mandatory minimum sentences were introduced for all narcotic and marihuana offenses. . . . In 1956 the mandatory minimum sentences were raised to 5 years for the first and 10 years for the second and subsequent offenses of unlawful sale or importation. They remained at 2, 5, and 10 years for the offense of unlawful possession. Suspension of sentence, probation and parole were prohibited for all but the first offense of unlawful possession. Many State criminal codes contain comparable, though not identical, penalty provisions . . . p. 11).

Purchase and possession . . . are criminal offenses under both Federal and State law. So is sale, to which many addicts turn to provide financial support for their habits. In many States, the nonmedical use of opiates is punishable, as is the possession of paraphernalia such as needles and syringes designed for such use. In other States, vagrancy statutes make it punishable for a known or convicted addict to consort with other known addicts or to be present in a place where illicit drugs are found. Thus the addict lives in almost perpetual violation of one or several criminal laws . . . (p. 10).

FROM THE BACKGROUND CHAPTER

[T]he nonmedical use of dangerous drugs, as with marihuana and narcotics, can lead to arrest and incarceration. Many sociologists and criminologists contend that arrest and subsequent experiences when one is treated as a criminal produce many injurious consequences and increase the likelihood of expanded rather than reduced criminal and socially maladaptive behavior. Especially in the field of drugs where use is a crime regardless of whether or not any other damaging behavior occurs, there has been discussion of the undesirable features of "turning the person into a criminal" through treating him like one and exposing him to contact with "genuine" offenders. *As an alternative it is often recommended that criminal prosecution be limited to criminal behavior as such* (*i.e.* crimes against person and property) and that drug use be handled (a) as a normal phenomenon, since this is a drug-using *society* except (b) where dependence occurs or other behavioral toxicity (aberrant actions, suicidal impulses, psychosis, etc.) emerges at which time the person may be subject to medical psychological-social rehabilitation efforts. The evidence for arrest and prosecution as methods more likely to create a criminal out of a drug user than to correct him remains very contradictory. . . . Even so, *it can be argued that on grounds of economics and humanity it may be better to handle any person abusing drugs* (that is anyone dependent and acting in damaging ways) *by other than criminal procedures* . . . (p. 31).

A general revision of criminal codes pertaining to illicit drugs should be undertaken. A reasonable change might eliminate criminal prosecution provisions for the possession of dangerous drugs including the amphetamines. Consideration may also be given to reducing penalties for acquisition and perhaps for sales under certain circumstances ... (p. 32).

In reviewing the claims made about the undesirable outcomes of amphetamine use (and of marihuana and opiate use as well) one is struck by the lack of support for the claims advanced by reputable and well-intentioned persons, including government officials, to the effect that these drugs cause crime and accidents. We have taken special care in reviewing the claims of risk to trace back reports to their sources. ... [O]ne finds that in some cases the reference has little relevance to the statement. In other cases, one finds that the reference itself is not a scientific report or other careful observation but only an impression or opinion written in as a letter or clinical note in one or another medical journal. Sometimes several references are cited which upon inspection are only quotes from an earlier source or simple repetitions of a claim. We find this distressing for several reasons. First, *it suggests that scientific and official reporting about drug effects may itself be subject to strong bias and may reflect preconceived ideas rather than an adequate appraisal of the evidence.* Second, it makes the job of layman, official, or scientist harder in the sense he cannot reply on reports by presumably objective agencies but must return to original sources and thus spend unnecessary time and effort. Third, it reflects what is seen daily in the popular press, what is heard in official hearings, and what we see and hear around us in social conversation to the effect that opinions and emotions about drug use and drug risks are strong but that the evidence may be weak ... (p. 31).

We have also taken time to survey some of the recent popular articles about amphetamine abuse, tracing their development in magazines. One finds the evolution of alarm and a sense of crisis, one article expanding on the one before, elaborating claims, exaggerating unsubstantiated cases, and become more intense in the cry for legislative control. Sensationalism can only be part of the reason; the public must be receptive to such snowballing appeals and such receptivity reflects, we believe, general public anxiety. This anxiety expresses itself about drug use and insofar as new drugs do present unknown dangers and known drugs clearly do have bad effects as well as benign ones, that anxiety is justified. Nevertheless the extreme feelings apparent, and the catering to bias in popular and purportedly authoritative publications, reflect more, we believe, than a reasonable worry about drugs. ... What people are said to do because of drugs—to rob and steal and rape, to injure and kill one another on the highways, and to become dependent and psychotic—these are the things that people do and we—all of us—have reason to be upset about them. But people do not need drugs to act in these frightening and damaging ways; and *the general evidence is that drugs in fact play a very small part in the production of our overall rates of trouble.* They do play some part of course and insofar as they do, they add to the already great social burden. What we suggest is that the *worry about drugs is extreme because somehow these substances have come to be symptoms of individual uncertainty and distress and can be used as explanations of why bad things are happening.* As explanations of the otherwise inexplicable willingness—or compulsion—of humans to damage themselves and one another, drugs are scientifically insufficient, but in terms of a public explanation they seem to serve that purpose . . . (p. 32).

Lawmaking about drug use need attend to at least two matters: One is that a law which is not based on facts and which has an unknown effect as far as control is concerned . . . is not likely to solve real problems associated with drug use. The other matter is that the apparent satisfaction produced by passing a criminal law directed at drug users must have some social function. Perhaps it does at least alleviate public anxiety or allow one to single out for punishment at least someone who represents the bad things happening. If that is the case, then any revisions in handling drug users which focused only on users and on the facts of risk, but which failed to realize the intensity of public worry, and perhaps satisfaction with punitive approaches, might well generate further troubles—this time not for drug users but for the public deprived of at least this form of expression. If any of these speculations are correct it would follow that public sounding, public education and direct efforts to recognize and try to resolve relevant public distress over unacceptable deviation and criminality—which is in fact one task of the President's Commission—must precede and accompany all provisional efforts at handling drug abuse. . . . (p. 32)

Other means of reducing drug risks aside from laws must be stressed. Expanded public education, direct efforts to correct social and personality disorders conducive to drug abuse, expanded education of physicians, druggists and other drug "gatekeepers" may well prove beneficial. As with most other public efforts directed to reduce social ills and mental disorders, it will be unwise to be overly optimistic about producing immediate change. It would also be unwise to expect specific programs to solve more general human problems. *So it is that broad scale programs such as those envisioned in welfare, antipoverty, mental health, public health, and other progressive efforts can be expected to contribute to the control of if not to a reduction in drug abuse. . . .*

In planning any program aimed at preventing or correcting drug abuse, it is important to be realistic about the limitations of any effort. *As a society in the habit of using drugs and with the approved expansion of pharmacological research and the medical application of drugs, and with the ever-present strain of technological life, there is reason to expect medical, social and private drug use to expand. Much of this is benign and without serious risk and no free modern society would seek to prohibit such use.* Risks and some bad effects will be inevitable, at least within the present generation. A quote from Dr. Maurice Seevers, Professor of Pharmacology at the University of Michigan is appropriate:

> The obvious lesson of history is that a certain segment of the population, probably a much larger one than we would like to believe, must find release or relief in drugs. . . . It is up to society, therefore, to find the means by which this may be accomplished with minimal hazard to the individual and to itself (*Journal of the American Medical Association,* 1962, 181 [92–98]) (pp. 32–33).

(*Task Force Report: Narcotics and Drug Abuse,* President's Commission on Law Enforcement and Administration of Justice [Washington, DC: U.S. Government Printing Office, 1967])

SUBJECT INDEX

Page numbers appearing in italic type refer to pages containing tables.

NAME INDEX